Dickie, may this book will be a blessing to you!

Ingrid

UNSTOPPABLE

it's a choice

INGA LIZDENYTĖ

Copyright © 2018 Inga Lizdenytė.

All rights reserved. No part of this book may be used or reproduced by any means, graphic, electronic, or mechanical, including photocopying, recording, taping or by any information storage retrieval system without the written permission of the author except in the case of brief quotations embodied in critical articles and reviews.

Photographer credit: Cover Photo © Penny Wolin, Photographer. All Rights Reserved
Author Photo and image # 30, Jurgita Mažeika

Scripture taken from the New King James Version®. Copyright © 1982 by Thomas Nelson. Used by permission. All rights reserved.
Scripture quotations marked (NIV) are taken from the Holy Bible, New International Version®, NIV®. Copyright © 1973, 1978, 1984, 2011 by Biblica, Inc.™ Used by permission of Zondervan. All rights reserved worldwide. www.zondervan.com The "NIV" and "New International Version" are trademarks registered in the United States Patent and Trademark Office by Biblica, Inc.™

This book is a work of non-fiction. Unless otherwise noted, the author and the publisher make no explicit guarantees as to the accuracy of the information contained in this book and in some cases, names of people and places have been altered to protect their privacy.

WestBow Press books may be ordered through booksellers or by contacting:

WestBow Press
A Division of Thomas Nelson & Zondervan
1663 Liberty Drive
Bloomington, IN 47403
www.westbowpress.com
1 (866) 928-1240

Because of the dynamic nature of the Internet, any web addresses or links contained in this book may have changed since publication and may no longer be valid. The views expressed in this work are solely those of the author and do not necessarily reflect the views of the publisher, and the publisher hereby disclaims any responsibility for them.

ISBN: 978-1-9736-1514-9 (sc)
ISBN: 978-1-9736-1515-6 (hc)
ISBN: 978-1-9736-1513-2 (e)

Library of Congress Control Number: 2018900843

Print information available on the last page.

WestBow Press rev. date: 02/22/2018

~~~~

"Internationally-known motivational speaker Inga Lizdenytė's first book is an intensely personal biography offering hope to those who've faced catastrophic, life-altering events. Not only does this powerful book provide readers hope and direction toward a spiritually-focused solution to their problems, but also it shows how her journey back from a tragic accident can become a roadmap for whatever curveballs life has thrown them.

A must read!" Robert Davis, Award-Winning Writer, former CMO

~~~~

"When I think of Inga, the word UNSTOPPABLE is such an appropriate title for her book. As an Immigrant myself from Ireland growing up with a handicapped Mother I know first hand the struggles that Inga faces on a minute by minute basis with just the basics of life. I have never heard her complain EVER about her situation. She has a WINNER'S MENTALITY! My Mom always taught me that if we have no TEST we have no TESTIMONY! I am so honored to know her as a friend of many years. Her Courage and Tenacity has and always will to PUSH THROUGH any POINT OF PAIN in my life to REACH MY POINT OF POWER. Because of her INNER DRIVE AND SPIRIT I am forever changed. I would say RUSH OUT and buy her BOOK .....as your LIFE WILL BE FOREVER CHANGED By her nothing short of INCREDIBLE LIFE STORY. Love you Inga.

Gillian Ortega, *Mary Kay National Sales Director*

~~~~
~~~~

There are three special features that distinguish this book from other counseling manuals.

First: All of the conclusions and recommendations on how to survive depression or find meaning in life where no one sees any, are all based on the personal experience of the author. In Inga's case, this is a rare and difficult experience.

Secondly: The accident, which resulted in Inga losing her legs, happened in response to her prayer to God when she said, "Stop me at any cost, otherwise I'm going to hell." Against the backdrop of dominant liberal theology, Inga finds God rather radical in His desire to save the soul from damnation.

Finally: The book consists of real letters, which Inga wrote to her brother, a skeptic of faith, who had asked her for help at a critical moment in his life. This is an extremely transparent story, written with extreme care, the result of which was God changing a man's life.

"Unstoppable" will not leave you without a reaction!
Alexander Shevchenko
Senior Pastor, House of Bread Church

DISCLAIMER: To preserve the authenticity of the author's true voice, the manuscript was edited without the constraint of some grammatical rules. Therefore, the manner and the style of communication as a non-native English speaker is captured in the pages of this book.

DEDICATION

I dedicate this book to my brother *Evaldas Lizdenis.* Without you, I would not have written it. Thank you for your encouragement and faith in me when I didn't trust I could do this.

You always have been my protector, and you always were there for me when I needed it. Thank you for all those things you did for me to make my life secure and brighter. Thank you for everything, brother. There are not enough words to describe how much I love you and care about you.

I dedicate it to my *Mom, Zita Lizdenienė.* You always have been my angel, Mom. Thank you for your unconditional love and care. Thank you for the sleepless nights, making sure I was well. You carried me when I couldn't walk, you rejoiced with me when I felt happy, you comforted me when I cried, you were strong for me when I was weak, you picked me up when I fell. Thank you for empowering me to spread my wings and rise above the adversity. Thank you for having faith in me even when my goals seemed impossible. Thank you for never trying to stop me, even though it was heartbreaking for you to let me go away. I love you, Mom.

I dedicate this book to my friend *Renata Palevičiūtė,* who never abandoned me after I got into a car accident. Your love and care carried me through my hardest times after the crash. You were by my side every step of the way. You held my hand while I was on a verge of death in ICU. You helped me while I was recovering physically. You came to visit me when I felt trapped. You made my life brighter when it seemed as though I was walking through the endless desert. You were by my side as I was restoring my life. And now, together we share the thrill of a victory. Thank you for remaining my true friend whom I could lean on. I love you, my friend.

In Loving Memory: I dedicate to my *father Algimantas Lizdenis,* thank you Dad for everything you had been. Thank you for trusting me and making every effort to fulfill my dreams. I would not have conquered my insurmountable circumstances, and would not have achieved my goals without your support. I miss you daily.

ACKNOWLEDGMENTS

First, I want to thank each person who remained by my side after the car accident.

My mother *Zita Lizdenienė,* father *Algimantas Lizdenis* and *brother Evaldas Lizdenis* – it is your unconditional love and care that brought me through my hardest times. I cannot thank you enough for everything you have done for me.

My immediate family and the entire *Lizdenis* and *Šumskas* family in Lithuania – thank you for your support you have shown to my parents *Algimantas Lizdenis* and *Zita Lizdenienė.*

My heart goes to *Renata Palevičiutė, Regina Palevičienė, Marius Čepas, Eglė and Andrius Cunik, Aliona Filipovičiūtė, Vitalij Boreiko, Roma Agapov, Dmitrij Orlov, Inga Makovskienė, Andžej Žeimo, Aušra Butrimaitė, Tautvydas Bitinas, Romas Žvirblis, Beata ir Algirdas Palevičius, Aurelija Poškutė, Silvija Janusauskienė,* and many others dear to my heart. I am so thankful for each of you. You made me feel loved and valued, even though I and my life had changed drastically. You were the reason why I smiled on my birthdays and other holidays. And now, as I live far away from you, my every trip back home to Lithuania is filled with laughter and fond memories because I get to see each of you, my true friends.

I thank all *my American friends,* who accepted me and supported me every step of the way as I was aiming for my goals. Just as my Lithuanian friends carried me through the hardest times when my life crashed, you, my American friends, empowered me to restore my life. Thank you for embracing me. You made California my home. Countless number of people has impacted my life. I am so grateful to each of you for the encouragement, inspiration, for giving me rides to places, and for every kind of support. Especially, I want to thank *Terry and Bob Bell, Felicity Doyle Kelty, Rayme and Michael Shapiro, Lanita and Mike Dillaha, Royce Brier, Don McAllister, Kim Page, Fred Phillips, Trish Reuser, Joni Pritchard, Gillian Ortega, Marina Moore, Irina Hall, Sidney Fox.* You went above and beyond supporting me in achieving my dreams. I would not have made it without you.

I want to thank every person, who encouraged me to continue writing this book and trusted me when I doubted myself. Your support meant so much to me and inspired me to continue writing. Especially I want to thank *Marina Moore* for continuous encouragement and support. You were there when I finally made the decision to write a book, you were the first one to read a chapter, and you were there by my side all these years while I was working on it.

My big thank you goes to *Irina Hall, Eva Rezvoy, Sharon Dawson, Adam Brown, Joni Pritchard, Tanya Malinovskiy,* and many others for the encouragement to keep writing. Your words of support that I received from you gave me the confidence to continue my work.

Thank you to those who were involved in the creation of this book:

I want to say a special thank you to those, who turned my manuscript into a book.

Anzhelika Polyak, thank you for trusting me and my vision. Thank you for walking with me every step of the way to turn my manuscript into a book. I am blessed and so grateful that I have such a wonderful team player like you. Thank you for everything, my friend.

Nicole Romeo, I met you at a perfect timing. When I doubted about my work, you ignited the confidence in me assuring that my work had to be published. And, you helped me to make my first steps turning my writing into a manuscript for the book.

Robert Davis, the editor of the book, who tirelessly worked on it. For many years I've been waiting for the editor with particular skills, and you were exactly whom I wanted. I was amazed by your professionalism and skill to edit the work, while leaving the author's voice. Thank you for everything, Bob.

David Scott, the second editor of the book. You diligently refined the entire manuscript. Your skill to work with the content is brilliant. Thank you for your dedication and hard work to make the manuscript shine.

Barbara Schulz, who encouraged me on a continuous basis and proofread the manuscript. Thank you for your continuous encouragement and for your profound feedback.

Contents

Foreword

If you're a fan of faith-based inspirational literature, Unstoppable is right up your alley. If you're like me, however, an agnostically-oriented cynic who finds little inspiration in anything, Unstoppable may be an odd choice of literature, but an incredibly rewarding one nonetheless.

As her employer, I have known and appreciated Inga for many years. She is hard-working, responsible and eager to face any and all challenges. While the fact that she has profound disabilities certainly serves to inspire many people she encounters, it has little bearing on her employment. She seeks, and perhaps to her detriment, receives the same treatment as any other employee with an overbearing boss. The idea that anyone meeting Inga, would expect anything less, is preposterous.

Her story, however, is not merely one of unusual perseverance and accomplishment. It is far more about a mindset and dedication to create and maintain a life of purpose and fulfillment. Unstoppable, provides an intense, often raw, insight into this unique attitudinal fortitude. The reader, even this reader, is provided the means for seeing life as more than its obstacles and is left impassioned, and perhaps even inspired, to do more with his or her existence.

Adam Brown
Attorney at Law
Executive Director
Disability Services & Legal Center

About the Book

Several years since the tragedy, I began hearing suggestions about writing a book, but it was something I never thought to consider. I never had problems giving interviews when journalists reached out, asking me to share my story, but I couldn't see myself as the author of an actual book. I always thought, "Who am I to write a book about myself?"

But the Lord had a different plan. The reason I decided to write came through my brother, whom I love dearly. I was living in California when I received a text message from him one day that read, "Inga, I don't know how to live my life anymore. Help me." I was shocked. The sense that something serious had happened overshadowed my surroundings, but I didn't know what I could possibly do to help him. After all, I was across the globe from him and there was nothing much I could do. As I wondered, in my mind asking the Lord how I could help, a thought came to me, "Write him a letter."

That moment I knew I needed to write to him the truth about my recovery. I needed to reveal my source of strength and the reasons behind my life-transforming changes, so that he could have it, too. Observers might have thought of them as incredible coincidences or mere luck, but it was not. There was much more to the story than what the world knew. The time came when I needed to pass on to him everything that empowered me to rise above the adversity and rebuild my life. It was a crystal clear thought that pointed me in the direction of what I needed to do.

At first I was perplexed by my feelings because I didn't think I could write well enough to convey what I needed to say. The next few days my thoughts followed me like a shadow. After wrestling with my insecurities, my love for my brother and a burning desire to help won the day. I decided to have an open and straightforward conversation with him. After returning from work one day, I closed my bedroom door and began writing him a letter. The words flowed from me like a river. For many hours I wrote without stopping. After finishing, I sent him the letter via email, hoping he wouldn't reject my offer to help. A pleasant surprise waited for me the next morning. He sincerely thanked me for writing him saying, "Inga, you probably can't imagine what you did. I feel so much better. Maybe there is hope for me after all."

He asked me to continue writing, to share what I wanted to share. And so I continued. I wrote of my journey from a perspective he never knew of, openly sharing with him my heart, motives, feelings and details which had never been disclosed to him before. Through these letters, we had a very honest conversation.

After a while, in one of his messages, my brother told me, "The reason why my little son still has his daddy alive is because of your letters. Your letters were the only bright light in my life."

My brother revealed to me that when he texted me initially, he felt devastated. The sudden crash he had experienced seemed too much to bear and he saw no way out of the despair. He said he wished he didn't even exist. He thanked me for writing because my letters showed him the light, brought him out of hopelessness, and equipped him with the knowledge how to improve his life. He asked me to keep writing and put it into a book to help other people. He added, "If you help at least one more person, it will be all worth it."

I still was hesitant, but then my friend and I attended a seminar, where I made the decision to continue writing and publish. Observing circumstances and my inner feelings when I prayed, I knew the Lord was leading me. I had a strong desire to encourage others to fight for their lives no matter what circumstances they were facing and tell the world what the Lord had done in my life. I wanted to share the experience and knowledge I gained so that anyone could use it to improve their lives.

But I didn't have an editor nor did I have funds to publish. It seemed impossible. Yet I had faith that it would all come when the time was right, and I continued writing. The manuscript itself went through many trials. By variety of circumstances, it seemed as though someone continuously was trying to distract me and stop me from writing. Finally, after the manuscript had been completed, there was an attempt by someone to wipe out my work by deleting the manuscript from my computer and stealing my flash where all book files were stored. Nevertheless, the manuscript of this book prevailed.

And after seven years of working on it, when the time came to get it out to the world, the editor and the funds indeed showed up all at once. It turned out that seven years I resisted the idea of me writing a book, and seven years I wrote it. The book contains real letters to my brother, and stories from my personal experiences. I wrote the book in the way that includes the most significant events of my life after the car accident.

And while this is a story about my personal journey, this book is not about me; I am only a character of the story. This book is about a living God who can restore the broken, heal the deepest wounds of a soul, and transform one's life no matter how desperate the situation is. The story is about unwavering faith. It is about resolve and relentless perseverance that can break through the insurmountable stumbling blocks. The story is about the power of resilience that can lift you up and carry you forward no matter how tired you are or how many times you fall. It is about God's immeasurable mercy and grace even if you make a horrible, unpardonable mistake.

This book shows how the Lord can make a way when there is none. And, it carries a lesson of how we can lose that blessing, if we allow ourselves to cross the fine line of when instead of saying "No", we begin to justify our decisions. This book is about the power of decisions that are made by us, once we stand at the crossroads of a choice.

I invite you to get on a journey with me. I hope my story will bring forth determination within you to aim for more than you ever thought possible. I hope it will strengthen you and empower you to keep on going until you reach your dream. I hope my walk with the Lord will ignite faith in your heart and you will find the source of living waters and spread your wings like an eagle. I encourage you to accept the ideas and practical tools you will find in this book and use it in your personal journey. My biggest wish is to make a difference in your life. These letters were written to my brother, and now the entire book is my letter to you.

1

My First Letter to My Brother

4/13/2007

Dear Valdas,

I keep thinking about you and your situation. It tears me apart knowing how hard it is for you and that there's nothing I can do about it. After I got your text, I kept thinking about you, and I prayed to God asking Him what I could possibly do to help you. You know there are some things that I cannot help you with, nor can I do anything about your situation to make it easier. But I know what I *can* give you. I love you very much and I can't focus on my own life knowing that you are so hurt, and that you're going through such a severe hardship. It hurts me to know that you are hurt. I know that deep in your heart you are very caring and kind. It isn't natural for you to be living in a circle of hatred and revenge and pain; my hope is for you to experience the joy of life. I so desire for you to be happy with who you are, and to be content with your life.

I've decided to share with you something that can change your life. You are a witness to how my life has been completely altered, and I want to share with you that which helped me to attain that transformation. You remember how devastated I was after the accident, how it left me without my legs and with my left arm paralyzed. It stripped from me everything that made my life fulfilling. February 12, 2000 still remains in our memories as the day which brought enormous trauma and anguish to our family. On that day, my destiny, indeed my entire spirit and reason for living, seemed completely and utterly broken.

Do you remember it as vividly as I do? As you must know, since then my life's journey has become so very incredible. At the time we couldn't imagine how my destiny would play out. I measured each day in terms of seconds, minutes and hours, never realizing that life would eventually become so beautiful. Today, my dream is my daily life. To be honest, today I am happier and I live a much more fulfilling and interesting life than I did before the accident.

Throughout my journey I have learned so much, and I want to pass it on so that you can transform your life as well. I want to pass on that which helped me to recover emotionally and rebuild my life, in spite of the devastating circumstances and how impossible my goals had once seemed. And as I think on your current situation, I am eager to pass on to you the jewel that I have found, hoping that you will grasp that jewel as I did.

I know you are going through unbearable pain, otherwise you would not have sent me such a disturbing text message. Maybe in few years you will look back and feel grateful for all these hard and painful years, because they brought you to something that you never knew, made you stronger, and gave you experiences that you could never buy or gain otherwise. I know this might sound ridiculous, to think like this at this point in your life, but that is exactly how I feel after years of pain and struggle.

Even though the loss I went through brought such unspeakable pain, with the crash I have gained much more than what I have lost. The event, the obstacles and the challenges that I had to face have molded me, making me the person I am today. Looking back, I appreciate all the difficulties because I have learned far more than I could have ever learned otherwise. I became much stronger, determined and persistent. I am thankful for what once seemed totally hopeless because I have discovered the incredible power of faith, and my experience has taught me how to hold on to that faith at all times. Faith has given me the strength to endure; faith has given me the courage to move forward no matter how challenging life's hurdles I had faced.

I am thankful for the experience because it made me much more compassionate than I was before the accident. Looking back, I was far more self-centered and concerned with outward appearances than I was with inner qualities and human needs. Hardships and agony have developed me as a human being. I am very thankful for the obstacles because they have taught me how relentless effort can break through any kind of barrier. I am thankful for the challenges because they taught me how to push myself, to go beyond what I thought I could do. I am thankful for all I had to go through because it has shaped my character and taught me some very valuable lessons.

And I am thankful for one of the biggest gifts I received from my life journey: I got to know the Lord my God, whose love and care cannot compare to anything in this world. I know it's very common to talk about God as some mysterious object, and that many people don't take faith in God seriously. It's as though people are ashamed to discuss their faith with others. My life experience has shown me how wrong I was in going along with the crowd.

Many people are sorry for me because it seems to them that I live a very difficult life due to my physical condition. Yes, it is not easy. And every day I live enduring ongoing physical pain. Yet these daily challenges pale in comparison to what I have gained since the time of the accident.

I want you to know that your circumstances – no matter how sorrowful and hopeless your situation makes you feel right now – are only temporary. You can get out of this desperate place in your life. With God's help you can get out of any circumstance, climb the highest mountain, and meet your sunrise at the top. You can deal with any adversity you face and emerge victorious. You can restore your life. You can bring to life your dream, if you have faith and do what needs to be done to make it happen.

My experience taught me that anything is possible if you truly desire it. You only have to do whatever it takes to achieve it and have unshakable faith that you will succeed. God can and will help you, even though right now you may feel you don't deserve His intercession. He had a plan for your life when He created you, and I know in my heart of hearts that you have a very long time in earthly years to complete His destiny for you.

Brother, if I managed to recover from such a tragic crash and achieve what I have, you can do it, too. It seems that you are in a deep and hopeless place in your life right now. I've been there. And while you may not have known, I've shared your thoughts. I know there is a way out for you, just as there was for me. I believe you can change it all. I want you to leave your dark thoughts and your irony aside. It's not the time for them.

It may sound strange to be telling you all this, as though I were some kind of "teacher of life." I am not. I am simply your sister, who dearly loves you, who wants to share with you that which can help you to change your life, just as my own life was transformed from a nightmare into a bright day.

You said that you felt like you were enclosed in a dark triangle and couldn't get out into the light. You want to be happy and have success in what you do, but you see your life actually spiraling downward at full speed. I know what can help you, but you have to be open to accept it. I am not going to convey theories that I merely heard about, but things that I experienced which transformed my own life after the accident.

I will talk a lot about faith. I am not going to preach, but I will share what made me believe in God and how trusting in the Lord changed my life. I have not really talked about it with you, but it was the foundation of my radical life-change.

After my accident, and in the years that followed, people could sense a difference in me. It seemed everyone I shared my life story with told me that I should write a book about my experience. The idea sounded absurd because I never consider myself to be an author. But for quite some time now I've been thinking about it, because I'm eager to share with others what helped me to overcome adversity and re-establish my life. Those who read what I've been through may take what I have learned and apply it to their own lives, to rise above their adversities to be the people they desire to be.

I dared not to do it because I didn't have a vision as to whom I would be writing. But I now know. I will write to you. I will disclose things that I have never talked about. I know it may sound strange, but you have seen my life transform in amazing ways and what you see is only the surface. It is not by mere "coincidence." My success comes from something deeper.

I want to believe that you will not just read it, but that you will take action to improve your circumstances. You are responsible for your life, and what you have today is the result of what you have created by making certain choices. Today is the result of the decisions you made yesterday. Today's decisions will shape your tomorrow.

As you read, keep in mind that your life is going to remain the way it is if you don't make necessary changes. Nothing is going to change on its own. You have to make radical adjustments in order to make a radical difference. And you and I both know you are capable of doing it.

How do you start your personal journey to change it all? Let's begin your journey together. I will write and send you emails, and I will send text messages to let you know when it's ready for you. Then go to our parent's house to check on these. Is that okay? Please let me help you.

Be as a child much like your own: open and trusting, and willing to learn. Accept your new truths with an open heart without doubt or sarcasm. In order to change and make your life more fulfilling, be open to what I will share with you. I am not going to write any nonsense. By that I mean that I won't share things that I have no knowledge about or won't be of value. You are a witness to how my life has changed, and I will write to reach out my hand to you, to try and help you get out of your despair.

I assume that you might be thinking, "This sounds well and good, but where do I start?" Your first step is to have faith that everything is going to be alright. I know it seems hopeless right now, but leave it alone. Believe, even if you think that some miracle must happen. Hold on to the hope that your life has to improve, that it has to be better. We don't know how it's going to get better or when it's going to happen. But I want you to trust that your faith and your actions can turn the impossible into the possible. You can change anything, and you can begin at any moment you make the decision.

Imagine that I'm reaching my hand out to you, from across the thousands of miles that separate us, and hear me say, "Get up and come with me. Let's make your life beautiful and meaningful. I will show you something that will lead you to the land of joy and abundance that no one can take away from you."

Be strong, all is going to be well,
Love you,
Inga

2

Coming Back Home

Dear Brother,

I want to share with you some of my deepest feelings about the accident and my rehabilitation in hopes that seeing from the depths of hopelessness which I was blessed to emerge from, you may accept the belief that you can get out of your pit as well. Much of this you already know. Much you do not. Further you will read what was taken from my journals and from what I can remember. And as you read you will discover the source of my inspiration and internal strength.

* * *

It was a great day. A wonderful and joyous day. I was finally coming home! It felt so good to cross the doorstep of our home. I felt as though I had just returned from a long trip. I sensed that it was a little unusual for me to feel this way, but I felt like a stranger.

Yet everything was so familiar: that same smoky smell mixed with the fragrance of mom's home cooked meals; the elegant contemporary style furniture; mom's originally created, beautiful, decorative arrangements to make our home so lively and cozy. Everything was so dear and familiar, where it felt so safe and peaceful.

I felt exhausted after the trip from the hospital. Mom prepared a place for me to lay down in the living room. Dad wheeled me towards the couch and transferred me so that I could rest. As soon as I lay down, my beloved white-as-snow cat Betsy jumped onto the couch and nestled next to the end of my thighs. Betsy became a member of our family from the moment dad brought her home seven years ago. Every one of us had a special bond with her. I was longing for Betsy while I was in the hospital and couldn't wait to see her again.

I remember that I kept asking my family to kiss her little pink nose and tell her that I would be back soon. I lifted my head to see my girl. Betsy looked up at me with her bright blue eyes as if asking where I had been for so long. Mom brought her two little kittens so they could be next to their mommy, and all together we rested. Betsy snuggled and licked my remaining thighs as if trying to tell me how happy she was that I was back home. I could sense that she knew my body was different from before. She didn't seem to care. All that mattered to Betsy was that I was home.

After I rested a little bit, I told my parents I would like to see my room. Dad moved the wheelchair first into the place I wanted to be seated. And then he came back for me. His strong arms picked me up and carried me into the room where I grew up, and he carefully placed me into the wheelchair. We silently looked into each other's eyes, each of us feeling awkward in our own way. We didn't know what to say. We both had faced a sudden, drastic change in our lives – no longer was I able to move around on my own. Then I asked him to close the door and leave me alone for a while. During my stay in the hospital, someone had been constantly with me, and I never really had a chance to be with myself, to think about this major turn in my life.

It was quite strange being in my room again. I hadn't seen it for about two months, but it seemed that I'd been gone for a very long time. I felt like a stranger where only months before, everything seemed so dear to me. I could not fully explain, but it felt as though I were a different person than who I was at the time when I was here last.

I looked around. Everything was the same. The walls were covered with pictures of mine and my brother's favorite pop and rock singers. We had so much fun applying one picture after another, until the walls were covered with a collage of both brightly-colored and black and white photos. My entertainment center was stacked with books, compact discs, and all kinds of knick-knacks in the order I'd left them two months before; and my part of the closet was full of clothes. I was so meticulous about personal appearance, especially about my shoes. But now, would I ever wear any of it again?

The windowsill was decorated with my mother's beautifully arranged flowers and a collection of gorgeous seashells (just as every room had). Next to the wall there was a desk I had shared with my brother since our school days. That desk brought back memories of the many hours I spent doing homework, which was never exciting. Yet I had precious memories, spending numerous nights at my desk by candlelight, writing in my diary of my first love.

And there was my brother's newly acquired music center. On top of it there were several framed photos showcasing some of the special moments of my life. With my right hand I managed to wheel myself closer to the desk, and I picked up those pictures to take a closer look. As I was gazing at them, for a moment I disappeared from my room and was taken back to those precious times before the shutter clicked, times I knew could never be duplicated. I knew those moments would live in my memory forever; they were unforgettable.

Vacation at the Baltic Sea, summer of 1999.

In this picture I am at the Baltic Sea posing like a snake on the lowered branch of a pine tree. My best friend Renata and I were on vacation the previous summer, and she took the picture while walking along the beach at sunset. This spot of the country was famous for its gorgeous sunsets, and it was a tradition for every visitor to meet the night by seeing off the sun on the beach. You would say "goodbye" to the sun, thanking it for a beautiful day filled with friendship and fun. This was that quiet moment of the day when upon gazing, you would look at life as an observer, sometimes feeling gratitude and sometimes being in wonder of what was to come next.

After sundown, our relaxing time would end, only to continue in a noisy bar or a dining spot outside, where we would listen to live music and dance throughout the night. Good times.

With my brother in the resort Palanga, summer of 1999.

This is my only photo of me with my brother. He is my blood, my friend, my bodyguard. In our childhood, as many children do, we fought constantly. Our parents always had to intervene, telling us that we were like a cat and a dog living in the same house together. As we grew up our relationship began to change, each day forming a stronger and stronger bond. Valdas was very protective of me, and at times it seemed he would do just about anything if someone would try to hurt me or try to take advantage of me.

I felt the same way about him. I love him more than I can describe. This picture was taken during the same vacation I enjoyed with Renata. We were riding bicycles in the resort town of Palanga and were surprised to run in to my brother. He, too, was spending a relaxing weekend by the sea. He does not like to be photographed, and so this picture with him is the only one that I have. I treasure it as much today as the day it was taken.

Vacation in the resort Palanga, Botanical park.

This picture was taken during my vacation with my other girlfriend, Eglė. We were walking in the park at the same resort in Palanga, near the Baltic Sea. Usually during the day, we would spend time at the beach enjoying the sunshine and swimming. Then, in the evening, we would walk through the Palanga Botanical Park, famous for its beautiful landscapes and the Amber Museum. While enjoying the fresh smell of pine trees, gracefully swimming swans and beautifully manicured landscape, we would walk to the sea to enjoy the colorful sunset and continue our tradition of saying goodnight to the sun as it sank into the sea.

At the entrance of the Business Lounge with the Administrator of the Lounge.

At the Airport Departure Hall during a lunch-break. Walkie-Talkie kept us on duty even during breaks.

At the Business Lounge with Renata (on the right)
and Žydrūnė, the Administrator (on the left).

These pictures captured my most precious moments at work. Vilnius International Airport has held a very special place in my heart since my childhood. I was proud of my father, who was first a pilot and then the airport's Security Director. I decided to continue his legacy and began working at the airport when I was 19. These photos were taken soon after I transferred from the Personnel Department as the manager's assistant to the Business Lounge manager position. What an exciting time it was! Transferring to my new position in the Business Lounge was one of the best decisions I had ever made.

Renata and I enjoying time out in the Vilnius city.

This is a photo of me with Renata taken at the nightclub. The candle we are holding is a symbol of our friendship. But we never needed a mutually held candle to show others that we were friends. In fact, Renata is more like a sister than a friend. My friendship with Renata is one of the relationships I hold most precious to me.

It began when I came to work at the Business Lounge. At the time she already had worked at the lounge for a while, and with her help I learned to perform my new duties very quickly. Since then we have become inseparable. We worked at the same place during the day and spent our leisure time together after work. While she and I often had fun together, we had each other to lean on when one or the other of us was going through a tough time. We knew we could call each other at any time, to be right there for support in any way we could.

Renata's birthday celebration in her hometown
Merkinė, Lithuania. Summer of 1999.

This picture captured the unforgettable moments I shared with some of my closest girlfriends. We were celebrating Renata's birthday in her little hometown of Merkinė. For us, the "sophisticated city people," it was a real treat to spend a few days away from the busy city life in a beautiful area, with the great company of our mutual friends, enjoying sauna, swimming in the river, and delighting in each other's company. It was one of the more memorable birthdays I had ever been to, even more than my own. We were laughing for two days straight. And when we weren't laughing at each other's silly jokes and escapades, we were dancing all night long. After the party we talked as only girlfriends could, sharing our feelings about this birthday and how unforgettable it would remain.

As I was placing the picture back where it had been for so long, my comprehension of what had happened pierced my whole essence like a bolt of lightning – times like these would now become history. I came to the gut-level realization that everything had been wiped out, that nothing would ever be the same as it used to be.

My dynamic work at the airport, my frequent, delightful get-togethers with friends, the fun times at coffee shops and pubs which periodically ended with dancing until sunrise, vacations at the sea, birthday parties at gorgeous locations framed by the natural beauty of the area, swimming in the lakes, BBQs and cozy times next to the fire - no longer will I be able to have those experiences.

I would never be able to walk barefoot through the sand dunes again, and I would never have the pleasure of running into the sea. No longer would I be able to join in on the fun activities together with my friends. I would never dance again. And the airport – was the job and the people I enjoyed being with really all gone? Are they now just memories? I gazed on the horizon through my window, realizing the horrifying truth. Everything that I had cherished in life had been destroyed in a flash. Everything that I delighted in, what brought me joy and confidence, had been completely shattered. Through my tears, I looked down. There was nothing but emptiness at the end of my thighs. Instead of my legs I saw the carpet.

"My beautiful legs," I thought to myself. "I will never have my beautiful legs ever again!"

It was another lightning bolt forcing me to understand and fully comprehend the merciless reality of my future. Horror and the torment from the full awareness of what had happened completely devoured and enveloped me. I barely held myself from screaming out of anguish. I didn't know how to cope with what I was realizing.

In my desperation I cried out to God, begging Him to tell me how I was supposed to live now, but it seemed that heaven was silent. I faced a dreadful fact - it was all a reality. In one life-changing second my life had become a never-ending nightmare.

* * *

February 12, 2000 was fatal for me and a young man named Dalius. I had just started dating him several months previous. It was a cold winter in Lithuania and the night before, Dalius and I were out partying with his friends in downtown Vilnius. I remember very little from that night of continuous beer drinking and the comments of his friends, complimenting him on his gorgeous new girlfriend with the long, beautiful legs. The last thing I remember was the moment I stepped out of the pizza pub restaurant, walking toward his car. Everything from there was erased, like damage to a movie film roll.

The next thing I remember, I was waking up in an Intensive Care Unit (ICU), hooked up to a life support machine fighting for my life. Our party turned out to be the tragedy that shocked the entire country. It was around 1:30 AM. The road was covered with notoriously dangerous black ice. Dalius disregarded the danger and sped off in his usual manner. He always loved speed and he was pretty competitive on the road. I have to admit, he was the best driver I'd ever driven with and I trusted him. Looking back, I can see now how the alcohol impaired his judgment, increasing his confidence to accelerate the car on an icy road. Little did either of us know that this one, careless decision would mercilessly end our evening.

I don't remember anything from the moment I'd gotten into the car. After the investigation of the crash I was told that we were racing down the hill at a speed of around 100mph. Dalius lost control and we hit a light pole. The car was torn in half. Ejected from the car, Dalius was killed instantly. He was 26 years old.

By divine miracle, my high school classmate Richard, at that moment, had been driving on the same road. He was struck by another car passing him at a lightning speed. And then, in a moment he saw that same navy color car careen down the hill, being split in half by the light pole. After witnessing the disaster, he immediately called for help. The accident scene was horrific. After cutting the wrecked car into pieces, the emergency crew extracted me half-dead, without my legs. Upon the moment of impact, some part of the car had severed both of them above the knees.

On the way to the hospital my heart stopped, yet the emergency crew did not give up on saving my life. After strenuous efforts to renew my heartbeat through emergency defibrillation, I was brought back to life. Due to a substantial loss of blood and the extensive trauma, I was immediately placed into the ICU and hooked up to a life support machine. I was given a 30% chance for survival.

By another divine miracle, a friend of my ex-sweetheart at that moment had been driving in the opposite direction, and he saw how we crashed. After recognizing me, he immediately called my former boyfriend Andžej, who rushed to my home to bring the news to my family. They were told it seemed hopeless. My heart had stopped again while I was in ICU. My family and friends were encouraged to pray, because that was the only hope left. After 17 days in the ICU I was transferred to a regular patient room. I was able to communicate a little and could recognize people, but I felt very strange. It seemed that I had left somewhere for a very long time and I was missing two things: people and nature.

I couldn't tell where I was, but it seemed that I had been absent for quite a long time, and I missed everything around. On the left side of my bed there were windows, through which I could see the gloomy gray skies and the tops of pine trees. How I wished I could run into the forest, so I could be part of nature and smell the pine trees! Obviously, since my wish to go into the outdoors could not possibly be fulfilled, my brother brought to me a CD with the sounds of nature, which was constantly playing. The sounds of nature and birds in the background gave me peace and comfort.

Day after day I would hear news about the traumatic injuries I had suffered on that chilly February night:

- I had lost both of my legs above the knee.
- My left hand was fully paralyzed and did not show any signs of life except delivering constant, sharp, burning pain.
- My right hand was severely broken and in a cast.
- A severe head injury resulted in memory loss – I could not remember many things; especially my life for the past several months had been deleted from memory.
- My jaw had been completely smashed, now held together by special medical wires until it healed; I hardly could open my mouth to speak.
- My broken ribs caused pain if I moved, and my lungs were full of blood making it difficult to breath.

Needless to say, I was confined to the bed, unable to do anything independently, except open and close my eyes. I was not able to sit up nor could I turn to either side. My injuries forced me to lay flat without the ability of moving at all. I was taken care of by my family and close friends. They were there with me twenty-four hours of the day, every day of the week, providing me with healthy, nutritious food, and taking care of my personal needs.

Since my jaw was fastened shut, I could not open my mouth nor could I chew a meal. So my mom used a straw to feed me. Every day she would bring food, which she had prepared at home, mashing it all together to form a half-liquid mass. It was always so delicious. It seemed to me that whatever I ate, it was the first time I tried it. I kept saying that her meals were the most delicious, and that she was the best cook in the whole world.

My mom was like my angel. Her warmth and love comforted me and I felt safe when she was around. She always came in with a smile and it seemed like the whole room would light up from her love and presence. Like all mothers, she knew what was needed for her child. I always waited for her to come. Nobody and nothing could replace my mother's warmth, love and care.

Looking back, I recall the best part of my meals were the freshly squeezed juice that my brother prepared for me. Valdas would always be the one who would come up with ideas on how to spoil me. He would daily bring delicious juice, smoothies, a variety of desserts, and get me things for my entertainment. In addition to pampering me with such items, he would always be on guard, making sure I had absolutely everything I needed and wanted, and that I was well taken care of.

Valdas had always been especially protective of his little sister. A few years previous I even started calling him my "personal bodyguard." If there was someone who tried to hurt me, I knew that all I needed was to tell my brother and that person would reap the consequences. But even though my darling brother is a very strong man, he has a tender heart. Every time I looked at him, I could see the agony in his eyes, not knowing what else he could possibly do to make it better for me and to make it easier for my parents.

Valdas "wore his heart on his sleeve." That is, he was not able to hide his suffering. He felt guilty that he was not able to prevent the crash. While feeling the immense pain and an untold hatred toward those whose actions brought about the occurred circumstances, he was consumed with finding solutions and ways to keep me cared for.

My dad took the administrative role. He was constantly meeting with specialists to make sure I was never neglected, organizing all the necessary documents and details for my stay at the hospital and further care. He had excellent qualities of diplomacy and discipline from his profession as a pilot and Security Director at the airport. He could always resolve any challenging situation and I knew he would do the same now.

Dad was my rock. I was not sure exactly what he was arranging, but I always knew he had my best interests in mind. I trusted that he would take care of everything, whatever the case. I always was Daddy's Girl and I knew he would do whatever it took to make sure I had all the best.

I always loved my father very much. While being disciplined and professional, he had a very kind and soft heart, and I always knew I could trust him and count on him. I always wanted him to be near, just as my mother and brother. His presence always gave me a sense of peace, comfort and security. I was amazed watching them working as a team and doing their best to provide the best possible care for me. I felt greatly loved. Their unconditional care pushed away any fears, or questions about what was going on. They focused on the "now," making certain they were doing all they could to keep me calm and comfortable.

I knew nothing about what had actually happened nor was I told details about my injuries. I knew only one thing, that I was very much loved. Seeing the pain and concern on their faces, I understood that something very serious had happened. But instead of telling me about it, they constantly showered me with care, smiles and joy for my rapid recovery. I was always very grateful for my family and now I was even more thankful that I had them. This event drew us all closer together. I wish they knew what I knew, but I knew they would not have taken me seriously. So I tried to comfort them by repeatedly telling them that everything was going to be alright.

In addition to my family, it seemed like everyone who knew me came to shower me with love and to support my family. My friends would take shifts, staying overnight at my bedside, so my family could go home and have some well-deserved and much needed rest. My room was constantly filled with visitors. Friends and acquaintances were visiting me throughout the day, bringing me flowers, various soft toys and gifts. My stay at the hospital felt like an ongoing hangout with the people I loved. My friends and I together would revisit memories and create our new plans, looking into the future with joy and optimism. One time, a friend even decided to celebrate his birthday in my hospital room so that I could be present for the party as always. It was the same friend, with whom I had my conversation that early morning, and after which I got distant from the church. Later I found out that he insisted to be let into the ICU when no one was allowed to be there except my family. He was visiting me on the ongoing basis.

I guess it was only then did I realize how blessed I was to have so many people who cared about me and loved me. It seemed that I had not seen many of them for a very long time, and I made every effort to be present with them regardless of my physical condition and my difficulty speaking. Day or night, the atmosphere in my room was always uplifting. My friends were cheering me up and complimenting me on getting stronger with every day. And I was cheering them up by telling them not to worry, because the accident was not going to affect my life that much.

Painkiller drugs kept me always cheerful, so I couldn't fully comprehend the true picture of what this accident actually meant. I knew that I suffered serious injuries during the accident, but what had happened was only a fact for which I had no feelings. I wasn't worried at all. In fact, I was probably the most cheerful person in the room.

I was trying to convince everybody that it wasn't the end; I would get prosthetic legs and live my life just as I used to. I kept saying I would come back to my normal life routine and my friends would have me back with them as soon as I got better. To my airport friends I promised that I would come back – they would see me yet again walking into the Business Lounge. It would be "business as usual."

I knew many people thought I was speaking with such optimism and eagerness because I was affected by the pain killers given to me daily. I could see it in their eyes. What they weren't aware of was that there was something more beyond the peace and positive beliefs that I had. There was a reason why I was reassuring everyone that my life was going to be well in spite of this accident.

I knew I would recover soon. I also knew that life would be extraordinary. I didn't know where this awareness came from or how my life could be possibly special, but I had that awareness engraved in my heart and I knew that it wasn't drug-related. Strong narcotics made me cheerful and taking it easy on everything, but the peace and positive outlook about my future came from a different source. I could clearly distinguish between the drug effect and that indescribable peace that I had within me at all times. Nobody knew what I had really experienced in the ICU, the true reason why I was so positive and calm about everything.

As a confirmation of my peace, I was healing and recovering miraculously fast. The hospital staff and doctors were shocked and they could not explain my rapid healing. They kept saying that my case was one of the most incredible ones in their practice and that what they were witnessing was unbelievable. They said it was an absolute miracle that I actually survived after losing so much blood and suffering such severe trauma.

Doctors were amazed every time they performed their visitation procedures, usually on Monday mornings. My surgeon would tell them the facts of the accident, the physical condition in which I was brought to the hospital, and my healing process. As I was watching my surgeon giving them the report about me, I could see the astonishment in the eyes of those listening. Hearing the diagnoses, they would look at each other or roll their eyes, expressing their wonder – or outright disbelief – in the facts as they were presented. As they provided their feedback, trying to explain, some said it was probably "divine providence." Some said it was because I was so optimistic. And the remainder didn't know what to say. I was the only one who knew who was behind my inexplicably rapid recovery, and I knew it was just the beginning of my unusual journey.

I was getting stronger with every day. As my jaw healed and I could open my mouth a little more, my mother started spoon-feeding me more substantial home prepared meals. But the real first step forward was the time when my doctors allowed me to sit up. Oh, how much joy we all felt when, with someone's help, I was able to accomplish this task! I would get dizzy and weak after a few minutes and someone had to hold me, but I didn't care. It felt so good to be able to sit. After ten minutes I would feel exhausted, and the person who was holding me would help me to lie down again. Every time I would sit a few minutes longer than before, and that was considered a huge success.

I was excited to see that I was getting stronger, and I started to look forward to getting back to my normal routine. I was missing life. While I was in bed unable to move, I dreamt of getting prostheses and walking again, getting back to work, and step by step returning to my lively world.

I felt a certain comfort from the idea, how nice it would be when I came back to the airport to continue the job that I loved. I so missed the good times with my friends, whether partying and laughing, or cozy nights with heartfelt conversations over a cup of tea. I even considered attending church again. I missed my life and I couldn't wait to get back to it.

After a month I already started saying that I was looking forward to the end of my "vacation." It's fun to have a little break from a routine, but that was enough. I wanted to get back into action and live my life instead of lying there in a hospital bed at the mercy of others for my every need.

Yet the more that I was sharing my anticipation, the more I began noticing the behavior of my parents and my brother that had me concerned. I started hearing words like "disability" and "wheelchair," which were not in my vocabulary, and certainly not part of my plans for a return home. I did not know anything about prostheses and how they were made, but I assumed I could get them even while I was at the hospital. In fact, I expected to walk out of the hospital.

Even more, I couldn't understand why nobody was talking about Dalius. Every time I asked family or friends about him and how he was feeling, I would hear the same response: "I don't know." I ended up asking them every day to tell me. Knowing of my own trauma, I assumed that it'd been a pretty bad accident, and so I really wanted to know about Dalius.

Then one day, my father sat on my bed, looked straight into my eyes, and he told me, "Inga, there's something you need to know. We didn't want to make you upset, but now we think you need to know this."

I looked at him with a question in my eyes, wondering what kind of additional injury I had that I hadn't been told about. After a moment of silence, Dad quietly said that Dalius was no longer among us. He was gone. I did not want to believe what I just heard. My father sadly repeated that Dalius was dead. Neither of us had worn our safety belts. It was cruel fate that I remained in the car and Dalius was forcefully ejected, killed instantly by a fatal injury to his skull.

Up to this moment, as days were passing by, I'd been learning about the terrible consequences of the crash, but this was something beyond my expectations. I was so shocked that I simply didn't know what to say. For the first time I felt the strange cold feeling of death, horror and terrifying fear. Tears made my father and the room fade away.

I asked my father to leave me alone and then I covered myself with a blanket. I couldn't speak anymore. The ultimate news shook me like none of the previous ones. It was the first time I understood that everything was far more serious than I had thought. I could hardly process the news that I would never see him again. Dalius and I only dated for several months. We'd met when Renata and I decided to hitchhike for a ride instead of waiting for the bus to get back to the city. We watched the cars passing by at crazy speeds and all of a sudden, we heard a loud squeaky noise. We looked where it was coming from and saw this car quickly going backwards toward us. In a few seconds the racer was right there. He opened the door and asked with a smile, "Need a ride, girls?" I saw that he was attracted to me instantly, and he invited us to join him and his friends for the evening at a Finish sauna.

After we declined his offer, and after some playful conversation, he asked me for my phone number. Then he started calling every day, to show that he wanted to go out with me. But somehow I didn't have a good feeling about the connection, but I couldn't understand why. Yet I disregarded my feelings and we began casually dating. After a while, it slowly started transforming into a relationship. And then, I lost him as soon as my feelings for him started to develop.

"Why? Why did You allow this?" I kept asking God in my mind. It was hard to comprehend that I would never see him again. Or hear his voice. Or hear him laugh. Or have him hold my hand. Nor would I be able to enjoy fast rides with him, watching how perfectly he handled the car at high speeds. Little by little I began to see the real consequences of that fatal night. It felt like I was slowly waking from a beautiful dream created by my loving family and friends, overflow of gifts, flowers, entertainment and narcotic drugs. Reality was setting in and I started noticing things that raised a lot of questions and made me concerned.

Talks about sessions with a psychologist, getting a wheelchair, and joining disability organizations made me restless. Actually, it made me frustrated. I had already decided that I was going to walk, go back to work, and return to my previous lifestyle; the word "disability" or anything related to it was not going to have a place in my life. I couldn't understand why in the world they were so worried, trying to get special care for me.

When it was strongly suggested that I speak with a psychologist, it simply irritated me. I couldn't understand how a person, with no understanding as to what I had been through and what I was currently going through, could help me and give me advice on how to handle it all. I knew my pain better than anyone else and I was the one who knew best how to deal with it. I would have to figure it out. I was visited by a psychologist nevertheless. She was very nice and we had a pleasant conversation about my feelings and my intentions after I returned home. After that single conversation, she never came back. I guess she didn't feel the need to see me anymore.

Overhearing my father asking nurses and doctors about organizations which help people with disabilities, and where he could obtain a wheelchair, made me very concerned. I was expecting to get prosthetic legs immediately and there was no way I was going sit in a wheelchair. As soon as I found out that he was trying to obtain one, I firmly told him that he was wasting his time because I was not going to sit in a wheelchair nor was I going to join any organizations for the "disabled." I told him how I didn't consider myself disabled and would not need a wheelchair, because I was going to walk again. Mom, watching this scene and barely holding her tears, tried to calm me down by saying, "Inga, daughter. How are you going to move around without it?"

"Mom," I replied fiercely. "I am going to walk again. And I don't want to have any discussions about wheelchairs or me joining some disability association. I am the same Inga regardless of what has happened. And as soon as I get out of here, I will go to facilities that will make me prosthetic legs and I am going to walk again, period. I will go back to the airport, just as I promised. I will get back to work and will live my life the way I did prior the accident."

Any topics related were rejected and I refused even to discuss anything remotely associated with the word "disability." I couldn't understand. It seemed that everyone knew what was best for Inga, without ever consulting her and asking what intentions she had. At this point, I was already impatient to get out of the hospital. I wanted to obtain prosthetic legs and return to my normal life. I didn't want to stay there anymore, watching their concerned faces. And yet, despite my expectations and my plans, there came the day when I realized that there was a big gap between the reality of my situation and what I had imagined.

My left hand's condition appeared to have serious nerve damage and I was referred to another hospital that specialized in that area. I had to get ready and be driven to another part of the city to see another specialist. It was the first time I had to get out of bed for any real length of time. After long negotiations with my parents trying to talk me into allowing my dad to place me in a wheelchair, I finally agreed. He carefully and very gently picked me up and transferred me into the wheelchair. Then, mom took a pair of pants and gently began putting them on. As she was helping, I felt irritated that I had to go through this embarrassing moment of being transferred into a wheelchair and being helped to get dressed. I said, "This is the first and the last time when I sit in a wheelchair! I will walk anyway; I won't need it."

I was so consumed by the thought of the wheelchair that I never considered what would happen next. Seconds later, a shiver of horror shot up my spine. I looked down and saw only my thighs; the lower parts of my pants were hanging freely empty. And then there was the floor. My knees, lower legs and my feet were not there.

I started crying hysterically, engulfed by those hanging empty pants. Since I was lying in the bed all this time and the lower part of my body was always covered with a blanket, I rarely saw my legs (or where they should have been). I always had the feeling of my legs as a whole – I felt they were still there (called a "phantom feeling"); and therefore, I knew that I had lost them, but I didn't really comprehend it.

Now I did.

My parents called the doctors immediately and I was given drugs to calm down. Slowly, very slowly, I felt the calming effect. I became calm only when the drugs began working. However, the view of my empty hanging pants confronted my medically induced illusion of calmness and comfort. No matter what kind of pill they prescribed, now I fully grasped the reality. The day which everyone was afraid of, finally showed up at our doorstep – the day I finally realized I no longer had legs.

I was so overwhelmed that I couldn't think of anything else. I don't even remember my visit to the specialists that day. In addition, being rolled out of the hospital in a wheelchair, my father transferring me in and out of the car, made me actually experience the dreadful reality, which I was not able to comprehend up to this moment. All I could think about was returning to the hospital as soon as possible, so I could get back into bed and be covered with a warm, comforting blanket. I did not want to spend another minute in a wheelchair. Looking at my remaining thighs and hanging empty pants were beyond what I could endure.

Now my stay at the hospital did not seem that easy and fun as it was before. Now I knew everything. Dalius had been killed. I lost my legs. My left arm got paralyzed, yet nonetheless causing sharp non-stop pain. I had multiple severe injuries, which caused pain with every single movement.

Doctors reduced the dosage of my pain killer drugs, so I had a clearer mind and was more aware of what was going on. While I still had that inner awareness, that my life would be remarkable, I was afraid of the day when I would have to get out of bed and again see that I had lost nearly half of my body. At the same time, I couldn't wait to end my stay at the hospital, get stronger, and receive artificial legs, so that I could return to my life.

And after being brought back to life multiple times by the emergency teams, on the verge of death, bleeding with severed legs and multiple traumatic injuries, in less than two months I was discharged from the hospital in "stable condition," ready for the next step in my life – the rehabilitation process.

It was a happy day, because it meant that the first chapter of my recovery had been finally closed. Now I was eager to open a new chapter – my physical recovery, so I could get back to my normal life routine as soon as possible. I kept repeating to myself and to others that I would "come back" regardless of my physical condition and I did not want to hear of any other alternatives.

My dad had to make few trips to transport all the flowers, toys and our belongings. And then he came to pick me up and bring me home. And there I was, after almost two months, in my room alone, feeling as if I'd gone somewhere for a long time. Through my tears I looked at my framed pictures, with every part of my being screaming out in horror.

THIS CAN'T BE TRUE!

I did not feel like the same Inga that I was looking at in those pictures. That beautiful young woman, with the gorgeous body and those long beautiful legs? She's now sitting in a wheelchair legless, injured throughout her body, and feeling pain with every single move.

My head, my neck, my chest, and my thighs were hurting with the slightest movement. And the healing wounds of my thighs felt as though a razor sharp knife was slicing through the muscle and bone all over again. I didn't feel, nor was I able to move, my paralyzed left arm. It was simply "there" without any feeling or any movement. The only way I could tell it was still alive was the constant, intense, burning sharp pain in my palm.

Alone in my room, I was sitting in a wheelchair missing nearly half of my body. From being healthy, confident, beautiful, cheerful and independent, I became weak, incomplete, helpless, crushed and totally dependent on someone else. My whole body was hurting, but it was easy to handle compared to the enormous emotional pain from the comprehension of my new reality. It seemed like just yesterday I was healthy, beautiful and filled with anticipation as to what the day and evening would have in store for me and my friends. Today, my whole body is aching. I am not able to go to another room or do anything without the assistance of a family member or a friend. I can't even roll over in bed without assistance! Just recently, confidence and liveliness were always bursting out of me. Today, I find myself feeling shocked, worthless and scared. Just recently I had a wonderful career and was financially independent. However, it's all wiped out today - I completely depend on my family. Before the accident, I did not depend on anybody and led a dynamic lifestyle and today, I am alone in my room confined to a wheelchair.

All the dreams, aspirations and hopes that I cherished up to that fatal moment were completely demolished. I lost nearly half of my body and with that I lost everything that made my life fulfilling. I began to wonder whether anyone would look at me again the way they did before, instead of looking at me as a disabled woman in a wheelchair. I could not endure. How I wanted to cry out, begging for someone to tell me it wasn't true! My innermost spirit wailed in grief and even worse, my future was a complete unknown.

"Please," I thought to myself. "Somebody, tell me it's a dream, tell me it's a hallucination, tell me anything, but tell me this is not my life!"

I felt exhausted and totally lost. "How am I going to continue? I'm only 22 years old. The rest of my life is still ahead! And I have to continue my life being *like this*? Why? Why did it have to be so cruel?" I felt my soul crying out constantly asking the same questions.

I could not accept what had happened. I could not understand why God allowed this accident to end so horribly. Why did he die and I survived? "Why? Why? Why……", I could hear myself moaning from the gut wrenching awareness that there were no answers to my anguished plea for help.

Even during these soul-crushing moments I did not feel any anger toward Dalius. There was no point in being angry with someone who wasn't alive. I just wanted to know where we were going and why we had to be racing at such crazy speeds on a road that was covered in ice.

But my efforts to recall that night were in vain. I opened my diary to read what I had written prior to the event. Due to severe head trauma, I'd lost my memory about many things. I didn't know how I lived my life for the past six months or so, especially the last few months. The time spanning from New Year's Eve of 2000 until February 12, 2000 had been completely deleted. It seemed like I was reading someone else's stories from someone else's life. I could only recall some of the experiences, but that was all. I realized that if it wasn't in my diary, the time was lost, and would remain a mystery to me.

I opened a new page to start writing about the terrifying world in which I'd awoken. I did not want to talk about my true feelings with my family. They were already suffering, watching me so helpless and in pain, and I did not want to add to that. They tried always to be uplifting and cheerful with me, but I could see the pain and grief carved into their faces. I don't know how they were able to endure through those days and nights when nobody knew if I would live. But I was grateful to them for their love and care, and I did not want to bring them any more pain.

Therefore, I decided not to show my true feelings, what I was really experiencing. It was enough suffering for us all. I decided that the only place where I would reveal my true feelings would be my diary. I opened a new page, dated April 8, 2000.

"I don't even know where I should start," were my first words. "I can barely see anything through my tears of anguish."

I was writing my latest update feeling absolutely terrified. I kept asking myself the question, why it had to be so cruel, and how I was going to live. Deep in my heart I had a tiny bit of hope. I trusted there had to be a reason and I knew there would come a day when I would get my answer.

Enough for now, Brother.

Be strong. All is going to be well.

Love you,
Inga

3

Rehabilitation Center "Baldžio Šilas"

Dear Valdas,

Aside from the accident and coming home, my rehabilitation was mentally the most devastating experience I had ever faced. It was a significant period as this was the time which changed the course of my life. It was during this time that I resolved not to accept my circumstances, but to fight for my life despite the level of tragedy. By sharing this with you, I hope to give you insights for your own life journey.

Much Love,
Inga

* * *

After spending several days at home, I was told my next step was to go to Rehabilitation Center Baldžio Šilas for forty-eight days. It was close to Vilnius city, so it comforted me that I would not be separated from family and friends.

I didn't know why I had to go there, nor did I know what was going to be in store for me once I arrived. I was always healthy and vigorous, and so staying at the hospital was new, while staying at the Rehabilitation Center was even further outside whatever I had imagined or experienced.

What I knew was that I wanted to recover as soon as possible, because I wanted to get prosthetic legs and return to my normal routine. I wanted to be over with any kind of hospitalization, but at this point I had no choice.

No longer could I do what I wished. Now I completely depended on my new circumstances and there was nothing I could do about it. Nothing. And if I dwelled on them, I would slip into a deep, dark despair. I had no idea that from that time forward, life would become a dreadful, never ending night.

My mom showed me new outfits she bought for me, which I could wear to go to the Rehab Center. She got some stretchy Capri length pants and some nice casual tops and sweaters. Regular length pants were no longer to be worn; Capri length pants had less material hanging below. It was still cold outside, so the warm clothing was just right. Mom chose beautiful outfits, though it wasn't what I would usually wear. I was always very selective about my clothes. No casual outfits.

At this point, though, it was better for me to forget the outfits I used to wear. High-heeled Italian shoes, classic style pants or elegant jackets were not destined to be worn anymore. I faced a new reality – I had no say in what I liked or didn't like, what I wanted or didn't want. If that wasn't enough, I had to be helped with getting dressed to go to rehab.

As I watched mom preparing all the necessary items for our stay, I saw that she tried to hide her agony behind the enthusiasm about "us" getting stronger and moving forward. She would repeatedly say things like, "We are going to get through this" and "We will heal and get stronger." It was clear this was not simply my accident; it was our accident, shared by the entire family. And in a very real sense she was right. Getting a dreadful message in the middle of the night, rushing to the hospital and seeing me on the verge of death, after having been injured and bruised to the point of being recognized only from my manicure, was a terrifying ordeal for everyone. The world stopped for them. My family and all who knew me prayed and anxiously waited to know if I would come back to them. When my condition became more stable, they had to face horrifying consequences that were shocking to everyone.

Watching me so weak and in constant pain, but not being able to help me, made it nearly unbearable for my family. I heard that they would've given their own legs and arm if they could, so that I would be complete and happy again. I could not possibly know their pain since I had never been a parent, nor had my brother ever experienced anything like it before. However, I could see the immense anguish and overwhelming grief in their eyes every time I looked at them. And I knew, they were suffering just as I was, maybe even more than I was.

It was then that I felt guilty, knowing that I was the cause of it all. It was easier to handle the contempt for my complete dependency on others than it was this taunting helplessness, unable to do anything about the anguish in their hearts. But the clock could not be turned back; events were irreversible.

As much as we hated this change, we all had to face the tragedy. While each of us dealt with the shock in our own way, it seemed like we all had an unspoken agreement to get through it together. My mom, dad and my brother were all in sync, arranging the necessary care for me. They were doing everything possible to help, regardless of how it was for them to deal with their own agony, watching me incapable of helping myself and so frightfully weak. It seemed like all they were thinking and living for was my comfort and well-being. In an unguarded moment, when she thought I couldn't hear, I overheard my mom saying that she knew she had to be strong for me, and that's what helped her to get up in the morning and deal with each new challenge.

Mom, Valdas and my father put me ahead of their own needs and interests, showering me with unconditional love and care, which carried me through every single day. As much I as desired to make it easier for them, there was nothing I could possibly do to lift the burden, except to stay emotionally uplifted, giving them my encouragement and passing on my strong belief that all was going to be well. I did everything possible not to show them my true emotional and physical torment in order to protect them from additional suffering. I knew that seeing me crying and depressed would only make it worse. I did not allow myself to get to that point. Instead, I put forth my strong determination to get back into the rhythm of life, and the belief that I had absolutely no doubts that it could happen.

After completing the initial survival process, we faced a new stage of my recovery that brought some relief but at the same time, revealed the cruelty of the consequences and the beginning of my new daily challenges, coupled with an endless feeling of hopelessness. My dad transferred me into the wheelchair, and after barely getting through the elevator door due to the chair's width, we slowly went down to the ground floor of the house. My brother parked the car in front of our home's entrance and widely opened the front passenger doors. While mom held the building's doors opened, my dad then took me into his arms, carried me downstairs, and seated me in the car.

I saw an enormous pain in their eyes, but nobody said a word. None of us could have ever thought of such a drastic, unexpected turn in our lives. I felt unconditionally loved, but worthless and helpless at the same time. My mom buckled me up to make sure I was wearing a safety belt. I hated wearing seatbelts and I never used to wear them. But at this point, I did not argue. Dalius would've probably been alive today had he worn a seatbelt that night, and who knows whether the result would have been the same for me had I been wearing one. My brother started the car and began to drive. He turned on my favorite music to eliminate the dead silence. None of us knew what to say. We all shared the same feeling of unbearable pain and fear of what the future held for us.

The Rehabilitation Center was located in a gorgeous setting. It was in a forest surrounded by lakes; it was one of the most visited sites in the summer. On hot days people went there to swim, barbecue and relax, enjoying nature with their friends and loved ones. The road to the center was the same one that my friends and I used to take to go have fun at the lake. As we drove by familiar places, I was brought back to those good times, when we would drive fast laughing, listening to the loud music. The atmosphere was always cheerful and easy because we were always enjoying our time together, expecting even more fun at our destination.

And now, I was driving on the same road to some Rehabilitation Center without my legs, a paralyzed arm, and feeling weak and totally lost. As we got closer to the main section of the center, I had a very unpleasant feeling. Our entrance into the building was met by the stuffy smell of urine and medicine. I couldn't believe that I had to be here. A staff member welcomed us, asking us to follow her to the room that was reserved for me. Going down the hallway, through widely opened doors, I saw old people lying in beds. As we were passing by other rooms, I pleaded in my mind that I wouldn't have to stay with other people. I wanted to be left alone, to shut myself off from the world. Dad rolled me into the last room of the hallway.

"This is your room, Inga," the staff member said, trying to comfort me. "I hope you will be comfortable here."

It was cold and dark in that room. Through the windows I could see the forest of pine trees. The trees next to the window looked cold, grey and naked without leaves. I thought to myself that it must be beautiful here in the summer, with the green trees and blossoming wildflowers all around.

But I did not like this place. It seemed that I was locked in some elderly nursing home, with nobody even asking whether I wanted to be here or not. And I was told I would be staying for forty-eight days. If I had the choice,

I would not have stayed for even one day. I would call my friends and ask them to come retrieve me immediately. Or I would call a cab as I used to do, and that would be it. I'd be gone, out of there in a flash.

"This is not where I am supposed to be!" I screamed in my mind. I could not accept this. I kept thinking how wrong this all was; I could not accept this new reality. "This is not how everything was supposed to be. I don't belong here!"

I would have given away anything so I could disappear from what I was forced to experience. Inside I felt like the same Inga, and I wanted to continue my lively adventurous life. But I realized the change was permanent; it was all part of my life now. I had no legs any more. I could not feel or use my left arm any more. And I was weak and totally dependent upon others.

No matter how much I hated the idea of staying in this place, I had no other choice. I knew I had to shut down my naturally rebellious nature and accept it all. I told my parents that I needed to rest. I had to get away. Mom helped me to lie down and then she handed me a new CD player. After making sure I was warm and comfortable, she continued unpacking, making the room a little cozier. Seeking at least some measure of emotional comfort, I turned on my favorite songs and retreated under the blanket. I needed to disappear at least for a while. The news about my physical condition, my limited ability to function independently, and all the drastic changes that came with the accident, were too much. To the sound of my favorite music, in my mind I returned to the last few years, which were the most beautiful, the most interesting, and the most significant times of my life. I was so independent, vigorous and healthy. I made decisions that seemed right and I never had to ask for anybody's permission. I never had to depend on anyone in any way.

I was always among friends, with whom we worked and spent our leisure time together. My days were quite lively. I was never alone. Spending time with friends, fun times at the coffee places and pubs, and dancing at the nightclubs, that was my lifestyle for the last few years. It all started when I transferred to work into the Business Lounge. My work at the airport became more than just a job, it grew into becoming the center of my life. I absolutely loved my new job. It didn't even feel like work. The airport became like a second home since we had to work twenty-four hour shifts. I was always looking forward to the days when I would have to get up early, put on my professional suit, and arrive at the airport.

On the way to work I might allow myself to be consumed by my thoughts, concerns and emotions, but as soon as I approached that busiest place in the city, I would push it all behind. Rushing people, cars dropping off and picking up passengers, taking off and landing airplanes, the activity would stir the excitement within me. I would forget about all that was going on in my personal life. As soon as I entered the airport's Departure Hall, I would dive in into the noisy atmosphere. Joy and excitement would push away my personal world and I would transform into an outgoing and cheerful Inga. Since I began working in the Business Lounge I met a lot of people from the Duty Free shop, Security and Border Police, and from various airlines as well. Going through the Security and Duty Free shops were always filled with the smiles and loud "Good Mornings," sharing unusual stories of their job duties, funny airport stories and laughter. These were some of the best moments of my work day. And as soon as I entered the Business Lounge, I would become an official representative of the Business Lounge of Vilnius International Airport. I always felt responsible for the experience that business passengers had before leaving our country, and I would do my best to make them feel welcome.

Oftentimes during the day, I thought of my dad. He always set a great example for me. While I was growing up I always knew him to be polite, professional and diplomatic in any situation. He always looked strong. At the same time, he was so loving and caring. He would never say "No" to his little girl; he was always my shelter. And when he would put on his pilot uniform, I saw him transform into a sharp and disciplined man. I remember how he would come home after his flights with a beautiful bouquet of mom's favorite Mimosa flowers, and kiss her and say, "It's so good to be home, I missed all of you so much."

Later, when he worked as Security Director, he taught me some professional skills that grew to become imprinted into my heart. And now, as I was wearing my bright blue professional Business Lounge suit, I would always keep in mind my father, whom I so admired. Working at the airport, I felt privileged to continue in my father's legacy.

I started working there when I was 19 years old. My first position was in the Personnel Department, and when I was promoted to the Business Lounge manager's position, a new world opened up. Excitement, constant change, meeting people, and an uplifting atmosphere pushed away a deep, spiritual sadness.

My work environment carried me through a very hard time when I was feeling lost. It seemed like I entered a new world, so much more colorful and easy. My time at work was filled with cheerful, meaningful conversations, joy and laughter. It was so uplifting and easy to be there. I was always looking forward to my shift. In addition to my special connection with the airport and the new exciting environment, it was there that I met friends who became very dear to my heart.

Soon after I started my new position, I noticed there was one Border Police Officer named Andžej, who attentively watched whenever I passed by; he always made the effort for me to notice him. I did not give much thought to him at first, since he was not my type of a guy, but soon Andžej's persistence won me over. Starting with casual greetings, gradually he began showering me with compliments and affectionate attention. Saying that he made me feel like a princess is not even close. I didn't even notice how Andžej became much more than some co-worker.He became a very important part of my life. Little did I know that he would be the one who would bring the dreadful news to my family that night.

I was especially grateful for my friend Renata; we were like sisters. We shared our life journeys together from the day I started my new position. We helped each other at work and we spent our free time together, considering each of us had three days off after a twenty-four hour shift. It didn't matter whether we had our wild party time in the city or in nature with a barbecue, times were always lively and pleasant. When we grew tired of parties and noisy evenings, we would stay at home, make dinner and relax sharing our girlfriend time. Sharing enjoyable times together was something we both appreciated, but what really got us connected were our similar values, mutual trust and support for one another. We had each other to lean on during difficult times. We knew we could totally trust each other and we were always just a phone call away if one of us needed anything.

We were like sisters. Renata and I spent so much time together that it seemed like she belonged to my family. And I felt like a part of her family when visiting her hometown. Renata became even closer after I got into the crash. She was at the hospital every single day when she was free from her work shift, and she took care of me. I trusted her to take care of my needs as I trusted my mother. We knew each other so well that we could understand each other just from our looks.

Renata always knew what I needed and how to help me. Knowing how I cared for my physical appearance, fulfilling my request she even applied my mascara while I could hardly speak. Only my best girlfriend could do that. She was the one who told me that she was able to recognize me in the ICU only from my black polish manicure. I assume she recognized the manicure because we did it together at her home while having a girl night. I was staying at her place for a few weeks prior to the accident and what a memorable time that was.

"Inga, how are you doing?" I heard my mother's voice say. I uncovered myself to look at her. My whole body was aching. "Would you like some juice?"

"No, mom," I quietly responded, trying not to move too much. It seemed like the pain never left. But sometimes I could find a position where it was almost bearable and I could get some sleep. "I don't want anything, but thank you."

I was looking out the window and saw nothing but gray skies and naked trees. I so wanted it to be over and for things to be back the way they were. But it was cold and dreary, a poignant reflection of my feelings. I simply could not believe that what I was seeing and experiencing was my new reality. I was lying in bed feeling totally lost. All I could do independently was see, speak and feel. One moment turned my life upside down. Only now did I realize that I had taken so many things for granted. I had been enjoying my life, but I did not appreciate that which I had and what I could do. All that I had seemed as it was supposed to be and I never considered how it was a precious gift, that I could walk and live independently. Only now did I see how fortunate I was. I never even thought about how fragile we really are as human beings. And we never know what awaits us either today, tonight or tomorrow.

We dream, plan and create, but we don't know how it all might end at any second. Today we can be healthy and beautiful, but we don't know if we'll be the same tomorrow. One day we have all that we need, and the next day it could all be gone. When we leave our home, we do not really know if we will come back the same as we left, or whether we will ever come back home at all. I left home the night of the accident with lots of dreams, aspirations and plans. I spent my evening with a special person without considering how the night might not end in the way I had planned. Instead of greeting a new morning at home, I woke up in the ICU hooked up to a life support machine. And my stay at the Rehab Center revealed that my physical condition was far more serious than I had previously thought, and nothing was going to be as easy as I thought it would be.

My dream of getting prosthetic legs and returning to my previous life was drifting away. There was no way I could immediately go to the Prosthetic Center to get artificial legs. Injuries throughout my body made me completely unable to move or take care of myself. Before I could get artificial legs made, I had to heal completely, gain my physical strength back, and learn to function without legs and only one functional arm.

It felt like someone had forcefully locked me into a cage of emotional and physical suffering, from which there was no escape. No longer was I comfortably lying in bed at the hospital, covered with warm blankets, entertained by my family and friends. Now I was facing a different situation. I realized that my injuries had made me totally unable to take care of my basic daily needs, which I could not see when I was in the hospital.

The slightest movement of my thighs felt like someone was using a sharp razor to cut through my flesh and bones all over again. Sharp burning pain in the palm of my paralyzed hand would not go away, even for a second. I thought I would go insane just from the pain in my hand. And the pain that I absolutely could not tolerate was touch of my left ear. It was excruciating. I was not sure what the injury was; nobody ever talked about it. Due to a severe head injury, I couldn't touch my entire left side of my head. Brushing my hair was an absolute torture.

My helplessness was beyond frustrating. I was not able to simply sit up by myself from a lying position, and I always had to ask someone to help. Getting up, dressing, going to the restroom, daily morning routine, making a meal or moving around, I had to be helped by another person. What once seemed to be a simple daily routine was no longer simple; I couldn't do it by myself anymore. From being fully independent, arriving to this state was unendurable. I could never have imagined this is how my life would change. I began to feel deep contempt for every single moment of my existence.

Experiencing my many limitations and continuously facing new and radical changes each day made me wish only one thing – to disappear from my awareness. I couldn't wait for daytime to pass, so I would not have to live through the constant awareness that my life was not what it used to be.

During the night was the only time when I felt some relief, because I was in bed not having to look at my body, not having to deal with my limitations, and not having to face the consequences of the tragedy over and again.

But the never-ending burning pain in my paralyzed arm would not let me relax and fall asleep. Pain and ongoing thoughts kept me awake throughout most of my nights, holding me hostage by this abrupt life alteration. Thoughts of what had happened, the death of Dalius, and the unexpected turn in my life were raising ongoing questions, especially about how my life would continue. And admittedly, I was afraid of what the future would bring.

My back was constantly aching from lying flat; my only escape from that was to have someone turn me on my side. I hated to wake up my mom or anybody who stayed overnight to ask for their help, so I would wait until I couldn't stand it anymore. After I was helped to turn on a side, I felt great physical relief. But there was no relief from the mental agony. Thoughts of the horror of the accident and fear of the future would not subside. I would meet the sunrise feeling exhausted from a sleepless night. The morning however, would not end my nightmare. In fact, that's when it would begin all over again.

The Rehabilitation Center had a variety of physiotherapy and massage programs for those who had suffered traumatic injuries. Physiotherapy sessions were on a daily basis. I didn't really want to go to the gym and do the exercises. Being an athletic runner in the past and having a strong physical health prior to the crash made it extremely difficult to appear in the gym with no ability to move. Every day, it made me face again and again the heart-wrenching fact that I had lost half of my body.

I knew I had to do it whether I liked it or not, and I forced myself to do what I needed to do. I liked the team of physiotherapists; they were young, fun people. Time with them was a little distraction. And I had a goal to get strong as soon as possible, and that was the biggest motivation which I kept in mind at all times.

Another rehab aspect was the massage. Rose, the massage specialist, was an extraordinary woman and my mom and I liked her. It was always a pleasure when, in the mornings, I would see her coming, always smiling, energetic and cheerful. She would always lift my spirits. By contrast, usually I loved massages, but these massage sessions were plain torture, each one testing my endurance. Just the thought of it made my functional hand's palm sweat. My body hurt from the slightest movement or a gentle touch, and Rose would do a deep tissue strong massage, starting from my left ear and head ending with my remaining thighs. After my daily rehabilitation sessions, feeling rescued from the procedures I could hardly endure, I would go back to bed, put on my music, and make my new reality fade away.

Day and night I would talk to God asking why He had allowed this to happen in such a cruel way. I have never been so terrified in my life. I could not see how I was going to continue. The scariest part was the hopelessness, because I couldn't see how I could possibly change my circumstances – lost parts of my body were not going to come back; life in a wheelchair meant an imprisoned existence within the walls of my own home.

At the time Vilnius was not accessible for wheelchair users: there were continuous barriers of stairs to get into buildings, no curb cuts, and no wheelchair access throughout public transportation. It was hard to imagine what was ahead for me. The only thing that offered comfort was that I had my family and my friends, who loved me unconditionally and took care of me twenty-four hours a day, seven days a week.

My friends continued visiting me at the Rehab Center and showered me with their love. They would spend time with me, giving me the news that I was missing, saying that everyone's waiting for my recovery and my return. Every single visit meant more than they could ever imagine. I was so happy to see how they remained so faithful despite my terrible adversities. I don't know how I would have gone through that time if I hadn't the love and support that I got from them.

It seemed there was no end to my hopelessness. The only thing that gave me endurance was my faith in God. I knew that by bringing me back to life, my Heavenly Father had given me another chance for a purpose only He knew. Now that the first shock had passed and I was fully emotionally present, visiting people shared with me what they knew about the accident and their amazement about my survival. The more I learned the facts, how severe and devastating the crash was, the more astonished I was. The way the emergency team got there only minutes before I died, the fact that I actually survived, the unusual rapid recovery, it all made a big statement to me – the Lord was with me.

Never before had I ever been so firm about my faith in the Lord. Those incredible experiences I had while I was in the ICU, and the divine presence with me at all times while I was in the hospital, were constantly on my mind. I did not tell anybody about it, because it was very sacred and personal. I had the sense that nobody would understand. Most likely they would have considered that I was under some morphine influence and would have suggested to me not to take it seriously.

But it was too precious to have someone respond with disdain if I told them, nor was I willing to argue with anyone. There is no way the drug effect can compare with the love and peace that totally surpasses human understanding, much less my ability to put it into words. Now I *knew* that

Jesus Christ of Nazareth was not just some historical religious figure. He was truly alive in the spirit.

I could have been angry at God for allowing this to happen, but I was not. I made the choices that led to the crash, not God. But I was perplexed as to why it had to end so tragically. What was His overall purpose behind all of this? I was tormented by waves of emotions, confusion, terror and questioning, and I kept asking why it had to be so cruel, trying to understand where God had been when we hit that light pole.

One morning Rose came into my room for my regular massage procedures with an astonished look on her face and shouted with a smile, "Inga! Do you know you were born under the lucky star?"

I answered with more than a bit of sarcasm. "Me? Oh yes, sure, me. In fact, I was born under quite few lucky stars," I replied. Internally I thought, "I lost half of my body and my ability to function. What a nice concept of being born under the lucky star."

"No, no. You don't understand." Rose came up closer and looked straight into my eyes, holding x-rays of my skull and my spinal cord. "I looked at your x-rays and couldn't believe what I found! There was the slightest chance between you breaking your neck, which would have resulted in full paralysis of your whole body, and the way it is now. Your one cervical vertebra got slightly cracked, and that's the reason why you feel neck pain and can't hold your head straight. If at that moment you had turned your head in a slightly different angle, or would have hit it a little bit stronger, you would be lying here with no ability to move your body at all. You would have been fully paralyzed for the rest of your life. Do you understand what a miracle it is that you actually can move at all?"

It sounded like a beautiful fairy tale, or some fantasy to make me feel better. I wanted to brush it off and prepare myself for the impending hour of endurance. Rose, however, didn't rush to start my massage. She continued, explaining everything in detail from her medical perspective. Listening to Rose share anatomical theories and her observations on how unbelievable it was that I was able to move, my sarcasm began to fade away.

"God *really was* watching over me that night," I thought. The next moment I caught myself putting together facts that I heard about how impossible it was to have survived, my experience in ICU, and my inordinately fast physical recovery.

And now, to hear this?

That moment was like a wakeup call. I realized that the Lord not only saved my life, but prevented me from full paralysis. As devastating as my injuries were, I had finally come to admit, it could have been worse. I was born under a "lucky star" or, as I preferred to say, the Lord was watching over me that night. Although I did not have the answer as to why it had to end so tragically, I saw that the Lord had pulled me out of death and prevented me from injuries which would have kept me bound to a bed for the rest of my life. It was then I saw a glimpse of hope brightening my outlook for the event which turned my life upside down. Rose's astonishment and the facts that she laid before me were on my mind.

I don't remember exactly when this happened, but it was soon after this marveling revelation. One day my mom and I were walking outside enjoying the beautiful spring day and we saw a young guy in an electric wheelchair, sitting alone, enjoying the weather as we were. We walked up to him to chat. He was approximately my age and he was completely paralyzed up to his neck. He was not able to use his legs or his arms and he had a hard time speaking. Like mine, his life had changed in a heartbeat when he got beaten up by a gang, resulting in total and permanent paralysis. This young and handsome guy was sitting in a wheelchair with no ability to move his body, even having difficulty speaking. Were that not enough, his family had abandoned him, forcing him to stay at various Rehab Centers and nursing homes, all the while being taken care of by strangers. As he was sharing his story, a thought came to my mind "See? You could've been in his place. That is what Rose was talking about."

That moment it seemed as though the entire world has stopped. Suddenly, the astonishment of my new revelation of how well it ended for me overshadowed the horror of my loss. "I am so blessed! In addition to the miracle of not breaking my neck, though I had a strong head injury, I can think clearly, I can express myself easily, and I can move!"

I wanted to shout out with happiness. It seemed like my eyes were opened and I saw with clarity how fortunate I was. While talking with the young man, my mind was captured by the astonishing facts of my blessings. All I felt was gratitude. After we ended our conversation, my mom and I continued walking toward the lake. I was completely astounded with what I had just realized.

"Wait a minute," I thought. "I have a clear mind and I can communicate. And while I do not remember many things due to the brain injury, I can think and express myself the way I did prior to the accident. I still have my right arm functioning. What if I still can be independent? I could learn how to do things with one arm, and then I could take care of myself independently. I can move my body freely, so I will walk again wearing prosthetic legs. I won't really have to depend on others. My body is not the same anymore, but I am still able to use what I have left. I will do everything in a way that I can. The important part is that I can! I am blessed that it ended the way it did. I will come back to life."

I was so consumed by my sudden realization that I didn't hear what mom was saying. And as I was having this inner dialogue, I felt how everything was changing within the core of my being, specifically in what I noticed and how I perceived my situation. Instead of looking at my losses and limitations, I saw how much I actually was able to do.

Instead of despair I felt enlightenment. It felt as though with every breath, I was gaining the hope that I would have a way out of this hopeless place in my life. As I was being rolled in the wheelchair through the forest, in my mind I was building a strategic plan to end this rolling in the wheelchair business to bring myself back to life.

"I will come back," I said inwardly. "I will be the same Inga. I have a loving family, who is there for me day and night. I have so many friends who love me and visit me every single day. This crash is not going to dictate how I am going to live. When my wounds are healed and I get stronger, I will get prosthetic legs. I will find ways to do things using one hand. I will learn to walk again using artificial legs. I *will* rebuild my life and I *will* live righteously in the sight of God. I *know* that I will have a beautiful life's journey despite it all."

It felt as if I had broken through the thick layer of tragedy and despair. For the first time, I saw my situation from an entirely different perspective. I had a clear vision of what I wanted my life to be, and I felt fueled with the unbreakable strength to fulfill it. My desperate wish was replaced by strong determination. My hope was replaced by the assurance that with God's help I would restore my life.

I recognized how the Lord was talking to me through the arrangement of these meetings and conversations. He was showing me that He hadn't left. He had been with me all this time. If He was with me and yet this was allowed to happen, then some serious reason had to be behind all of what had occurred. God doesn't make mistakes. I decided that I wasn't going to blame Dalius, fate or God, and I certainly wasn't going to sit there and whine. The accident was not going to determine how my life would evolve.

That moment my inspiration grew into the determination not to give in, but to restore what I had lost.

That sunny spring day made a significant impact in my life. Looking back, I see this time presented me with a choice as to which way I wanted to continue. I chose to fight against the odds. I finally saw that I could change the circumstances if I chose to focus on what I had and what I could do. I deliberately began to work on getting myself out of that mental and physical dead end. My outlook for a new era encouraged me to get out of bed in the morning, go to the gym, and to endure those painful massage procedures.

My confirmation about the new discovery occurred when I met several young people who, due to various reasons, ended up being paralyzed and using a wheelchair. These were my first "similar fate" friends. Two young men with the same name, Saulius and an elegant young woman named Eglė drew me into their circle. They would invite me to spend time with them chatting outside or would come into my room and we would have tea with sweets. They were very supportive and encouraging. What surprised me was that they were always cheerful, joking around and having fun. I could not understand how it was possible to be so uplifting and cheerful while facing the prospect of being confined to a wheelchair for life. Watching them I thought, "Maybe it is possible to enjoy life, even if you have to use a wheelchair?"

They had found life to be beautiful in spite of it all and they found what they could enjoy and appreciate. It had a big impact on me, conveying the message that it is possible to enjoy life, even if you have to live differently. I quietly concluded, "It's what you make out of what you have which will make your life either fulfilling or miserable." Once again I reaffirmed inwardly that I won't give in to my limitations and will not give up restoring my life.

The more I faced the consequences of my adversity, the more I was affirming to myself that what had happened would not determine how I was going to live. My deep contempt for my helplessness and anger toward the drastic change turned into a non-negotiable resolve to work hard and do everything in my power to become independent again and re-create a dynamic, values-based, God-centered lifestyle.

My first goal was to walk. Since the city of Vilnius didn't have wheelchair accommodations at that time, it meant that I had to walk again no matter what. Otherwise I would be stuck at home with no way to go to work and live as I envisioned. I couldn't imagine life restricted by my home walls, hospitals and rehab centers. I desired to move around independently, be able to get out of the house, go to work and lead an active lifestyle as I used to. The more I thought about it, the more enthusiastic I got about implementing my new goals.

As days were passing by, I was rapidly getting stronger. My determination was getting stronger as well. The more I faced obstacles that were caused by my physical challenges, the stronger I felt I was going to overcome each and every one of them. I wasn't going to come to terms with what the crash brought into my life. I did not see myself as disabled, nor was I ever going to accept it as my identity. By the time I ended my rehab time, I felt strong and ready to start my journey towards implementing my vision. I believed that with God's help, I was going to overcome all my obstacles and succeed, creating a vastly different life from where the crash had brought me. I knew that with this event my life did not stop. In fact, it had just begun.

4

My Rock

Hi Valdas,

Sorry that my letter to you got a bit delayed, it was because of a trouble with finding time to write. It is so busy at work right now that I barely have lunch time to write you. And when I get home I'm fairly tired after a day of working non-stop. I hardly even notice how the week has passed by.

My new position at work consumes me. It is still like a dream that I was promoted to this new Public Relations position. It was totally unexpected. It's funny that it came to me just as I was getting tired of my previous position. It feels like someone in the universe had orchestrated everything with perfect timing, just as everything else since the accident. I feel the responsibility to do my job well, and so it requires all my focus, even after I leave the office.

In addition, I have a lot to do for my personal Mary Kay business as a consultant, so I've been busy every single day. Regardless of what's going on though, I want to continue writing, just as I promised. First, I will tell you what I think is the most important factor to consider as you start your journey recovering your life. It will be your strong foundation, on which you will stand and no life storm will be able to knock you down. You will not fall into hopelessness and it will give you strength to move forward despite tribulations.

Often I hear people sharing their observations about me, that they see me as very strong and they admire my ongoing perseverance. It's not that I am "naturally strong" as many may think. I am the same as you are or anyone else. I also make mistakes, experience pain, suffer disappointments and go through life's tribulations. And, after the accident, there were times when I did not want another day to come.

But I have the source of my strength, which has been my rock-solid foundation for many years. And in addition, there is something I do when I face struggles. But I will talk about it in my other letters. Now I want to devote this letter to tell you about the foundation of my inner strength.

My strong character and certain inner qualities were developed over time. They didn't happen overnight. The mindset and attitude that empowers me are the result of my constant work with myself. It can be developed by anyone; it's a matter of choice. The endurance and ongoing tenacity, though, was given to me; it is not mine. I want to share with you the source of my inner strength, so you know where to find it for yourself.

Understand that the trouble you're now facing in your life cannot break you down. Nothing and no one can break you down unless you allow it. Everything has a reason. There is a purpose behind it all. Many are mistaken thinking that "it's too much" for them to conquer their challenges. I hear quite a lot of people saying, "I am not as strong as you are. I don't know if I can overcome this difficulty in my life. I would've never been able to go through what you faced, and I would not be able to overcome those obstacles as you did."

I remember hearing you say that to me, as well. And I want to say to you the same thing I tell everyone else – and what I have told you before – yes, you can successfully handle your current situation. It's only a matter of knowing your source of strength and your choice as to whether you are willing to fight and win, regardless of how hopeless it may seem at the time, or whether you just give up and take the easier path.

I made the choice to fight and my decision was not up for debate. Determination, action and perseverance were my best friends throughout my journey. They were crucial to my recovery and were the keys to the locked doors of opportunity and success. But there is one thing without which I would not have made it. I had to go through many heartbreaking losses and face times when it seemed like there was no end to my hopelessness. But then, I would reach out to what seemed my last and only hope, and to my amazement – my strength was renewed every time.

I found the "Rock on which I stand." It got me out of absolutely hopeless situations every single time. In fact, this was the only thing that gave me endurance to live through my darkest hours. This is the true reason why I remained calm and positive after the accident and looked at my future with hope and anticipation. This is why I became resilient and had the power of relentless perseverance to continue going forward through the ongoing challenges. My empowering perspective, courage and inner strength have a strong foundation, which cannot be shaken by anybody or any circumstances. In other words, the reason I became strong and have a positive mindset is because of something I have and do.

Faith and prayer. Together they are my source of strength providing the driving force. And the Lord Jesus Christ of Nazareth is my Rock. He is my strength and He is the true reason why my life has changed so incredibly.

"Oh no, don't start talking to me about this," you may say. "Let's not get into that religious stuff."

I totally understand. The subject of religion over the years has brought lots of discussion and even heated arguments. You might feel that you have heard about it numerous times, you are disappointed in Christians, you don't believe in Jesus, and you are not interested in "religious fairy tales." I assume that what you really want to hear is something concrete and tangible.

But please hold on. Don't rush to reject what I want to share with you. I do agree there are many who do and say simply outrageous things using the name of Jesus Christ. At some point in my life I was greatly disappointed in people who called themselves Christians. And I left the Christian Evangelical Church because I didn't want to have anything to do with them all. Even today I am disgusted watching how the name of Jesus Christ is blasphemed and ridiculed. I am not blaming you for feeling resentful about this and I can understand your point of view. I want to ask you, though, please don't put this letter away, thinking that you'll "read it later." Read it through and then decide for yourself what you want to do about what I share. After all, you always have a choice in what you are going to do with the knowledge that you receive, right?

Many say to me that I am just a strong person and that's why I overcame the adversity and attained my goals. The true reason for my strength and endurance is my faith. My Lord Jesus Christ is who I get the strength and the blessing from. There were numerous times when the hope that I might see God's help was the only thing that kept me breathing and gave me the will to keep moving. There were times when I felt so tired that even all my knowledge about personal development and success principles did not help.

I got knocked down and deeply disappointed so many times that I simply didn't have the strength to pick myself up. And when nobody could help me and my personal growth knowledge was powerless to help, Christ was the one who picked me up and carried me. He got me back up on my feet after each time I fell. He healed my soul's wounds and encouraged me to take the next step. When I could not walk anymore, He carried me. He was always the one who gave me inner strength, inspiration, courage and endurance to persevere. I sincerely say that I would not have rebuilt my life after the crash like I did, if I did not have my Rock.

Brother, Jesus Christ is alive in the spiritual realm, though we don't see Him with our physical eye. And prayers in His name are truly answered, as it's written in the Bible. I will be honest with you – I don't know how I would have handled the consequences of the accident if not for my faith in the Lord. It's scary to even imagine what my life would be like if I did not have the Lord God on my side. You very well remember me injured beyond recognition in the ICU and how hard it was to face those changes, and how this crash altered all of our lives.

You watched me endure physical pain and emotions dealing with the loss of my body. Despite it all, you often saw my enthusiasm and certainty that all was going to change. I have one question for you: Who do you think gave me hope? Do you remember how all of you were so surprised by my optimism?

You and I and our parents could not even imagine how I was going to continue living with such severe changes. My life seemed to have been given a life sentence characterized by a dull, daily existence. Who do you think gave me the tenacity to change my circumstances? Where did I find the courage and assurance to aim for what seemed outrageous when everyone around me claimed they were impossible to attain?

You witnessed the hardships and stumbling blocks that were in my way. Where did I get the endurance to go through those struggles and then continue with my intentions in spite of it all? How come I had that never-ending enthusiasm for life and ability to continue moving forward despite difficulties, hardships and heartbreaking experiences? How do you think those amazing opportunities were created that completely changed my life? How could it be that today I can sincerely say that I am happier than I was before the accident? I worked very hard to attain the vision that I had for my life, but in order to do that, I had to have certain inner qualities such as hope, determination, endurance, faith, tenacity and relentlessness, all combined with an inner peace.

I additionally had the advantage of having favorable circumstances that opened the doors of opportunities for me. I had people who were willing to help at particular times for specific reasons. I had a blessing in attaining successful results. I am sure you know people who cannot accomplish their desired results no matter how much they try.

Here are some questions for you that I had to grapple with on my road to recovery, both physically and mentally:

- How was it that I survived when I was expected to die at any time, and then healed so unusually fast – a fact even medical specialists could not explain?
- How come I had the inner qualities to create a new life for myself, which (as you know from before the accident) were not in my nature?
- How come I had amazing opportunities presented to me at the perfect times and a blessing in everything I did?

As strange or even unacceptable as it might sound – it was the Lord my God who let me survive, who healed me, who instilled within me inner qualities that were necessary, and who blessed me to restore my life. Brother, that is the source of my many blessings.

Many times people think of God as some mysterious force somewhere up in heaven, who may or may not exist. There are many people who call themselves Christians because they attend a Christian church once a week or on a major holiday. And even though they might go and say their memorized prayers, without thinking what they mean or what difference they make, they don't know the Lord. They sit through the service and after leaving, they conduct themselves in ways which are against God's commandments and they don't really care about it. They live the way they want, satisfying their sinful natures, justifying themselves by saying, "Well, times have changed; everybody does this now and there's nothing wrong with it." If you ask them why they go to church, a common response would be, "I don't know. Because it is a tradition. That's what people do on Sunday mornings. My parents used to do it. I did it from an early age." Or they might say, "Well, I believe there is a God. There is some kind of higher power."

Mostly it boils down to tradition, but that's where it ends. Daily they speak and act the way they desire yet they fail to remember God until the following Sunday, Christmas or Easter. How do I know that? I used to live this way, which wasn't much different from the people around me. I know many who still live this way, as it's common for religion to play such role in people's lives. Faith in God is more like some mysterious topic that people may be aware of, but it doesn't have an impact on their decisions, actions and way of life. In fact, they would rather not discuss faith. This is a religion that has nothing to do with living in faith, following the Lord Jesus Christ as He called us to live.

But I want to tell you about faith that breathes within you day and night. Let me share my thoughts and deepest feelings about the Lord who heals and gives life. The Lord God, our Creator, is not some mystical object, but is as present and real in our daily lives just as you and I are.

God is omnipresent (present everywhere and every time), omnipotent (all powerful, almighty), and omniscient (knowing everything at once). His love and care for us is beyond our comprehension.

And yes, He does answer our prayers. I want to share with you about the Lord who transformed me and my destiny. He is the One who renewed my strength and gave me back my life when nothing and no one else could. That is why it's so important for me to share with you about my faith, a faith that has incredible power and does wonders for those who believe. Faith is not a tangible thing that you can feel and measure. Faith is a great, infinite force which can turn the impossible into the possible, a dream into reality. When you get to know Jesus Christ and surrender your life to Him, your life is never the same. This is the precious treasure that I have found in my journey after the crash. This is my Rock.

A Life Changing Day at Age 16

During my early teenage years, I always knew there was something beyond that which we physically see, that there was some supernatural power beyond our senses, beyond our power to grasp. But I never delved deeper into the subject.

As you well remember, your former classmate Emilija became my private English teacher when I was 16 years old. One day after our session, she asked me if I truly enjoyed smoking. I told her, "I guess I would like to quit, but I can't."

She told me that God could help me with that and invited me to come with her to church. It sounded a little strange that God could help me to quit smoking, but I agreed to go. I was curious to see what it was about. It was quite unusual to learn that what she called "church" was not in a regular church building like our usual Catholic churches, but instead was held in a large room in some conference building.

The moment I walked in I could sense there was something different about these people. They were like a family, and they seemed to be united by some invisible bond. I watched them pray and listened to the preacher teaching from the Holy Scriptures. It was something I had never seen or experienced in my life. They talked about God and how to consider Him when making certain choices in life, as if He were real just as every physical thing that we have in our lives.

You might remember that I used to go to church on holidays when mom would organize all of us and we went together. I always liked it, but to me, God was some undiscovered myth or some symbolic object who set the rules of good behavior for all of humanity. I couldn't imagine that God could be treated as though He were present in the here and now, or that He could take part in our lives.

I saw how these people had a firm faith in their God and they prayed, believing that they would get their answers according to their prayers. To me, prayer was more like a symbolic act to have hope that things would get better. Their faith in prayer was more like an actual anticipation that their prayers would be answered – which I had never seen before.

The preacher read the scriptures and he took it very seriously. I always thought, "Who cares what's written in that book called the Bible?" I had read some of the New Testament, but found it hard to understand, quite boring, and not applicable to my life. I didn't see how I could apply its stories or teachings, so why should I bother reading it?

But here, in a bare-walled room with no stained-glass windows or centuries-old murals, paintings or sculptures, I was sitting with rapt attention, watching the preacher read the New Testament. He explained it in a way that made sense, and I saw that I could use these teachings in my everyday life.

I don't remember what he was preaching about, but I do remember how I felt. As I observed these people I thought to myself, "Maybe God is real." That second I remembered the experience that I had a few months previous. I will never forget the night when I was lying in my bed trying to fall asleep, and suddenly I felt something invisible approaching me; I felt a terrifying fear. I didn't understand where it came from, but I felt like something invisible was getting closer, and I felt darkness and unspeakable terror. I was scared and somehow I started calling for Jesus Christ. I don't even know why I thought of Jesus that second and why I thought He could help me. I remembered the stories that I heard about Him during Christmas, and somehow I thought that's who I should call. So I did. I started calling Jesus, asking Him to come and protect me. I told Him of my penitence, that I believed in Him, and I asked Him to protect me from this foreboding sense of *pure evil* I felt at the moment.

Suddenly the feeling of that dark invisible force vanished and the fear was gone. It disappeared after I called for Jesus. As the fear was taken away, I felt complete peace instead. It was strange to see such a sudden difference, but the experience was all too real. I asked myself, "Is He real? Did He really hear me and come to me?"

Puzzled, I fell peacefully asleep. Now I was seeing how these people were talking about Jesus and Father God as if it was all very real and not some myth. I decided that I, too, wanted to know Jesus, especially after my experience that scary night.

After the service, when Emilija asked if I would like for them to pray for me, I agreed. When I went up to the front, the preacher asked me what I would like to pray for. I said I wanted to accept Jesus Christ in my life as my Lord and that I wanted Him to help me quit smoking. The group began praying. I started saying a prayer in my own words. I believed that Jesus was right there and that He heard me.

I prayed that I believed in Him, that I wanted to have Him in my life as my Lord, and I wanted to get to know Him. I asked God to forgive me for all the bad I had done and asked Him to help me quit smoking. Suddenly I felt an unusual warmth around me and I felt as if someone lifted something heavy off me. I felt so light inside! It even became much easier to breathe.

After the prayer, Emilija and I went out to the balcony. I took a deep breath looking at the gorgeous bright blue sky. I felt so light within, like I could have flown if I jumped into the air; I had never felt that way before. It was such an indescribable feeling of inner peace and joy, which came upon me from out of nowhere. As we were saying goodbyes on our way out, I knew that I would be back. I wanted to be back in that place, where people were caring and united, who had such strong and real faith. My few experiences relating to Jesus where so real, I wanted to know more about Him and anything related to Him. As I was going back home, I could not get used to the uplifting feeling within. It felt like I returned home a different person.

The next morning I woke up and noticed how the easiness and peace that I received the previous night was still there. And I didn't want to smoke any more. After I returned home, that night I still took a cigarette out of habit, but to my surprise it was no longer satisfying. And so I quit smoking. My experience during and after the prayer, and the sudden change regarding my smoking, made me consider carefully the power of prayer and about Jesus being not just a myth.

I joined Emilija again for the next service at the church. Since then, my life took a totally different direction. I was 16 years old when Christ came into my life and attending Christian Evangelical Church became a regular part of my life. I began to see changes happening within me. No longer was I interested in going to parties for the primary purpose of getting drunk. I stopped joining my friends for smoke breaks and I stopped being offensive and cruel in my speech which, before my first visit to church with Emilija, had been my normal language pattern. It wasn't that I was being a vicious person, but it was simply the way we conducted ourselves as teenagers.

I didn't want to live the way I did before; it seemed that after I found Jesus (and He found me), an entirely new world opened up to me. It was so much more interesting than parties, drinking and smoking, or having ongoing concerns about boyfriends or any relationship dramas. I enjoyed communicating with people on a much deeper level about our purpose in life than about daily soap operas or empty jokes. I enjoyed the openness, love and purity. The indescribable peace I felt within – and this change within me – drew me back to learn more about that which was invisible, yet at the same time so real. I decided that I wanted to associate with the people I met at the church, and they became my new friends.

Since then, my circle of friends and my lifestyle completely transformed. As you may recall, I went to church every weekend, and daily I spent my time with my new friends. There were a lot of young people and we would visit each other, go camping and do various things together depending on the weather and our respective inclinations. My life became much more interesting and purposeful, and I could tell my inner being was transforming. Most of all, I got to know Jesus. My life became filled with marvelous stories when after prayer I would get healed when I was sick, and would get solutions in unexplainable ways for situations that were out of my control.

The most astonishing healing after prayer still lasts up to this day – I received freedom from seasonal allergies. You and I both suffered from them since our childhood. For us spring and summer were the worst seasons of the year, due to the allergies associated with flower pollen. Instead of enjoying the seasons of warmth and blooming gorgeous flowers, we suffered from constant sneezing and itching eyes. The itching was so irritating that it was impossible not to rub my eyes; touching them would cause them to itch even more, turning them red and swollen, often followed by severe headaches. I know we both absolutely hated it, but there was no cure for it then, nor was there any medicine to have at least some relief. Today this is just a memory as I am free from it all.

This amazing miracle came into my life one Sunday morning. It was a gorgeous sunny day, but this disgusting allergy overshadowed its beauty. I was standing on the stage in the church among other choir members, and due to my itching eyes and constant sneezing, I was not able to sing and worship God. I very well remember that moment, when I felt so tired from this allergy, and decided to ask Jesus to heal me. It was my only hope.

Deeply trusting that Jesus was right there, in prayer I told Him how this allergy was plain torture and that I could no longer cope with it. I asked the Lord to take it away. I remember the moment I realized that Jesus could heal me, and I had faith in His touch. After the prayer, during the sermon, I noticed that my sneezing had stopped. I took note, but then I thought maybe it had stopped on its own, as it used to do at times. After the service was over, a group of us were outside chatting. While enjoying my time with friends, I realized that my eyes were no longer itching, the swelling was nearly gone and, I hadn't sneezed even once after my prayer. Brother, believe it or not, after eleven years of suffering, this allergy left me that night and since then I have never had its symptoms. It's been fourteen years since. I know you still have this problem so you understand what a miracle this is. Even now I live in a part of California that has many pollen producing plants, one of the worst places to live for those who suffer from this type of allergy. But I have no symptoms; it's as though I never had it.

This miraculous healing is one of the many testimonies of answered prayer in the name of Jesus. Do you remember those times when you would come into my room and ask me to pray for you because you were in trouble? I didn't know exactly what was going on in your life at that time, but I saw you were very worried and anxious. I prayed for you every night, asking God to show you His mercy and His power. Later you shared with me that somehow things started happening in your favor in unexplainable ways, and you got out of the troubles you were having when you asked me to pray to Jesus on your behalf. I have experienced and witnessed countless testimonies when prayers in Jesus Christ name were answered.

A Lesson for Many

Brother, I'm assuming that you might be confused as to why I'm telling you so much about Jesus Christ since I left the church. You knew that church was a big part of my life, but then you noticed I stopped attending and started partying, smoking and at times, not coming home at all. I remember you felt contemptuous for my new lifestyle, but there was nothing you could do about it. The truth is that after four years of being an active member of a Christian non-denominational church, I stopped attending because of the disrespect and manipulation I witnessed. I was affected deeply and had reached my threshold.

Regardless of my personal relationship with the Lord, I no longer wanted to associate with people who called themselves "Christians," but whose behavior and actions contradicted the very teachings of how followers of Christ should conduct themselves. The truth is that I never really wanted to leave the church, because I loved my friends whom I met in the church and I loved the Lord. It was my life! But I reached a point where I could no longer tolerate some of the behavior and some of the disciplines and practices that were going on. I firmly disagreed with some practices, nor could I withstand the actions of some who were in authority. For years I was neglecting, justifying the attitudes and choices that church leadership and some other church members were making until one day, it reached the point of no return.

There was a day when I felt I could no longer tolerate the behavior that was arrogant, superior, unfair and manipulative. I decided to open up to my friend and share with him how his and few other fellows' behavior were hurting me and my girlfriend. I was not sure how he was going to respond to my honest opinion addressing his conduct, but I believed we would have an open and friendly conversation. When I finished sharing my feelings, what followed after a pause felt as though I was spit in the face. I watched him casually sitting and ironically smiling. And then, I heard careless short response to my open and heartfelt conversation. I think he responded without putting much thought into how it could affect me. It ended up to be a turning point in my life. His negligent remark reached the threshold of my endurance.

After I asked to be left alone in the room, he went on to continue celebrating our mutual friend's birthday. Left alone, I stood at the window feeling trampled. Watching a beautiful sunrise, I felt something had been torn deep inside of me. I could no longer tolerate the way I was being treated and I didn't want be a part of what I had witnessed.

"This is it. I cannot take this anymore," it felt as if I heard my soul utter as my commitment to the church had taken the last breath.

As I was gazing at the beautiful sunrise, I quietly stood there alone. I was full of tears and feeling betrayed, deeply hurt by the person whom I so sincerely trusted, who was my close trustworthy friend for a long time, of whom I highly respected as one of the leaders in the church. Disappointment and heartbreaking pain suffused every part of my being. Something died within me. I felt my strong inner bond with those people and the church was torn. I was tired from it all. As I witnessed the sun color the morning sky, I knew it was the beginning of a different life for me. I knew that after I left, they would not see me again.

"If this is what Christianity and the church are all about," I stated, closing the chapter for good, "then I don't want it."

I believed that God was a righteous God. I trusted that the Lord knew my heart, and it gave me hope that He was not going to abandon me for my decision. I believed in the Lord with all my heart, but I couldn't tolerate anymore the attitude and behavior that was so hurtful.

After that day, I intentionally started missing church services and youth gatherings, instead spending my time with new friends that I met at the airport. I found it was easier, and I had more fun with them than I did at the church. I felt more loved and respected.

My close friends from the church tried to talk to me, encouraging me to return, but I repeatedly responded that I would stop attending the church services or youth gatherings for a while. One day, the fellow from church who hurt me came to see me at work after the flights. He apologized for his actions and asked me to come to the services, to join them again for youth gatherings because they missed me and didn't want to see me leave their fellowship.

I wished I could have felt the same. But I did not.

That sunny morning his arrogant attitude and words tore my soul apart. I couldn't continue tolerating what I was patient about for such a long time. No longer could I consider him to be a friend. Quietly, but firmly I responded how I appreciated that he understood his mistake, and I forgave him. What I didn't tell him was that something had died within me, and that I didn't want to be with them anymore. I reiterated my decision that I needed a break from it all, and that they shouldn't expect to see me in the near future.

I will never forget the night when my friend and I were walking in the park, talking about everything. We were close friends and normally had open, straightforward conversations. Deividas tried to comfort me and encouraged me not to leave the church. Gazing at the city all lit up at night I responded, "No, I can't live like that anymore. For now, I am stepping away. I know I will be back. I don't know when or how, but I know I will be back because I can't live without God."

It was an extremely difficult time in the beginning. I knew the spiritual law that I learned in the Bible and I knew what my choices meant in the spiritual realm:

> *"The thief does not come except to steal, and to kill, and to destroy." (John 10:10)*

> *"Be sober, be vigilant; because your adversary the devil walks about like a roaring lion, seeking whom he may devour." (1 Peter 5:8)*

I understood this wasn't a game. I wouldn't get out of bed for days because I was heartbroken and confused. I prayed, telling God how I knew that I was making a crucial choice, but how I couldn't continue living the way I had for the past few years. I could not understand how people, who claimed to follow Christ, could make those kinds of choices, and manipulate in the way that I heard and saw. I cried before the Lord that I believed His teachings were not reflected in the actions these people took, and I didn't want to have anything to do with them. I knew I needed to step away from it all at least for some time, and I asked God to protect me from evil and never to abandon me, hoping for His protection and His mercy.

It was heartbreaking to make that kind of a choice. I had to leave my closest friends, who were like my family; I had to leave behind everything

I had previously lived for. I didn't know how to live my life. I didn't know where the truth was.

My only distraction from pain and confusion came from work. My shift at the Business Lounge was the only pleasant part of my existence. That's when I met Renata and other young people, who were like a breath of fresh air. My work and my time spent with my new friend Renata was very healing. It would take my mind off my misery and pull me into a world that was bright, pleasant, fun and delightful. That was the only time when I would laugh and was able to forget the dilemma with church. Renata and I got very connected so that we began to spend more and more time together. The more time I spent at the airport and with my new friend, the further I was from the distress. And, the church. I finally started to recover emotionally, to the point where I could feel the joy of life again.

It was good to have freedom from any kind of artificially-imposed regulations and manipulation, to be myself and manage my time, my decisions and activities the way I wanted. I felt valued and respected by the people who surrounded me.

Coincidentally, this was also the time when Border Police Officer Andžej showed up in my life, showering me with his charming attention. He and his amorous affection was irresistible. I got to know my new friends and stepped into their world, where it seemed to be so much more pleasant, easier and exciting. And each day brought more fun. I thought I would stay away from sin and was committed to do my best, but as I spent my time with my newly met friends, who didn't live according to the Bible, I slowly immersed myself into a world of earthly pleasures, smoking cigarettes again and drinking, dating and partying, going to nightclubs and meeting more new people.

Within a very short period, my life had totally changed. I loved my new friends, but leading a careless lifestyle was something that I felt cautious about. I was aware that my actions were the opposite from what Scripture taught about leading sanctified and righteous lives before God. Deep inside I was restless and I couldn't get away from it. I was well-aware of what my choices meant in the spiritual world and I was scared. In the back of my mind I always had the verses from the Bible:

> *"Do you not know that the unrighteous will not inherit the kingdom of God? Do not be deceived. Neither fornicators, nor idolaters, nor adulterers, nor homosexuals, nor*

> *sodomites, nor thieves, nor covetous, nor drunkards, nor revilers, nor extortioners will inherit the kingdom of God." (1 Corinthians 6: 9-10)*
>
> *"Now the works of the flesh are evident, which are: adultery, fornication, uncleanness, lewdness, idolatry, sorcery, hatred, contentions, jealousies, outbursts of wrath, selfish ambitions, dissensions, heresies, envy, murders, drunkenness, revelries, and the like; of which I tell you beforehand, just as I also told you in time past, that those who practice such things will not inherit the kingdom of God." (Galatians 5: 19-21)*

I knew this was a spiritual battle and at this point I was losing. The point of the matter was not about what I was going to do in five years or so; it was about my eternity after this life. Each of us will leave this physical world sooner or later, and a thought that did not give me peace was that the end of my life journey could end at any moment. Everyone has a freedom of a choice and everyone will have what he chooses.

But I felt so hurt that despite my restlessness, I could not even think of returning back to the same church. I assumed there were other churches that were different, but I was so fed up with the subject that I did not even want to look for another congregation of the Evangelical Christian Church. Yet my comprehension of the spiritual world and the choices I was making would cause conflict within me every day. So I tried to find emotional comfort and a way to silence the worry by spending time with my new girlfriends and Andžej, distracting myself by partying with them. The only way to overshadow my restlessness was the activities with them, to get my mind off dwelling about the world I was leaving.

At work I was continually surrounded by people and it was a busy time. On my days off, I was engaged in activities with my girlfriends. I loved them and was thankful that I had them in my life. Fun time in the city, visiting friends, dating my new sweetheart, going to nightclubs, and attending loud parties until morning became my lifestyle. It distracted me and I enjoyed the company of the people I encountered.

When I would stay alone though, I would always think about my path and what I was doing with my life. Oftentimes after the flights, I would close the Business Lounge, shut off the lights, and have my "Inga time," the only time when in absolute silence I could look into the eyes of truth and analyze my life choices.

There was a relentless battle raging within.

In the beginning the fun times overshadowed my sadness and I enjoyed it but very soon, I realized how nothing could replace the tranquility that I used to experience with Christ. That sheer inner joy could not be found anywhere else. The indescribable peace was not to be found in alcohol or cigarettes. Instead of deep fulfillment in my heart I felt emptiness. When those lively distractions faded away, I was alone with the truth. Instead of contentment, I felt heavy-hearted. It felt like the loud parties and jovial atmospheres were a cover-up, a distraction from what was truly important. It was nothing more than a temporary distraction to fill my hollow heart, which was longing for the true fulfillment only Christ can give.

At times, I felt such a strong longing for God's word and His presence that I would go to the church. I'd sneak in quietly and go straight to the second floor, so nobody I knew would see me and start asking questions. With the first chords of the worship song, I would take off my invisible armor and burst into tears before the Lord. I was longing for Him, and felt heartbroken for having to keep myself distant. But while I was longing for what I considered to be so important and most valuable, I felt I could not continue my journey with those people any more. My trust, love and unconditional devotion had been simply trampled.

It felt as if the pain was choking me and I couldn't say a word to my Lord. Feeling heartbroken, I only cried. But I knew He heard me and understood. My tears spoke for me. And as the sermon took its course, I cried before my Lord the entire time. The voice of the preacher was like a knife, stabbing me in the heart because I hated hypocrisy. I despised manipulation and unfairness. I cried, not knowing what to do with my life. I was longing for God's love, peace and truth. And, I knew my choices were going to bring destruction sooner or later. But I couldn't think of returning to be a part of this church. Besides, it felt as though I were already a different person living a different life. I couldn't see how I could leave my new world behind.

I loved my new friends and loved my new life. Yet I loved the Lord. I was longing for Him. So I cried out to God asking to save me no matter what decisions I made at the time, and bring me back to Him at any cost. And then I would leave before the service ended, so I wouldn't have to talk to anybody. Hoping that God would not abandon me, I would dive back into my fun and adventurous, yet spiritually vapid world.

The further I went, the more distant I became with my actions from God and His commandments. Uneasy feelings of worry in time started fading away. No longer would I remember the church nor did I feel so restless about my choices. I was immersed in my new world. And my life followed a steady and downward spiral with drunken parties and casual dating. But at that point it felt like I had stepped into quicksand, which would slowly but surely suck me in deeper and deeper. And I couldn't get out of there no matter what I had observed about my life.

As I was fully immersed into my new world, there were three occasions within a year or so, when my friends and I nearly got into car accidents while partying and driving fast. Every time it ended well, although it did make me pause for a moment and think seriously about my life choices. However, at this point I did not have the courage nor the strength to make any changes. Just a thought of returning to the church associated with pain and I felt I could not go back to that, which I ran away from. Besides, I had established strong relationships and I was way too engaged in my new lifestyle. After each nearly tragic incident, for a moment I felt an awe and thanked the Lord for keeping me safe. I would get a sense of worry and warning, but then I brushed them off my mind and moved on, continuing my path without making any changes.

But I always had a feeling that this careless time would come to an end. My only questions were "when" and "how." I just never thought that it would be a car accident and that it would end so tragically. As many people do, I thought that accidents would only happen to others, but not to me.

The Moment that Changed Everything. Meeting the Lord

The Lord never left me. He heard my prayers and He remained faithful. People might betray you, hurt you and abandon you, but the Lord never will. Now I will tell you about something that I rarely tell anyone.

It changed me and it changed my life.

These were the moments that carried me through all these years. They gave me hope against hope, when there was not even a glimmer of light in my life. They kept my faith unshakable no matter what I had to face. They strengthened me and kept me from giving up. When it was so difficult that I did not want another day to come, I would return to this experience, and it would give me the inner strength necessary to hold on to my faith and cope with whatever I had to go through. I am so fortunate to have had the experience. Seven years passed, and I still remember the feeling as if I had experienced it yesterday.

While I was staying in the ICU I did not have a sense of time, so I cannot tell you when it happened. I only know that I was very weak. I could not move nor could I speak. I was hooked up to a life support machine. I remember how the oxygen would go in and out of my lungs without having to make the effort to breathe. It was so strange and I slept most of the time. Sometimes I would open my eyes, look at people who were visiting, and after few minutes I would go unconscious again.

There was one moment when I woke up – and right at that moment I felt love. Before I even opened my eyes, I felt the most amazing sense of love flowing towards me. I'd never felt anything so magnificent and immeasurable. I knew it was not my mother or my father because it was not earthly love. It was incomprehensibly deep and beautiful. The feeling was so delightful that I don't have the words to describe it. There is no such love on this planet. But I recognized it.

It was Jesus Christ. It was my Lord. It was His love. I knew He was standing at the end of my bed. I opened my eyes to see Him. I had been longing for my Lord! I did not physically see Him though. But the feeling of immeasurable love and His presence was there. I *knew* the Son of God was standing there. And He was with me.

The awareness was so real and clear that I had absolutely no doubts Jesus was standing right in front of me. In a moment I heard the words in my mind, "I love you." I knew the words were not my own thoughts; they were placed in my mind. I don't even know how to describe how He communicated; it's as if He was speaking to me through my mind. The love was so *immense* and so *beautiful*. I will never forget how blissful the moment was! It was a supreme happiness. His love surrounded me; it felt like He hugged me with His love.

The awareness that I was totally safe came upon me.

I'd never felt so safe in my life, ever. I knew there was nothing to be afraid of or concerned about, because if Jesus Himself had come, then everything was going to be alright. The Lord was with me and that's all that mattered. I closed my eyes and thought, "How happy I am to still have Him!

I did not lose my Lord. He did not leave me even though I had left Him. And He is right here. He came to me. It doesn't matter what happened and what's going. The most important thing is that I still have Him."

That moment I understood that the most important thing was that I had Jesus back in my life. Nothing was more important. I knew that nobody ever again would have the power to push me away from the Lord. Never again. Being surrounded with that amazing love, feeling fully at peace, I drifted off back to sleep.

Then came another experience that was inexplicably divine. Again, I don't know which day it was out of my seventeen days in the ICU. After I woke up and before I opened my eyes, I felt that someone was standing next to me on the right side of my bed. He was tall; taller than average human height. I had a clear understanding that he was controlling everything in the ICU and specifically that he was making sure I was alright. I realized how this was again, a supernatural presence, because the feeling of comfort and security was so unusual. I had an awareness that it was an angel, and that he was there specifically to take care of me. In my mind I asked him, "Who are you? What is going on here?"

As soon as I asked the question, I felt a stream of peace flow towards me, and in a moment, it felt like my whole essence, everything that I was, had been completely filled with incomprehensible and indescribable peace. As it was happening, in my mind I heard his words, "Do not be afraid. Everything is going to be well with you."

It was the same way as had happened before; it was as though he were talking to me through my mind. It was incredible! That moment I felt so secure and peaceful. I have never – ever – experienced anything like it. The feeling of peace and security was not earthly. It was a messenger sent by the Lord.

I wasn't aware yet of what exactly had happened or what I would have to face in the future; I only knew that I was in a car accident and something serious went down. But that moment I received a strong message, assuring me that I should not be fearful now or in the future; everything was going to be well because God was with me. I had an awareness that I was not abandoned but just the opposite – I was taken care of by the divine, that the Lord and his angels were closely watching over me.

Since then, while I was in the hospital, I have always felt a divine presence with me. Just as I was fully aware of your presence, or anybody else's presence, I was fully aware there was always an angel in my room. I felt him so clearly that I could even tell where he was. In my mind I would greet the angel every morning and night, thanking him for protecting me and taking care of me.

As I was hearing observations of others about my rapid recovery and watching the medical specialists who examined me proclaim their astonishment at my unusually fast healing – claiming that it was one of the most extraordinary cases even seen – I would smile inside. I knew this was the Lord's work. I knew I was being taken care of by the divine.

The fact that I was so cheerful and talkative throughout my stay at the hospital was largely because of morphine and the other drugs that were administered. However, the feeling of peace and security, inner stability and my optimistic view of the future were based on these moments: The moment I felt the Lord at my bedside and the moment I realized an angel was sent by the Lord to watch over me.

I know many of you questioned whether or not I was out of my mind when I kept saying that everything was going to be alright, that I would walk again and would live a beautiful life no matter what had happened. Most people thought it was the drugs.

They were wrong.

I knew I felt euphoria because of those drugs. But my tranquility and assurance about my future came from a different source. In my spirit I knew that from then on my life was in God's hands. Everything – absolutely everything – was in God's hands. It was knowledge I knew at the deepest core of my being, within every part of my soul and my conscious awareness. I also knew that my life would be extraordinary.

While I was at the Rehab Center, I had a lot of time to think. It seemed as if I was stopped by tragedy at that specific moment in my life and forced take a step back, to think things through thoroughly, to analyze all that had happened and draw my conclusions. My emotions were from feeling that it was unfair (the accident), to the realization that it was me who made the decisions which led to the destruction of my body and my life. I saw that my own choices as to how I responded to other people's behavior, choices on how I spent my free time, choices to continue dating Dalius (despite my intuitive feelings), and all the choices I had made, had brought me to where I was now. Sure, I had questions – most with no answers.

What if I had not allowed my dissatisfaction with people to influence my decision to follow Christ? What if Renata and I had not tried to hitchhike to get to Vilnius and I never had met Dalius? Where would I be today if I had not dated him? What if I had listened to my mother's request to stay home that night instead of going out on the date?

I was in constant agony realizing that I had a choice each and every time, and each bad decision led me towards the experience that was the deadly crash. After observing the sequence of events and how they led me to my life's destruction, the glass had been wiped clean. I was seeing very clearly. I saw that behind particular people and events that occurred, there was a spiritual influence. In the Holy Scriptures it is written that the enemy in the spiritual realm comes to steal, kill and destroy. I knew this verse before I left the church but now, I experienced exactly what's written.

The enemy stole when I allowed my dissatisfaction with people to stand between me and the Lord my God. He stole when I no longer considered my lifestyle as sinful. And then the enemy, like a predator fully consuming every area of my life and my mind, nearly killed and destroyed me for all eternity.

While I was occupied with my new and exciting life, it seemed that various circumstances occurred out of nowhere, but when I analyzed the events and how they led me to where I ended up, I could see how spiritual laws worked behind my physical world. I finally grasped the notion that even though we might not believe, that we might neglect and overlook this aspect, the fact is that our belief or disbelief does not change the laws of God. We can jump from a skyline believing it's not going to harm us. But like everything else in the universe, God made the law of gravity and the results of jumping will be drastic because the laws work, regardless of our beliefs. I realized the spiritual aspect of life was not a game. Everything I read in the Bible was far more serious than I had ever thought.

I admitted to myself that leaving the Lord because of my dissatisfaction about the conduct of other Christians was my biggest mistake. People, whether they are true followers of Christ or not, remain human. We all have needs, ambitions, feelings and desires, different perspectives and different intentions of the heart. Christians also have flaws and make mistakes, whether they are in the church leadership or not. Pastors are human just like those whom they teach, only they are tasked with the responsibility of watching over the flock, and they will give an account before the Lord God for every person for whom they have accepted responsibility. Whatever they do – they will give an account before the living God. I realized that I had to watch my own steps because there would come a day when I, too, would stand before God to give an account of my own life.

I allowed mistakes of others to push me away from the church and ultimately from the Lord. And, I nearly stepped into the dark eternity without the light of the Lord, with no way of returning to change anything. Why should I determine the path for my own soul based on other people's conduct? My choice to lead my life according to God's word is a decision between me and the Lord, and I cannot depend on others or circumstances to make that choice for me.

After all, when I meet the Lord, what am I going to say when He asks why I drifted away, why I had a shipwreck of my faith resulting in the loss of my salvation? Am I going to justify myself by blaming other people, that they didn't act nice? Really? I imagine Jesus saying, "All you had to do was follow Me, not people."

Now, after Jesus revealed Himself to me, I fully grasped that He is not just some historical or religious personality. Jesus Christ is truly alive in the spritual realm; we just don't see Him with our physical eyes. And, we shouldn't make conclusions and decision about Him depending on how Christians conduct themselves. Jesus is not like people. The Lord's love and light and truth are beyond measure and comprehension. I learned from experience. I had reached the point where I fully understood that the spiritual aspect of life is *not* a game that you can take lightly. A lot of those stories written in the Bible reflect the spiritual world and how it impacts our physical world. I made the decision to live in a righteous way before the living God. I decided that from then on, it wouldn't matter what people in the church did or what they said; the most important thing was that I knew the Lord and He knew me.

I wasn't ready to go back to the congregation that I left, but that detail was not going to determine how I was going to live before the Lord. While many from that church judged me and made their conclusions about why the accident happened and what was ahead, to me the most important thing was that the Lord was there for me.

He remained faithful to me.

He heard my cry and answered my prayer.

He did not forsake me and saved me regardless of my decisions.

And now He was carrying me through a devastating time. He even revealed Himself to me. Faith had been ingrained into the deepest core of my being. Interestingly, I noticed that since the moment I returned to life after nearly dying, my thoughts about the Lord and my relation to Him changed like never before. I did not simply believe there was a God. I *knew* there was a God.

But it was more than just thoughts of God as some mystical being somewhere in the universe, in whose existence I believed. This time I found myself not only believing, but actually counting on Him as I would count on any human whom I fully trusted. It was the first time in my life I found myself relying on God, expecting to receive His help. And true to His word, He didn't fail me in my times of crisis, nor has He failed me since.

Getting to Know the Lord

This was the time when the Lord brought me back to Him. I recommitted myself, gave my right hand to Him, and since then we began our extraordinary journey together.

Looking back, I realize that before the crash, I didn't really know the Lord. Being a Christian was more about the lifestyle according to Biblical values rather than knowing Jesus Himself and having a connection with Him. Life according to Biblical values was more about meeting the church's traditions and regulations rather than choosing to obey the Lord's commandments because you love the Lord. Merely fulfilling tradition by going to the church on a weekly basis does not make you a follower of Christ. It is written:

> *"Not everyone who says to Me, 'Lord, Lord,' shall enter the kingdom of heaven, but he who does the will of My Father in heaven. Many will say to Me in that day, 'Lord, Lord, have we not prophesied in Your name, cast out demons in Your name, and done many wonders in Your name?' And then I will declare to them, 'I never knew you; depart from Me, you who practice lawlessness!'" (Matthew 7:21-23)*

The words of Jesus offer every practicing Christian a roadmap to his or her salvation. It is knowing the Lord your God, loving Him with all your heart, with all your essence, and living according to His commandments, that makes you a true follower of Christ. To tell you the truth, I got to know God only after the car accident. Only in the past seven years have I learned and experienced how caring and powerful He is. Since the time I fully surrendered my life to His will, the Lord God has been watching over me, caring for me, and teaching me as a father teaches his child.

As I continued my life path having Jesus by my side, I got to know Him more than I ever knew Him before. It might sound strange to you and you may ask: How can a person possibly get to know Jesus? He is not here physically to get to know Him. But understand that He is truly alive in a spiritual realm. He manifests Himself to those who seek Him with a sincere heart. When you read about Him in the Bible and then you experience in your own life that which is written; when you receive answers after you've talked to Jesus in your prayers; and when after your prayers to the Lord your inner strength is renewed when you feel like you cannot possibly continue your battle or live another day; when you receive inner peace and assurance in the midst of hopeless circumstances or hardship; and when you see how after your conversation with the Lord your needs are met by circumstances changing in your favor; when you feel joy and fulfillment when others say they would have committed suicide if they were you; when your soul is healed despite the deepest wounds, and when you receive miraculous physical healing after the prayer, Jesus becomes so very real.

Jesus manifests Himself through answers to your prayers. Knowing Him and seeing Him manifest Himself in my life is the most precious gem I have found. Even though I have experienced the sweet taste of success and victory, being loved and giving love, fulfillment of knowing my calling and purpose, I have found nothing that would give me as much joy as knowing the Lord. I am often asked how to find the Lord. I personally found the Lord when I started seeking Him with all my heart. It's written:

> *"And you will seek Me and find Me, when you search for Me with all your heart." (Jeremiah 29:13)*

It's a different kind of searching. It's not just simply a nonchalant search of something you wish to find. It's an imperative search for that which you truly and desperately desire.

After I returned from the hospital and Rehab Center, and the shock and everyday visitations calmed down, I faced a dreadful reality: I was in my room, alone and totally helpless. I couldn't imagine how to continue with nearly half of my body gone. The anguish was unbearable. I was sitting in bed, faced with the realization that my life had come to a dead end. I can't describe how devastating it felt to watch the total destruction of everything

I held important, while having to live another day fully realizing how there was no way to restore what I lost. No doctor or money could possibly bring me back to life.

Love from you, our parents and friends gave me a great comfort dealing with a new life. But when it came to my future, there was no end to my pain. To tell you honestly, no, I could not "accept the loss and live differently" as some had suggested. At times it seemed I would go insane from the despair and this never-ending, sharp burning pain in my paralyzed arm. It felt like it was beyond what I could take and there was nothing I could do about it. I heard several people saying that they would have committed suicide had something similar happened to them.

Indeed, often I wished that I wasn't here at all, but I never thought of committing suicide. I knew that if I made that step – it would be the real end. It might end my earthly pain, but for murdering myself I would step into the beginning of eternal torment on the other side. After we leave the physical world, there is eternity ahead for our soul and no way to go back to fix anything. With suicide, there is no turning back.

Have you ever thought of what eternity really is? It's hard to comprehend, isn't it? Thousands of years will pass and that will be just the beginning. Since suicide was not an option to run away from the pain, I had to live with the change that altered my life's journey. Even though I was in what seemed like such a cruel situation, I still had hope. Because I knew God was watching over me; deep in my heart I had an awareness that my life would not only continue, but it would be extraordinary. The first two and a half years the reality I had to face day to day was not even close to my vision. I didn't know where I could possibly hide from the despair and agony, and I began seeking for strength from the Lord.

I began asking Jesus to help me deal with my new life head-on. I asked Him to give me the willingness and strength to meet another morning, because I didn't want to live another day in such physical condition. Facing the heartless nature of my position, I became like a child, trusting that God was powerful enough to pull me out of that pit of despair. The only hope left was my faith that all matters were subject to the Lord my God and therefore, He could change anything. I trusted that our Creator was a loving God, that He didn't allow this to happen for some senseless reason.

I was convinced that there must be a cause for why my life took such a turn. But why did it have to end so cruel? What was His will for my life? What was the purpose behind the accident and the gift that I had survived?

These questions were on my mind daily. I needed to know the answers and I decided to seek the Lord. I needed to hear from Him. I think that was the first time when I truly sought the Lord.

There I was, in bed, alone in my room. Fully understanding how the Lord, who saved my life and had everything under His control, would hear me if I began searching for Him with all my heart. I started simply talking to Him, and that was my prayer. I had an open, sincere conversation with the Creator. I would end by affirming my faith over and again that I believed He had a purpose for me and that He would bring me out of the despair, and I would lead a beautiful life in spite of it all. I sincerely trusted in my Lord and that was my only comfort I had when I thought of my future.

I began to notice changes within me, which quite frankly surprised me. I noticed how differently I felt after the prayer, particularly after I asked Jesus to strengthen me: I would wake up in the morning feeling much stronger and hopeful. I had the desire and even the excitement to get out of bed, and the willingness to do what I needed to do to move forward. These changes revealed once again that we are spiritual beings and our true strength and joy comes not from material things or some favorable situation, but instead comes from the spirit which is God.

Observing such significant changes after prayer, I began talking with Jesus more frequently and coming to Him when I needed comfort and strength. And, each time I felt stronger and more at peace, assured that the Lord was going to bless me. This way, I found my source of strength. Jesus became my Rock. My Comforter. Seeing that the Lord was answering my requests strengthened my faith every time.

I was also noticing that after praying, outside circumstances began to occur in my favor as well. During the first two years after the accident, my life consisted of multiple surgeries and physical recovery, staying at Rehab Centers, and adapting to an altered way of life. While I was going through that desert of pain and recovery, I would notice that everything seemed to be going well with no difficulties or troubles. My stay at each hospital, my surgeries and my healing progress, went smoothly with no complications.

When, after the surgery, even the pain medications would not help, I would cry out to Jesus and somehow my strength to endure would increase from "out of nowhere." And I would feel the determination to get through the hardship of post-surgical recovery.

Also, it seemed like endurance and relentless perseverance fueled me when I began taking my "first steps" toward my aim to be self-sufficient. Outside circumstances fell into place when I began achieving further goals, and I had success in goals that I set for myself. As I was observing my life, it seemed like circumstances and people who worked with me had been arranged in my favor by some invisible force. My faith grew even stronger, seeing that prayer in the name of Jesus Christ was not some abstract religious act, but that it actually carried power. It had the power to make changes in my heart and my mind, and it had the power to influence the circumstances.

When I became strong enough physically to start changing my circumstances, numerous times I felt discouraged. It seemed like no efforts had the power to change my living conditions, and at times I didn't see any reason to try to do anything about it. There were times when I felt like I was left alone with no place to go, with no direction in front of me, and I saw no end to it.

During these times, I would remember my meeting with the Lord, ponder on the moments when He would strengthen me, and reflect on all the miraculous coincidences in my favor which had occurred. I knew the Lord was with me, and I trusted that He would not leave me half-way through. I would remind myself, there was a purpose behind everything, and that it had to get better if I continued putting forth the effort in becoming self-sufficient and improving my circumstances.

So, I would pull myself together and ask Jesus to give me endurance to keep going. To my pleasant surprise, often after the prayer I would receive not only strength to endure, but enthusiasm for what I was aiming for. In addition, I had outstanding success in all I did.

Watching how my life was changing according to my prayers, with time my faith grew even stronger. Instead of hoping that my prayer "might" be answered I started *expecting* an answer. I had more confidence in the Lord. Jesus became a close friend, someone I could call any time and He would always be there.

And finally, when I acted on the inspiration and my life started taking a direction that was literally the answer to my ongoing prayers, it grounded my faith even more.

Now I not only heard or read about how powerful God was to change any circumstance, I was actually living it. I became more confident in my Lord, relying on Him as one would rely on any person they fully trust. So, when new opportunities showed up and it was scary to leave my comfort zone, I turned to the Lord again because I knew He had the authority over circumstances, and I could fully trust in Him to arrange everything I needed.

"You are such a courageous woman," many say to me. But that is where the courage came from – I was empowered by my faith and complete confidence in the Lord. When I took those steps forward in faith, to my amazement circumstances would change in my favor. I would witness how people from out of nowhere would come into my life willing to help, and I would have success in all I aimed for. Astounded by receiving exactly what I had asked, I would think to myself, "How is this possible? After all, it is impossible *not* to believe in God!"

Observing my choices, I noticed that living against God's commandments had been very destructive for my life. I began learning to make decisions according to the Scriptures. I fell time and again, making mistakes and wrong choices, and the Lord taught me as a father teaches his child. And after I learned my lesson, He healed my wounds and I continued my journey. The more confidence and trust I put in the Lord by faith, and the more obedience I showed to His commandments in His word, the closer I got to the Lord, and the more astonishing answers to my prayers I would receive.

> *"He who has My commandments and keeps them, it is he who loves Me. And he who loves Me will be loved by My Father, and I will love him and manifest Myself to him." (John 14:21)*

Up to this day it boggles my mind when I think of how my life has transformed since I opened my eyes in the ICU. I live my vision, even though at the time I was not able to speak or move. Yes, I worked very hard to achieve my goals. My new life did not simply land on my lap. But I sincerely say this to you: I would not be who I am today and would not have achieved any of it had I not the Lord in my life. While I am happy to be able to live a dynamic life, be independent and valuable to others, my most sacred joy in life comes from knowing the Lord my God. It might be difficult for you to understand it now, but I hope with time you will. For now, I just want you to hear me out and be open to what I am sharing with you.

Surrender Your Life to the Lord

So, that's the story behind my faith. I had gone through the kind of spiritually transformative process where each day I contemplated, spoke to, and walked with the Lord. In a way I went through a personal resurrection where the "Old Inga" died in a car accident, then found Jesus during my rebirth, rehabilitation and reawakening. And the reason I am spending so much time on writing this letter is to tell you that Jesus is not just a mere historical or religious character. Jesus is real.

He is resurrected and is alive in the spirit.
He is the One who has the keys to life and death.
He is the One who has the power to heal your soul wounds.
He has the power over any circumstances.
He is the One in whom you will find life.
He will renew your strength.

> *"But those who hope in the Lord will renew their strength. They will soar on wings like eagles; they will run and not grow weary, they will walk and not be faint." (Isaiah 40:31 NIV)*

With all that I am sharing with you in this letter, I want to inspire you and encourage you to seek the Lord. This is the first step in rebuilding your life on a strong foundation. I want you to be blessed. This is the key to a fulfilling life, my dear brother, because our life in this world depends upon the spiritual realm.

You will receive forgiveness for your sins and receive salvation for eternal life. I think you already know and will agree with me that we have a soul that never dies. Even scientists prove that there is life after death of the physical body. There are many scientific tests being done to confirm the existence and immortality of the soul. You might think, "Why should I think about the death? I am alive now and I want to think about my life here and now." But let's face the fact: Do you know if you are going to be alive tomorrow? You don't even know what's going to happen in your life after you put this letter away, do you?

What happens to human soul after the death? The soul enters eternity, which is in the spiritual realm. According to the Bible, there are only two ways to spend eternity – either in Heaven with the Lord or in Hell, a place of torment, which was created for Lucifer (now Satan) and the fallen angels. It's our human nature to be sinful, and we have all transgressed before the Lord God. Jesus Christ paid the ultimate price on the cross for all of us. Those who accept Him as their Lord receive forgiveness for their sins and are rewarded by spending eternity with Him in heaven rather than being cast into Hell.

I know what I have told you might sound like a Sunday school tale. But have you ever considered the testimonies, videos of those who've had the experience visiting Hell? Before you roll your eyes and sarcastically dismiss what I am saying, I encourage you to do a little research; you might be surprised.

He is Standing at Your Door. Do You Hear Him Knocking?

Every person comes to a point in their life when the Son of God knocks at the door of their hearts. Everyone has the opportunity to invite Jesus in. He does not force Himself into anyone's life. He gives signs of His love and waits until a person recognizes Him and welcomes Him into their heart and life.

> *"Behold, I stand at the door and knock. If anyone hears My voice and opens the door, I will come in to him and dine with him, and he with Me." (Revelation 3:20)*

Many people unfortunately don't recognize Him, or they reject Him. But there are also countless who hear Him and accept Him as their Lord. There are many who've experienced the incredible moment when Jesus touched their lives. And you can find countless stories of the wonderful impact that the Lord has had in the lives of many. He brings fulfillment, love and joy in a way that nothing else in this world can. Jesus can take away fear and any tormenting feelings that your soul quietly suffers from. He frees you from any addiction, from destructive habits and terrible sins. The Lord restores destinies which seem to be broken. He changes the lives of those who accept Him and are willing to change in His name.

This is that time in your life, when Christ is standing at your door knocking. I truly believe in that. I would even say I know it because I see what's happening in your life and I feel it in my spirit. You cannot imagine what amazing peace I feel as I am writing this to you. He is standing at the door of your heart, ready to bring His light. All you need to do is believe and talk to Him sincerely. Ask Him to forgive you for all your sins, acknowledge Him as your Lord, and ask Him to change your life.

His love and mercy is unconditional and all your sins will be forgiven if you admit you did wrong and repent. I know you told me that you have made many mistakes and have done bad things to others, and that you might not deserve forgiveness. But He forgives all sins, no matter what and how much you have done. Scripture states:

> *"If we confess our sins, He is faithful and just to forgive us our sins and to cleanse us from all unrighteousness." (1 John 1:9)*

> *"Therefore, if anyone is in Christ, the new creation has come: The old has gone, the new is here! All this is from God, who reconciled us to himself through Christ and gave us the ministry of reconciliation: that God was reconciling the world to himself in Christ, not counting people's sins against them. And he has committed to us the message of reconciliation." (2 Corinthians 5: 17-19)*

> *"Therefore I say to you, every sin and blasphemy will be forgiven men, but the blasphemy against the Spirit will not be forgiven men. Anyone who speaks a word against the Son of Man, it will be forgiven him; but whoever speaks against the Holy Spirit, it will not be forgiven him, either in this age or in the age to come." (Matthew 12: 31-32)*

All your sins will be forgiven unless you speak against the Holy Spirit. Stop holding on to your past and what you have done. You will be forgiven and a fresh new page in your life will open. You are not less than I am or anyone else. God loves you in the same great and unconditional way as He loves me and other people. You are a special soul for Him and He had a special plan when He created you. By accepting Jesus in your life as your Lord, you will see a big difference. Rather than wanting to gain what you have lost, seek the Lord and you will find treasure that is beyond measure and far more valuable than what you have lost.

Your life will never be the same.

Simply gaining back the money you lost or any other tangible possession you had is not going to give you a fulfilling life. Have you heard stories of people putting every effort into gaining tangible wealth or fame, but then they still don't feel fulfilled and don't know what to do? The practical arrangements for life are very important, yet the fulfillment does not come from material gain.

Having God on your side and living according to His word, you will be empowered and blessed. He will create new opportunities, will provide solutions, will send you help, and will get you out of any pit because your Creator has the power over all circumstances and people's hearts. He does not have limits and there is nothing impossible for Him. You will have that which no one can take away from you – your life will be in God's hands and you will be blessed wherever you go.

You will not have to fear of anything because you will know that the Lord your God is going to be with you and nothing can harm you. Instead of anxiety and fear you will have confidence because you will know that absolutely everything is subject to your Creator. You will be able to handle and conquer your challenges because He will give you the wisdom to make the right choices and He will make ways for you to resolve any difficulties. You will have the peace that surpasses human understanding even when troubles come your way. He will make a way when there is none and He will bring you through all your hardships. You will also be protected from evil by supernatural power. When destructive events and circumstances occur, you will receive help or they will go around you and you won't even feel them.

It is good to have faith in almighty God and surrender your destiny to Him. He who created the universe has a plan for your destiny. He loves you and in fact, God calls you His child. In His Word He states that even if a mother would leave her child, He would not leave and would never forsake you. Do you know what that means? You will never be alone in your struggles and you will have supernatural help no matter what circumstances you face. I have lived thousands of miles away from all of you for many years and I can testify that it is really true – I had Lord's supernatural help throughout the years.

The Lord is calling you and if you choose to love the Lord your God, everything in your life will be under God's control and everything in your life will work together for good. It is not shameful to believe in God. It is not shameful to read the Holy Scriptures and live your life according to God's word. It *is* good to know the Lord because that's where you will get the blessing for your life here on earth and then you will have eternal life with Christ. It *is* good to study the Scriptures in order to learn what it takes to live in a righteous way, so you have a blessed life. It *is* good to know it because it tells about the future events on the earth. The Scriptures come to pass right before our eyes. Things that were written thousands of years ago actually are reality today. Everything they say is becoming true right before our eyes.

I know that believing in God might be associated with boring church attendance every Sunday. But remember, it's not about merely attending the church on Sunday. And it's not about saying, "Okay, whatever. I can go to church." The tradition of going to church or any religious routine without putting your heart into it is not what I am talking about. Many who attend church on a regular basis don't even know the Lord nor do they know His power.

I'm talking about faith that breathes in you, that which becomes a part of who you are. Life with God means a lifestyle of having faith and living according to God's commandments and spiritual laws that come from the Bible. It's about seeking the Lord with all your heart on a daily basis. It's about knowing Him and living according to the Lord's will. And this kind of life is truly amazing. Faith in God has the power to change people and transforms their lives.

> *"For I know the thoughts that I think toward you, says the Lord, thoughts of peace and not of evil, to give you a future and a hope. Then you will call upon Me and go and pray to Me, and I will listen to you. And you will seek Me and find Me, when you search for Me with all your heart." (Jeremiah 29: 11-13)*

What I have written in this letter is my real experience. I found the way out of my dark labyrinth and now it is time for you to come out of yours. It is time for you to have the freedom from any concerns, fears or anxieties. The time has come for you to receive incredible lightness in your heart and peace within. It is time for a new life. It is time for a new you.

Now you know who has the power to change your life. And it's not a game. I would not have spent this much time writing about something that is not important. You are a witness to how my life has been transformed, and this is where I began – surrendering my life to Jesus Christ.

Go into your room and when you are alone call for Jesus. I know, it might sound crazy: How are you going to talk to someone you cannot see? But you still try. Put away your armor of criticism and personal cynicism. There is no one here for whom you need to hold your image or pretend to be who you are not. The Lord knows who you really are deep down in your heart. He knows your every thought, every feeling and your intentions. He was there watching you enjoying your days and He was also there when you faced hardships. The Lord knows that your ways are just a shield; deep down you are different.

I know you are kind and caring and that you need everything that every human needs. He has protected you so many times and led you out of serious circumstances. You just didn't recognize His fine hand. He knows how you were betrayed by those you loved and trusted; He was there watching you at all times. He's been waiting all this time for you. He is waiting for you to open the doors of your heart, so He can come in and calm the roaring waves of your life.

Only He will give you comfort and heal the wounds of your soul.

Only He will give you peace that surpasses all human understanding.

The Lord will lead you out of this trouble.

Only He has the power to break all curses in your life and replace them with blessing.

I am not saying your destiny will be sugar coated. We don't get the promise that life's not going to have struggles. But we do get the promise that the Lord is going to help us in our afflictions. There will be times when He will walk by your side, and there will be times when the Lord will go before you and protect you. Also there might be times when you will not have the strength to walk anymore, but then Jesus will carry you in His arms. Whatever circumstances you will face – the Lord is going to be with you and help you.

Collect your thoughts, close your eyes, and realize that now you will be talking to the Lord God, who is omnipresent and He will hear you. Talk to Him from your heart; you don't need any memorized prayers. Say to Him whatever is on your heart. Yet there a few things to consider when you invite Jesus to be your Lord, and I can give you an example that will help.

"Father God, I can't see you, but I believe in you. You said in your word that those who seek you with all their heart, will find you. And here I am. I ask you please hear my prayer. I believe that you sent your son Jesus Christ to the earth to die for our sins, so we may have eternal life after our life here on the earth. I have done a lot of wrong and sinful acts, and I ask you please forgive me for all my sins that I have done. I recognize I did wrong, I repent in all my evil deeds, and I renounce them all in the name of Jesus Christ. Jesus, please come into my life and be my Savior and my Lord from now on. I need a change in my life. I surrender my life to you, and I ask you please arrange my life according to your Father's will. Strengthen me and my faith and help me to cope with pain and resolve my problems that I have. You see all my struggles that I am facing right now and I need your help. Please help me and give me peace. Thank you for coming into my life and for all you will do. I pray in the name of Jesus Christ, Amen."

Inviting Jesus Christ into your life and surrendering your destiny to Him is your very first step. Start reading the Bible. I know you might have questions and doubts about the Bible being truthfully the Word of God. Think of this: the Bible consists of 66 books that were written during a long span of time by many different people, and yet, you read it as a one whole book as though it's written by one author.

Many theories and facts that scientists proved about the earth, universe and other matters, were written in the Bible long before. The Bible is the only book in the world that has accurate prophecy. The Bible accurately foretells specific events in detail many years and even centuries, before they occurred. Approximately 2,500 prophecies appear in the Bible, and over 2,000 of them already have been fulfilled just as it's written. After many hours of research and analysis, archaeologists and scientists have repeatedly confirmed that Bible is truthful and reliable.

In the Old Testament, there are over 300 prophecies about Jesus Christ that are fulfilled in the New Testament. What Jesus foretold about the end times, (which we find in the New Testament) is being fulfilled right before our eyes. The Bible has been laughed at, burned and ridiculed, but it prevailed. It is the world's most translated and the most widely read book in the history of the world. Do you think the Scriptures would have gained these facts, if it was merely a collection of good stories?

Ask the Lord to reveal to you the depths of the Scriptures. Since authors wrote it being moved and inspired by the Holy Spirit, the Word of God will be understandable and life changing when the Holy Spirit will speak to you through messages written in the Scriptures. Find Spirit filled Christian church that truly loves the Lord, teaches His truth and practices it. Be aware though, not every person who uses the name of Jesus Christ is a true follower of Christ. There are many who call themselves to be prophets, but they are wolves in sheep's clothing, just as Jesus told us to beware of. The Scriptures foretold that times would come when people would not want to hear the sound doctrine, but rather would go to teachers in accordance with their own desires. It says there will be a great apostasy before Christ returns, and nowadays we can see that the apostasy is mind-boggling. But I am sure you will find a church that preaches the true Word of God. You will know them by their fruit and by checking their teachings against the Scriptures. Ask the Lord to bring you to a church where He wants you to be. Start making changes in your life according to the Word of God. Talk to the Lord on a daily basis.

> *"But you, when you pray, go into your room, and when you have shut your door, pray to your Father who is in the secret place; and your Father who sees in secret will reward you openly." (Matthew 6:6)*

Say your prayer as if you were having a conversation. Speak what's in your heart. Open up to Him sharing your pain and joy, troubles and victories, concerns and worries, wishes and dreams.

> *"Be anxious for nothing, but in everything by prayer and supplication, with thanksgiving, let your requests be made known to God; and the peace of God, which surpasses all understanding, will guard your hearts and minds through Christ Jesus." (Philippians 4: 6-7)*

The important aspect of a prayer is asking for forgiveness for the sins which you committed throughout the day. Scripture states that our sins will be forgiven if we repent.

> *"If we confess our sins, He is faithful and just to forgive us our sins and to cleanse us from all unrighteousness." (1 John 1:9)*

Always pray in the name of Jesus Christ, because His name is above all and has the power. The Scriptures say that your prayers will be answered if you pray in the name of Jesus Christ.

> *"And whatever you ask in My name, that I will do, that the Father may be glorified in the Son. If you ask anything in My name, I will do it." (John 14: 13-14)*

> *"And whatever things you ask in prayer, believing, you will receive." (Matthew 21:22)*

> *"And in that day you will ask Me nothing. Most assuredly, I say to you, whatever you ask the Father in My name He will give you. Until now you have asked nothing in My name. Ask, and you will receive, that your joy may be full." (John 16: 23-24)*

Again, you don't need to memorize any prayers. Speak from your heart. The only prayer that Jesus Himself taught us to pray is:

> *"Our Father who art in heaven, Hallowed be thy name. Thy kingdom come, Thy will be done, On earth as it is in heaven. Give us this day our daily bread, And forgive us our trespasses, As we forgive those who trespass against us. And do not lead us into temptation, But deliver us from evil, For thine is the kingdom, and the power, And the glory forever. Amen." (Matthew 6: 9-13)*

I hope you did not get tired of reading? I know, it's a lot. But this is imperative because this is the foundation.

Many see me as a strong person, but I was not born strong. I became strong. It's not because I am strong that I overcame the tragedies or betrayals, creating the life I desired in spite of it all. I *became* strong because I *made the decision* to never give up, and I asked the Lord to give me strength. There were too many times to count that it seemed my life was beyond what I could bear, but instead of giving up I sought the Lord, asking Him to grant me the strength to see it through until the next morning. And He always did.

It's not a matter if and how strong you are to handle difficulties. It's a matter of knowing your source of strength and your decision to show up stronger than your circumstances. If you decide to fight your battles until you win, and seek strength from the Lord in your prayers, you will overcome. And you will come out of it stronger than you were before.

Invite Jesus into your life just as I did. It will change you and your life will never be the same. Everything is going to be alright, you will see.

Take care until the next time,
Love you,
Inga

5

New Page ~ The Orthopedic Center

Dear Valdas,

I know it seems to many that getting to where I am was always as easy as I may portray today. However, you know very well that is not true. Even though you were there with me during the entire time, there is much you could not have known. I will share my experience, hoping that you will get something of value that you can use when you reflect on your own life and come to your own personal insights.

Take care,
Inga

* * *

"Finally, it's over," I was thinking as I watched my mother packing up our belongings for the return home. "Now I can look forward to returning to a normal life."

The last day at the Rehab Center was one of the happiest days that I can remember. The long days and nights were like an ongoing nightmare constantly reminding me about the horror of the accident. I was relieved that it had come to an end. I was so tired, constantly facing the cruel consequences that my choices had brought me. I was tired of being disabled and weak. I was tired of facing the devastation and I couldn't wait for this period to end, so I could bring this chapter in my life to an end and begin in the direction I had envisioned.

I had a lot of time to examine my earlier choices and now I was eager to start from the beginning, making the effort to follow the Lord and learn from Him, no matter what other Christians or non-Christians did or said. I had learned my lesson and from that point forward, I was ready to make wiser decisions. Just as I had choices before, I had them now. Also, I had a choice to give in to consequences of the tragedy and a choice to fight for my life, restoring it no matter how devastating my circumstances seemed. This time I decided not to "go with the flow," but instead to stand up for what I believed in no matter how difficult it might be.

I knew my vision contradicted people's perceptions and beliefs as to what kind of life lay ahead. I knew I would have to deal with not only my physical condition, but I would have to go against the stream in order to succeed in the life I had envisioned. But, I was ready. I looked at my future with hope and strong faith that with God's help I would become independent again and would recover my life. I was feeling much stronger physically and spiritually, and I was ready for the new chapter of my journey towards recovery.

It was comforting to be back home. It seemed like I had returned to my world, which had a totally different atmosphere. Without waiting too long, I asked my father to contact the Orthopedic Center, to see when I could arrive to get fitted for artificial legs. The main obstacle standing in between my current life and my vision was my inability to get around. I kept talking about it daily to my mom or anyone who was visiting. It grew into an unwavering goal and I was ready to make it happen.

The Orthopedic Center was located in another city, about an hour away from home. All the way to the center I was dreaming of how great it was going be when I got my prosthetic legs. I imagined that I would put them on as I would shoes, and I would get dressed and go wherever I needed to go. And I dreamt of how awesome it was going to be when I returned to my job, and my friends at the airport.

It was the first thing I was planning to do as soon as I was able: fulfill my promise to return to the Business Lounge. And what a joyous day it was going to be when I walked into the airport's Departure Hall! I envisioned how delightful it would be when I was able to leave home independently and once again share an enjoyable time with my friends. I felt so grateful to have so many friends, who were there with me during that scary time, who did not abandon me in my difficulties. After I learn to walk wearing artificial legs, little by little I was going to restore everything that I had lost. As we were approaching the city, I saw the Orthopedic Center from far away. It looked very impressive, like a fortress from far away.

"So this is the place that will give me a new life," I remember thinking.

We came to meet with a professor to evaluate my condition for the prosthetic fitting; when my dad rolled me into the office, the professor was sitting behind his desk doing some paperwork. He greeted us with a smile and welcomed us. He asked my dad if we had my medical records. My father handed over the documents of all which had occurred so far. As the professor went through the papers, he asked if my thigh wounds had healed yet. They were almost healed. Then he lifted his eyes and asked, "How is your left hand? Do you have any feeling? How much can you use it?"

I responded that I could move only my shoulder, and that I could move a little from my elbow. But I couldn't move it at all below the elbow, nor did I have any feeling in the lower part of my arm. The only sign that it was still "alive" was a constant burning, sharp pain in the palm of my hand. He looked again at my records, paused for a moment, then looked straight into my eyes, and with dream-shattering clarity he stated, "I think you should wait until your left arm recovers its function, because your condition right now is too complicated to walk with prosthetic legs. It is impossible to walk missing both legs above the knees, and having no use of one arm."

"What do you mean wait? How can it be impossible?" I immediately replied. "I am not going to wait. I don't know when it will recover, and I am not going to sit and wait until it starts functioning again. I want to try. *There must be a way.* I will learn to walk anyway, even though I can't use my one arm."

Observing the professor's facial expression, I assumed that he did not expect to hear that, nor had he ever heard this kind of response. My answer was so strong and firm that it didn't leave room for the alternative. For a moment I thought maybe I pushed it too hard, but I didn't really care much what he or anybody else thought about my desire to walk. I was not going to allow anybody to stop me from it.

"I cannot understand how it may be impossible," I added, while the professor was hesitating to give me his final decision. "There must be a way; we only need to find it. I will learn. I will work hard. Give me a chance. I decided that I would walk and I am going to make it happen."

After a few moments of silence, he said they would order certain parts for my prostheses from Germany, and that I could return once my wounds were healed completely. They would see what they could do. After his positive decision, I took a deep breath. That's what I came for and was not going to leave without. Now I could relax.

On my way back to Vilnius I felt disappointment. Hearing a medical professor's pronouncement that it was impossible for me to walk was not what I expected. I didn't think about this kind of option. In fact, for me it was never an option at all.

"How can he say it's impossible if he has not even tried to find a way?" I felt annoyed and perplexed. "Why am I told what I can and cannot do? But since he said they would order prosthetic parts, and then asked me to come back, that means that walking is still doable? I know there must be a way for me to walk again, even if it is such a complicated case. I will do everything possible and I *will* walk again. End of discussion."

Hope, disappointment, sadness and determination were all mixed up within me. Who was I to argue with a professor? Still, I knew I was going to do what I had decided to do regardless of any opinion, whether it was a professor or any medical specialist who pronounced it was *impossible.* I was going to walk again and I wasn't going to consider the alternative.

As I was looking through the window at the beautiful scenery and passing cars, I kept repeating in my mind, "Even if my medical diagnosis shows my physical condition is too complicated, and even if theory states that it's impossible – I don't care. I will make it possible. I will do more than walk; I will even dance, and they will see it."

After we returned home, my family and I agreed to take care of other important issues while waiting for my legs to heal completely. My father took the initiative, arranging appointments to see what could be done with my paralyzed left arm. He also made appointments to assist with my broken jaw, my employment at the airport, and all the paperwork from the Social Security Department.

Just as it seemed that I was climbing out of a dark hole, I got bombarded by the facts, overshadowing that tiny light of hope that I had. I was forced to watch how the accident continued ruthlessly depriving of me all that I cherished and valued.

First, I had to hear another "impossible" from a medical specialist. My father, seeing no progress in my arm's recovery, made an appointment with the best neurosurgeons in the country, who agreed to take another look at my arm. After checking my x-rays and examining the feeling and functions, the surgeons said the condition was critical. Apparently, the nerves that controlled my arm were severely damaged, even unrecoverable. They said it was one of the worst traumas I could have gotten.

They still planned to operate in a few weeks to take a closer look, to see if they could soften the pain, and maybe give me some movement from the elbow down. The news that I heard from surgeons was not what I had expected. At the hospital and Rehab Center I was being comforted that my arm would recover soon. Learning that my arm's injury was irreversible totally broke me down for several days. I could not even imagine how I was going to live without my legs and without my arm for the rest of my life.

Then I learned that my jaw had been severely damaged as well, which also required multiple medical procedures and a complex surgery. Since the operation for my arm needed to be done immediately, to forestall more nerve damage, we moved the surgery for my jaw to a later date. And so I had to endure another surgery and wait yet again for my body to heal completely.

Remaining idle at home was most challenging. I was full of determination to change everything that the crash has created, but the circumstances appeared to be stronger than I was. Mom said that prior to the accident, I was like a lively butterfly, constantly flying from place to place. Now I felt like a trapped colorful butterfly, and no matter what I tried to do to get out of the cage, all I faced was a locked cage door with no key.

I tried to get artificial legs – I was told that without the function of my both arms it would be impossible to walk. I tried to see how I could restore the function of my left arm – I was told it was irrecoverable. No matter what I tried to do to make a significant step to return to life, I was stopped each time. And finally, I ended up imprisoned by the walls of my room.

Every aspect of my life had become unrecognizably different. I could not move and take care of myself independently. I had to stay in my room with no ability to leave. My room's doorways were too narrow for my wheelchair to go through so I slept, ate, took care of my personal needs in my room, and spent the entire day in bed.

I could not even get out of the room to be with my family in the kitchen or living room unless my father carried me out in his arms. I hated to be carried, so I chose to stay in my room. Days and nights were tormenting, having only television and friends' visits for a distraction. It was springtime and I knew that behind the walls of my room there was liveliness, laughter, and an enjoyment that I was no longer a part of.

Every day I looked through the window at the blue sky and the sunshine.

It brought back memories of being with friends in both the city and the nature. I was flooded by memories of fun work shifts at the airport. I knew they were having a great time working there today, enjoying gossip-filled coffee breaks and continuous laughter as they made plans for after work.

They were able to get out and do whatever they wanted. But me? I could only witness the sun through a window, could only imagine the delightful feeling of being outside on a warm and sunny spring day. Restricted by the walls of my own home, without the ability to get out of my room, I longed to be the person I was before the accident. At times it felt like my spirit was screaming out that I *was* the same Inga, who had feelings and a strong desire to live her life just as everyone else.

But no one heard me.

And I was absolutely powerless to change anything. Every day I woke up to face the same dreadful reality. My only comfort and distraction from my hatred toward my changed reality were my friends. I was showered by their unconditional love. Every day our home was full of people. I treasured every person who came to spend time with me. I was blessed to see those whom I considered to be my true friends, how they remained faithful to our friendship. It was even a nice surprise to see the people I hadn't really seen for the last few years since I left the church.

My 23rd birthday lasted for several days, as it always used to, with ongoing visits from friends and relatives. I was happy to be alive for this birthday and once again, I saw how greatly loved and valued I was to others. My room grew filled with flowers and gifts, but nobody really knew it was a sad day for me. I was forced again to face the reality that I wasn't the same anymore, that nothing was ever going to be like it used to be.

After my birthday, painful emotions continued showing up at the doorstep of my heart. Since there was no way I could continue my job, I had to write my own resignation letter to the airport, the center of my life for the past several years. I was crushed. Being back at the airport had been part of my dream to be "whole" again.

The time that I worked there delivered the best years of my life and most wonderful people, and now I was forced to leave. Dad passed on best wishes from the administration and a message stating they would be waiting for me to come back. However, until I recovered and was able to return, I wouldn't be able to stay on. My dad handed me the document and quietly stood next to me. Pen in hand, I gazed at the words. I squeezed the pen in the palm of my hand. I could not sign it. The force of this crash mercilessly continued to obliterate everything that I held so precious.

My father repeated that the airport administration was expecting me to return, that the resignation was only temporary. Hardly able to see anything through my tears, I signed the request. My employment at Vilnius International Airport was terminated.

In time I had to prepare for another medical procedure. Again we had to pack and leave home; and it was without knowing that I was to face the most painful and difficult surgery to date. Anesthetic drugs made me sick for days and created a migraine which would not go away, despite the medication. In addition, due to the excruciating pain in my neck where the surgery occurred, I could hardly speak or eat; even the slightest movement of my head felt as if someone had cut my neck with a surgical blade. Up to that point I had hope and was enthusiastic about rebuilding my life, but I found myself in bed crying in agony and despair, feeling that I couldn't take it anymore.

The emotional and physical suffering within had finally taken me to the edge. I was lying absolutely helpless in a hospital bed, tears uncontrollably rolling down my face as I kept asking in my mind, why it had to end like it did. I reached the point to where I wished I wouldn't wake to see another sunrise.

I thanked the Lord for my mother. She was my angel, there with me day and night, making ever sure that I was alright. Her loving eyes and her warm hands would give me peace and comfort. She took care of me without rest. She became my legs and hands and basically my everything. She would make meals for me, would feed me and make me drink plenty of fluids, as well as helping me with my daily routines. My slightest move at night would immediately wake her up, and she'd be right at my bedside to see if I needed something. She completely forgot about herself. I was thankful for all of my family, because every one of them had done everything they could to provide the best care possible.

My last day at the hospital was a big relief; but unlike the other times, I did not leave with the determination that things could ever get better. The fire of hope and enthusiasm for life had been quenched. I was tired of being torn from everything I cherished. I couldn't take anymore the excruciating pain raging throughout body. Nor could I stand the endless emotional anguish. I felt lost and powerless. I only wanted to hide from the world.

Getting back home brought some comfort. The healing process was very long and difficult. I was constantly in pain. As the days passed, the wound from surgery would heal and the pain would lessen and fade away. But unfortunately, the surgery hadn't produced any changes to my arm; I still had that never-ending, sharp, burning pain in my paralyzed hand. These months of my life were like an endless nightmare and I could no longer bear it. The more contempt I felt towards my imprisonment in that lifeless cage, the more my determination started to reawaken. I realized this misery was going to last for as long as I was willing to give in. And there was no way I was going to continue.

6

My Agreement With God

Dear Valdas,

Now I will share something very sacred to me, something I have never told you about. It is the moment that I breathed in the inner strength and tenacity to restore my life. This was when I finally heard from the Lord my God, and I made an agreement with Him. It was His promise that sustained my hope during the darkest times, and the times I yet had to face. Looking back, I understand that when the Lord your God makes a promise – He's going to make it happen. The only thing required is to keep your eyes on the Lord and not your circumstances; obey Him and by faith take each step forward, fully trusting in the Lord. Once you trust in the Lord, He can do the impossible. He can restore your life in ways you could never have imagined. Surrender yourself to Him.

Be well,
Love you very much,
Inga

* * *

Things didn't go the way I thought they would. It seemed like I hit a brick wall every time I wanted to step forward. Instead of making progress, I was being pulled back and losing everything I valued and cherished. I wasn't making any forward progress, yet I did not accept my new circumstances very well. I couldn't imagine how I was to continue, being in such a mentally and physically tormenting condition. Every day I prayed to God, pleading for Him to speak to me. I needed to know why He allowed for it to end so cruelly. I believed that God had power over it all. He brought me back to life, and I am so thankful for that. I asked Him to save me regardless of my decisions, and He did. But why did He allow me to lose my legs and my arm? What was the purpose behind such devastating consequences? I knew that God didn't make mistakes, and if He allowed this to happen the way it did – there had to be a reason.

One day, as my friend Martynas was visiting, our light conversation turned into a discussion about my major questions. I knew I could be open with him and I shared with him my thoughts and how I felt. After listening, he looked at me and said, "Inga, I don't know why it happened the way it did. But what I do know is that God did not leave you then, and He is not going to leave you alone now. He would not have allowed you to appear in this position if you would not have been able to take it. With God you will handle it."

It felt like someone enlightened my mind and suddenly I got a very clear awareness: God is love. His purpose was not to torture me. He knows what I can and cannot endure. He never abandoned me and He showed me that He was with me the entire time. If He saved my life, even though I was not supposed to survive, and used His power to heal me so rapidly, there must be the purpose behind everything.

Martynas reinforced my belief that there was a divine purpose in everything that had happened, that the Lord was with me. I was strong enough to take it. In fact, I wasn't only going to live through it, but with the Lord's help, I was going to have a victory.

It felt like someone gave me a drink from the spring of life and suddenly, I felt alive. This was the first time I felt strong enough to accept the consequences of the crash. But I felt strong not just to cope with it, but to emerge from the tragedy and triumph over it. I felt endowed with unexplainable resolve to restore my life like I had never experienced before. I felt at ease. I felt confident. No longer had I questioned whether I could take it. I knew that I could and that I would have a wonderful life.

I knew the Lord was speaking to me through simple conversations like this and various situations like I had at the Rehab Center. It gave me confidence knowing that God hadn't left me alone. I was a part of His eternal plan, and together we would turn the situation around. I couldn't imagine how it could possibly happen, but I felt at peace about it.

I again started feeling that flame of determination.

Knowing that the Lord God was there gave me strength to get up in the morning. Day after day, I grew stronger learning to live with no legs and only one arm. The one thing that gave me strength to endure was the certain knowledge that there was a purpose in all that had happened. The driving force was my hope and anticipation that there would come a day when I would be able to walk again, breaking the barrier of my limitations to function independently.

Dealing with my limitations was very hard though. My contempt for my inability to be self-sufficient was agonizing. My relentless question, "Why did it have to end like this?" was constantly inducing a debate with God within the depths of my mind. I could not look at myself in the mirror. I couldn't take the fact that I was not able to do things like I used to and that my position was irreversible. Every day I kept asking God in prayer what His purpose was and how I was supposed to continue.

One day, after my prayer pleading with God to speak with me, a thought came to me to open my Bible and see if I would get my answer through His Word. I didn't look for any particular chapter or verse, I simply opened it having faith that I would open the verse through which God would communicate His answer. I opened one of the gospels and began to read:

> *"Now as Jesus passed by, He saw a man who was blind from birth. And His disciples asked Him, saying, 'Rabbi, who sinned, this man or his parents, that he was born blind?' Jesus answered, 'Neither this man nor his parents sinned, but that the works of God should be revealed in him. I must work the works of Him who sent Me while it is day; the night is coming when no one can work. As long as I am in the world, I am the light of the world.' When He had said these things, He spat on the ground and made clay with the saliva; and He anointed the eyes of the blind man with the clay. And He said to him, 'Go, wash in the pool of Siloam' (which is translated, Sent). So he went and washed, and came back seeing. Therefore the neighbors and those who previously had seen that he was blind said, 'Is not this he who sat and begged?' Some said, 'This is he.' Others said, 'He is like him.' He said, 'I am he.'" (John 9: 1-9)*

As I was reading, I felt this story speak specifically to me. Particularly meaningful to me were the words, "But that the works of God should be revealed in him." I had clear insight that the Lord was going to heal me and restore my life, and the way He would do it would bring glory to God. The accident was the result of my decision to venture into enemy's territory and lead a sinful lifestyle. My choice brought me to the crash, but because of God's grace, He saved my life. The accident ended my sinful lifestyle, and now God would heal me just as He had healed the man blind from birth. And the way He would restore my life would bring glory to God.

"What? Your glory?" I was shocked. "What are you talking about, Lord? I have to go through the pain and loss of my body, and everything that I had, and now you are telling me that this will bring glory to You?"

I got angry. I closed my Bible and my conversation with God was over.

That moment left me unsettled all day long. The words and the feeling I had while reading was like a movie replaying in my mind. I've never felt this way reading God's word. Those words stood out and became alive, as though speaking to me out loud. Furthermore, the insight that came upon me while reading was not my own. There's no way I could come up with that awareness myself. Besides, it didn't make sense to me - I couldn't understand how it could bring glory to God if, in fact, this crash broke my life. I could not understand how I was supposed to bring His glory to people if I was locked away in my house with no ability to leave.

I was restless. The next day, I again prayed asking God to speak to me clearly. I felt totally lost and helpless against my circumstances. I was in emotional agony and confusion. I needed to hear from my Lord. I needed His guidance. After my prayer, I took my Bible with the intention of receiving God's message. Again I opened it without choosing any particular chapter or verse, believing that I would open what God wanted to say to me through His word. I never used to read Bible like this, but I was in such a desperate need to hear from God that I said in my prayer, "Please speak to me. I will open Your Word, and oh God, please direct me to the passage through which You want to speak."

Having faith that God would answer my prayer, I opened it blindly and began reading from the verse before me. A chill shot through my body – it was exactly the same story, how Jesus healed a person and that the purpose of his blindness was for the glory of God!

This time the words, "works of God might be displayed in him," were particularly brought out to me, creating an insight. The reason why the accident ended so cruelly was because through God's healing and restoring my life, God's glory would be revealed.

I again felt His supernatural presence. I felt it significantly stronger and even physically I felt something unusual. I was in awe, having no doubts the Lord my God was speaking to me through His Word, just as I had asked Him to do.

Suddenly the awareness came upon me: I needed to stop questioning God why it all happened the way it did. Stop questioning and stop dwelling, trying to figure out the "why." I would understand it later. Meanwhile, I needed to accept and trust God. I needed to surrender to the Father's will, to be obedient to God, and to put my trust in Him in everything. I needed to watch where He was leading and walk in faith, moving forward the way I needed to go.

I stopped crying. The feeling was so strong and my new awareness was so clear that I didn't dare continue agonizing over the question. I just sat there. Like a statue carved many hundreds of years before, I couldn't move. The deep comprehension was so profound that I knew I would *not* ask that question again and would not argue with God about it. Being in great awe before my Lord, I put down the Bible, closed my eyes, and said out loud, "Okay, Lord. I give up fighting and questioning. I know You don't make mistakes, and if You allowed it, that means there was a serious reason why it happened the way it did. I accept it. Yes, the fact I am alive is Your miracle. And yes, I healed exceptionally fast and it's all because of You, Lord. But how am I going to bring You glory? I do not have my legs anymore, I cannot go anywhere. I cannot even go out of my home, so how can I bring Your glory to others? I don't know what You are doing, God. What kind of glorious things You are going to do in my life and how I will be able to bring them to others. But I will trust you Lord, unconditionally and unquestionably. You are my God and I give up fighting and questioning. I accept it all and surrender myself to You. Show me Yourself. Show me Your greatness. Show me Your power and I will bring Your glory to the nations."

Suddenly I felt peace. I felt comforted and assured about my future. I knew my Heavenly Father heard my prayer. It felt like I made an agreement with the Lord. There was no agony within anymore. It was replaced by confidence and joyous peace. The sudden radical change within me was a sign that I just had yet another encounter with the Lord.

I knew with deep and internal reassurance that I would see God's almighty power and be given the answers to my questions when the time came. It was an incredible feeling. Deep within I had the knowledge that God's promise would come to be my new reality. I knew that at some point, my life must change again.

7

Self-Management: How Perspective Affects Our Inner State and Future Decisions

My Dear Brother,

As we continue our journey together, I would like to stop for a moment and take a look at the next important aspect. In this letter, I want to share with you something that empowered me tremendously. It is my second strong foundation that comes after faith. If you learn to master this step, you will be able to respond to life's events in a way that will empower you, and you will be able to manage your feelings no matter the circumstances that come your way.

Imagine your life is a house that you plan to build. First you build the foundation. It must be strong for the house to stand solid when the storms come. If you have your strong faith as your foundation, you will be unbreakable. Faith will give you strength and endurance to move forward despite the obstacles and challenges that arise. I shared with you in my previous letter about the rock-solid foundation. Continuing further in this metaphor, let's see what else we need to do to have an unbreakable house.

As a construction specialist explained to me, the ground floor, which sets upon the foundation, is equally as important as the foundation. The ground floor frames the walls and other parts of the house. It must be accurate and calculated precisely, because everything built from there will rely on its dependability. If you don't pay close attention to the dimensions of your foundation and the framing of the ground floor during construction, later you will see how your walls are not straight, the windows are not aligned, and the house will not be well-built.

What is the next step after you lay a rock-solid foundation based on faith? It's the skill to manage your perspective of the world around you, the circumstances and events that happen in your life.

Have you thought about why some people give up and others overcome seemingly insurmountable situations which confront them? Why some people get depressed and give in to circumstances and others refuse to give in and find a way to improve their lives? Is it that some are stronger than others? I don't think so. I believe that what sets those people apart is their ability to manage themselves.

What is self-management? It is the skill to master your perspective, your thought patterns, your thought focus and your feelings. It's the ability to manage yourself. When you have the skills necessary to manage your inner state, you will be able to respond to life's events in a way that empowers you. It is imperative to be able to manage your outlook and your inner state at all times, because you make different choices and different decisions depending upon how you view a situation and how you feel at the time your decisions are made. Would you agree that you make different decisions when you feel hopeful, confident, tenacious, strong and determined, and make entirely different decisions when you feel hopeless and helpless, defeated, doubting and pessimistic?

I am sure you have heard the saying, "I feel bad because 'this and that' happened," and you have many experiences when outside events influenced your feelings which in turn impacted your decisions. Have you ever thought what are the roots as to how you feel on a daily basis or when certain situations occur? Do your feelings depend on what's going on around you? Or can you be the master of your own feelings and outlook about what's going on, where you control the situation, not the situation controlling you? Here is a basic truth I've found: The way we feel greatly depends upon our *thought focus* and *perspective.*

What causes excitement and depression? Both inner states are the result of our thought processes. Nobody gets into a depression by focusing on exciting opportunities or how grateful they are for everything good that a person has. Depression sneaks in when a person pays close attention to what he or she is unhappy about and constantly thinks about it. Same way, the more a person focuses on hope, things that he's grateful for and any positive events, on new opportunities and compelling goals, there will be no room for sadness, only the excitement and determination to make the desired change. Our feelings always follow our thought focus.

I learned and realized that thoughts and emotions don't simply happen to me, leaving me powerless against them. I *choose* what I think and what I focus on, what meaning I give to the events and what I am going to do about them. Nobody and no event has the power to make me feel in any particular way, unless I allow it. I am the one who chooses my response, and that depends on my *perspective* and my *interpretation of what it means to me.*

In our minds, we constantly communicate to ourselves what things mean to us, how we feel about events, and what we are going to do about them. When we are doing well, we are excited and think about how thrilled we are or what it took for us to achieve success. Having an even stronger belief of what is possible for us, we move on with our lives. Likewise, when various complex circumstances occur, we weigh the situations, we examine the reasons why they happened, and move forward having reached our conclusions and made our decisions for the future.

While we are in the middle of one or the other situation, it's only natural that we feel certain emotions. It's easy to see the good side and feel the positive emotions when the circumstances are in our favor. But it's far more challenging to feel positive if it's a painful and difficult event for us, isn't? The way we will feel about the event greatly depends on how we interpret it and how we communicate it to ourselves and others.

I am sure you have experienced situations when, after hearing some news or having some particular experience, you automatically reacted to what happened accepting the event as a bad thing. Being overwhelmed with negative feelings, you got so fearful, frustrated or disappointed that you offended someone, hung up the phone or broke off your relationship, stopped pursuing your goal, gave up on a project, broke your commitments and, well, the list is endless. After some time, when everything calmed down, you regretted how you reacted that way, realizing your actions were taken because you were driven by the emotions that you had at that time. Unfortunately, our words and actions most often are irreversible. If you learn how to stop yourself from the negative reaction and allow your empowering perspective to shape your response to a situation, it will be much easier for you to accept and handle problems. In addition, you can save yourself from unpleasant situations you may face as a result of your reactive response. Having the same event, we have a choice of how we look at it. Our point of view will lay the foundation for how we are going to feel about it.

Let's take a simple example. Ken, after a break-up with a woman due to her lies and cheating, can look at it in various ways. Ken can feel that he is not good enough, and that something's wrong with him; he has been lied to because there is someone better than him, and probably this woman only wanted to use him. What is he going to do next? Very likely, this kind of perspective will lower his self-esteem and will greatly impact his decision as to what love and relationships mean to him. He might start believing that he is not good enough to be loved, that women are deceptive cheaters, or that all women feel negatively toward him. He will feel that any relationship won't work out because he is simply not worthy of being loved. This will shape a new perspective about himself and his relationships; something is wrong with him and he's not attractive to women, and that he can't trust women. As a result, he will not even want to get into a new relationship because he doesn't want to be hurt and disappointed again.

Given the same situation, there is a choice to look at it differently.

Ken can see the break-up as a good thing, because if his girlfriend chose to be dishonest with him, then this was not really the woman for him. He knows what kind of woman he wants to be with for the rest of his life and this is definitely not who he wants. In fact, it would have been worse if he'd wasted more time (and money) with her, and especially if he had made a life commitment with that person.

Now he has a new opportunity to meet his true life partner, who will love him unconditionally, who will not hurt him and will be faithful to him. Actually, he is thankful for this break-up, because now he is free to meet the right woman for him and he is ready for that special connection and relationship.

How will this perspective make Ken feel? What kind of decision will he make concerning what he's going to do next? The same situation can have different perspectives with totally different results.

Another simple example in a different situation: let's say I come to work and find out that I was laid off. How am I going to feel about it? What am I going to do about it? It greatly depends on my perspective. I can see it as I am not good enough and they are getting rid of me; it's a big problem; it's the end of my security and well-being. Consequently, the anxiety, lowered self-esteem and fear are just a step away.

But what if this is an opportunity for me to get a better position? What if this door closes, so another door opens to a career that I really want? Maybe this is an opportunity for me to apply for the position that I've been dreaming about? Or maybe even create my own business? This could be the end of my 9-5 routine job, so I can have the beginning of a fulfilling career. How differently am I going to feel if I take this as an opportunity for something greater than I already had? Again, two different perspectives for the same situation and both create different outcomes.

What if we take circumstances or events as facts? The fact itself can't make us feel any particular way. It is what it is: a plain fact, the same as any object. It's how we look at the facts that will shape your attitude and your feelings about it. Events, the same way as objects or activities, are simply neutral matter and they have neither likes nor dislikes. They are, in reality, the sum of what a person thinks they are, depending on what it means to people. Let's take a gambling game, for instance. It is just a game, nothing more. But how we feel about it depends on how we look at it and what gambling means to us. We can look at it as a fun time with friends, the anticipation of what's going to happen next, and a great opportunity to gain huge sums amount of money with no effort and work.

Or we can look at gambling as a waste of time, opening doors to something that can bring destruction to our lives (and the lives of our loved ones); it is throwing away our hard-earned money which can be better spent on something more meaningful. It's all in how we look at it that will make us feel about that pastime or any event.

As you can see, our perspective is how we give meaning to an event or circumstance. Depending upon our point of view, we will feel about it in a particular way and then choose further action accordingly.

Analyze this with me. Do you think you would respond differently to a situation by changing the way in which you look at it? Let's say you take your last difficult situation and applied each question equally. Notice how differently you will feel about that situation when you look at it differently:

- Is this a failure or punishment, or is this an experience with a valuable lesson for me in the future?
- Is this a loss, or a hidden opportunity for something new and better?
- Does this situation show me that I am a failure, or does this situation show me there are areas where I can improve so I can do better next time?

- Is this a dead end, or a challenge for me to find a way because my faith tells me there is a way?
- Is this a devastating crash, or is it the end of something that will be replaced by something that really needs to take place in my life?
- Is this too much for me to handle, or is this an opportunity for me to overcome a new challenge and become stronger and better at what I do?
- Is this a problem, or a challenge for me to find a way to improve and create what I want?

When any situation occurs, instead of getting into reaction mode, focusing on how bad it is, stop yourself and shift your point of view in such a way that will give you hope, will show you the benefits, will make you feel better, and will give you a sense of well-being because of the newly opened opportunity.

Beliefs and Perspective

What if you can't see your situation in the way that empowers you? Then look deeper within – pay attention to your beliefs.

What is your general belief about yourself and success? What is your belief about your personal destiny? What are your beliefs about circumstances in your life – where do they come from? What is your belief about you and your relationship with the opposite sex? Where do your beliefs come from? How do they affect your outlook on life's events? How do they impact your decisions when you're forced to handle difficult times? How does your belief system support you in times of trouble?

Think about it: Our perspective depends on our beliefs. For the most part, beliefs are unconscious, and they come from a person's cultural background, life philosophy, religious beliefs, life experience, or the opinions and experience of those whom they trust and respect. Belief is nothing more than what we hold as the truth.

We have a choice to believe that we are not good enough and will never be, and we may choose to believe we are capable and will improve as part of our learning process. We may believe that we do not belong to the circle of successful people, and we may believe that with our relentless efforts we can climb any ladder of success we want, regardless of our background.

We may believe that all life's events and circumstances are pre-destined and are out of our control, so whatever happens we say, "such is life." At the same time, we may believe that with our decisions we can shape our destiny, and by making smart choices and with God's help we can create the circumstances we want and will ultimately direct our destiny.

We may believe that there is no God, that life is just a series of random events happening to us in a random fashion; it's all about luck and most often, life's not fair. We also have a choice to believe that everything that happens in our lives is in God's total control and everything happens for the purpose and for the better as part of His plan for us.

We may believe we are not good enough and are not worthy of love and building a strong family, or we may choose to believe we are worthy just as everybody is, and that we will have it when the right time comes.

We may have a belief that we will not succeed anyway, so what's the point of trying; success is only for the "chosen" ones, or, we are not as lucky as others. But we can believe that success is not luck but rather, the result of our efforts, and we will be blessed and will succeed in what we decide to do.

We may believe that our well-being or opportunities depend upon given circumstances, and we can have only as much as those circumstances allow us. At the same time, we may believe that circumstances are a subject to change. It's not the circumstances that determine our well-being and what we can have in life, but with our own decisions and actions we can create the favorable circumstances we need and attain what we desire.

These are only several examples of general beliefs about destiny, success, God, love and people. Do you think people make different choices in life depending on those beliefs? Consciously or unconsciously, our beliefs shape our perspective about events and various aspects of our life and these beliefs directly impact our decisions.

In order to illustrate better how a belief shapes perspective and how it directly affects our choices, I will share with you a real-life example. In my first letter to you I mentioned that what you are witnessing in my life is not a coincidence, and how there is so much more beyond what you can see. What you are witnessing is:

- The fruit of the Lord's blessing.
- My conscious intentional work with myself.
- The actions I took to implement my plan, to achieve a desired outcome.

My actions to initiate the change of my circumstances reflect my decisions. My decisions were based on my perspective on how I viewed my situation and how I viewed my future. My perspective depended on my belief. It is all a process. Any action that a person takes begins internally within that person's heart. I am not talking about their physical heart, but about their soul, their mind, will and emotions. In order for you to start making any changes in your life, you will need to begin making changes in your *mind*, your *will* and your *emotions*.

Determine what your beliefs are, because based on your beliefs you have a certain perspective and a certain thought pattern. Based on your perspective, you consciously or unconsciously make different choices concerning what you are going to do and which direction you will take.

People often wonder about the boldness and tenacity that I have and ask me where I get it. It's not because I am stronger or more gifted than anybody else. It all comes from my faith, which grounded me with a rock-solid perspective empowering me to aim high and overcome whatever adversity got in my way. Since the accident, I had a strong foundation for my personal, empowering outlook. I had then and have today an unwavering faith in what the future holds. That's what gives me hope each day, and gave me the hope I so desperately needed during the darkest times. That's what empowered me to fight for my life and this is the reason I aimed for goals which to everyone else seemed unattainable.

You have watched me going against the stream, aspiring to achieve my goals despite the circumstances that were against me. You have seen me breaking through the obstacles, relentlessly aiming for what I set my mind to despite the advice of many to accept my new way of life.

I know it might have raised questions such as, "Why isn't she listening to anyone?" But I was unyielding in my determination to change my life the way I envisioned it, despite the perception of others in the impossibility of my idea. I saw how you were bewildered and at times frustrated watching me suffering when I would repeatedly reach a dead end and yet, refused to give up on my aim. Well, the reason I decided not to play by the rules and not to listen to anybody, but to do what I envisioned, was because my beliefs were a lot different from those of anyone around me.

There were many different opinions as to why the car accident happened, questions about my destiny, and advice about what I should do from that point forward. Some people thought that God was punishing me for my transgressions and for leaving the church. Others said, "Such is your fate. This man broke your destiny," implying that the only option I had was to give in. I also had to hear from those who told me not to try so hard pursuing my dream, because achieving it was unrealistic. I disagreed with them all and decided to do the opposite – to fight for my life. Why? My perspective about what was going on at the time and about my future was much different than everyone else's.

First, I had the *unshakable belief* that the Lord my God was watching over me and that my life was in the hands of the Almighty and therefore, I would not give in to fear and despair. There was a reason why I got into this crash and there is a purpose for why I survived, even though my heart stopped twice and I was given only a 30% chance to live. I was absolutely sure that this crash did not break my destiny as many people thought. And it didn't happen for me to spend the rest of my life being regretful and depressed, watching my life pass by in sadness because of my restricted mobility. I received a message from the Lord through the Holy Scriptures that He was going to restore my life, and that's what I was holding on to. His promise was the ground I was standing on. I didn't understand many things, but I believed with all my heart there's a purpose in everything and my Lord was going to restore my life.

Second, based on my belief, *I had a perspective that empowered me:* I looked into the future through faith with confidence that I would live a full life despite my injuries. My understanding about it was so bright and clear, as if I was given a wide range color palette, being told that I could draw only a black or gray house, and I knew that I could use all colors I wanted, and paint not only a house, but also blossoming gardens, green trees, colorful flowers, bright yellow sun, blue sky and more. The crash did not break my destiny. It only redirected it. I was in the unknown, which of course wasn't really comforting, and at times had me questioning what was going on. But my faith always strengthened me. I looked at my future with curiosity, to see how the Lord was going to restore my life. I began calling my life a *journey.*

I was not going to give in to anybody's opinions or the circumstances. I completely rejected the statement, "Such is your fate." As soon as I would hear such opinions, feelings of rebellion would instantly stir up inside of me as a volcano ready to erupt. And often I did, responding to them, "No. That is *not* my fate. I will create the destiny that I *want.*" I did not have any idea how my situation could possibly resolve for the better, but deep in my heart I believed that I would live well.

So, empowered by my beliefs and perspective of how I viewed everything that was going on in my life, *I resolved to take action.* I decided to turn my vision into reality, and I never doubted I would successfully attain it. I decided that I would not sit around wrapped in a self-pity blanket and collect sympathy from others. I did not see myself as disabled, nor was I ever going to. I would not adopt the mental attitude of a victim of drunk driving, as it was accustomed to say in cases like mine. And I wouldn't waste any time dwelling on the tragedy either. Instead, I would focus on improving my health and put forth every effort to become as independent as I could. I resolved to do whatever it would take to come back to a dynamic life. I set goals for myself, which transformed my life from not being able to move or do anything independently to leading a fulfilling and exciting life.

Today when I look back, I see that if I had agreed that God had punished me, or that my fate was to be disabled, implying that I was destined to lead an isolated life, I guess I would have given in and would not have tried to change my life. If I had accepted the identity that I was disabled, it would have limited me greatly. I never would have known what I could achieve. If I had looked at my circumstances "realistically" (as many did, thinking they were doing me a favor), and followed their advice to work around my circumstances and physical limitations – probably I would still be stuck at home with no access or aspirations for a full life. That's why I am so grateful to my Creator for the mindset I had then and now, because my perspective empowered me to take whatever action I thought necessary to change my circumstances. Faith and an empowering perspective enabled me to take steps that ultimately transformed my life from dim and desperate to fulfilling and hope-filled.

As all of my earlier examples show, the same situation can have totally different outcome, depending on which outlook a person chooses. I believe you see how important it is to be aware of our beliefs and the perspective we have, because our choices in life depend on that. If we are aware of our beliefs and our perspective, we can master our response to any outside influence on our lives.

Choose the Belief that Empowers You

The good thing is that we *have a choice* as to what beliefs we want to have. If I had an outlook of what the future holds based on my cultural beliefs or other people's opinions, I would have never dared to aspire to change my life the way I did. If I had given credence to a common belief in our culture that you can have only that what given circumstances allow, I doubt I would have achieved my goals. In fact, I would not have even tried. Every goal I had meant breaking through the given circumstances, and I chose to believe my Lord – all things are possible for God and to those who believe, and so I dared to aim for what seemed unattainable goals and change what seemed unbreakable circumstances. My trust in the Lord is what equipped me with the boldness and tenacity to go against what other people thought were limitations.

When total hopelessness stared at me with its deadly look and there was absolutely nothing I could count on, I chose to have faith. I put my trust in the Lord almighty that He is able to change any circumstances and thus, I was able to cope with daily agony and darkness knowing eventually there would be light on the horizon. That's what held me from giving up. My faith gave me a perspective, "This is not the end; there must be a way and there will come a day when I will find it. The Lord has the plan."

This is what gave me hope and endurance to continue on and make every effort to improve my circumstances. When you have a belief system that strengthens you, it is much easier to accept life's challenges and handle the difficulties you encounter. Here's an example:

When you put your sunglasses on, you see the same surroundings and objects as you saw without glasses, but you see everything *differently*, don't you? What you see stays the same, but how you see it changes. Now replace sunglasses with glasses of faith. When you look at your life through the perspective of faith, you will see the same events of your life and surrounding world, but you will see it differently. Your perspective through faith will give you hope and will empower you and thus, you will feel differently and you will make different choices.

Only there is one important detail: What is the foundation of your faith? Who do you believe in? If you trust something that you cannot really be confident in, your beliefs and perspective will break when the storms of life hit you.

I shared with you about my Rock on which you, too, can stand firmly.

As I mentioned in my first letter, the physical realm directly depends on the spiritual realm, and Jesus Christ has the authority above all. Now you know what to do when troubles come. Our Heavenly Father is the God of Abraham, Isaac and Jacob. He is a Creator of the universe, a living God, who has the power and authority over any circumstances in your life. He is God who is powerful to help you and He will. Those who trust in the Lord will not be ashamed. Now you have tasted the peace that the Lord gives. I will never forget your words when you said you have never felt such peace in your life, and you were in wonder that you could feel tranquility in the midst of a storm. "Yes, that is my Lord," I smiled. It is beyond our comprehension, isn't it? Now you know it is not some myth or someone's imagination. The God you believed in and surrendered your life to is the God who changes circumstances. You can have assurance in who you believe in. Looking into your future through the glasses of faith will give you confidence, boldness and anticipation for the future, for your life to come.

Knowing that the Lord your God has the power over any circumstances and people and there is nothing impossible for Him, build your perspective about your present and your future through perspective of faith. You may still wonder: When you apply God's promises into your life, how will this change your outlook? I will give you several examples:

> *"And we know that all things work together for good to those who love God and are the chosen according to His purpose." (Romans 8:28)*

When you have events that seem bad and destructive, your belief will shape your perspective – whatever happens, all will work together for the good. In the end, it will bring some benefit, because the Lord works in mysterious ways and He works out everything for good. It will equip you with endurance and the positive mindset you need to withstand any adversity.

During times of turmoil and uncertainty you will still be at peace, knowing that the One who created the universe will deliver you from troubles.

> *"Many are the afflictions of the righteous, but the Lord delivers him out of them all." (Psalm 34:19)*

"I lift up my eyes to the mountains - where does my help come from?
My help comes from the Lord, the Maker of heaven and earth.
He will not let your foot slip - he who watches over you will not slumber;
Indeed, he who watches over Israel will neither slumber nor sleep.
The Lord watches over you - the Lord is your shade at your right hand; the sun will not harm you by day, nor the moon by night.
The Lord will keep you from all harm - he will watch over your life; the Lord will watch over your coming and going both now and forevermore." (Psalm 121 NIV)

"Whoever dwells in the shelter of the Most High will rest in the shadow of the Almighty.
I will say of the Lord, 'He is my refuge and my fortress, my God, in whom I trust.'
Surely he will save you from the fowler's snare and from the deadly pestilence.
He will cover you with his feathers, and under his wings you will find refuge; his faithfulness will be your shield and rampart. You will not fear the terror of night, nor the arrow that flies by day, nor the pestilence that stalks in the darkness, nor the plague that destroys at midday. A thousand may fall at your side, ten thousand at your right hand, but it will not come near you.
You will only observe with your eyes and see the punishment of the wicked.

If you say, 'The Lord is my refuge,' and you make the Most High your dwelling, no harm will overtake you, no disaster will come near your tent. For he will command his angels concerning you to guard you in all your ways; they will lift you up in their hands, so that you will not strike your foot against a stone. You will tread on the lion and the cobra; you will trample the great lion and the serpent.

> *'Because he loves me,' says the Lord, 'I will rescue him; I will protect him, for he acknowledges my name. He will call on me, and I will answer him; I will be with him in trouble, I will deliver him and honor him. With long life I will satisfy him and show him my salvation.'"* (Psalm 91 NIV)

When you face an immense challenge and you are unsure, your belief will equip you with the strength and confidence to do what you have to do. You will not be afraid to take action, nor will you be fearful of people because you will know that the Lord will watch over you and protect you. And you will succeed because the Lord your God will help you.

> *"Are not two sparrows sold for a copper coin? And not one of them falls to the ground apart from your Father's will. But the very hairs of your head are all numbered. Do not fear therefore; you are of more value than many sparrows."* (Matthew 10: 29-31)

Your belief will give you the confidence that comes from knowing that no harm will touch you, because your Father in heaven is watching over you and things happen in your life only when your Father allows it to happen. If He allows it, it is for your benefit, because all things work together for good to those who love God and are called according to His purpose.

> *"And we know that all things work together for good to those who love God, to those who are the called according to His purpose."* (Romans 8:28)

Building your perspective on faith will give you a strong foundation to stand on. Never take off your glasses of faith, because you will open the door to doubts, anxiety, fear, rejection, hopelessness, and other negative feelings that will impact your life. While you wear your glasses of faith, ask the question that is going to change how you view the situation; ask a question that will direct you toward your solution:

- Keeping in mind that the Lord God is in control, what is the purpose of this situation?
- What if this situation is an opportunity? What might this be? How will this opportunity reveal itself to me?
- Trusting that all things are for a reason and all things work together for good, what good will this situation bring? If not right now, what benefit could it bring eventually?
- What can I learn and appreciate from this life lesson that I can use as valuable experience?
- Trusting that this situation is not to harm me, but to bless me, in what form will my blessing take?

Having a belief that will be the Rock on which you stand will always hold you steady. Empowering perspective will direct your mind and decisions in a way that will bring the best out of any situation. Asking the right questions will move you toward the right actions, which will have a direct impact on your circumstances.

Always remember: You do not have control over other people and many times you do not have control over what happens in life. But you have a choice as to how you look at situations and people and what you are going to do about anything that happens. Depending on your decisions and what you do next, you will create subsequent events and this way you shape your destiny. If you carefully and deliberately choose your beliefs and perspective, you will always have control over your response to various life events, challenges, or any situation in life.

I know there is a reason why you are facing the circumstances you shared with me. Instead of dwelling on how tough it is, ask yourself what you can learn from this, what might be the reason this situation occurred. What's the purpose behind it all? What do you need to do to take your life to the next level? Once you know the answer, focus on the solution and confidently move on.

I want you to extract the most valuable lesson out of this experience and put this gem into your basket of wisdom, which you can carry with you everywhere you go. May this time frame remain as a memory of the most significant time in your life, which directed you unto the incredible journey, for which you will be eternally grateful.

I hope you take time to consider and ponder what I have written. As I mentioned earlier, this is one of the most powerful tools of managing yourself that I intended to pass on to you. Master this. It will change you. It will change your life experience.

Take care of yourself. All will be well.

Till the next time,
Much love,
Inga

8

Back to the Orthopedic Center

Dear Valdas,

The next chapter of my journey taught me some valuable lessons. I know you were a witness to this period. Yet I want to share what you couldn't have seen nor could you have known. I realize your current situation might be raising concerns and many questions. You might have thoughts that are too difficult to deal with. But I want you to be inspired as you read, and use what I am telling you to mark your own path toward the future.

This period of recuperation has taught me the power of relentless perseverance. If something you want to achieve looks impossible, it only seems like that. Human perseverance can do the unattainable. Your pain might become your strength when you use it wisely. I only hope you will notice and collect the gems that will help you become unbreakable in your pursuit.

All is going to be well,
Inga

* * *

My left arm surgery and the ensuing extremely painful recovery depleted my endurance and enthusiasm for life. Every one of us felt tired after months of distress, sleepless nights and fear of the unknown. My parents decided we needed to go away for a few weeks to the Baltic Sea. I was looking forward to getting away from the confinement. Sadly, the trip turned out to be nothing more than a continuation of the grief. The previous summer, Renata and I had a wonderful vacation at the same resort, but appearing in the same place in my wheelchair, with empty pant legs where my legs used to be, was heartbreaking. At times I wished that I didn't even exist anymore. As I was being slowly wheeled through the streets of that cozy resort, succumbed by the reality of no longer being able to walk, no longer able to feel the sand dunes under my feet, no longer able to run into the sea and swim, or ride a bike, or dance, it all hit me on a continual basis. Having fresh memories of all the things I was able to do while sitting helpless in a wheelchair often seemed more than I could handle.

Since it was my first time out, I had no idea how people would react to seeing me this way. But when I saw people staring at me, as though I were an alien from outer space, it made an even stronger statement that I didn't belong in the world anymore. Every person who stared and looked at where my legs used to be made me relive the tragedy over and over. I knew it was unusual to see a person in a wheelchair in the street among the crowd, and especially it was shocking to see a person missing both legs. Still, in my mind I asked why they could not understand how agonizing it was for me to have them looking at me like that. At times, I could barely restrain myself from shouting, "Please stop staring at me. I'm no different than you are, I just happened to experience a tragedy. Tomorrow you may end up like me or worse; you don't know what your tomorrow has in store, just like I didn't."

Finally, the anguish reached the threshold to where I could no longer endure. Then something shifted within me. Feelings of being hurt transformed into a resolve. I decided that I was going to change it all. I wasn't going to remain in a position that would make people feel sorry for me. Maybe they saw me as weak and helpless due to my incomplete body, but they were mistaken. Strength was *within* me. Those who stared couldn't imagine what it required for me to get up in the morning and start my day in spite of my injuries. They didn't know what courage it took for me to go out in public being different. It required unbreakable stamina to go forth and continue my life when I was differently capable than I used to be. And now, I would use that courage and strength to bring myself back to life.

The anguish and contempt for my situation was so strong that I turned my pain into the resolve to become "normal" again. My grief became my strength to end the torment and establish my life once again. I was ready to fight. And this time my determination was even stronger. I knew that nobody and nothing would be able to stop me from implementing my intention. With that, I found a way to deal with those looks and it didn't hurt anymore. I didn't tell any of this to my mother or my father. I'm sure they had enough of their own sorrow to deal with. With each day, I was eager to end the vacation so I could get to the Orthopedic Center as soon as possible.

Upon our return home, we received a phone call from the Orthopedic Center telling us they had all the necessary parts for my prosthetic legs, and were welcome to visit if my wounds were fully healed.

I took a deep breath. This dreadful first half of the year was coming to an end. The ongoing agony of my helplessness was nearly over. I finally got the keys to the cage where I was imprisoned – walking again would open that cage. I would no longer be stuck at home, separated from my friends and my life. And the greatest joy – I would come back to the airport and return to work!

Mom was on summer vacation from her work, and she said she would go with me to stay at the center to be there to help. She couldn't imagine letting me going alone. She was consumed wondering who was going to help me in the mornings, not to mention who was going to help me with everything else I needed to do. She did not even consider any other option but to spend the rest of her vacation with me, and she packed our belongings all over again.

Father, as always, took care of all the administrative details, making sure all the paperwork was correct and ready, and he drove us to the Center. The Orthopedic Center's giant red building could be seen from miles away. I felt like the flames of hope and excitement were rising as we drove closer and closer to our destination.

The closer we got the bigger and more foreboding it became. As we approached I remember thinking, "I am going to get back what I have lost. I *will* walk again. I am *not* going to give in to what this accident created. I am going to claim back my independence and live an active life. I don't care how much effort it will require. I will get this done. No matter what."

Upon entering, we were met by a staff member who escorted us to the office to register. Everyone seemed to be very caring and welcoming. Even though it, too, was a Rehab Center, I liked the atmosphere. It didn't feel like a hospital or like some elderly nursing home. It seemed to be exactly the place I wanted to be – the gateway to my fulfilling life. I easily accepted the fact that I had to stay. A doctor escorted me to the room reserved for me and my mom.

After we made ourselves comfortable, I met my prosthetic specialist, Simas. He was in his twenties as I was, and seemed enthusiastic about his work at the center. He took measurements of my thighs to make sockets for me, and said he would let me know when my prostheses would be ready.

While I was waiting for my new legs to be built, I was assigned to the rehab program in the gym to strengthen my overall physical health. In addition, I was scheduled for spa and massage therapies, which were supposed to prepare my thighs for wearing prostheses. I enjoyed the procedures, and I was looking forward to the day when I would stand up again.

During my procedures or when conducting my exercises at the gym, in my mind I was already much further along in my progress: I envisioned myself being fully recovered physically and finally walking again. I had never seen anybody walk with artificial legs, and I didn't know what it looked like or what it took to walk using them, but at this point, I didn't care. All I cared about was that it could be done and I knew I would do whatever it took to walk.

In between sessions, I would make myself comfortable in bed, put my headset on with my favorite music and again escape into the world of my vision. I saw myself standing beautiful and being myself again. I couldn't wait to get back to the airport and join my 'airport gang' in that energetic atmosphere. I was so longing for our time together. The thought of returning to my pre-accident life and being connected with people I loved felt like I was breathing in life. My vision was so strong that I again felt the delight of life and excitement for my accomplishment as if I were actually living it. It felt so real that my commitment to turn my vision into reality was becoming stronger and stronger. I did not take seriously what the previous medical professor said about the impossibility of walking. I would not even entertain that idea. I knew I would walk without a doubt and it didn't matter how much I had to work to reach that goal. All I had in my mind was my vision of returning to the airport and living my life to the fullest.

Every day I eagerly waited to be informed as to when my prostheses were going to be ready. In a few days, while I was in my room listening to music, I saw Simas enter, as always cheerful and enthusiastic. Little did I know he would utter the five words I had been waiting to hear since the accident.

"Your prostheses are ready, Inga." He could tell my eagerness was about to erupt like a volcano, but he asked, "When would you like to try them on?"

"When?" I yelled out. "Now! I want to try them right now!"

Simas smiled and gave directions to where we should go for the fitting. Without waiting I immediately put away my CD player and asked mom if she could help me get upstairs. My heart began to quiver from the mixed emotions of excitement and anxiety. This was the moment. This was the moment I was so eagerly waiting for! This wheelchair business was coming to the end.

Following the directions we got to the fourth floor and found a room filled from floor to ceiling with exercise tools, benches and parallel bars. In a moment, we saw a woman enter, who introduced herself as my physical therapist; she was going to teach me to walk. I instantly had a very good feeling about Greta; her warm eyes revealed that she was a very caring person. There were others in the room, but I couldn't pay attention to what they were saying. All I could hear were my thoughts, "I will walk again. I will walk again!"

In a moment, I saw Simas enthusiastically storming into the room holding some metal devices attached to some plastic things shaped like a tall cup. I had no idea what they were, but shivers penetrated my heart watching him walk towards me, holding these things in his hands.

"What? These metal sticks are supposed to be my legs?"

I stared. I could not believe this was to be what I would have to use to walk. I was frozen. I couldn't say a word. All that time I was dreaming about walking again and I had imagined it would be like it used to be, without considering what my new legs would actually look like. Now I was hit hard by the reality – these metal sticks with white plastic sockets attached were the prosthetic legs with which I was to walk.

"My beautiful legs are gone," I thought. "Now these things are supposed to replace them?"

A wave of emotion hit me, nearly collapsing my enthusiasm and my only hope I had. But then, I shook it off and pushed those thoughts away. In a moment I would stand, that is what was important. I had no idea how they worked, so I followed every direction to the letter. Apparently, the white plastic attachment was called a "socket," used to fasten the prosthesis to my body. The sockets were applied on my remaining thighs the same way as putting on a pair of socks.

After the prostheses were fastened, the team of two lifted me up to situate me in a vertical position. As soon as I stood up, sharp pain pierced me through. The plastic socket edges pushed into my groin.

"I am standing!" I shouted out.

I looked at my mother. Standing aside, she was barely holding back her tears. I looked in the mirror in front of me. The shocking view was paralyzing. I saw only half of my body. Below my hips, instead of my legs, there were metal sticks. I could not believe that what I was seeing in the mirror was actually me.

I was in a vertical position, but I didn't feel my feet nor did I feel the ground underneath. I didn't even have a sense as to what was holding me in a vertical position. All I felt was strongly squeezed thighs and razor-sharp pain in my groin.

The view that I saw in the mirror and the penetrating edgy pain completely overshadowed my previous excitement about my beautiful dream of walking again. I felt dizzy. I lost all sense of my surroundings. All I was aware of was the enormous pain and clear realization that I would never be able to walk like I used to. I would never be the same. Nothing was going to be the same. Ever.

"See, you are standing again, Inga!" Greta's gentle voice from behind pulled me back from the stinging realization of the truth. "You look great standing. Now straighten your back and tighten your buttock muscles."

I collected my thoughts and focused on what I had to do, numbing all my previous thoughts and feelings.

"You're doing great, Inga," she continued. "Now let's take your first step. Lift your right leg and put it in front of you on the heel."

I tried to do what I was told. I lifted my right leg and put it in front of me on the heel.

"Good job. Okay, now shift your weight onto your right side and put all your weight on the right foot, starting with the heel and slowly shifting toward the tip of your foot. Take a step."

Never before was I so scared as I was at that moment. I still could not feel what kept me vertical, nor could I feel the ground underneath, and I had to put all my weight on my "foot."

"Don't be afraid, Inga," Greta said. "I'm right here with you. I am holding you strongly. You will not fall. Shift your weight onto your right side and put all your body weight on your right foot."

Once again I sharpened my focus and, keeping in mind that she was guarding me, I shifted my body weight to my right foot. Excruciating, knifelike pain in the groin area again pierced me through, overshadowing all that I saw around me and all that I felt.

"You did it, Inga. You made your first step!" I heard Greta's excitement behind me. I felt nothing, except feeling as though someone were stabbing me with a knife. "And now Inga, standing strongly on your right leg, lift your left one and put it in front of you on the heel, just like you did with your other one."

I felt sweat flowing over my back. Fear and tension. I could never have imagined this would be so scary. It seemed like the joy of finally standing, terrifying fear and unexpected stabbing pain were battling each other, competing to win my consciousness. I collected my thoughts and despite my mixed-up, overwhelming feelings, I did what I was asked to do – I took another step.

"Mom, I did it!" Feeling the victory I looked at my mom. "I made my first steps!"

She stood there quietly with tears rolling down her cheeks as she watched me taking my first timid steps. I turned my eyes away, because I didn't want to start crying too. I collected my thoughts and emotions and took a few more steps.

It hurt.

Excruciating, penetrating pain was the cost of each step.

Reaching the other end of the parallel bar seemed an infinity away.

"And now, let's go back," Greta said. "Do exactly the same as you did before. Straighten your back, tighten your muscles, lift up your right leg, and put it in front of you on the heel and slowly shift your weight on to it. Then do the same with your left side. That's how you make steps. I am right here behind you. Let's walk back together."

Along with shouting words of encouragement, Simas and Greta gently coaxed me to return doing the same step techniques all over again. And again. And again. Now I knew what to do.

It was terrifying but I knew I was safe. I took a step, then slowly took another. And then, by repeating the same technique, I took my next step and then another. I was so focused trying to walk that there was no room for any other thoughts or feelings. After I returned to the end, everyone in the room congratulated me with victorious shouts and applause. Greta suggested it was enough for that day because it was important not to push too hard the very first time. They helped me to sit down and together they removed my prostheses. Once again they congratulated me, and Greta said she would come pick me up the next day to try it again.

My mother helped me transfer into a wheelchair and suddenly I felt physically exhausted. It felt like my energy was completely gone – wiped out. She suggested that I get some rest and we started walking back to the room. We were both silent as she was slowly wheeling me in the wheelchair through the labyrinth of interconnecting hallways. Neither of us could say a word. I knew she was feeling the same way as I. Suddenly I burst into tears uncontrollably.

I couldn't hold it any more. It felt like everything that I was holding within exploded. Long awaited victory, deeply-hidden anxieties, dreams to walk again, excitement, pain, shock and expectations followed by deep disappointment stirred in my mind. On the one hand, I felt joy. I finally met the moment of which I had been waiting for so long – I stood up and took my first steps. On the other hand, I was so terrified from what I had to realize and view in the mirror that I was ready to scream. And the stabbing pain, with every single step. It was something I hadn't expected. I never felt such excruciating pain before. And this was something I would have to feel every time I took a step?

I kept seeing the view that I saw in the mirror, not knowing how to accept that this was the new me. I didn't even know whether I cried out of joy that I finally made my first steps or whether I cried out of unexpected shock and heartbreaking disappointment.

Mom tried to comfort me, but I saw she was devastated as well. Yet she made an effort to remain collected and strong for me. She was my comfort and strength. She was the only person who really understood what I had to go through. She was the only one who knew me, knew who I was and what I had lost.

I got back to my room and immediately called my dad and my brother to tell them the news. My dad cried with me and my brother said he couldn't imagine how it was possible. I was going to call Renata, but my mom suggested we wait and call her in the evening, because she had her shift at work, and was afraid Renata would get emotional during her work responsibilities. After all, flights were still landing and taking off. I agreed and left my special phone call to my best friend for later in the evening.

After talking to my brother and dad, I felt so exhausted that I did not have the energy for anything else. I did not want to watch television nor did I want to talk to my mom or anyone. Intense emotions, physical tension and pain wiped out whatever strength and liveliness that I had. I saw that mom was dramatically affected as well. I suggested that she go to downtown of the City, to get some fresh air and clear her mind. Having her watch me bursting in tears and suffering was definitely not the vacation I wanted her to have. I asked her not to worry but rather, to go to places she might enjoy. After she left, I reached for my usual getaway tool: I turned on my music to disappear from the present. At that point though, even my faithful mode of escape wasn't much help. I was not able to get away from the view in the mirror and the new realization of my actual reality. I wanted to weep out of horror and despair.

All this time the hope that I would be able to walk again was my only comfort in accepting the unexpected turn in my life. I had imagined that everything would be the same when I received my prosthetic legs. But the day showed me that the actual reality was much different than what I thought. My memories of what I looked like and how I hoped to live were not relevant anymore; it was never going to be the same.

And the pain! I knew it wouldn't be easy to walk wearing prostheses, but I could never imagine that it would be so scary and so painful. I cried the whole afternoon. I couldn't see what I was going to do with my life in this physical condition. I was glad that my mother had left so she couldn't see me crying, not so much from pain, but from the sheer hopelessness I felt.

I finally pulled myself out of the bubble of emotions and looked at the facts: no matter how much I was going to grieve, it was not going to change my present nor would it improve my future. The only thing that would improve my position was if I did something about it. The fact was that I didn't have my legs anymore, and if I couldn't learn to walk with these artificial legs, then I wouldn't be able to get out of my house; I wouldn't be able to go to work or anywhere else. The only thing that would get me out of the deadlock was to walk wearing those prostheses.

I knew – no matter how heartbreaking it was to look at myself with those metal sticks instead of my legs – I would have to accept it and get used to them. If I had to walk with those metal devices, so be it, that's what I would have to do. If it took enduring the stabbing pain to take each step, then I would have to deal with it. The important thing was that I had the hope to return to a life that I nearly lost. After consideration of my actual position and what I could do to make my future better, I began to calm down. My dream life was on the other shore, and the only bridge to get to that shore was accepting these metal devices as my new legs.

"The most horrifying has passed already," I said to comfort myself. "Now I can start climbing out of the pit. I will fulfill my promise and revive my life. This is a new chapter and I will make it a good one."

I fell asleep knowing that I wasn't going to allow this to break me. The date was August 3, 2000 when I took my first ten steps.

Making the Impossible Possible

The next day, my physical therapist came to my room to pick me up. It was the beginning of daily, intense, arduous, ongoing workouts. I would start my day at the gym, where I would do my stretching, sit-ups and other muscle strengthening exercises. Then I would go into another room which had parallel bars and a mirror. Simas would fasten the prostheses, and then with Greta's help I would practice taking steps. Simas told me that the permanent prostheses were going to be covered with special material to make them look like real legs, so the unseemly metal parts would not be seen by others as they were now.

It made me feel easier knowing that ultimately, my new legs would look like real legs and not as I saw them as metal sticks. At this point though, I was mentally equipped not to pay attention to what I saw in the mirror. I decided to focus on learning to use them rather than how they made me feel. I would step along those parallel bars and would walk back and forth learning to take each and every step.

In the beginning, I was allowed to walk only for twenty minutes a day while my body adjusted to my "new legs." While it seems like a very short time, those twenty minutes seemed like hours of plain torture mixed with glimpses of joy. While it was a thrill to be able to stand and take steps again, the physical suffering was enormous. The plastic socket edges would press into my groin every time I put my weight on either leg. It was a little easier when I stood still because I would equally balance my weight on both legs. The test of my endurance came when I would transfer my weight onto either leg; that's when the sharp edges would press straight into my groin.

After twenty minutes of wearing prostheses I had to stop, so I didn't overwork myself, and to protect myself from causing deeper wounds. Soaking wet from the arduous effort and tension, and feeling completely wiped out, I would end my sessions feeling the victory of being one step closer to my ultimate dream. My comfort was Greta, whose warmth and supportive attitude consoled me and fueled me with enthusiasm.

When another young physiotherapist replaced Greta, my training sessions became fun. Erikas was a young man about the same age as Simas. He knew many jokes and in addition to his instruction, how to maintain my balance as I took steps, he would share various fun stories. He made me laugh for the first time since the accident. Erikas' supportive and fun personality was probably the only thing that made these trainings bearable. Many times I told Erikas that without his jokes, the sessions would be torture.

Simas tried to adjust those sockets numerous times to reduce the pain, but the results were always the same. I had graduated from twenty to thirty minutes of walking, but after the thirty, I was forced to take the devices off because I could no longer endure the pain.

I was told this was the reality of wearing prostheses – that pain would be a part of my effort to walk. I questioned how I was supposed to use them all day long on a daily basis. As an answer, Erikas would shrug his shoulders, conveying that I would have to deal with it since there was nothing much that could be done about it.

My desire to walk was so strong that I accepted the fact that I would have to walk through pain. After all, my only other option was the wheelchair and being imprisoned for life among the walls of my home. I could not bear thinking of that kind of life; therefore, I was ready to endure any kind of hardship and pain to escape that alternative. Having the ability to walk again was my only path to experience life and freedom, and I was willing to pay any price for my chance to return to life as I once knew. So, I continued training despite the suffering.

Every day, without any consideration or any exceptions, I would get up early in the morning for training. While listening to the upbeat music, I would apply my make up and put myself together for another active day, envisioning myself fully independent. I would go to the gym for exercises and then practice walking. After half-an-hour of training, feeling exhausted, I would finish my routine with a massage. By lunchtime I would be so exhausted I had no energy left for anything else, except go to bed and sleep until late afternoon. Next day I would get up early in the morning and start it all over again.

When Erikas saw that I was feeling confident and was holding my balance well, he encouraged me to walk outside of the parallel bars and walk out into the hallway. This was one of the scariest things that I ever had to do. I conquered my fears by seeing it as a challenge I had to overcome towards my beautiful dream. As soon as I thought of my promise to my friends to come back to the airport, I told him I was ready. Erikas gave me his hand, so I would have ensured support, and I stepped outside of the now-familiar safety of the parallel bars. Step by step, I walked out into the hallway, building my confidence with each step.

The hallway was constructed in a way that I could walk rounds. That day I had my new victory – I walked one rotation of the hallway and then back to the welcome comfort of the training room. The pain was enormous. But I felt so much joy about my progress that I neglected it. Now I was even more determined and confident. I saw progress and that encouraged me to train even more.

From that day, Erikas and I would do our training in the hallway. After several days, I was given a quad cane, and that represented even more progress and yet another victory – I began walking in the hallway on my own using the cane to support my balance, Erikas walking by my side for my protection.

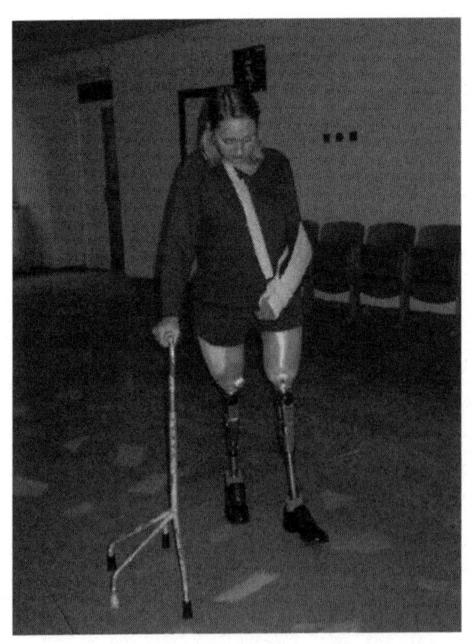

Walking rounds with my new legs.

Soon I was asked to showcase my walking to a combined group of medical specialists. It quite surprised me and I found it puzzling. What for? Why me? Erikas and Simas then told me that my case was one of the most unique ones. Nobody believed that I would be able to walk, and when they heard rumors that I was walking, they wanted to see. I was honored, but I was nervous to walk while people were watching.

"Don't worry, Inga," Erikas and Simas proclaimed with their upbeat attitude. "They want to see you walking because it is unheard of in our center, that a bilateral, above the knee amputee with only one functioning arm would walk. Just think of it as your usual daily training. Relax and walk as you do daily."

I was a bit perturbed that the specialists expected to see that I would fail. But, they didn't know me or my dream.

When the time came to reveal what I'd learned, Erikas and Simas helped me put on my prostheses, gave me my cane, and let me go. I walked out of the training room and saw a group of people in a hallway. As I was walking, looking down to watch my path and where I placed my feet, I heard their loud impressions and excitement. That moment I remembered the professor, who told me that having such severe physical limitations it would be impossible for me to walk.

"I told you I would walk," I thought to myself. "And this is just the beginning."

I don't know if he was in that group of people, but it didn't matter. What mattered to me was that I did it regardless of the diagnosis. I strongly believed there was a way, and I was going to prove it despite any accepted medical theories or other people's beliefs. After I made my round and approached the group of specialists, I heard lots of congratulations and encouragement to keep up the good work. I guess I shattered their theory as to what was possible. I had a vision of living an active life, and I was committed to making it happen regardless of anybody's opinions or the amount of effort it would require.

My determination to bring myself back to life was getting stronger with each day. One day, as I was having my break, I suddenly realized, "Wait a minute. Why am I still asking mom to help me get up? It's ridiculous. I can learn to walk wearing prostheses, but I have my mom helping with simple daily activities. If I can walk – which was supposedly impossible for me – then I can do anything."

Up to that day my mom was helping me to get up from a lying position, dress and perform other daily activities. In my mind (as well as my mom's), there was a mindset that I was no longer able to do things, so I had to be helped. Now that I had overcome the hurdle of something that had been generally agreed to be impossible, there was a big question mark in my mind about what I was actually capable of.

"If through persistence and hard work I can walk, then what else can I possibly do? I can be just as persistent and tenacious about doing things by myself." Suddenly I felt an indescribable joy. I was fully aware that I could do much more than what it seemed at first. I declared my independence stating, "I can do it. I will figure out how to do anything I need to do and will become fully self-sufficient."

From then on, I started seeking how I could sit up by myself from a lying position, and with the help of a physical therapist we found a way. It required some effort, but the more I did it, the stronger I got, and the easier it was.

I began looking for ways of dressing independently and performing various daily activities by myself. I didn't allow myself to think whether or not I could. I began eliminating the phrase – *If I can* – from my thought patterns. My new mindset was – *I can without a doubt.* I only needed to *find a way how to* do it. I told my mom that I would begin learning to perform daily necessary activities by myself, so she would not rush to help me. It was not easy for her to stop; she would quickly rush to me and do things when she saw I was challenged by any task. I began refusing to receive help from her, and tried to find a way to do things independently. It did require patience and perseverance, but little by little, I was figuring out how to take care of myself independently.

Very soon I realized that when you believe something is impossible, it really is. But it remains that way for only as long as you hold on to that belief. As I look back, changing my mindset was one of my biggest breakthroughs, which empowered me tremendously. Since that time, when my limiting beliefs of what I thought was possible were shattered and I began mastering my way of thinking, my recovery of independence has taken to a whole new level.

After that day of showcasing, Erikas and I developed a plan to consistently increase the length of time I wore my prostheses. My everyday goal was to increase the number of rounds I would make, and that fueled my determination to conquer myself and beat my best every time. Making an additional round in the hallway was a huge victory. At times, due to the pain, even spending ten to fifteen minutes longer wearing prostheses seemed a major accomplishment. Every step felt as if someone was penetrating my being with a knife. When I felt I could no longer endure another step, I would envision myself walking into the Business Lounge and being there again with my friends. I would remember my promise. And I would draw forth all the strength I had left and take that step and then another one, and then another one and another one. Every time I had to put my foot down knowing I was about to feel the stabbing pain again, in my mind I would envision my ultimate dream, escaping the dull imprisonment. When it would seem like I could no longer cope, I would tell myself that I could. I would remind myself why I needed to do it, repeating that I was strong enough to handle even that level of pain.

Erikas' jokes would distract me from my questions as to how much longer I could stand it. Simas would join us at times, to visit and observe my walking skills. It was always fun to work with them. My progress motivated all of us to continue putting forth effort, and while joking around we aimed for the ultimate goal. We would be consistently increasing the number of rounds, ending sessions when I no longer could endure the pain.

While I had a burning desire to increase the length of time wearing the prostheses, at the same time the end of our daily sessions meant a great relief to me. I felt rescued every time when my new legs were removed from my body. I especially felt that way when I increased my training up to one hour. The longer I wore those prostheses, the more my physical suffering increased. Since I was not able to sit down and rest, I had to be standing or walking all the time, coping with each leg's knife-like edges. Every session would end with my thighs swollen and red. My skin was so damaged that I could not even touch it. Finally, when I reached over one hour, my groin area often would end up with blisters and open wounds.

After practice, feeling totally exhausted, I would wheel down to my post-training massage, the highlight of my day. The massage therapist would release the pain and tension in my back and my thighs, and then the nurse would apply medicine to my sores to guard against infection and to aid in their healing.

There were times when it was too painful to sit in a wheelchair with my thighs so close to each other; then my only choice was go back to my room and lay down. After all my procedures and a light lunch, I would sleep throughout the afternoon feeling wiped out. But despite the wounds, I didn't want to stop training. In the morning, I would apply the bandages to protect my damaged skin, and again I would start my day at the gym, and then my ever-increasing rounds of intense and exhausting walking. I hated the suffering of each step, but there was no other way. Giving up on walking was not an option. I continued every single day, holding onto my dream, determined to make it a reality.

It was more dangerous than I had imagined. I had to be very focused and control several things at once. I could not relax even for a second because if I lost control of my balance, I could easily fall down from the slightest, careless movement. The frightening thing was how there was nothing I could do to prevent myself from falling. I was 5'6" tall, and I would fall down flat with no ability to control, stop or at least slow down the fall. What's more, should I fall, it was a natural reaction to put an arm out to try and break that fall. But since my right arm was my lifeline, it was all the more important that I not fall and jeopardize my one and only arm. I had to be extremely careful with every single movement.

Because I wasn't feeling my feet and did not feel the ground underneath, I had to watch where I put each step. The slightest mistake could end in another tragedy, so I always looked down when I walked.

To the amazement of the medical specialists at the center, I also learned how to ascend and descend stairs. This was another thing that once seemed nearly impossible. My physical condition made it very complicated. But I knew I had to learn it because there were ten steps at the front entrance of my home, and I had to find a way if I ever wanted to get in and out of my house. What's more, the Business Lounge at the airport was on the second floor, so I had to know how to navigate staircases. I was so glad that Erikas was open-minded and willing to try and teach me. He figured out how I could do it, and created a program designed especially for my unique needs. To my surprise, it wasn't that difficult. I thought it would be more challenging but it was more scary than difficult.

The one thing I didn't like was that I had to descend stairs backwards. But wearing prostheses with the model of the knees that I had, it was way too terrifying and impossible to descend stairs forward as normal people do. I was happy that I was able to do it at all, so I accepted it and I learned to ascend and descend stairs in a different way. But while I was thrilled and grateful that I was attaining goal after goal, there were things that concerned me.

To my big disappointment, walking and climbing stairs was all I could do. I wasn't able to put on the prostheses by myself. I kept asking the medical specialists how I was going to use them once I left the Orthopedic Center. I kept asking who was going to put them on for me? In response, I heard the same and only option: "Ask your father." I was told that having someone else to put them on was the only solution.

My next concern was that I could not sit down on a chair nor could I stand up on my own, and I was told that I would never be able to do that independently. I would be physically drained after twenty minutes of standing and walking, but unable to sit down and rest. So how was I supposed to wear them all day long without the ability to sit down? How was I going to work? And how was I going to get into the car to get to work or any other place I wanted to go? These questions were imperative – they had to be resolved, but nobody could give any answers except shrugging their shoulders or suggesting that I would be forced to have someone help. This was not the "independence" for which I was aiming.

After one and a half months, my time at Rehab Center was complete. I had my temporary prostheses made. I could walk, and I could ascend and descend stairs. Despite opinions that I would not be able to sit down wearing prostheses independently, I persisted in finding a way to sit down in the car. I was contemplating how I would fulfill my promise of returning to the airport. I knew I was nearly there. I would be able to ascend stairs to the second floor where the Business Lounge was located, and I could walk. But how was I going to get to the airport from home? I needed to learn how to get in and out of the car.

On my last day at the center, I shared this with Erikas, asking him if he would assist me with walking out of the building and escort me to the car. Getting into the car was the last thing I had to learn and now was my chance. I saw that my idea seemed very unusual to him, but I don't think my request was that surprising. He heard me speaking about my dream nearly daily. He knew my goal was to lead my life wearing prostheses and he knew I was serious about it. Erikas agreed, so we could try to figure out yet again, one more challenge.

On the last day, after all our belongings were packed and we were ready for the trip back to the capital, I said goodbye to the doctor and to the nurses who had helped me throughout my stay. It had been a very pleasant stay and I thanked and hugged all of them on duty at the time. They were like a second family to me, getting me through this stage of my journey.

And then I proceeded, step by step, slowly walking towards the elevator to get to the ground floor. My parents, Simas and Erikas walked with me.

Walking out of the building was both frightening and very emotional at the same time.

I remembered the moment when I first saw this gigantic red building from afar. I had no idea what an intense and arduous work program was ahead, but I envisioned myself walking out of the center. I'm glad I didn't know how painful and exhausting it would be, and I am glad that I never gave up. Yet now, as I was walking out of that same red building that had grown to become a home, I was afraid of not knowing what laid ahead. I had never walked outside wearing prostheses before. I was solely focused on holding my balance, looking down at my feet to watch every step. A slight uneven spot or surface could have resulted in losing my balance and falling. That day for some reason the pain was more excruciating than usual. At some point, as we were halfway to the car, the pain was so immense that I thought I would not be able to reach it. Still, I needed to see how to get into the car. So I pulled myself together, and slowly and carefully proceeded further. In the middle of my agony, I heard my mother's trembling voice yelling at me.

"Inga, look up!"

I stopped, made sure I was standing on solid ground, held my balance, then looked up at the windows. I saw doctors, prosthetic technicians, nurses and other patients looking through the glass. When they saw me looking back at them, they started waving, showing their admiration and excitement for me and all I had accomplished. This was the best gift and support I could have asked for. I smiled letting them know how thankful I was for their support. But what I heard next was almost enough for me to lose my balance.

"Inga," Erikas quietly said. "You are the first patient who has walked out of the center."

"What? Are you serious?"

Erikas looked at me with a smile, ensuring me that it was true. I wished I could have stood there longer to chat with him, but the pain in my groin was so intense and pierced my flesh so mercilessly that I couldn't wait any longer. I told them I couldn't stand anymore and needed to get to the car as soon as possible. I had to sit down.

As we approached, we looked at various options as to how I could sit down by myself, but it seemed very complicated and we couldn't figure it out quickly. And at that point, I couldn't endure the pain any longer. I asked them to help me sit down as soon as possible. All I wanted was to take them off. Dad helped me get into the car and immediately he pulled off my prosthetic legs.

"How am I possibly going to walk with them?" I asked as I was being rescued from those devices of both pleasure and torture. I'd been avoiding this question all that time. But now it stared at me with its blank look, and I knew the answer. I looked at Erikas and Simas, who went with me through the long, tiring process to see this sweet victory, smiling at me with pride for accomplishing what none other had done before. I knew they did their best to help me achieve the impossible.

"We'll see you in January!" Simas exclaimed with a wink as we drove off. And as we drove along the center's main building, I looked up. People were still looking through the window waving to us. This was my first round of "getting my legs back."

Now my singular task was to practice walking, and then in January, to return for them to fabricate permanent prostheses. As we were leaving, I looked back at the giant red building, the one I had emerged from walking on my own despite the doubts of many. But I didn't know whether I felt happy or disappointed.

I had mixed feelings about it all. For the first time I asked myself if my dream to walk and live an independent life was an illusion. But I knew I could not let go of my hope. I was well aware that this prosthetic project and driving back and forth from one city to another was happening only because I persisted. My parents had done everything possible to support me, but at times it felt like I was the only one who believed in what I was aiming for. I knew that all I had to do was to say a word of doubt, and I would lose the battle.

My brother was trying to talk me out of it. He told me many times that what I was doing was "simply nonsense," and that I should find a different strategy for my life instead of wasting my time and our parent's efforts with this silly dream of mine. I knew my parents saw how walking with prostheses caused more pain and danger than independence and the ability to move around. I could see it in their eyes - they knew I wouldn't be able to walk with these devices. Nevertheless, they supported me and went along with driving on a weekly basis from one city to another, because they saw my great desire to go beyond my limitations and return to life. They knew it would be unbearable to me if my last hope had been taken away, so they made every effort to support me in my pursuit.

My friends were cheering me up and at the same time, they could not believe I was really doing this. Some of them were surprised that I was willing to go through so much pain, and asked if it might be smart to let it go. Basically, everyone around me saw the true picture, but they did not say "no" to me and my dream, and still gave me their support because they simply loved me and they saw how determined I was.

I refused to consider dropping it and would not even get into such discussions. In this way, nobody would argue with me and they let me continue what I was doing. But I knew that if I had just said a word that I was contemplating abandoning the pursuit – everyone would immediately agree it would be a smart decision, and would probably even encourage me to leave it alone for many reasons. So I knew I had to hold on as long as I could.

What if I gave up and lost my support, and then it turned out that it was possible for me to walk? It would have been me who had given up on the dream and destroyed all that I had achieved so far. I had a chance to make my dream come true for as long as I tried. If I kept pursuing it despite people's doubts or any obstacles, there was hope. But if I said "no" to it – that would be the end. I would never realize my dream. And then what?

Therefore, I decided not to tell anyone about my true feelings and thoughts. I decided to keep it to myself and keep trying. I knew I needed to continue. I still had the hope that I would learn the necessary activities when I returned in January. For the time being, I was going to focus on practicing my walking and balance skills at home with my father's help. I turned on my CD player and escaped into the new world that I envisioned.

9

Overcoming the Quicksand of Depression

Part 1 ~ My Journey of Winning the Battle

Dear Valdas,

Now I would like to move on to the next aspect of your personal growth – your inner state. This is as crucial as your unshakable faith and your empowering perspective because how you create your life a lot depends on your beliefs and your inner state. As a recap, faith in the Lord God will give you the right mindset and beliefs that will empower you. Your beliefs will shape your perspective and how you view the surrounding world and events personal to you; they will shape your views about the future and your awareness of what's possible.

We built a strong foundation and precisely calculated the ground floor if we continue with our metaphor of building a home. It's not just the foundation that is important; the remainder of the structure is equally as important, isn't it? In the same way, your mindset, thought patterns, emotional state, personal standards and values, character traits and work ethic are essential to your overall character. Together they are what defines you as a person.

Your inner state is one of the most important parts of the construction process. Would you agree that you make different choices and different decisions when you feel grateful, excited, determined, and are anticipating a successful outcome, than when you feel sad, apathetic, dissatisfied, hopeless, anxious and depressed? Paying attention to your inner state is imperative.

How do you feel most of the time? Do you feel hopeful, anticipating good in your future, or are you affected by constant dark thoughts? Do you anticipate a forthcoming blessing and feel at peace or do you feel pessimistic, anxious and helpless?

Remembering our last conversations, I heard deep sadness in your voice. Knowing your situation and the hardship you've been dealing with, it is not surprising you feel that way. Watching how everything you built and hoped for had crashed overnight, it is only natural that it has affected you emotionally.

I am familiar with these feelings. Actually, I assume there are times you don't even want to wake up in the morning. Are you surprised I shared the same feelings as you? Please don't be. Depression made my life cold and dim for several years. I overcame it and want to share with you how I escaped my depression and got to the point where I maintain the inner state that empowers me no matter what difficulties I am facing.

In this letter, I want to share with you something that will empower you, as it greatly empowered me throughout the years. I've divided this letter into two parts. In the first part, I will share my personal experience. Some of the details you might remember, but most of it you could not have known. In the second half of the letter·I will share some practical tools which you can apply in your own life whenever you struggle with daily sadness and emotional heaviness. So, let's continue our journey together.

Before the accident I never thought about depression and what life looked like being depressed. My friends and I often made jokes about it, but I had no idea what it felt like to be depressed or how dangerous it could be. Depression can break a person inside. It comes slowly and quietly; it's easy not to notice how it enters your life and begins to dominate your every waking thought. But moving from depression to happiness is quite a battle.

While I respect and value the science of psychology (and I believe professionally trained psychologists can help people), after the tragedy I said "no" to the suggestion of receiving psychological help. I especially refused to think about taking anti-depressant medications. I overcame it in a different way. It takes effort and discipline to overcome depression, but it is possible. I want to share with you what I have learned about depression and the ways I defeated it, so you can use it in your own life if you need to. The best, of course, is not to let depression into your life at all because it is easier to stay away from it than to fight with this monster when it already dominates every aspect of your life.

The car accident was a big crash in more ways than the obvious. I could never imagine that my life would take such a drastic turn. To be honest, I did not see how I could possibly continue living feeling that enormous physical and emotional pain.

Actually, it was easier to go through the physical pain. I knew it would pass after the wounds healed. But the emotional agony was so strong and I couldn't see the end. Only prayer and faith in almighty God, augmented by the love and care from my family and friends gave me the strength to want to wake up in the morning.

You, mom, dad and my friends always saw me cheerful, smiling and repeating over and over that "everything was going to be alright," but my inner being was crying. It was very dark inside. While I put my hope in the Lord that He was going to get me out of the bottomless pit into which I'd fallen, I was in a constant horror and agony fully grasping how my life had changed and how desperate my situation was.

I absolutely hated the world that suddenly I was forced into. Previously, I lived a fun and exciting life, and suddenly one day I woke up in a world where there was only an ongoing emotional agony, suffering, shock and the unknown, compounded by excruciating pain that emanated from every part of my body.

Each waking moment I thanked my God for you all, because I never got the feeling that I was a burden. Yet I can't express the contempt I felt for the person I'd become, because the continuation of my life was based upon complete dependence upon others. The loss of my independence was unbearable.

In addition, I lost my world. I always valued connecting with the people I loved at work or at play; deep in my soul I yearned for that dynamic phase of my life. And now all of it was gone. Everything that I cherished had been torn from my life in a flash. The worst part was that I could not see how I could possibly change the circumstances. I was in shock and facing the total unknown. Even though friends were visiting me almost daily (especially right after the accident), still it was not the same. They were dear to me and it felt good to be loved despite the drastic changes; yet nevertheless, I often didn't even want anybody to come over. I was hurting so badly that I wanted to be left alone and didn't want anyone to disturb me.

I was not interested in what was happening on the outside. I say "on the outside" because due to the inaccessible entrance to our apartment building, I was locked in my room for the entire year. Only the television, the Internet and visiting friends were my access to the external world.

The only times I got to take a breath of fresh air were when father or you would take me to yet another hospital or rehab center. I lost interest in what was going on beyond the walls of our home because I was not able to be a part of it. Presents that I got for my birthday or Christmas didn't give me joy. I felt it was meaningless for me to have all those beautiful clothes or expensive perfume when I had nowhere to wear them, or no one to wear them for. You, our parents and friends tried hard to do something sweet and nice for me, giving me presents that I always loved and wanted to have before the accident. I always appreciated and valued yours and everyone's efforts. On the outside I showed I was happy, yet on the inside, I didn't show anyone my pain and true feelings. It didn't make sense to me to have all that; I didn't need it any more.

The daytime itself hurt. I absolutely hated the fact that outside my home, life was going on as usual, and I could not be a part of it. That's why I tried to sleep most of the day. It was my way to escape from my current life and the comprehension that no longer was I the same Inga.

My daily routine was upside down. My mornings would begin around 12-1:00 PM. Once I'd awaken, I would have my coffee, exercise a little and then train to walk using artificial legs. After an hour or so of walking back and forth in a hallway, I would take the legs off and, feeling exhausted, would go back to bed and try to fall asleep. If I couldn't fall asleep, I would listen to music that reminded me of my life prior to the crash. This way I would escape from my reality back to my beautiful and exciting world. Then I would get up in the evening around 8-9:00 PM, get on the Internet, and disappear into another world. I would go to bed around 2-3:00 AM and sometimes not until 5:00 AM. The endless sharp and burning pain in my paralyzed left arm kept me awake. Another reason I stayed on the Internet that long was because my dark thoughts and the horror of comprehending my changed life wouldn't let me relax and fall asleep. Every night I had to take strong sleeping pills that would knock me out for the night.

My morning would start again with a deep contempt for the world I was forced into. I hated waking up; I didn't want another day to come. I didn't want to face the facts again that I did not have my legs anymore and that my life had turned into endless hopelessness. I will never forget the day when I caught myself thinking that I envied Dalius, forever gone from us, because he didn't have to go through the anguish I had to go through now and for the rest of my life. I simply wanted to disappear so that I wouldn't exist here at all.

My only reason to get out of bed every morning was my commitment to walking again, which was my only hope to get out of my imprisoned existence. While I lived in deep, silent sadness, at the same time my negative feelings toward my circumstances created an inexpressible desire to change my life. I wanted to live, not exist.

I am very grateful to God that these feelings of contempt toward this drastic change in my life didn't destroy me to the point of giving up. Instead they created exactly the opposite – they created an unbreakable commitment to do whatever it took to end this daily nightmare and create a life which I would be able to love again. I wanted to return to life, and I believed that the only way for me to accomplish it was to be able to walk again.

I know it might have seemed to you that I was simply stubborn, and you were perplexed as to why I would be so stubborn about something that seemed impossible and so hurtful to my body. It was not a simple wish. It was a burning desire and a non-negotiable resolve to make it happen at any cost. Not achieving this meant locking myself into a lifeless existence confined by the four walls of my room and remaining helpless.

That is the reason why I was determined to pay any price to fulfill my vision. I refused to even hear anything that was counter to my decision. In my mind, it was very simple math – there is a cost to everything: I could either endure the physical pain now and live the way I desired, or I could take the easier path and endure a life of grief and misery. I made my choice and therefore, I trained devotedly every day despite the exhausting work and enormous pain. I did not consider whether I liked it or not, whether it was easy or not, or whether it was too much hard work. My mindset was - quite simply I had no other option. Achieving my dream must not depend on how I felt – I have to work and pursue my goal in spite of my mood.

There was a day when even my dream to walk again – which was the only hope that gave me the reason to move forward and restore my life – was broken as well. After several months of training my walking skills at home, I returned to the Orthopedic Center in January 2001. It was my second time there and this time my permanent prostheses were being made.

At the center I continued an arduous workout schedule, to further develop my walking skills. Again, daily physical exertion, enormous pain, swollen thighs, bandages on wounds were my everyday routine. The one thing that gave me strength to persevere was knowing why I was doing it. And I was holding on to the belief that my goal was still possible. Therefore, I disregarded the cost of my dream and kept persevering.

While I was taking one step at a time, over and over I envisioned what it would look like when I finally mastered my prosthetic walking skills. I envisioned how I would return to my beloved airport, envisioning what a delight it would be when my friends and I reunited, and how beautiful I would look standing, looking whole again, with no wheelchair as part of my life. I thought of how I would go wherever I wanted to go without having to worry about wheelchair access, or getting in and out of cars. I would work, meet my friends, and have a wonderful time with them just as it was before February 2000.

In my mind I saw clearly how joyous it would be when I finally brought myself back to life, and this pain that I had to go through was definitely worth it. After a month of strenuous exertion my full circle of orthopedic rehabilitation was coming to its scheduled completion. I was getting ready to leave the Orthopedic Center with a finished pair of permanent artificial legs created just for me. My prosthetist and I discussed the decorative finish for my prosthetic legs. I wanted him to cover the metal parts with a special material that looked like skin. I didn't want to shock people when they saw the metal sticks instead of the "legs." He tried to explain to me it was not a good idea for the mechanics of the knees. After I insisted on making them look like real legs, Simas looked at me with ironic smile and said, "Do you really think you will go out somewhere wearing them?"

A statement like that from a prosthetic specialist – someone I knew and trusted – was so unexpected that for a moment I stood there, impervious to the pain, completely and totally speechless. I asked him why he thought I worked so hard and went through so much daily pain and exhaustion, and why I trained so hard, despite all the sores and blisters all over my body. He shrugged his shoulders, thinking I'd known the result long before the question was asked. But at that point his response was not really important.

His question (sounding more like a statement) made me face the reality which I had tried to escape all that time – the reality that I would *not* be able to walk for any extended period of time. With one comment he had erased two years of arduous work through suffering excruciating pain, believing I would be able to walk daily and be active. My vision of walking again was just a dream. Nothing more. No matter what I had anticipated, these were the cold hard facts:

- I could not put my legs on by myself.
- It hurt simply standing still.
- It hurt even more to take steps.
- The longest time I could endure the stabbing pain in my groin from the prosthetic legs was for about an hour to an hour and a half a day.
- I was not able to rest because I was unable to sit down and stand up.
- I could not get in and out of a car, so there was no way I would be able to go anywhere.

His simple question had opened up the floodgates to the questions buried deep inside my inner self, questions I had avoided for two long years. What's more, I was told I had to accept the fact I would always have to endure pain and ask for help to put them on or sit down, because that's the reality of wearing prostheses given my physical condition.

My dream to walk again crashed on the day I left that Orthopedic Rehab Center. From then on I was completely submerged in a world of deep sadness, where there was nothing to look forward to. I was facing a life with no purpose, no goal and no hope.

I lived this way until the summer of 2001. My parents and I went to visit our aunt for a week. In order to find something to stay occupied, in our mom's library I took a book to learn more about psychology. I was interested in why people felt a certain way and why they act the way they do, so I thought I might like the book. As I was reading, one day I came upon a chapter dealing with depression. I had never read anything about depression and I didn't know anything about this inner state. Since I had nothing else to do, I decided to read it and learn what depression was and how people felt when they were depressed.

I cannot describe the shock I felt when I started reading this chapter. While reading the symptoms of depression, it seemed like the author was talking about me – he knew exactly how I felt and wrote about it in his book. And if that weren't enough, I learned that I was not only depressed – I was deeply depressed. To be honest, I was so caught off guard that I didn't know how to internalize it. I was aware that I had been sad on an ongoing basis, but I thought it was normal to feel that way. Now I realized my inner state was not just a mere sadness due to my loss. It was a deep depression.

I knew there was a reason why this book got into my hands; it seemed like it grabbed me by the shoulders and shook me. It told me to wake up, look carefully at my inner state, and do something about it. I felt disturbed. Actually, I was appalled at what I had discovered.

"Who me? Depressed? No. It can't be. It cannot continue like this. I am not that kind of a person, someone who will wallow in self-pity. I am not weak. I am not the one who gives up. I will get myself out of this pit."

For the first time since the Simas' comment, I felt how my feelings of disturbance could be re-directed into my determination to change things. I absolutely did not like the diagnosis of my inner state. The fact that I was depressed was not acceptable. My friend Renata and I used the word depression to point out the irony in various funny situations. I remember us laughing and making jokes saying, "My stockings are torn, that's it. Now I am depressed." To me the word "depression" associated itself with the joke to make ironic fun out of a little inconvenience.

As I was contemplating my new discovery, suddenly I felt how tired I was from my 24-7 helplessness, watching my days passing by, living that empty and sad existence. It seemed like my life journey was stopped. I was tired from being disconnected from the world I once knew, filled with friends, laughter and daily challenges. I felt drained from being in a deep depression, filled with silent grief, sorrow and longing for what I'd lost.

As I continued reading, I realized the feelings I lived with for the past year were not my nature; it wasn't me. I looked back to who Inga was. She was always cheerful, outgoing, positive and upbeat, regardless of the circumstances. I wanted to be the same Inga again – the same as before the accident. After realizing into what a deep emotional pit I had unknowingly fallen, I told myself, "If I managed to get into this depression, I will manage to get out of it, too."

In a way, I felt the same determination I felt as I did when faced with the daunting task of learning how to walk with prosthetic legs the very first time. But to tell the truth, I didn't know how to help myself. I didn't have any knowledge as to how depression was supposed to be treated. I refused the option of seeing a professional psychologist. I didn't want some stranger – who didn't have a clue as to the nightmare my family and I were going through – to tell me that life would continue, how it can be beautiful despite the fact that I didn't have legs and only one arm, and that I had lost my world and I could no longer be self-sufficient.

I didn't even consider taking prescription antidepressants that would make me feel better. My opinion was that covering up my true feelings with the help of those pills would not root out my depression; this was a temporary, artificial way to hide the real problems by chemically altering my state of mind while the reasons behind my depression remained unresolved. My belief was that you had to look into the issue and its causes, and then do something about it, not to run away from it by covering it up with antidepressants, drugs or alcohol.

My new discovery about my inner state left me uneasy. The next day, I took that book again and went outside. It was such a sunny gorgeous day. I treasured this opportunity to be in the fresh air, surrounded by nature rather than by the walls of my room. I took a deep breath. It was so good to hear the birds around me, chirping grasshoppers, and see blossoming flowers. It was the melody that only nature could create. Over my shoulder I heard mom saying, "Look what I found in the garden. Here, this is for you. Enjoy them."

She poured from her little basket some apples and berries she had harvested from the garden. I looked at the precious gift of nature and felt sad that she had to bring them to me instead of me being able to pick them myself and take them to her.

While I was enjoying my fresh fruits, mixed emotions and thoughts were going back and forth in my mind. I appreciated simple things like being outside, eating freshly picked fruits. But at the same time the deep sadness overshadowed my joy because I could experience it only a few times a year. My longing for everything I had lost and the indescribable contempt for my changed life outweighed the little joy I had.

"Am I really going to live like this for the rest of my life?" I cried out to God in my mind. "Wait a minute. These circumstances were created by the event – the car accident. If circumstances could be altered by events, then these circumstances can be changed as well!"

At that moment it felt like a light bulb had lit in my mind and I understood a very simple but profound truth: "Since circumstances can be altered by the events, I could change them by taking the initiative and deliberately creating the events that I want. My life simply will not be able to remain the same if I deliberately do something to change it! I am not going to settle for what the crash has created. I refuse to be defined by the accident. This is my life and what it will be like depends on me, not on the accident, other people or events. Nothing – neither this accident nor any other problems or difficulties can determine how I feel and how I will live. I am not going to allow circumstances to dictate who I am and what my destiny will be like. I will re-establish myself. With God's help I am going to get out of this horrible place and create a new life."

It was a defining moment. I resolved to change my life conditions. I knew I was not going to settle for the disabled lifestyle. My desire to be connected with people, to work, travel and be useful to others was still there, alive in my spirit. And at that moment I knew this was exactly how I was going to live.

It felt like my will and my determination started breathing again. I was tired from the endless pain but it didn't matter how much work and effort it would take. I was ready to turn this lifeless imprisoned existence into a lively and fulfilling life journey. I realized that nothing was going to happen if I sat and did nothing to make this new direction happen. I decided the "New Inga" would take the initiative and start making changes to get herself out of a dead end.

"But where do I begin?"

I had the resolve, but not the knowledge. I didn't know how to help myself. Following my philosophy – that it was necessary to look into the root of the problem and begin change from there – I began asking myself questions and coming up with answers that would guide me out of my depression.

Q. "Okay, it's enough," I thought. "It cannot last like this anymore. What kind of life do I want in order to feel happy again? How must my life change for me to be the same Inga as I was?"

A. "I want to be active and independent again. I want to be able to go out by myself whenever I want to; I want to go back to work; I want to be connected with my friends just like I used to. I want my life back."

Q. "How can I turn that dream into reality? Where should I start?"

A. "If I could walk, I could leave home and return to work thus achieving a certain level of personal and financial independence. I would be able to go out and spend time with friends. Little by little, I would return to my active life. Yes, I need to walk again. This will be my "first step."

Q. "What exactly do I have to do to make it happen? What steps do I have to take?"

A. "I must train again every day and develop my walking and balance skills."

That moment I felt the heartbeat of life within me again. I finally saw how there was a way out of this pit. I didn't have to live this way; I could change it all if I could walk. In order to walk I needed to train again, that's all. Step by step I would get back into my normal life routine.

It felt as if my heart would jump out of my chest. I remembered that walking with prostheses meant dealing with excruciating pain, but the realization that I could actually change my life filled me with the hope and enthusiasm to get to work.

Suddenly I felt lightness. I had hope once again. I was fully aware that it was up to me, not the accident, as to how I was going to continue living my life. I knew I would have to work, but I was not afraid of work. In fact, I couldn't wait to end this vacation, so I could return home and start the process of my journey out of this lifeless, dark and depressing place.

That day I told my father that I would like to start walking again once we returned home. He had a question in his eyes, observing my enthusiasm and determination, but he did not disturb me with any questions. He said, "Sure, I'll help."

Upon my return to Vilnius, the only thing I thought of was continuing my training to walk. My prostheses were standing in the corner behind the curtains. Before each session, we would take them out for training and then put them back behind the curtains again when training for that period ended. It had been a few months since I'd last seen them.

I did not use them much after I came back from the Orthopedic Center. My enthusiasm quickly faded away when dad pulled them out from behind the curtains. I could still feel the sharp pain every time I put my foot down. Remembering the excruciating pain they caused made me sick. As I was looking at them, just the memory of that torture made me sweat. I couldn't think of putting myself through that again. Nevertheless, this was the only way to escape my imprisonment. I decided to try. However, as soon as my father helped me stand up, the sharp stabbing, familiar pain pierced me throughout my entire body. I couldn't take even one step forward.

I immediately asked for help to sit down. This pain was beyond what I could endure. I asked dad to take them off and put them back in the corner, so I wouldn't see them again. The enthusiasm and the excitement that I felt at my aunt's house began to fade away.

"I just saw the way out of this; I knew exactly what I needed to do. And now what? I can't do this anymore," I thought. As the pain subsided, the sadness and hopelessness started pulling me down again. And I realized I was getting closer and closer to the edge of the pit once again.

Not long after, my friend Renata came to visit. I knew I could be open with her, and I could trust her. Generally, I would never tell anyone how badly I felt. Nobody knew my true feelings. At this point though, I felt so heartbroken and empty that I couldn't hold it within any more.

Finally I shared the truth, and the truth was that I was not okay, even though it seemed like that to family and friends. The truth was that I felt dark sadness and deep hopelessness. The truth was that I didn't have any goals or anything that inspired or motivated me. I had nothing to look forward to and I didn't know what to do with myself.

When Renata heard what I said, she looked at me with a surprised expression on her face and responded, "What do you mean you don't have any goals? Inga, you said there would come a day when you would walk into the Business Lounge on your own. In fact, we all are waiting for you at the airport. Don't you remember your promise? You're not going to sit here at home forever, are you?"

I don't think Renata realized the impact of her words. To hear how they were all waiting for me to come back to the airport meant more than she could've ever imagined. Knowing that I was not forgotten, but wanted to be seen again among them breathed new life into me. Memories of us greeting each other in the morning and sharing our lives, our experiences, the coffee breaks and loud laughter, the heart-to-heart conversations and support for each other during those long work hours filled with delayed or cancelled flights went through my mind in a flash, such precious memories of people and places and time together, all so dear to my soul. Once again, it felt like my determination had been re-awakened, like a long dormant volcano ready to erupt.

Renata's surprised look and persuasive response to my thoughts reminded me that the "true Inga" was a go-getter, a person cheerful and optimistic. She was always surrounded by her friends and that's how they knew her. A discouraged attitude, depression and isolation were not her character traits.

"How did I get to this emotional place? No, I am not going to give up. I promised them that I would be back, and yes they will see me again."

And then Renata and I set a goal. We decided that I had one month to renew my walking skills and by the end of September, I would show up at the airport. By the end of our time together, I was filled with renewed strength and enthusiasm. The thought that I would return to the airport and be among my friends gave me so much anticipatory joy that I couldn't sit still. I told my father that I made a decision to return to the airport in one month and I would start training again every day regardless of the pain.

I asked him if he would help me again to go out to the nearby school's stadium to train to walk. He looked at me with a surprised expression on his face. Yet I could see in his eyes he was pleased with my decision, and he said that "of course" he would help.

Now I had the goal and the date I had to reach it by. I knew exactly what my aim was and what I needed to do. Imagining the moment of my return was all I needed to say "yes" to endure the price of this venture.

Since then my thoughts and my focus completely shifted into an entirely new direction. I stopped thinking about how hard and painful it was, what I'd lost and what I was not able to do. Now all my thoughts were directed toward:

- My ultimate dream.
- My immediate goal: to return to the airport.
- The work that I had to do to achieve it.

I was obsessed with training to renew my balance and my walking skills, along with ascending and descending stairs. I trained every single day with no exceptions, never considering whether or not I was in the mood.

It didn't matter that the sharp edges of the prosthetic sockets were pressing against my groin, and every single step felt like someone were stabbing through my whole body with a serrated knife. I knew the reason why I was doing it and it was far more important than the cost of pain and exhausting work. My improving abilities to hold my balance and walk gave me hope that my dream was still realistic, and that there would come a day when I would be active and independent again.

Fulfillment Day ~ The Day I Kept My Promise

September 27, 2001 was a personal day of victory – the day I fulfilled my promise. It was an evening which will always remain in my memory. I fulfilled the promise that I had made to my friends during those first few weeks after the accident.

Dad helped me to put on the prostheses at home, but I did not walk out from there. We decided it was better not to irritate my body ahead of time, so my thighs and skin would be able to endure the pressure when I arrived at the airport. I sat in a wheelchair with the prostheses on and he rolled me out. Upon our arrival the airport's Departure Hall, with dad's help, I got out of the car. While I was sitting in the wheelchair, he fixed my prostheses so they fit properly and were tight, then he helped me to stand up.

I stood and immediately closed my eyes from the knife-like pain. My dad immediately understood what happened. He looked at me with the kindest eyes I'd ever seen and said, "Well Inga, now it's up to you. You have to go through it."

I silently nodded. Without saying another word, we agreed that we would get through it together and complete our mission. Then I took my first step. Edgy pain penetrated my whole essence. I took the next one. Sharp edges of my prosthetic legs were cutting into my entire groin area. There was nothing I could do about it, nor was I going to cancel my plans. This was the moment I dreamed about for many days and nights. I had worked so hard to make my dream come true. And now I was there, at my airport. The pain shouldn't matter at this moment. I pulled together my endurance and willpower. And then I took a step, and then another. All I could think about was how not to lose my balance. I kept thinking, "Don't fall, Inga. Be careful." Holding my father's hand, I walked inside and looked up.

"Here it is! My airport!" It seemed like my pain and the whole world disappeared as I crossed the threshold. "I am here; I am back. My dream has come true!" I took a deep breath. This dream held me together for all those months. So many days and nights this was the moment I lived for.

I glanced through the terminal and took a deep breath; I had missed it so much. For many it's just a quick stop before they get on their journey to another country, but for me it was like my second home. This place brought so many new, wonderful people and many unforgettable memories into my life. I looked around the Departure Hall. Normally the place was like an anthill with rushing passengers and staff performing their duties, but now it seemed like the place was resting – it was break time between flights. I glanced at the Business Lounge, but through the darkened glass wall I could see nothing, as it used to be. I only saw its brightly lit advertisement.

Upon second glance, though, it looked as though many things had changed from before.

In a minute, a couple of Lithuanian Airlines agents came up to me, not hiding their shock. Valdas and Paulius were my favorites to work with. They stood in front of me completely stunned. Valdas, cheerful and funny as always, began the conversation by welcoming me. Paulius stood there speechless, staring at me. He could not say a word, so I spoke to him saying, "Hi Paulius. Yes, I am alive and I came back, just as I promised."

He was still silently gazing at me, barely holding tears. Paulius and I were good buddies at work. Many times we collaborated trying to accommodate passengers during their delayed flights; and we had fun coffee breaks, switching to beer at the end of long busy days. Our loud, cheerful laughter and the many moments we'd shared went through my mind. I could only imagine what it felt like for him to hear the news of my horrific crash. I looked around to find my other friends from Security or Border Police, but none were there. I was saddened a bit, because I had expected to see many of them that day – my very special day.

Some of the security staff waved at me while performing their passenger registration duties on the other side of the Departure Hall. It seemed a little strange that I did not see any of my people, but then I thought maybe they were on break and I would see them later when the last round of flight registrations began.

I decided to continue my journey toward the Business Lounge, and then I planned to go to the Duty Free area to surprise my friends who worked there. Paulius still had not said a word; he continued to remain speechless. I was not sure if it was how I had changed that shocked him, or if it was seeing me standing in front of him, after hearing news of me dying and losing nearly half of my body. I left Paulius and Valdas standing, and slowly I turned around and proceeded toward the stairs to get to the lounge.

While slowly taking step after step, I wondered what Renata was doing. Probably she was preparing the lounge for the upcoming flight. "It will be so good to be there again," I thought. "I won't be able to help her, but maybe we can have tea together like in the good old days. The Business Lounge was where we saw each other the last time just several hours before I got into the accident; together we got through that horrific time, and we will be there together in the lounge again despite it all. And then, I am going to surprise my "Duty-Free gang!" I hardly could hold the joy as I was imagining my visit with my friends.

I looked up to check how many steps were left. There were a few more until I reached the end of the first set of stairs. I quietly whispered to my dad that I wished we could move my prosthesis to a slightly different angle, because every time I put my weight on my leg, prostheses were severely cutting into my groin. The knife-like pain was penetrating my whole essence.

The pain was more intense than usual, and it was gradually increasing. My only relief were those few seconds while I was transferring my leg forward until my foot touched the floor and I put my weight on it. "Hang in there daughter, there is nothing I can do about it now. Hold on, you are strong enough to do this," my father whispered as he was trying to strengthen me. Slowly I made it to the second floor. After a moment of giving myself a break, I continued ascending the second set of stairs to enter the lounge. After conquering the stairs, with a trembling heart, I looked up to get my first view.

I could not believe what I was seeing. Right there in the Business Lounge I saw a line of fifteen or more of my dearest friends and co-workers holding flowers and gifts to welcome me back. I realized that the reason why I hadn't seen anyone was because they were gathered in the Business Lounge waiting for me. I had no clue that I would be met this way. I asked Renata not to tell anyone that I was coming, because I wanted to make it a surprise. But it looked like Renata decided to make it a surprise for me.

After I walked to the center of the lounge, I positioned myself in front of the group. I looked at each person. Every one of them meant so much to me. So many beautiful memories of working together, or after work times spent together. They loved me unconditionally, had faith in me and were patiently waiting for me to return. Some of them were smiling, some were wiping away tears, tightly holding bouquets of flowers and gifts. Everyone was speechless including me. It was so quiet, you could have heard the pin drop.

In their faces, I saw the expectation for me to say something. I thought that walking and ascending stairs would be the most difficult part, but I was wrong; this moment required so much more effort to hold myself together and not burst into tears. Tears of joy. Tears of finally conquering the tragedy. Tears of victory.

All this time, training through the excruciating pain, I saw this moment in my mind. This is why I did not give up. And there I was, after eighteen months, finally making my dream come true. I fulfilled my promise to my "airport gang" and walked into my cherished work place.

"I know February 12, 2000 was a shock to many of you," I began, in a voice more anxious than they were used to hearing. "The crash took my legs, my arm, my independence, the joy of life and everything that I so cherished, held dearest and valued the most. I know this crash has impacted many of you. All of you wondered whether Inga would ever enter the lounge again. But the idea of never coming back to this place and losing you was too much to bear, and I promised that I would return to you, at any cost."

Barely holding my tears, I started sharing my heart with them. I thanked them for not forsaking me, but for caring about me and not giving up on me. We all were emotional, sharing the same feeling – it was a victorious day for all of us.

After my speech, the evening continued, celebrating our joint victory. The evening was delightful, filled with stories and cheerful laughter, jokes and sharing good memories. I think that night passengers of the last flights and all employees knew that something was going on there on the second floor, as our laughter in the Business Lounge resonated throughout the entire Departure Hall.

After so many days and nights of the unknown and questioning whether I would ever have a glimpse of my cherished world again, I arrived. In between the hugs and the tears and the laughter, I caught myself gazing at the group of people I loved, understanding that I had arrived at my dream because I did not give up. The only person who could have stopped me from having this experience was me. And that's how I must continue – never giving up, no matter how difficult challenges may be.

This was such a special time for all of us. I knew it would be engraved in my heart forever. I treasured every moment of the evening. After some time, Paulius and Valdas joined us, holding a giant bouquet of roses. Paulius was more relaxed. Apparently, he had no idea that I was coming and was not prepared to see me. The celebration continued for several hours, sharing stories, taking pictures, giving me a tour of the newly designed lounge.

I have to admit that my happiness at being there and sharing memories with old friends overshadowed any kind of pain I felt walking. I returned home physically exhausted, but it was nothing compared to the joy of the night and the triumphant feeling of finally achieving my goal. I felt like I finally reached the summit of a giant mountain, one that had never been conquered before. The joy that enveloped me, and my newly treasured memories were my own personal torch of victory at the top of that once insurmountable peak.

Once I got home, I could no longer take even one step. Nevertheless, I returned with a smile that wouldn't go away coupled with wonderful memories of a night with lots of good friends, gorgeous flowers and beautiful gifts. My mom, instinctively knowing that I was hurting, took off my prosthetic legs. I was so delighted about the day that I didn't give much attention to my sore thighs. The pain didn't really matter at the time. I lay down, thanked my God for this unforgettable evening, and fell soundly asleep.

When I got up in the morning and looked at my thighs, I was horrified. My thighs were swollen, shaded a dark purple color, and my entire groin area had open wounds. I could not even touch my legs for the next two weeks. I took those artificial legs, put them in the corner, and declared, "This is it. Enough is enough."

Now I really saw that my desire to live an active lifestyle using artificial legs was not possible. If I couldn't even touch my thighs for more than a week after wearing prostheses for only six hours, how could I go to work and wear them all day long?

For some time I was in euphoria because of my achievement. For that day, that one very special day, the pain was worth it. However, as the following days went by, my daily routine became dim once again. My life turned into a dreary existence within the walls of my home. Once again, I had hit a brick wall. Now I saw that there was no way I could walk again and return to my pre-accident life.

I always had the drive and enthusiasm to improve my life. I sincerely hoped that I could learn to walk. I believed my current circumstances could be changed and I worked so hard and diligently to bring that change to life. I didn't care how much effort it would cost and I did not spare myself. I put so much strenuous work into my return, I was willing to suffer because I believed that what I was doing would lead to the culmination of my dream.

Countless hours of driving from Vilnius to Orthopedic Center back and forth weekly for nearly two years: Was it all in vain? I took thousands of steps with these artificial legs and for what, the illusion that I would be able to walk again? Each step had been made through never-ending stabbing pain, blisters, open sores and bruises: But for what? Each day was spent in training through soaking sweat and daily physical exhaustion. Was it all in meaningless?

My only hope to bring myself back to life was shattered into pieces. I did not see what I could possibly do to move forward. After seeing that it wasn't going to happen, I once again faced the bottomless pit. At this point, there was nothing else that I desired. I didn't have anything to aim for. I didn't see any point in training or doing my exercises because I knew that I would not be able to walk with artificial legs anyway. It seemed like my life had become directionless, going nowhere. I would start my day any time I'd wake up. I had no plans for the day and no plan beyond that day. I did not want to do anything nor did I have any desire to see anyone. Total apathy took over. My prostheses stood lonely in the corner.

Facing the fact that all mine and my family's efforts were in vain brought heartbreaking disappointment to all of us. Now there was nothing more that I could do, and there was nothing left to offer any signs for a better future. My circumstances were counter to anything that I had aimed for and what I believed in. Even my hope that this could be changed was simply unrealistic.

Deep sadness pulled me back into its trap. Every day I was back on the computer surfing the Internet. It was like another world that I used to escape from my reality. I especially liked the instant messaging program, which was a way to have an instant conversation with people from all over the world. It gave me interaction and the opportunity to practice my English language skills. I numbed my disappointment and hopelessness in a digital world.

The only thing that held me above water was my faith. In my prayers, I kept saying to my God, "Lord, I trust you. I know you can do the impossible. I don't know when, I don't know how. I have no idea how this possibly can happen. But I know that You will give those legs back to me and I will live again. I do believe I will be independent again and I will have a life."

At this point, mine and my family's efforts were not something I could count on. We already tried; we really tried. Now I was left with nothing to rely on to see the change. Nor did I have anything to look forward to. Something deep inside of me though, did not allow me to give up. I did not want to give up. Since there was no way to change my circumstances and there was nothing I could count on, the only thing left for me was a child-like faith that God could make a miracle. I kept praying for God's miracle and I waited for His answer. I kept saying, "Lord, you have the power over everything. There must be way for me to walk again, there must be a way for me to live again."

Christmas and the New Year were times I dreaded and I was not looking forward to them. Having no opportunity to celebrate them with my friends as I did before created a sadness deep in my soul that had me facing my loss all over again. Before the celebration of New Year's Eve, 2002, I had a strong feeling that I should meet the New Year not with a glass of champagne in my hands, but with a prayer in the church. The church I used to go to had a tradition that I really liked – entering into each New Year with a prayer, asking the Lord God to bless the upcoming year.

That's exactly what I did – I asked my friends to pick me up so I could greet the New Year at church. I will never forget the moment when we entered into the New Year asking God to bless that year. I spoke with my Lord from deep inside my heart. I thanked Him for His blessings during my recovery after the crash, for giving me the strength to endure the pain and the loss, and closed my prayer by asking Him to bring change into my life. I knew there was nothing impossible for God and that miracles truly could happen. Deep in my heart I knew it to be true. What's more, I had a feeling that something special was going to happen to me that coming year.

My New Year's Miracle

I started my new year with hope. At this point, my faith that there is nothing impossible for God and He could change any circumstances was the only thing that gave me hope. My faith was the only thing that gave me endurance.

I believed there was a serious reason why my life and its series of events happened to me the way they did. I believed there was a reason why I was chosen to live. And I believed He had a plan for my life. Every day I continued praying to my Lord, telling Him that I believed He had the power over any circumstances since He is the always-present, all-powerful, all-knowing God who created the universe. I didn't know how, nor did I know when, but I believed He was going to restore my life. He had the answer and a way out of my despair. I sincerely put my trust in His divine help and every day I waited for my miracle.

It was March 2012. There was nothing in my life that gave me any signs for a better future. Every morning I would wake up with a feeling of emptiness surrounding me, facing another wasted day, depending on others for my every need.

Then came a day, which remains engraved in my heart up to this moment. I was sitting in the kitchen having my morning coffee. Gazing at a spot on the horizon, I was thinking about my life. I was so tired from this empty and purposeless daily routine, but I did not know what else I could do to escape it. Thoughts were coming to my mind over and over again, "Such is your fate." It was the most common comment I heard from old and new acquaintances over the past two years. People would say this because they had no explanation for why my life had changed so drastically, and they did not see how it could ever be changed. They wanted to comfort me, and yet they didn't know how, except coming to the trite philosophical conclusion that it was the way it had to be. I did not blame them for their perspective, but I absolutely hated hearing it, and I never agreed with them. These thoughts were bombarding me as I was trying to quench my last efforts to resist the hopelessness.

"Is it really my fate to live like this?" I asked myself as the hopeless reality stared at me. "No. No! This is not my fate. There must be a way. I cannot believe other people in the world are not able to walk with artificial legs. I can't and I don't want to believe this is true. There has to be a way."

Suddenly, at that moment, a thought came into my mind. "Go on the Internet and look for help worldwide." It was a very unusual experience; in fact, it seemed like someone placed that thought into my mind. It wasn't my thought. I felt in a split second that my mind was enlightened and now suddenly I knew exactly what I needed to do. "Yes, that is right! I need to look for help in another country."

This thought was precisely clear and I felt such strong assurance that this was my way out of this dead end that I was compelled to do exactly that. Immediately after I finished my coffee, I rolled back into my room and began my search. To be honest, I didn't know what to look for. I only knew I had to search for information about prosthetic legs somewhere in the world. I opened the Yahoo search engine, typed in the keywords in the search box, and after opening each link, I began reading information about prostheses.

It didn't take long to realize that it was going to be a challenge, requiring perseverance and diligence. The content was written in specific prosthetics terminology and I could hardly understand what I was reading. My English skills were not good enough to understand everything, especially that kind of detailed content. So I took my dictionary and began reading the websites, translating nearly every other word to grasp what was written. Every day I studied websites of companies worldwide that were fabricating prosthetic legs. I was learning prosthetic terminology in a foreign language, as well as the process of getting artificial legs made. Now I was on a new mission.

I would start my day doing research about prosthetics worldwide, and finish my day doing the same. I spent countless hours searching the Internet and learning about the development of prosthetic devices in foreign countries.

There was a night that was no different from others. I was browsing through prosthetic companies doing my search for what they had to offer. But unlike those other nights, among all of the companies I'd researched, there were three companies that I particularly liked, and there was something special about one company in America, in the state of California. I didn't know why, but while I was browsing through many links, for some reason I wanted to come back to that company and check it out again. I had a good feeling about it in my heart. It's difficult to explain, but I had an unexplainable closeness to it. I made a mental note to revisit that company in California and two other ones and, feeling total exhaustion from many hours of reading and studying in a foreign language, I decided to end my day. It was after midnight. I felt I like I would collapse right there at my desk if I did not shut it all down and go to bed. Feeling wiped out mentally and physically, I closed all the websites, turned off my computer, and rolled to my bed. As I was transferring from the wheelchair, suddenly a very strong, clear, feeling-thought came upon me. "Get back into your wheelchair, turn on your computer, find those companies that you liked and write letters to them."

It was a thought mixed with a feeling and it felt like a very clear direction as to what I had to do. Furthermore, it was a very strong and urgent feeling. It's hard to describe; I've never had that type of feeling before. It was so strong and profound that it got my attention despite my exhaustion. I couldn't dismiss it. I felt exhausted, though, such that I couldn't even think straight, so I promised myself that I would write on the following day.

Interestingly, the feeling was strongly urging me to do it immediately. The feeling was so crystal clear that I could not ignore it. I knew I would not be able to fall asleep if I did not listen to that voice. I got back into my wheelchair, wheeled over to my desk, and turned on the computer. In my browsing history, I found the companies that I liked and emailed them.

There were two in the United States and one in Germany. The letters were very simple and short:

"I got into horrible accident. And I have lost my both my legs above the knees. I would like to know more information about your artificial limbs. I would like to know how I would be able to stand up and sit down, and to know the prices of your artificial limbs."

It was my last chance. I thought maybe somebody would reply and tell me how prostheses should be made and how the experience of wearing them really should be. I wanted to know if it was really true, that it's supposed to hurt as I'd been told. Also, I needed to know about the ability to sit down and stand up independently. Even though prosthetic experts told me that it was impossible for me to do it, I never agreed with them. I believed there had to be a way. I knew there must be a way. I knew my family would not be able to afford to pay for prostheses, but I wanted to know what it would take for me to get them.

To my surprise, after I sent the emails I felt peace inside. It was an interesting and strange feeling at the same time to have such a significant change in how I felt. Feeling peaceful, I shut down my computer and went to sleep.

I started my morning as usual, with a cup of coffee at the computer checking my email. As I was deleting numerous junk emails, I checked one and was ready to delete it along with the others when my eye accidentally caught the word "legs" in the subject line. I stopped. Then I read the entire subject line and read, "a response about the legs."

"What is that? A response about the legs?"

And then I remembered my three emails before I went to sleep, and my heart started beating faster. I opened it and started reading. It was hard to believe this was a real email from a person, not junk email. Then I read the message a second time to make sure I was not misunderstanding the message. I realized it was a response to the email I wrote the previous night! I had received a letter from the prosthetic specialist and owner of a company in California, the one that I had a special feeling about.

It was a very warm response with information about prosthetic legs, and he asked me a question about what was wrong with my artificial legs. In response to my question, how it is possible to sit down and stand up independently, he sent me the link to his website and wrote, "Why don't you have a look around and then write back if you need more information."

I opened the link and clicked on the video. Holding my cup of coffee tightly, I watched a man who was also missing both legs above the knees independently walking, ascending and descending stairs. I clicked on the next video and started watching the same man independently sitting down on a chair and standing up. I squeezed my cup harder and harder. Totally shocked, I clicked on another link and saw that same guy lying down on the floor and getting back up, showing what to do in case you fall. After the video ended, I immediately clicked on another video and saw the same man riding a bicycle. "What?" I said in amazement. I was overwhelmed. I sat there for a moment stunned from seeing what this man was able to do. I didn't know how to react to what I had just watched.

I witnessed what I was convinced was impossible to do wearing prostheses, and all this time, I was told that there was no way I could sit down or stand up independently and yet, look at what this guy does! He doesn't have both legs above the knees, just like me. And yes, he *can* sit down, and he *can* stand up independently. And not only can he sit down and stand up, but he can also ride a bike? I sat for a moment astounded and amazed at what I had seen, asking myself if this could really be true.

"I knew it," I said. "I knew it was possible!" I put my cup back on the desk, turned around, and rolled as quickly as I could to the living room. I found my mom and said with excitement in my voice, "Mom, you have to watch this. Come with me."

She was understandably a little puzzled by what was going on, but came to my room and sat down on the bed next to the computer. I turned the videos on again without any explanation where I found them and said, "Look at this, mom." We both were watching the videos and had no words to say. We were speechless. It seemed that my heart was about to jump out of my chest. I was in tears, totally astounded by what I had discovered. I looked at my mother, who was sitting quietly with tears rolling down her cheeks.

For two long years, we were told how impossible it would be for me in my physical condition to walk on a regular basis and perform simple activities like sitting down or standing up independently, and here we see *this*? I can't even imagine what my mom went through hearing medical professionals and specialists spout their opinions and theories of my inability to ever walk again. Yet she saw me, day after day, working through the pain and exhaustion to prove them all wrong. I proved to them it was possible. And now, we saw this. We were both crying. I told her the story, how I emailed three companies and received an answer from California. I saw she was sad, because that meant there was no way for me to receive help directly from that specialist. Our family did not have money to travel overseas nor could we possibly afford these types of prostheses. She encouraged me however to keep in touch with this person; maybe he could give me some suggestions for what I should do.

This email was like the light at the end of a dark tunnel. Reading the message I felt the writer's sincere interest in my condition. He probably had no idea what his letter meant to me. I answered his question, what was wrong with my prostheses, and described my experience watching the videos. We started emailing back and forth with questions and answers about prosthetic legs. His name was Michael, and I looked forward to his messages daily.

What a shock it was to read Michael's messages telling me that it was not supposed to hurt to wear prostheses. I told him what I'd been told by my specialists, and I told him about the excruciating pain I had to endure to take even one step. He asked me questions about my physical condition and current prostheses, trying to figure out what could be the cause of my problem.

This contact brought new light and hope to me. It felt like the gloomy sky in my life was clearing after the storm, and I saw the first rays of sunshine. I was breathing again. I heard the heartbeat of my hope. It was coming alive. Someone across the world was actually interested in my problem. Finally someone was listening to me when I said, "It hurts!"

After a week of discussing my unique problem, one morning I received Michael's email saying that in few weeks he was scheduled to give a prosthetic training seminar in Istanbul, Turkey. He asked me if there were any way for me to meet him there. He said this was the closest to Lithuania his travels would take him, and he would be glad to look at my prostheses if I came to Istanbul to meet him.

"What? Travel to Istanbul?" It was hard to believe. "This specialist would meet me and take a look at my prostheses?"

Like the first time, I read his message a second time to make sure I was not misunderstanding him. But after reading it a second and third time, I realized that I had read it correctly – this American specialist was inviting me to meet him in Turkey, so he could take a look at my prostheses and possibly help me. I remember that moment up to this day as if I had experienced it just yesterday. It's hard to describe the relief and joy that I felt. Finally, there was a prosthetic expert who actually cared that I was suffering while walking with artificial legs. There was someone who was interested in helping me. And it's not even a local person or someone who knows me; this was a specialist from across the globe.

I finally saw the light. I knew this was the answer to my prayers. This was my chance. This was the opportunity given to me and right at that moment I knew I would travel to Istanbul and meet Michael. There was no doubt but that the Lord's hand was involved. I went into the other room, looked at my parents, and confidently told them, "Mom, dad, I am going to travel to Turkey."

My dad turned his head away from the television with a dead serious look and a question in his eyes. Mom stopped doing her household chores; it seemed like she was suddenly paralyzed. They both stared at me as dead silence blanketed the room, wondering what it was about. I saw they were bewildered, hoping to hear that I was joking. I revealed my idea of seeking help from foreign prosthetic companies and shared with them how I reached out and received an answer from California. And now, this specialist was inviting me to meet him in Istanbul. Now they understood that I was not joking. I was very serious. They were a little shocked about my intention to travel to Turkey to meet a stranger. The sense of horror of the night when I made my independent decision to leave home despite their concern was very fresh in their hearts. Our lives were forever changed because of my decision, plus they shared the fear of letting me go anywhere on my own – the accident was like a shadow following all of us. Besides, a trip to another country in my physical condition raised a lot of questions and concerns.

However, my parents didn't try to stop me. On the contrary, while I saw concern in their eyes about me taking the trip, they were very surprised about my tenacity and pleased to hear about the response I had received. My unconditional aspiration to improve my life, having a sincere childlike hope that it could be done, destroyed their strongholds of fear and concern. All they wanted was for me to be happy again, and if it took them to trust me to go to Turkey, they were ready to support me.

At times it seemed that their suffering was much greater than mine, watching their child suffer physical and emotional distress. I knew they were ready to do whatever it took to see me get out of this cage of helplessness and again spread my wings and live. I think it was the first time I saw hope in their eyes since the tragedy showed up at our home's doorstep. I asked them not to worry about a thing – I would get care of all my trip details and everything would be fine.

Many of whom I told about my plans, couldn't understand how I could possibly agree to such venture. It seemed crazy for me to travel to Turkey and meet someone, whom I had never met and had only exchanged emails. As you well remember, brother, you especially thought it was the wildest idea ever. I remember how concerned you were and how you tried to talk me out of it. You offered every possible reason as to why it was a stupid decision. I remember you saying, "Besides, Inga, what can this American man change? He may check your physical condition and maybe he will do some adjustments on your prostheses, but then what? He will inspire you and then he will go back to sunny California, and you will remain here in Lithuania with your hopes up, but no way of implementing them."

You continued your comments by saying, "In addition, the travel expenses will cost a substantial amount, and it'll be a plain waste of money."

I remember so well our dialogue. In a way, I understood. You were convinced how it would be a waste of time and money, and most of all you wanted to protect me from further disappointment. You didn't want someone to build up my hopes, because when they were shattered (as you were certain they would be), that would hurt me even more.

In your eyes I was going toward an even bigger disappointment hearing that I could walk without suffering pain, and not having it fulfilled. Having no money to purchase that type of prostheses, I would remain where I was, even more disappointed because what I needed to fulfill my dream was beyond my grasp. Realistically, I had no money or opportunity to go to the United States. Looking at my desire realistically, I was moving toward another disaster of crashed hopes followed by the pain of disappointment.

Daily I kept hearing your reasoning why I was making a crazy step and that I should cancel my plans immediately – before it was too late. You were not the only one giving me a strange look and raising excellent questions about my intentions. However, I was not going to give up on my dream only because you or someone else had a vision and opinion different from mine. You see, brother, I knew something that you and all the others didn't: I was confident this new contact and Michael inviting me to Turkey were not a coincidence. I was listening to my intuition and was ready to follow it. I had absolutely no doubt that this was the answer to my prayers and I had to use this opportunity regardless of what it looked like on the surface.

And that's exactly what I did – I started making my travel arrangements to Istanbul to meet Michael with my faith as my guide.

My New Chapter

When Michael appeared in my life, who seemed really caring and ready to help me, I knew there was going to be a major change. After seeing the emailed videos of his patients performing various activities wearing prostheses, I saw that my dream to walk again was not an illusion, as I was told. These were not computer generated videos, these were real people doing real things with real prostheses. It was possible. That's exactly what I was aiming for; and if they could do it, I could too. My hope was turning into confidence. I was slightly shocked, however, having to travel to Turkey in my physical condition to meet someone I didn't know. But I was ready to do whatever it took.

My doubts and fear of disappointment were replaced with faith. I trusted that my connection with this specialist was divine, and if the Lord opens a door – He will walk me through that door and will lead me to receive His blessing.

I didn't know why, but I felt I could trust Michael. I felt total peace about what I was planning to do. My anxiety about traveling to Turkey turned into anticipated excitement. I invited Renata to travel with me, and we decided to enjoy an adventure together and have fun with it instead of worrying about the "What Ifs." I again felt a positive, forward momentum in my life. Now I had the confidence that my hopes and assumptions for what was possible were correct and I was ready to do whatever it took to achieve my dream. But there was one thing holding me back.

While I was getting ready to meet this exciting change in my life head on, my habitual thoughts from my past were sneaking in, trying to get my attention and overshadow my hopeful anticipation for a new blessing. My constant thinking about my beautiful past was a way for me to escape my reality and give myself at least some comfort. I was unaware that at the same time it was causing pain and deep sadness, because while I was enjoying my beautiful memories, I felt a gut-wrenching awareness that I had lost them forever and I would never have such beautiful experiences again.

And when I was thinking back, observing my changed life through the eyeglass of my new reality, it was like I was in this bubble of constant awareness about all the things I was no longer able to do. While I was making the effort to become as self-sufficient as I could, thoughts were always present like, "I wish I could stand up and go get it" or "It was so easy to do this or that before my arm was paralyzed." I realized that unknowingly I would put myself through reliving the pain over and over again by constantly thinking about my past experiences, what I had lost, and what I couldn't do anymore.

Apparently I was the one who was torturing myself without even knowing it. Those memories and thoughts of my loss were like a poison to me. Here I felt enthusiastic, anticipating the change that I so strongly desired and dreamed about while those dark thoughts were infiltrating, as if I would put dirt into a clean, fresh water and turn it into mud.

I decided this had to stop. I had an opportunity to open a new chapter in my life, but I wouldn't be able to do it if I didn't close the previous chapters. I needed to leave my memories of the past where they belonged – in the past – and open the book and begin a new chapter.

That moment I made the decision that pulled me out of my depression completely. I committed to myself to not put the dirt into clean water: no more nostalgic memories about my past or anything that I no longer have; no more thinking about what I don't have any more or what I am not able to do.

I will soar above that which could not be returned. I will look at the new life that is ahead of me. I will set my sights on how to create a fulfilling future, instead of looking back and longing for my past. I will focus on the life that I desire to have and what I need to do in order to turn it into reality. I will be grateful for what I have now instead of grieving about what I have lost. I will focus on what I can do with one arm and will find ways to get things done in spite of my physical challenges, instead of emphasizing what I could not do anymore. I will use my energy to change my life instead of wasting it on painful memories that are never going to change. I will be grateful for every day given to me, knowing many delightful experiences are in store and waiting for me. From now on, I will think on only what makes me feel uplifted and stronger and I will put all my efforts into creating the life I desire. I am opening a new page of a new chapter in my life.

That moment I felt something had shifted in my whole essence. I felt peace and complete harmony within. I was filled with joy, hope and the expectancy of something good that was still ahead. I let go of my past and all that was hurting me. I was ready to receive new opportunities and a new life. I closed the chapters that were full of pain, loss and fear, and opened a new one that was clean and full of dreams, goals and faith. I believed that my life would be beautiful in spite of all.

"I can and I will live an extraordinary life despite the loss of my both legs and my left arm," I said to myself, and went on about my new day taking the further steps that ultimately transformed my life.

And you know, shifting my focus and changing my thought pattern totally changed how I experienced life. Did negative thoughts completely disappear out of my awareness? No, of course not. There were circumstances that made me face my loss and thoughts about my pain, but no longer was I like a puppet on strings, manipulated by negative thoughts. I simply did not allow negative thoughts to affect me. I took charge of my thoughts and upon that which I was focusing. I would stop those hurtful thoughts each time before they became dominant in my mind. As soon as I would catch myself thinking about anything that made me feel grieving, rejected or discouraged, I would interrupt my thought process and intentionally switch my focus onto something that was uplifting and empowering.

At the time it was my connection with Michael, the American specialist, and anticipation of a change, or sheer excitement about my trip to Istanbul that gave me hope about my future. And I made the effort to focus on that. This was the only thing that gave me hope, and that was enough for me. At least I had one good thing that I could focus on to divert my thoughts from depression. I deliberately kept my mind focused on this new opportunity knocking on my life's door and all the good it held in store for me.

Soon I noticed that the more I focused on what was good happening in my life, the more goodness I noticed around me. The more I focused on all that was good and on my anticipation of the desired change, the more uplifted I felt.

Figuring out ways to do things with one hand no longer was a burden; in fact, I was challenging myself and had fun with it. Every time I learned a new way to do things, I felt uplifted that I overcame that challenge and felt one step closer toward full independence.

I became excited and optimistic again.

I did not want to dwell anymore on my previous life and my loss.

I developed a new habitual thought pattern: gratitude for the present and hopeful anticipation for a blessing. My comfort was no longer in the past, but through faith in the future. I believed that God had reached His hand to me through Michael and this was a beginning of a new life. Since then my life took an entirely different direction than we could possibly imagine. Sometimes it's hard to believe that this is my life, my reality, and not some fictional movie of the week on the television.

Part 2 ~ Managing Yourself

As you can see, many times I fell and got up; and then I fell down again and got up again. It was very painful each and every time. I have fallen many times since and was hurt, and it's no different today. Life is a journey, and on our paths we face disappointments and painful experiences, obstacles and challenges, mistakes and discouragement.

I just have one rule that is non-negotiable: I keep going no matter what experiences I have to live through. Painful lessons and challenging obstacles were difficult to go through, but I am thankful for them because they made me stronger. They taught me principles that every person can use to reach their desired results.

The reason I wrote and told you so much about my disappointments and the depression I experienced, and how I got out of that heavy inner state, was to show you that just as we can lead ourselves into depression, likewise we can get out of it.

In my journey so far, I have experienced depression several times, and each time overcame it. These are just a few examples from the beginning of my journey. In addition, there were times, when I felt I was very close to being pulled back into the depression I described. After recognizing where I was headed, I intentionally worked on preventing this unwanted guest from making itself feel at home in my life and, to my joy, I looked into the eyes of victory each and every time.

I want you to understand that depression is *not* stronger than you are. You don't depend on it. Depression depends on you. Many think of it as a monster that the person is powerless against. Well, having gone through it, I agree it is a monster; however, it has power over you for as long as you give it that power. Let's look at it together.

What is depression? It is a feeling caused by certain thoughts, nothing more. And it is no one else's but your own thoughts that bring you into that pit. Nobody and nothing puts feelings into your being. It is you who creates these feelings by thinking in a certain way, and it is you who is responsible for what you think about. Yes, you can control what you think about. And sure, various thoughts may come into your mind. I am sure you have had the experience of certain thoughts attacking you, and it seems like you can't get away from thinking about them.

While it may seem like you are powerless against thoughts, the fact is you are the one who decides whether you want to continue developing a thought or, you deliberately intend to cut it and choose to think about something else. No one becomes depressed by thinking how grateful, content, enthusiastic and optimistic he or she is. Depression comes when a person pays close attention to what is not good in his life and constantly thinks about it. A person can lead himself into depression by thinking negatively and focusing on painful situations that have happened, what he doesn't have or what he cannot do, or anything he might be unhappy about.

In the same way, a person can get out of this state by having strong faith, an empowering perspective, a positive attitude, thought discipline and taking the necessary action that will change or improve the circumstances he's not happy about.

With all due respect to specialists in the fields of psychiatry, psychology or counseling, I disagree that a person is powerless to fight depression, and that only trained psychiatry who prescribe mind-altering antidepressants can help to overcome depression.

I agree that psychology is very valuable in our efforts to understand human behavior and dealing with certain issues. To my big disappointment, however, nearly every time I spoke to someone who visited a psychologist to seek help with his or her depression, I was told that after their initial consultation, the doctor prescribed powerful anti-depressants. I assume, if I had gone to a psychiatrist when I was deeply depressed the first few years after the crash (or even other times), I would have been given an antidepressant to make me feel better. I knew that it wasn't pills that were needed, but a change in circumstances that caused the depression in the first place. I worked on that instead. And I am so glad I made that choice.

Why do doctors prescribe antidepressants? What antidepressants do is make a person feel better. Pills do not address the root of the problem and they don't treat depression, they cover it up by artificially making a person feel better. Take the pills away from a person and they will return to dark and cold world.

I realize that I may offend many psychiatric professionals, the specialists in treating depression, and many would argue with me, but what about dealing with the problem itself, instead of rushing to get "happy pills"? How about figuring out the cause of depression and eliminating it?

I have neither the medical credentials nor the intention to argue about the scientific theory surrounding depression, or about an inherent chemical imbalance or genetic predisposition toward depression. I am simply not competent to do that. I personally believe it is a spiritual issue; but again, I will not go in depth regarding this matter because while I am learning the spiritual part of it, I have not studied the science of the human mind and I know my limitations when it comes to arguing about the many nuances of depression. That about which I am writing, I apply to a mentally healthy person who is depressed because of some bad events that had happened or circumstances that made the person unhappy. And while I don't have the scientific knowledge about depression, I conquered this monster and I learned how to prevent it and I want to share my thoughts about this inner state and how I dealt with it. You can take my thoughts and use them in your own life if you think them appropriate for you.

After experiencing and overcoming depression myself and hearing about the experiences of others who have successfully dealt with it, I am convinced that each individual is responsible for their inner state. I sincerely believe that it is not depression that has the power to rule a person, but it is the person who has the power to rule over depression.

Every time I found myself feeling depressed, I used the same steps to get myself out of it. I used the same strategies to prevent it as well. I will share them, but I want you not just to read it as another self-help cliché. I want you to implement the steps. I am sure you have heard the popular saying, "Knowledge is power." It is power only if you use it. Otherwise it will remain a mere piece of information if you don't put it into practice. Merely knowing something is not going to do any good in your life, but putting knowledge into practice can change your life.

So, what are those steps?

Step 1 ~ Perspective

Usually, when we hear people sharing stories about their depression, they say they feel this way because of some event that happened or, people hurt them in some way or have experienced circumstances they are not happy about. When you think about it, however, the event itself is just the fact and it cannot make anyone feel any particular way. Certain circumstances can't make a person depressed, because it is only an event which occurred. It's the meaning we give to that event that makes us feel in a certain way.

Losing a job for Ken may mean a devastating end to a career, yet Daniel will look at it as an opportunity to find a more fulfilling and a better-paying job. In direct sales, getting a "no" for Ken means rejection and failure, and for salesman Daniel it means a learning curve and a challenge to keep persisting until he gets a "yes."

For Ken, difficulty will mean a severe hardship, and for Daniel it will be a temporary challenge while having an opportunity to witness a testimony of how the living God answered his prayers and who helps in difficult times.

Having a break-up of a romantic relationship for Ken might mean the end, and Daniel will perceive it as the beginning, because now he has the opportunity to find true love and have a fulfilling relationship. Would you agree Ken would be most likely depressed and Daniel would be totally fine, and actually even eager and enthusiastic about his future? Why? It's the same situation. Why would Ken and Daniel feel totally different?

Would you agree with me – that the way we perceive any situation depends on what perspective we have and what meaning we give to that situation? The situation that occurred is just a fact by itself. It's the person's negative perspective about the situation, or his focus on the negative parts of his life and a certain way of thinking that causes his depression.

Brother, I have written a separate letter to you about the power of perspective, so I won't repeat myself now. There is a reason why I asked you to reflect on what I wrote in that letter. I believe this is the crucial element of self-management because depending on your perspective about any given situation, you will make different decisions about the path you are going to take – what you are going to do about it. Naturally, your decisions and the choices which follow will create further circumstances. I believe the very first step to handling depression is choosing your perspective, which will empower you and help you see the benefits in your specific situation.

Step 2 ~ Focus

The way you feel depends on what you think about most of the time. It's very easy to put yourself into a depressive state. All you need to do is constantly think about the negative parts of your life. If you start focusing on what is going wrong in your life, what you are unhappy about, who disappointed or betrayed you, how hurt and lonely you are, how you failed to achieve something, what bad things happened to you – depression will definitely find you.

If you want to change your inner state, you must change your thought pattern and what you focus on. You must stop constantly thinking about what you are unhappy about, what happened to you, what you've lost or don't have yet. Because you will experience that which you focus on. Focus on what you have. Focus on opportunities. Focus on your abilities. Focus on the progress you have made and be excited about moving forward to reach your final destination.

You might ask, "How do I stop thinking about pain when it overshadows anything else and it's all I can think about?" I know. It's not easy. There are some aspects, though, to be mindful about, which can help you focus on the right things. It might take an effort at first. Dark thoughts will come without a doubt; it's not realistic that now suddenly you will entertain only good, happy thoughts. But with discipline, you can train your own mind to choose empowering perspective and focus on the good.

> *"Finally, brethren, whatever things are true, whatever things are noble, whatever things are just, whatever things are pure, whatever things are lovely, whatever things are of good report, if there is any virtue and if there is anything praiseworthy – meditate on these things." (Philippians 4:8)*

You must understand and always remember – *you have a choice* in what you decide to focus on. On a rainy day, you can choose to focus on how sad and gloomy it is that there is no sun, that it's wet outside and inconvenient to carry umbrella. Or you choose to be grateful that you have a home, warm clothes and an umbrella when rainy days come. It would be much worse if there was no rain and so praise be to God that He sends the rain. What you focus on will determine your experience on a rainy day, and it is entirely up to you what kind of experience you will have. The choice is yours.

Start noticing small details that give you joy. Look around attentively and see how much good you already have in your life. Stop for a moment and think. What are you sincerely grateful for? What would make your life more exciting and interesting? What would fire up the enthusiasm in you to move on and create the life that you desire?

Make no mistake, it is not going to be easy at first, when you make the effort and deliberately try to control what thoughts dominate in your mind. When you catch yourself drifting into your "sad world," immediately stop entertaining those thoughts and remember good and exciting times, new opportunities that seem promising, what you could be thankful for or anything that will make you feel good. Let dark thoughts pass. Don't notice them. And even if you focused on them for a moment – let them go.

Appreciate what you have and what you can do. Think about those you love and those who love you. Connect with your loved ones or friends and share your joy and progress. Intentionally think about what you are grateful for, what makes you feel uplifted and happy, what gives you joy, what you've accomplished so far. If you can't think of what you can be grateful for, I must ask you one very easy question: What would it be like if you lost that which you already have? It is not a rhetorical question. Don't rush through it, but think about it. I will be honest, I never thought of my blessings until I lost what I had.

- Only after I lost my arm did I understand how blessed I was to be able to make a simple sandwich or easily button my clothing.
- Only when I lost my legs did I realize what a treasure it was to have legs to be able get out of bed and go anywhere I pleased.
- And only when I lost everything that made my life beautiful, even the simple things I took for granted, did I understand how fortunate I was.

There are millions of people who don't have what you have and cannot do what you can. I see many people who simply don't appreciate what they have, because they are used to it and it has become a norm for them. I believe going to a rehab center or visiting sections of the city where homeless are settled would make a big difference in their understanding how blessed they are.

If you don't have anything exciting going on, find at least one thing you could be grateful for and focus on that. The more you focus on the beautiful, the more you will notice it surrounding you. Thoughts about painful experiences or negative circumstances change into a question to yourself, "How I would like it to be?" And allow yourself to dream about it.

Do me a favor: Imagine your mind is a blank piece of paper, and your thoughts are your pencils. What color pencils will you use to draw on that paper? The choice is yours. Will you use the dark color pencils, or will you choose the myriad of other colors available to you? Consciously train your mind to think of uplifting, hopeful things. Soon you will notice that it's getting easier and easier to do that.

<u>Ask yourself questions that will shift your mind toward the gratitude and solution.</u> There are times when we ask ourselves questions and the answers that our mind comes up with determine our further conclusions and decisions. It is another crucial aspect of managing your focus and directing your mind in the right direction. Let's take some very common questions people ask during tough times: Why do I have to go through this? How could this person do this to me? Why does this always happen to me? Why can't I finally be happy?

What kinds of answers will these kinds of questions give you? These are the kinds of questions that already have a predisposition for answers that will make you feel like a victim, helpless in your situation. These questions are based on emotions and they are not going to bring a substantial answer. These questions become more like statements, and your mind naturally will focus on anything that confirms that statement. Guess how you will feel? Believe me, asking questions like these is one of the fastest ways to become depressed.

By changing the questions you ask yourself, you can direct your mind into an entirely different direction. Once your mind is directed the right way, you will think hopeful thoughts, you will see the solutions and will feel empowered to change your negative circumstances.

Start asking yourself questions that will shift your focus, those that are solution-based. Ask questions that will enable you to deal with the situation you're facing. As an example, let's see how we can replace the earlier questions:

- "Why do I have to go through this?" This question will only make you focus on how bad it is and how unlucky you are. This question could be replaced with, "What can I do to resolve this?"

- "How could this person do this to me?" This question will not provide an answer, but will make you relive the betrayal and pain. Replace it with, "Being in a position that this person brought me into, what can I do to improve the situation and move on?"
- "Why do things like this always happen to me?" Replace this question with, "What is the solution to this, and what conclusions can I make so it doesn't happen again?"
- "Why can't I finally be happy?" Replace this question with, "What needs to change for me to feel happy? What are possible ways to make the changes I need to make?"

Train yourself to ask questions that will be substantial and valuable to you, questions that will help you see the way out of the pit you fell into, questions that will enable you to take action. Start changing the circumstances that caused you to feel depressed.

Deliberately support your decision to maintain your focus on your blessing and get away from emptiness and negativity. Read books that will inspire you and encourage you, strengthen your faith, give you knowledge, and contribute to your personal growth. Read your Bible to gain wisdom. Start spending time with people, who have strong faith, who have uplifting attitudes and will encourage you. Surround yourself with friends who have a purpose and aim to improve themselves and their lives, people who are passionate to make a difference rather than the ones who aimlessly waste their days leading a mediocre life spending countless hours watching television or gossiping about others.

Carefully choose with whom you associate and how you spend your time. Have you heard the saying that, "You become who you spend most of your time with?" Why? You will adopt their beliefs, philosophy of life, their mindsets and standards. Surround yourself with those who have higher standards in life, who will believe in you and support you.

Just as you exercise to be physically fit, you need to support your inner being. It might not be easy at first, but you can discipline yourself and deliberately start doing it. Constant focus on either good or bad is simply a habit. The way habits are formed is by doing the same action repeatedly.

A good way to create a habit of focusing on good is to spend at least 10-15 minutes a day thinking about what you are grateful for. Gratitude makes a tremendous difference on your overall inner state. I personally listen to instrumental music or worship songs and spend time bringing my gratitude before the Lord for what He has done in my life. But don't do it just to put a check-mark next to the task because you have to. Also, saying "Well, yeah, I am thankful for it," without giving much thought to it won't make any difference. Many say they are thankful while actually feeling discontent or feeling the lack of something that they wished they had. Feel it. Truly feel how sincerely thankful you are. Take some time to ponder on your many blessings and why you are thankful for each one. Feel it until every part of your inner being is filled with gratitude.

Another good way is to start writing down notes for what you are grateful for. Every evening, after you're done with your day, write down the many good things that happened that day and what you feel grateful for. I don't understand the mystery of it, but there was a big difference in how I felt waking up in the morning when the night before I thought of things that irritated and made me unhappy, or when I went to sleep thinking of what I was grateful for. After I thought of little joys that I had and progress I made, in the morning I would wake up feeling sincerely grateful, happy and enthusiastic to continue my journey. I felt ready to bring my life to the next level. When you discipline yourself to spend time on thoughts filled with gratitude, it trains your mind to focus on the good rather than the negative.

Finally, take your eyes off of yourself. By that I mean, "Think of someone else besides yourself." Find someone who needs your help and put your mind and efforts into helping them. Focus on how you can be of service to others. It will make a difference not only in the life of the person to whom you are serving, but also it will be a blessing and will make a huge impact in your own life.

Step 3 ~ Deliberately Cut Memories of the Past Be Present: Focus on How You Can Create the Life You Desire

Completely cut off your deliberate memories of that which makes you feel depressed. Since your feelings highly depend on what you think about, you will only hurt yourself by constantly thinking about painful events that happened in the past. Maybe the event happened six months ago, a year ago, or maybe ten years ago, but you can still keep that event fresh and feel the pain or anger just by constantly thinking about it.

Would you listen to a song that irritates you and makes you feel bad? I don't think so. Why would you go back in your memories to the past events that make you relive pain, anger and any negative feelings? Why would you go back to those memories over and over and by thinking about them, not allowing yourself to heal?

Do you realize that it is not the past event anymore, but it is you hurting yourself by holding on to memories and reliving them in your mind? Past events are only the facts of your life. It's all gone today. It's history and you can't change it. Sure, today you might have some consequences that are directly related to the past events. Some of those consequences are not going to be changed or forgotten, because you have to face them daily.

For example, I still face the consequences of my car accident. I live with it from the moment I wake up till the moment I fall asleep. But I don't feel the pain of the event anymore because today, I look at it differently and I changed the circumstances that made me depressed. In case you have some consequences that are permanent, work on your perspective about them. What good can you extract from your experience? What are the benefits to you or your loved ones? Maybe they will be beneficial in the future? Give meaning to the event which will empower you, and it will not pull you down.

Every day is a new day and it's up to you whether you will remember this day as another wasted day on your painful memories or as your stepping stone toward the life you desire. Every day you are given twenty-four hours that are new and clean. It is not your past that has the power to decide what those hours are going to look like, but you, your new choices and new decisions. It all depends on what you choose.

You may choose to live your life in gratitude for what you already have and faith that it is going to get better. You can choose to use the given time to think about how you could create a better future or make a difference in someone's life. At the same time, you may also choose to use this time to go back in your memories and dwell on what happened to you, who hurt you, who betrayed you, etc. But what's the point? Where will you end up wasting your given time on such memories?

If you keep thinking about what happened yesterday, a year ago or earlier – you will stay where you were. Your life will move forward only if you look ahead of you. Try to imagine how you would be able to move forward while going backwards. You won't be able to move forward, will you?

Let's face it, dwelling on painful memories won't make you feel better.

What's the point of going back to them? You only torture yourself by reliving the pain over and over again. If you want to move on in your life, stop thinking about your painful, past events. If you can't let go of the mistake you have made or you can't forgive yourself for making a choice, try to change your perspective. Mistakes are not the reason for you to feel bad about yourself or beat yourself up for making the wrong decision. We all make mistakes.

The only way to ensure you will never make mistakes is to do nothing. Take past wrong choices or bad experiences as lessons for your growth and wisdom of what you will do better in the future. Simply ask yourself what you can learn, close that page and chapter and move on. Next time you will do better, because you had the lesson. And meanwhile, make necessary conclusions, learn your lesson and take a step forward. Today, dwelling on those painful memories won't change anything, because those events are sealed with time and it's all history. Today you can do something to create a better, more fulfilling future. Don't waste it. Don't look back. Turn your sights to the destination you want to go, take a deep breath, smile, and open a new page of your life.

Every day you can begin your change. Your faith, your empowering attitude, and the actions you choose can make the changes you need. Focusing on the blessings you have today will keep you away from depression. Finding ways to improve your circumstances will make a difference and might even change the direction of your life. What had happened to you earlier is not the judge that hands down the sentence for the years ahead. It is God's will for your life and your new choices will determine what your future will look like. If you did not succeed a year ago or yesterday, it does not mean you won't succeed today or tomorrow. Your past events cannot determine how you feel nor can they determine your future, if you decide not to dwell on your past, but move forward creating the life you desire.

Step 4 ~ Take Action to Change What's Depressing You

I always had a strict inner dialogue with myself: "If you don't like something, don't sit and complain about it. Change it. Complaining won't help. Change will."

You must change what you are not happy about if you want to get out of depression. It is imperative to keep your focus on that which uplifts you, gives you hope and empowers you. Having that in mind, there is one detail: chances are, if you make the effort to be positive, while continuing to live your life in circumstances that make you feel unhappy and depressed, after a while you might say to yourself, "This positive thinking stuff is nonsense." You can't lie to yourself anymore because the truth is that you have circumstances that make you feel depressed and you are not satisfied and not happy. So while you make the effort to keep your mind away from that which makes you depressed and focus instead on that which empowers you, work on making changes that will alter those circumstances which caused your depression in the first place.

For example, it was unbearable to me that I suddenly woke up in the world where no longer was I able to take care of my personal needs independently. I felt a burning contempt deep inside my inner being towards my helplessness to provide for even the simplest things, so I resolved to get back my self-sufficiency and continuously aimed for it in every decision I made, every action I took. This way, eventually I totally changed my position and no longer am I depressed about it.

Another thing that caused deep depression was being imprisoned by the walls of my home. Overnight my most valuable things were wrenched away from me: no longer had I access to be connected with my friends as I used to; there was no way for me to continue leading my life as I did before, and there were no opportunities to be useful to myself or others.

I was in such deep pain that I couldn't stand the thought that this was how I was going to have to live. I was so tired of hopelessness and sadness that I decided to change it all and I was ready to fulfill my desires, no matter how much effort it might take. I figured out what would make a difference and got to work to make it happen.

This way, my actions initiated a beautiful change in my life and today my life is completely transformed – I am self-sufficient, have full access to get out, go to work and travel, be connected with other people and contribute to others. I eliminated the cause of my depression and it's no longer there because it has no reason to be there.

If your circumstances are beyond any possibility of changing them, then change your perspective about them. For example, there was nothing I could do to get my own legs back or regain the function of my left arm. I still tried to do what I could do (get prosthetic legs and surgery/various procedures to recover the function of my paralyzed arm). But when medical reasons forced me to discontinue using prosthetic legs, and no therapy or surgery could improve the function of my arm, I came to the point when I had to accept my personal circumstances. I found an empowering meaning to my accident and by changing my perspective, I changed my point of view about having to use the wheelchair and having to live with only one hand. No longer do I suffer from the agony of loss.

I will repeat myself only to stress the importance of this simple truth: check your beliefs and perspectives. Ask yourself questions that will help you find the meaning which will comfort you and allow you to enjoy your life journey. For now, let's look into what you can change.

Action Item #1: Create Your Own Strategy for Change

Your empowering perspective, positive thought pattern and action for change have to occur at the same time. Your action is absolutely necessary in order to change what you are not happy about. Sometimes certain situations occur and people come into our lives without us doing anything. God makes miracles like that. The Lord also provides the opportunity, sends the right people to us, and inspires us to implement some idea. However, we might miss it if we don't use the opportunity (whether due to the laziness or fear of failure, fear of the unknown or fear of obstacles).

Do you think I would have connected with Michael if I was too lazy to spend countless hours of diligent work researching the Internet? Never. It started from the inspiration and it evolved into an opportunity only when I took action and worked hard. Also, I really doubt you would be reading my letters if I had not paid attention to the inspiration that the Lord put into my heart. They would not have been written if, instead of diligently working on them, I had chosen to sleep longer in the mornings before I went to work, spent my evenings watching television, or spent my weekends lavishing in my selfish leisure time. I am also sure I would have accomplished much more by now if I had used my time more wisely and worked in a more disciplined manner.

I have to admit that I did miss some of my goals because I was procrastinating. We might miss jumping into the last wagon of the train, so to speak, if we procrastinate. Time is ticking; it does not stop to wait for us to make decisions. The inspired and yet unfulfilled idea might become a missed chance that was given to us.

When I would say to myself, "Don't sit and complain, change it," my focus was always on the solution instead of what was wrong or how big the problem was. I asked myself questions that helped me to see that I could change what I was not happy about. It directed my mind into "possibility thinking." I started thinking about any possible ways as to how I could change my life conditions, instead of thinking of how bad and painful and desperate it was. I developed the attitude that certain circumstances were not eternal, that they can be changed if only I looked to see how it could be done.

When I faced depression and decided to get out of it, I asked what seemed to be very simple questions, but the answers transformed my life. I used them again later on because they proved to be my roadmap for change. Again, here are the questions I asked and, hopefully, they will get you started on the same journey:

- What do I want? What needs to change in my life for me to feel fulfilled and happy?
- How can I make that happen? What are the possible ways to implement change?
- Where do I need to start? What specific actions must I take to turn my desire into reality?
- What is the first goal that will get me closer to my desired result?

When you lay out your strategy, bring your focus on the stepping stone – the goal.

Action Item #2: Have a Compelling Goal

One of the benefits of setting a goal is that it will shift your focus onto something different from what you're depressed about. And when you have something that you really desire, you will be eager and enthusiastic to seek possible ways to achieve that goal in your life. Your mind will be captured by your enthusiasm as you seek out new possibilities to attain your goal. Remember, depression is the result of your thoughts about why you are not happy. When you have a compelling goal and are busy figuring out how you can bring it to fruition, you won't have time to think about bad things that happened earlier, or spend time focusing on current problems and how bad things may be. You will be occupied with your task and it will shift your focus in a different direction. So, have a goal that you are passionate and enthusiastic about.

If you've noticed reading my personal experience above – every time I had a goal, it seemed that something inside of me would "wake up." I would get excited about achieving it. It would totally change my inner state. My apathy and hopelessness were replaced by enthusiasm, determination to take action, and the tenacity to see it through. In short, while I was working on my goals, I didn't have time nor the interest to think about the tragedy and the loss.

In addition, when you take action toward your goal, you will be changing circumstances that were the cause of your depression in the first place. You will see that you are getting closer and closer to your desired result, that everything is changing for the better, and your inner state will automatically change. As you achieve your goals to improve your life, you will have a sense of progress, and that will make you feel alive and joyous. That's how nature is – be it plant, animal or a human being – it either grows or dies, right? There is no "in between."

If there is no way to change the circumstances that got you into your depression, by achieving another goal that is meaningful and important to you will shift your focus from depressive thoughts. The new excitement and anticipation of your new desire will become a part of your life. Either way, having your mind occupied with productive thoughts and changing your circumstances and achieving compelling, exciting, goals will make a big difference in how you feel.

Action Item #3: Use Your Goals as Stepping Stones

When you know what you want and how you could make it happen, set your first goal that will get you closer toward accomplishing your desired result. Remember, without a goal your dream will remain a mere wish. If you decide to aim for the stars and set a lofty goal (which I highly encourage you to do), and know it will take some work and time to accomplish, break it down into smaller, achievable goals. These little goals will be the stepping stones that will bring you to the finish line.

Also, set the date by which you must complete each goal. Your journey toward achieving your goal without a deadline may last forever, and there is a possibility you will never get it done. In the process you might have a lot of distractions, which can easily shift your focus away from your goal. Having a clear goal and a deadline to achieve each segment of your goal will work to your benefit, because it will keep you focused on it consistently.

Make sure your goal is always in your awareness. If you need to, write it down and have it in a place where you can always see it to keep you focused. Life might present you with many distractions, and you must not allow them to divert your attention from your goal. Otherwise, you will join the crowd which keeps setting goals but rarely achieves them. Ask yourself whether your friends are goal setters or goal achievers, and spend far more time with those who put their minds to something and achieve it. Surround yourself with positivity.

So, answer yourself what you really want. Try to imagine what your life would be like if you already had what you desire. Are you ready to make an effort to turn this dream into your reality? How can you make that happen? Where do you need to start? What is your first step? Don't rush to say, "Oh that's not going to happen; it's not possible." Anything is possible if you really want it, relentlessly work toward accomplishing it and have unshakable faith that you will succeed.

I was in a quite desperate position when I asked myself these questions. My dream seemed to be an absurd, unachievable fantasy. Yet I felt so much contempt for my situation that I was ready to do whatever it took to change. I never questioned whether it was possible or not, nor did I allow myself to think in terms of how big my aspirations were nor how small chances were of making them come true. I decided what I wanted to bring to fruition, then I strategized possible ways to achieve what had to be done and took immediate action.

I started with small goals and small steps to move myself forward. When I was discharged from the hospital and began my rehabilitation process, my first goals were to be self-sufficient in my simple daily routine: independently roll over in bed, sit up from a lying position; then independently dress, make a cup of coffee and my breakfast – all using one hand. Now those memories make me smile.

At the time, every such activity was a huge challenge to me, requiring tremendous effort, consistent attempts and perseverance. Every time I found a way to do things by myself was a huge victory for me. Every time

I was able to do something independently was a step closer to my ultimate aspiration – to not have to depend on anybody.

By aiming and achieving my little goals, it strengthened me and increased my confidence for achieving my greater goals. Over time, these small achieved successes compounded; they changed my position. I came out of ICU having absolutely no strength and no ability to do anything independently, except open/close my eyes or speak (and even the latter required efforts), and after half of the year I was staying at the Orthopedic Center in another city able to take care of myself independently and training to walk with artificial legs. Even though my mom was with me at the Ortho Center, I was aspiring to do things independently, knowing that it was a little stepping stone to reach my ultimate goal. As time flew by, I was setting bigger goals which, three years later, resulted in traveling independently across the globe to America, laying the groundwork for completely changing my life circumstances.

With God's help and the strength that I received from Him, I successfully overcame my obstacles and today I live independently in spite of my injuries. Goals and aspirations can have a significant value in life if you take the process seriously and work consistently and diligently to achieve the accomplishment.

Action Item #4: Take Action Once You Have a Goal

It is absolutely critical to take action once you set your goal. I am sure you know that a big reason why many never achieve their goals is simply because they don't do the work it takes to turn their goal into reality. We all know how easy it is to set a goal and then just talk about it. It is exciting when you share your dream with others and receive support from your family, friends and colleagues. It gets tougher though, when it comes to the actual execution of your intention. An example would be of someone deciding to lose twenty pounds after the first of the New Year. This person, with good intent, joins a gym or a health club and assiduously begins working out each day, until life intrudes.

The baby's crying kept them awake all night and they need more sleep. They have a big day at work and have to be fresh. They're tired and don't feel like it. They're embarrassed about their body and what it looks like in front of others. Or, whatever excuse is convenient that keeps them from doing the work that must be done.

There are many reasons why people don't take action to implement their initial intentions, or why they give up during their journey. Regardless of what these reasons or excuses might be, the fact is that no matter how much you are going to dream, no matter how strong and sincere your intentions might be, no matter how big and precise your goals, or how perfect your strategy and action plans are, and no matter how much you talk and think about it – none of it will have any value or chance for success if you don't do the simple but absolutely imperative part: the actual work.

Without action, your dreams and goals are going to remain just that, dreams and goals. They will be nothing more than mere wishes. Dreaming about your desired outcome without taking the right action, but expecting it to happen somehow by itself, eventually becomes a delusion. While it is very important to have a clear vision of where you are going, and make the plans and develop your personal roadmap planning how you are going to get there, it is only the appropriate action that will get you there.

There is the opinion that all I need to do is pray and believe, that I don't need to do anything else; all is going to come to pass, if I just believe. I think it is a great misconception that leads many to a big disappointment and, ultimately, falling away from faith. Yes, I did have numerous experiences when the Lord answered my prayers, delivering solutions without me making any effort. I admit that was absolutely incredible.

In other cases, He connected me with people, who helped me with certain needs, or the Lord miraculously healed me after prayer. While at times our Lord does make changes in our lives without our input, in many cases we must do the work. We live in a physical world, and we must take action and do the work in order to get the desired outcome. I fully realize that I'd still be living imprisoned by the walls of my home in misery and reliving the horrible grief of my loss if I had not initiated the change and had not worked as hard as I did. The Lord will inspire us to do something, but then we must act on it. Our prayers might be answered by inserting new people in our lives that we need to proceed further with our goal, but then we must work on it. We also might get the opportunity that we needed, but we have to use that opportunity and sometimes even to be the ones to initiate the action. The Lord may open the doors, but then we must equip ourselves with faith, step out of our comfort zone and make that first step to enter through those doors.

The biggest changes that greatly impacted my life were when I acted on inspiration, or when I stepped out in faith trusting that the Lord my God would bless my efforts. And with faith and inner peace as my guide, I always worked relentlessly. Remember: No action will bring you no results, and most likely you will not like it. Zero multiplied a thousand times will remain zero. On the other hand, what are you going to get when you multiply one a thousand times? Far more than zero times zero. Even small, consistent actions compounded over time will make a big difference in your life.

I believe you agree with me and I don't need to try to convince you that it is imperative to do the actual work if you want your desired vision to become your reality. Don't let any obstacles stop you. Go for your goal until you complete it. If needed, re-evaluate your strategy of how you are trying to reach your destination, but never give up on your destination.

Step 5 ~ Find Your Source of Inner Strength

Where do you get inner balance, peace and joy? As I've already shared, my strength has a rock solid foundation, which could not be shaken by any storms of life. The reason I have unbreakable inner strength is because of my faith.

Jesus Christ of Nazareth is my Rock. He is my strength and He is the reason I was able to do what I have done so far. It's because of Jesus and my faith that I always have hope in the darkest nights and endurance in the storms. Faith is my rock solid foundation on which I build everything else. I often hear people saying, "Inga, you are so strong. Where do you get this inner strength?" Well, that's the answer. My inner strength, peace and hopeful look into the future comes from my faith.

> *"I will love You, o Lord, my strength. The Lord is my rock and my fortress and my deliverer; My God, my strength, in whom I will trust; My shield and the horn of my salvation, my stronghold." (Psalm 18)*

> *"For who is God, except the Lord? And who is a rock, except our God? It is God who arms me with strength, and makes*

my way perfect. He makes my feet like the feet of deer, and sets me on my high places." (Psalm 18)

"But blessed is the one who trusts in the Lord, whose confidence is in him.
They will be like a tree planted by the water that sends out its roots by the stream.
It does not fear when heat comes; its leaves are always green.
It has no worries in a year of drought and never fails to bear fruit." (Jeremiah 17: 7-8 NIV)

"Jesus answered and said to her, 'Whoever drinks of this water will thirst again, but whoever drinks of the water that I shall give him will never thirst. But the water that I shall give him will become in him a fountain of water springing up into everlasting life.'" (John 4: 13-14)

When you live your life in faith in Jesus Christ and you put your confidence in the Lord about your future and any circumstances which may confront or concern you, you will always have the hope that the Lord will pick you up even when there is nothing in your life that gives you any sign for hope.

When you get on your knees before the Lord and ask Him to give you strength, He will give you the kind of strength that will not fade away and will get you through anything in life. It may sound like a cliché or some fantasy theory, but I am talking about real experience. It is not some religious fairytale. Your inner state and circumstances change when by faith you put your confidence in the Lord and bring your requests to Father God in Jesus Christ's name. I always feel stronger after prayer and reading the Holy Scriptures. He will give you inner peace and joy, which cannot be given by anything else in this world.

Often people feel secure and confident about their lives because of the good income, well-established career or reputable people they may know. But it is not a secret that circumstances can change overnight, people can abandon you and your peace and sense of security might dissipate before your very eyes. However, the assurance about your life will not be taken away from you by any circumstances when you put your trust and confidence in the Lord God. Inner strength and tranquility you receive from the Lord are going to be in your heart even if you find yourself in the midst of the storm. That kind of peace surpasses our understanding and yet, it is going to be in your heart at all times. There are countless people who experience the same feeling of peace and joy and reassurance; it is not just my testimony.

When you study Holy Scriptures and live by faith, you will always be filled with strength and will have hope no matter what is going on in your life. There were countless times when, after praying, my inner state would change – sometimes overnight or even immediately during the prayer. My total apathy, unwillingness or interest to see anybody or do anything would be replaced by a strong desire to live and the eagerness to take action to make a change in my life. To my surprise, I even found the joy for life and expectation of something good and beautiful. My irritation and anger would turn into resolve to do whatever it took to make a change. Inner emptiness and exhaustion would suddenly change into inspiration, easiness and strength to keep on going.

As I told you, there were times in my life when, out of despair, I was an inch away from falling into deep depression, and my hope that the Lord was going to deliver me from trouble was the only thing that kept me from giving up. And my hope in Jesus never failed me. When people betrayed me, abandoned me and hurt me when I sincerely trusted them, the Lord was there with me at all times.

He was faithful even when I was not. He never forsook me. I would always receive help after my prayer to the Lord. When I was left in despair and there was nobody who could help me, my Lord did. After praying, opportunity would show up out of nowhere and my circumstances would change in the most amazing ways. Also, I always felt different when I asked Jesus to strengthen me. The differences afterwards showed me that prayer is not just some symbolic ritual, but carries great power when fueled by belief.

We all are spiritual beings and our source of inner strength is not tangible. How many times have you acquired something you wanted so badly, and then soon it no longer gave you joy? How many times did circumstances that first gave you a sense of security, over time changed and pulled your security out from under you?

Look for the peace, security, inner strength and joy in a prayer, not in the desired circumstances or various things that you can buy. By faith, put your confidence in the Lord, then you will be like a tree planted next to a source of water, and you will never be thirsty, because the Lord will be your source of strength, assurance about your life, peace and joy for your life.

In addition to my inner strength, my faith empowered me to set my aim high and gave me keen ambition to achieve goals that would improve my life. It formed the foundation for my perspective, which enabled me to accept my new life and any challenges I had to face.

This is my foundation, my rock. I will repeat myself: If you build your life house on the foundation that is Jesus Christ, your house will be unbreakable despite any storms. Having your foundation strong as a rock will make you unbreakable. It will enable you to have unwavering faith. Then you will be able to choose the right perspective in any given situation, and thus you will make the right choices what you are going to do about them. You will not doubt and will look into the future with assurance that all is going to work together for good.

There won't be anxiety, fear for the future or despair. Hope will give you the endurance to break through the obstacles and go through any storm of life, until the time comes when you see your rainbow.

As you see, brother, positive attitude and inner strength do not happen out of nowhere. I worked a lot until my current perspective about life and attitude became my natural thought pattern. I never stopped working with myself. You and anyone else can develop the empowering mindset and inner state that will make your life experience fulfilling.

Finally, I just wanted to say last thoughts. It's easy to sit and complain. It's painless to blame someone else for your problems rather than taking responsibility for your choices and circumstances today. It is much easier to say to yourself and the rest of the world, "Probably this is my fate," or "I am not that strong," and simply go along with whatever life delivers. It is easy to stop fighting and give up. Giving up doesn't require any talent; nor does it take any effort. Usually this is the choice of those who seek an excuse as to why they live the way they do instead of making the effort to take charge of life and make a difference. It's an easier route, but this way a person can waste many years of a gift of life being in pain, hate and anger.

It requires boldness to look up and affirm that life is going to be beautiful in spite of it all. And yes, it does require fortitude and endurance. It requires a decision to be resilient and relentless no matter who or what you are going to face. It requires courage and determination to look straight into the eyes of problems and fear, and declare that you will change those circumstances. It requires resolve and tenacity to design your life the way you desire, and not how outside events try to arrange it. It requires perseverance and patience to go against the storm.

And only those who really have a desire to win in life go against the wind if they need to. They don't allow negative emotions to take over and dominate. They don't allow themselves to give up. They do whatever it takes to keep going. When in their journey the storm shows up, they don't try to hide from it to make it easier; they remember why they must go on and relentlessly continue on walking. When they walk in the dark night, they keep their eyes on hope, which shows them the path in the darkness and encourages them to keep on going. It is not easy, but it's that kind of people who are able to change their circumstances and live their purpose.

I want you to know that you are one of those people who can call themselves "winners." I know there is a lot of strength within you. You have courage and determination. Remember how much you already have achieved and what kind of hits from life you were able to take. I will be honest with you (as I always have), not everyone would be able to handle it. But you did, and you have not given up. The truth is that you can do so much more than you think. I believe that with the Lord's help you will overcome. There is a reason why you had to go through all this and I believe you will see it once you go through this tough time and look back. I know all these problems and challenges will make you even stronger than you are today. They will teach you valuable lessons. But now, you have to pull your faith and your inner strength together and make your best effort, so you will come out of this battle a winner.

Just as your choice of the attitudes and personal actions will determine whether you win or lose, it depends only on you whether you will live in pure joy or retreat to the depths of sadness and despair. I want you to really understand that deep inside – you can choose to which shore you want to arrive, and it all depends on you which direction you take.

So, be strong and win. I love you and know that I will be right here with you whenever you need me.

Love,
Inga

10

Trip to Istanbul, Turkey

Dear Brother,

I know this time still remains in your memory. But I know you and I looked at this opportunity from different perspectives. In your opinion, this was a crazy decision I was making. Quite frankly, my decision superseded even my own expectations for what I was capable of doing. Little did we know how life transforming it would be. I never talked much about my feelings or this trip. After more than a decade, I want to share with you the side of the story which you never knew.

Enjoy, and most of all, I want you to ask yourself: What direction would my life had taken if I had listened to the fear of unknown, the fear of disappointment instead of stepping out of my comfort zone in faith?

What would change in your life, if you stepped out of your comfort zone and go after your dream?

Much love,
Inga

* * *

My decision to go to Turkey shocked many people. No one knew I was doing the research to seek help worldwide and the results of my endeavor surprised many. I watched people experience all types of reactions to my news, from being flabbergasted to variations on comments like, "I was out of my mind to go all the way to Turkey in my physical condition."

Add to the fact that I was traveling to another country to meet someone whom I had never met in person, someone I didn't really know. On top of that, it was for a one-time visit: the specialist I was flying to meet was from another part of the globe, which basically meant that after this meeting I would likely never see him again. People could not understand the point of putting so much time and effort and savings into something that seemed so doubtful and temporary at best.

And in the back of my mind, I had a nagging thought. "Wasted money, wasted time for a consultation which may turn out to be futile." Our family had used all of our savings for my hospitalization and rehabilitation, and we did not really have discretionary funds to pay for my and my friend's airfare, plus the additional expenses for our stay in Istanbul for five days. Doubts and fear of disappointment were like my shadow every day.

Nevertheless, I felt total peace within. All I wanted was someone to look at my prostheses and give me some direction. I needed help, even if this was to be a one-time consultation. Deep in my heart I knew this was the answer to my prayers and I would miss my chance if I didn't go. I decided not to listen to anyone, and not pay attention to those who doubted the singularity of my goal. I knew it was my opportunity and I was not going to miss it because someone had a different opinion about it. My parents did not to argue with my idea. They had been watching me in pain as I was striving to walk again, and this foreign stranger seemed to be their hope as well.

Both parents felt easier about me seeing this unknown person as I shared with them how caring he was not only for solely prosthetic issues, but even for my travel arrangements and my stay in Istanbul. Feeling total peace about my journey and having full support from my parents, I started making travel arrangements. I asked my friend Renata to go with me, found money to pay for all our expenses, and made all the necessary arrangements to stay in Istanbul.

Since we were planning to remain there for five days, I thought it would be great to have someone local there to guide us and show us around. Giving careful consideration about it, I decided to notify some of my virtual friends from Turkey. For a few years I had not been anywhere besides hospitals and rehab centers, and the Internet was the only way I could get "out of my home." I spent many hours on my instant messaging program. It helped meet my need to be social and connected with people, and it was a great way to maintain my English language skills. Among my contacts from Turkey, I followed my intuitive feeling of whom I could trust. I notified three of them about my trip to Istanbul. All of them were excited that I was coming and said they'd take care of me and my friend while we are visiting their country.

It was morning when Renata and I left Lithuania, and with a connection in Frankfurt we arrived to Istanbul at 2:00 AM. My virtual friend Cengiz arranged our transportation from the airport to our hotel in Istanbul. Two of his business partners not only met us at 2:00 AM at the arrival gate at this unfamiliar airport and safely brought us to our luxurious hotel, but also they'd made arrangements with the hotel management not to charge us for our first night. With the help of the hotel's staff, we got into our room and immediately stretched out on our soft beds. It was a long, tiring trip.

Next morning, as Renata and I were starting our day and sharing our experiences of the trip, the hotel's phone rang. It was the prosthetic specialist, Michael. He said he would come to our hotel to meet with us in the evening after he had completed his lecture at one of the local prosthetic laboratories.

Since we had all day long with no agenda, Renata and I decided to enjoy our day exploring Istanbul. Our guide of the day was my other virtual friend Celil, who was a cousin of Cengiz. He was a handsome, outgoing young man who should have been a professional tour guide. He took us to downtown Istanbul, sharing with us the famous places, their history and their culture. Fascinated by the extraordinary architecture, culture and non-stop busyness of the city, my bestie and I were thrilled anticipating the most important moment of our trip.

At the agreed time, Michael called our room to let us know he was at the hotel, and we went down to the lobby to meet this kind-hearted stranger. As soon as we came up to him and introduced ourselves, I felt an indescribable peace inside. That second I knew how coming to Turkey to meet this man was the right choice.

Michael was very pleasant. To my surprise, we got connected instantly; it felt like we had known each other for a long time. Michael was accompanied by a local specialist, who welcomed us to her country. We shared a little bit about our trip experiences and discussed what the plan was for our stay in Istanbul. Michael told us he had some lectures to present at some local prosthetic companies, but he was going to look at my prostheses and see what was causing the excruciating pain each time I put them on. We agreed he would take a look at them the next day, first thing in the morning.

Meeting with Michael impressed us both. We saw that Michael really did care that my prostheses hurt me. It amazed both of us how a stranger could be so caring and willing to help and receive nothing in return.

Next morning the three of us met for breakfast at the hotel, and then we returned to our room so he could evaluate my prostheses. After unwrapping them and pulling them out of the box, Michael attentively looked at the sockets. He silently touched the edges of the sockets.

"You really walked with them?" Michael asked, looking at me with wonder in his eyes.

"Yes, I did," I replied. From observing his reaction, I could see he knew what I had to endure. "Well, it was very painful, but yes I did."

"Okay, let's try this."

Michael asked me if we could put them on and stand up, so he could see how they actually fit. With them on I couldn't make even one step, though. It was so painful that I could barely stand. I saw that he immediately figured out what the problem was and suggested I sit down and take them off.

After we put these devices of torture aside, Michael explained to me that it's not true that pain is an inevitable part of wearing prosthetic legs. Walking with prostheses must be comfortable; he never allowed his patients to walk while suffering pain. Michael said he could not imagine how I could possibly walk having the sockets shaped the way they were. After we talked a little more, Michael said he would be busy for the next few days, but he would like to take my legs to a workshop in another town, Izmir, to see if he could adjust them for me. We agreed on the date and the time and parted ways.

The following few days were filled with delightful surprises and fun, made possible by my virtual friends. They surpassed our expectations beyond our wildest dreams. Besides the hospitality and care from Cengiz and his cousin Celil, my third virtual friend, Cem, gave us fantastic two days of driving us around showing us the most prominent places in and around Istanbul. Among of the most memorable sightseeing events we experienced was crossing the bridge that connected Europe and Asia, and seeing first-hand the famous Istanbul mosque. We spent two days exploring Istanbul, trying authentic Turkish dishes and getting to know the culture so different from our own world. As we said our goodbyes, we hugged, thanking them for the wonderful tour and fun times, and wished the best to each of them.

I was happy to meet my internet friends, with whom I had spent countless hours online, instant messaging. Our surprises continued when on the following day Cengiz called and said his friends were waiting for us in the lobby. He apologized for not being able to meet us, but he asked his friends to take his place and make our visit in Turkey memorable.

After our brief conversation, he encouraged us not to fret, but to relax and enjoy our day. In the lobby Renata and I met Cengiz's friends, both dressed in business suits, who politely introduced themselves and offered to join them for the day. On our last day of random fun in Istanbul, Renata and I were spoiled and treated as queens the entire day. Cengiz's friends drove us to other prominent places we had yet to see, and we tried authentic Turkish coffee (which up to this day remains to be the best coffee I have ever tried), and then they took us to a restaurant which was a former castle. Renata and I were fascinated by their culture, the city's beauty and the local hospitality. Neither of us could remember the last time we felt so pampered.

After days of fun and exciting visiting, my long-awaited day came. April 18 started with joy and excited anticipation. Early that morning, Michael and another local specialist came to pick us up, and we drove to another city where prosthetic center was located. There a local team of specialists warmly welcomed us. After a brief introduction and an overview of my injury and recuperation medical history, Michael got to work.

He was surprised to hear stories of walking through the pain, being told how "this was normal, and that's how it's supposed to be." Michael explained to me once again that it is not supposed to hurt and wanted to be sure I would honestly tell him where it hurts, so he could take care of the problem. I must admit his statements still sounded completely unrealistic to me. I was used to attempt to ignore the pain, if it was tolerable. In my mind, it was not painful if I could easily tolerate it.

"Inga," Michael said. "I cannot imagine how you walked using these prostheses; it's nearly impossible to walk having this shape of the socket. But since you did walk anyway, it shows how strongly you want to walk again. I am going to help you as much as I can to fit you with comfortable prostheses. So, let's get to work. I need you to tell me exactly where it hurts, even if it's a little bit, okay?"

Without waiting for an answer, Michael began the process. He put on the prosthetic legs, helped me to stand up, and asked me where it hurt. I showed him the spots where it was painful, he marked it on the socket, took them off, and then went into the shop to make adjustments. Then we would repeat the process – Michael would come out of the workshop with my prostheses and would put them on to try his new adjustments. I would tell him where it felt uncomfortable and after he marked the spots, he would again disappear back into the shop. He worked nonstop all morning, and after lunch we got to work again.

It was amazing to watch how carefully and accurately Michael worked. It seemed like he was creating a ceramic piece of art. He was very attentive to wherever (and whenever) I felt discomfort. It was a long tiring day, but the change was noticeable; with each time I tried them on it was getting less and less painful to stand wearing my prostheses. A miracle was happening right in front of my eyes. We were getting tired, but the significant progress fueled us with excitement.

In the afternoon, Michael again came out of the shop carrying both of my artificial legs. He put them on and helped me to stand up. Michael lifted his tired eyes, looked at me and asked, "And how is the pain now?" In his voice I heard the hope that comes from someone who knew what he'd accomplished was going to work. I stood there for a moment swinging from side to side, back and forth, to see where it hurt. To my astonishment, I could not find a spot of discomfort.

"No pain!" I shouted loudly, still trying to grasp how it could really be true. Everyone in the room stopped talking and looked anxiously – waiting for my confirmation. I could tell Renata was looking into my eyes, wondering whether it was true or if I was merely willing it to be true after all we'd been through and all that Michael had done. "Yes, it's true! It's not painful anymore!" I confirmed to all those within hearing range of my voice.

After my confirmation, the whole room burst out in cheers, applause and congratulations to Michael and me. Everyone hugged each other, with a jointly-shared happiness for this amazing victory. I was shocked and amazed and still trying to grasp that my prostheses really were no longer hurting me. I couldn't believe how I was able to stand, yet to feel no pain firing throughout the nerves in my body. This was the first time in two years I stood feeling no pain.

I looked at Michael and did not know how to thank him for what he had accomplished. Single handedly, with no knowledge of my prior medical background and the pain I suffered wearing my prostheses, he solved the problems no one else could. The man seemed tired, but very happy the problem was solved. Yet in his demeanor, he was very humble, as if he hadn't done anything extraordinary. It was as though this was something he ought to do. And with his skills and knowledge, he did.

It took us about half an hour or so to drive back to Istanbul. I was in tears nearly the whole trip. As I was looking out the window, those months and days of the last two years passed by in my mind. Months of suffering were still fresh in my mind. Every single step felt like someone was stabbing me with a razor-sharp knife. People at the Ortho Center had no idea how excruciating my pain was, and I was told with a smile that pain was a part of the package. For two long years I had to deal with tormenting experience making a single step, blisters, swollen thighs and open wounds, and I was told that nothing could be done about this. And now, this extraordinary man I'd never met spends part of his day adjusting the prostheses I'd come to hate, and now I am able to stand with no pain at all! I looked at the sunset through tears of pain and happiness at the same time.

I called to him, "Michael." He turned around with a tired, yet with such a peaceful look on his face. "Michael, thank you. I can't thank you enough for what you have done."

He stopped me mid-sentence, almost embarrassed by my gratitude and said, "My pleasure Inga. I am glad I could help."

He turned back to the road towards Istanbul so he wouldn't have to see me crying. I saw that he felt uncomfortable seeing me cry, but I couldn't help it. I cried the whole trip, crying tears of joy and admiration and far too many emotions to try and describe. I guess my crushed dream and renewed hope which I held within could not be kept in my heart anymore. In my mind I kept thanking my Lord for giving me the insight to look for help on the Internet. I thanked Him for connecting me with Michael. I was astounded how everything had been arranged like a chess game. I received a clear thought to look for help worldwide; then, among countless links, I chose Michael's website; then I got this urgent feeling to write a letter and to my surprise, I received a response on the next day. And then in one week, I find out that soon after I contacted him, Michael was planning a business trip to come to a country close to Lithuania from another part of the globe. It was a miracle! It was my miracle that I have been waiting for.

As we were driving into the city, Michael invited us to join him for dinner at a Turkish national restaurant. We were all hungry and excited to try traditional Turkish food for the last time. We ended this significant, successful day celebrating our success in a beautiful Turkish restaurant, trying various authentic Turkish dishes and watching their national dances performed for the restaurant's guests. This day will stay in my memory forever.

I was watching how the Lord was making another miracle. During dinner, Michael told me that my desire to walk again and determination to reach my dream inspired him greatly. Then he said something I would have never expected him to say: That he would like to help me to get a pair of comfortable prostheses.

That was beyond what I could have ever expected, but after the day's miracle, regardless of the world distance between us, I told him how I wished he was my prosthetic specialist. Michael said he would like that as well, and we began discussing the possible ways to make it happen. He told me the trip to California would be a very challenging and expensive endeavor.

"Let's see if we can make it a little easier on everyone," he said. "I am willing to travel to Lithuania to visit the prosthetic facility where you got your prostheses. Why don't you go back there and tell them what we did, and that I would be willing to come to Lithuania and give complimentary training to your local specialists, so they can learn how to make comfortable prostheses for all their current and future patients."

It sounded like a great idea and we decided to try implementing his plan. We agreed to stay in touch, to see where it would lead. Our trip to Istanbul ended up being one of the most beautiful and amazing trips Renata and I had ever had. And I was bringing home wonderful news for my family, which I knew they could have never even dreamed about. It was hard to comprehend how a stranger would be so willing to help. I felt like I was dreaming, and kept reassuring myself that I was wide awake, and that all of this was really true. Finally, after enduring an endless desert of hopelessness, I saw a glimpse of light. This was my hope, a new beginning. And I knew it was an opportunity that God created for me. And who can close a door that God opens?

11

My Dream to Walk is Fulfilled

Dear Valdas,

Just as I have been honestly sharing my story with you, I will continue doing so, sharing my heart without filtering anything. Because you were there when these major events took place in my journey, you will read what you personally witnessed. However, there is so much of what you have not known.

May it strengthen your faith that even if your situation seems hopeless, the Lord can send you help that will pull you out of despair. He can make a way when there is none. Also, may the pursuit of my dream will give you an insight and the knowledge to the keys that open the doors of success.

The story of finally achieving the impossible is intertwined with many emotions and crucial choices I have made. The time has finally come for me to share it – to pass on the message and lessons I had to learn on my own. Since I've been writing my story openly sharing feelings, understanding and perspectives I had at the time, I will continue in the same manner. Many things have changed since then. I have changed. But I ask you please live this through with me, as we continue this journey together. While I am sharing everything just as it was then, may my experience give you insights into where we cross the fine line that leads us into the abyss.

"What are you talking about?" you might ask.

I can only answer, "You will know only as you continue reading."

Much love,
Inga

Part 1 ~ Michael's Visit to Lithuania

When my parents met us at the airport, Renata and I were probably the most excited passengers getting off the plane. We still felt like we were on cloud nine after the beautiful, most unexpected surprises of this trip. Without a doubt, the most important, most life-changing surprise was meeting the American stranger, who completely debunked all the theories about prostheses which we had been listening to for two years.

I couldn't wait to tell my parents about my new discovery. "Mom! Dad! The truth is that it's not supposed to hurt! I knew I was right. For two years, I've been suffering and listening to specialists who told me that nothing could be done to reduce the stabbing pain. And for Michael it took only several hours to fix the issue. I was able to stand and take steps – and I wasn't feeling any pain!"

Despite our travel fatigue, the whole trip home Renata and I shared what we each considered the most exciting highlights of our trip. My parents eagerly listened to stories about our adventures in Turkey, and most of all they were amazed by American specialist. They were as shocked as I was when they heard what he had to say about walking while suffering pain. And they were impressed when we told them how it took only several hours to do what we had been told by local specialists could not be done at all.

I knew what they heard was beyond what they could have ever expected. And that was just the beginning – their surprise turned into astonishment when I told them that on top of all Michael was willing to travel all the way to Lithuania to make me comfortable legs at no cost to me as well as teach our local specialists to create pain-free prostheses. We all were in wonder how this was possible. The only explanation I found for myself was – it was the answer to my prayers. Nobody knew I had been praying for this kind of miracle all this time. Nobody knew what inspired me to conduct a search worldwide for help.

Upon our return from Turkey, Michael and I continued our friendship via email. He shared with me that he enjoyed meeting me and was inspired by such a strong desire to walk again. He said he was thinking more about how he could help to fulfill my dream, and confirmed the three options he discussed at the Turkish restaurant during dinner our last night in Istanbul:

1. He would write a report to my prosthetist, explaining what he'd done to take away my pain and the techniques he'd used.
2. He offered to set up a training in Lithuania, where he would make completely new sockets for me and teach our prosthetists the technique of constructing comfortable prostheses for their patients.
3. If the first two options were not enough, he would like me to visit California and he would make legs personally.

His reflections on our meeting and his intention to continue his efforts to help me with prostheses touched me so deeply that I sat there for a moment trying to comprehend whether this was really happening. This connection totally surpassed my expectations. When in one of our initial emails Michael responded to my question as to how much the prostheses cost, I knew that having my legs done by this specialist was not going to happen. I don't recall exactly what the cost was, but I remember it was far beyond what my family could ever afford. Still, something inside pushed me to not give up, and I continued my email communication with him to find out how it was really supposed to be, so I could pass his proposal on to our local specialists. And there you go; one little email and a life-changing decision not to give up despite a "reality check" was developing into entirely new circumstances; an opportunity I could never have imagined as possible. Michael and I agreed to take action and start make things happen.

In a day or so I called Doctor Anna at the Rehab Center and shared my experience. I passed on Michael's offer to come to Lithuania and I persuaded her to invite him officially to come to the center and train the staff. As I learned, the issue I was suffering from was very common among the center's clients, and this presented a great opportunity for local prosthetists to have an American specialist train them on making prostheses comfortable and wearable. Because while I can't be certain, I believe the patients leaving the center with my condition had two choices: endure excruciating pain or store the prostheses away and use a wheelchair.

I told her I would like to visit the center and personally present Michael's offer to the director and other specialists on staff. Surprised by what I had to share with her, Dr. Anna said she was definitely interested in learning more about this person, and she arranged my meeting with the director of the center.

I never thought I'd ever return that place. When I arrived, besides the director, there was a group of specialists who gathered to hear my news. After they heard my story and news that an American specialist was willing to come to Lithuania to provide free training, they were astonished. After a short discussion, I heard a positive decision – they asked me to pass on to Michael that the center was presenting an official invitation.

After we got home, I emailed Michael immediately. He was very excited to hear my news and said that he was looking forward to seeing me again and making me comfortable legs. Michael planned to come for two weeks in about six months, around the middle of October 2002. Finally, after countless days of relentless efforts and ongoing discouragement, we had hope. My faith that it was possible turned into confidence. Now I knew. And I was not going to allow anyone to argue my aspiration claiming that it was a crazy idea and meaningless work. I was astounded how everything started unfolding – my dream to walk again was around the corner.

Soon my news reached not only many of my friends, but also the whole country: one journalist, as if he knew I had great news since my last interview, called me and assertively asked me to give him an interview for his television program. My story was not new to his viewing audience, nor was it new to the Lithuanian people. The tragic car accident I was involved in was first shown on television news right after it happened. Some of my friends learned about me losing my legs and nearly losing my life while watching television news the next day. Then my story that I was overcoming the tragedy and aimed to walk again reached the country when it was published in the major newspaper *The Morning in Lithuania* ("Lietuvos Rytas"). I received countless comments and feedback after the article came out; it seemed like the whole country was shocked yet very inspired by it. Then my recent interview for the television program *Women's Happiness* ("Moterų Laimė") was like an update of my aspiration to have legs again and rebuild my life, and it again touched many. I was not really up for doing another interview, but journalist's assertiveness won out the day. This time, I shared how my unbreakable desire and aspiration to fulfill my dream led me to seek help worldwide and the amazing results I gained through my perseverance.

After filming and the program was shown, I saw how my story inspired many not to give up after their adversity, but to do whatever it took to persevere and move on. Most interesting was that I was inspired myself. After I watched the interview from the perspective of an observer, I learned an important lesson – never give up, because ultimate victory might be one step away. I asked myself, "What would have happened if I had given up when my desire seemed impossible?"

The answer was simple: I would have continued life imprisoned and deeply depressed, not knowing that I was only one action away from realizing my beautiful dream. My experience strengthened me to continue despite the hardship and other people's opinions. It reaffirmed to me that the path I was taking was not crazy as it seemed to others, but that of an unstoppable person whose strength of will relentlessly to keep moving her forward until victory was attained. Now I was ever more certain that I was taking the right path, and felt even more empowered to break through the obstacles in my way.

Our family looked forward to Michael's visit. Countless times my parents witnessed my blind perseverance while watching the ironic looks and reactions from everyone else, especially from the prosthetic specialists. Michael was the only one besides me who believed I could walk wearing prostheses. He was the only specialist who sincerely said it was possible to fulfill my dream, which others doubted or claimed to be impossible. Mom, dad and you were eagerly looking forward to meeting Michael personally, so you could thank him for the new hope that was lit in all our hearts.

We all were thrilled preparing for Michael's arrival. My parents prepared a room for him, and just like our culture engraved in our hearts, we bought the best of every delicacy to cover the table abundantly for our guest. I set up a plan for sightseeing to show him Vilnius and its historical places, some legendary castles, and other prominent, well-known sites.

After months of communicating via email, in October 2002, Michael arrived. Despite jet lag, he seemed very excited about the trip and meeting my family. Even though my parents and Michael had to communicate through me interpreting, my family really liked Michael for his warmth and simplicity. They were astounded by the thought that Michael had traveled across the globe at his own expense so he could make prostheses for me and train our local specialists. They were overwhelmed by Michael's giving heart and sincere willingness to help. I was as astonished as they were.

Watching Michael's care for me, I kept asking myself how this was possible to have a stranger make so much effort to help someone they'd never met. Although by the time of his arrival date, I felt Michael was no longer a stranger, but a new friend.

After we returned from Istanbul, we consistently exchanged emails all those months. Besides the prosthetics, we got to talk about many other things, and thus through his emails I got a good sense of who he was as a person. My respect for him grew as I got to know him and observe his love for life. I don't think I've ever met a specialist who would love his profession so much and have such sincere concern for his patients as Michael did. Behind the specialist there was a very caring and interesting person. I started appreciating him not just as a specialist who was willing to help, but appreciating him for who he was as a person.

The first few days we stayed at our home in Vilnius. Our family and Michael were getting to know each other and bringing him to various places in the city that tourists love. Michael was fascinated by the rich history of Vilnius city and our culture. After the weekend, my father drove us to the Orthopedic Center, where Michael was pleasantly welcomed by the staff.

The center had nice hotel rooms built inside for visitors, one of which was given to Michael. I was assigned to stay upstairs on the floor where all other center's patients were. Michael came to Lithuania for two weeks and during that short period of time his goal was to make comfortable prostheses for me and to train local specialists. Michael decided he would use solely local materials and equipment to build my prostheses to demonstrate that they could do everything he did; they only needed the knowledge of making the shape of the sockets comfortable and pain-free for those they helped.

The day when I stood up wearing Michael's fabricated prostheses still remains unforgettable. There were a group of specialists who watched Michael making my prostheses all over again from scratch. And I knew I was not the only one who eagerly awaited the moment when I stood up. The only difference was that I had no doubts Michael would make it comfortable. My expectation did not disappoint me and quite surprised everyone else. When I stood up wearing my new prostheses that Michael just built, I did not feel any pain in my groin area, which was always a major problem. There was one tiny discomfort, which Michael quickly fixed. After his adjustment, I stood up again, and now with indescribable joy I exclaimed that I felt totally comfortable. It was even hard to believe that my steps were totally painless. The room was full of center's prosthetic specialists watching me in wonder.

"What? You really do not feel pain anywhere?"

Doctor Anna looked completely stunned watching me taking steps. I assured her I felt no pain, and walked out from between the parallel bars and walked in the hallway that had caused me so much indescribable pain in the past. I knew it was unbelievable to them, but it was true. It was easy to walk, and there was no pain. Now I was walking just like I had dreamed for so many days and nights. In a moment, I glanced at Dr. Anna. She was watching, speechless. Her reaction explicitly expressed, "This cannot be possible."

We both smiled and understood each other without words. I was grateful for Dr. Anna. She always nurtured my dream of walking and made my stay at the Center pleasant all those months I was there. She was on my side fighting for my ability to walk comfortably, and it was because of her effort the center agreed to meet with me. And now Michael was here at the center. Finally, I had a specialist who made comfortable legs for me, and the center had a specialist who brought new knowledge to the staff, so they could improve their care for many patients. It was a victory for our team-like efforts. That day was like an eye opener to many – there is a technique to make sockets comfortable so people can walk wearing prosthetic legs and not suffer.

Since that day, the center's staff completely occupied Michael's time. He gave lectures and teaching his techniques; then in the workshop he demonstrated his previously taught techniques in practice. He taught those at the center – physicians and specialists – the process of making pain-free prosthetics.

After Michael made me new legs, I started practicing my walking skills every single day. Michael warned me that my thighs would be changing due to strenuous physical work, and later it would be necessary to make adjustments again to fit the sockets right. While it was comfortable though, I continued improving my walking and balance skills and enjoying every moment of it.

One day, Michael surprised me again. While he was between lectures he found me in the hallway practicing my skills, and said he wanted to teach me the technique of sitting down. This was one of my questions I'd asked when I first contacted him. Michael remembered my request, and wanted to fulfill it.

"It would have been helpful to know that your one arm was paralyzed when you first emailed me." Michael was teasing me, saying that I set him up by not telling him upfront that my left arm was paralyzed.

"Well, my main focus was on my prostheses, not my arm." We both laughed at the challenge I unknowingly brought to him.

Having only one functional arm made it significantly more complicated to apply prostheses and perform all normal activities. Michael said he put a lot of thought into my request and said he wanted to try something. He showed me a step by step technique on himself. And then, ensuring me he was guarding me from falling, encouraged me to do it. It was scary to begin with, and my mind flashed back to the day at the center when I originally met my prostheses for the first time. This task required tremendous focus and balance skills. But with Michael's guidance and encouragement I did it with no particular difficulty.

"This is it?" I looked at Michael totally shocked that I did it and how easy it was. "So easy? And I kept hearing those two years I would never be able to do this because it was not possible in my physical condition!" I was overwhelmed watching how my two biggest dreams of walking without pain and sitting down and standing up independently were being fulfilled one after another.

Even though we used a bench that was higher than a regular chair's height, now I knew the technique. In addition, Michael brought me special assistive device, which made it significantly easier for me to put prostheses on. The socket fastening option that was applied to me at the center could not be done by someone like me with one hand, and I needed help with that. However, the device Michael gave me made it much easier for the person assisting me to put them on.

By the time Michael's visit was coming to the end, he made certain I was fully equipped to walk comfortably and I had mastered the techniques of sitting down and standing up by myself. Now I was even more determined to achieve my goal of returning back to life.

Michael had previously warned me that my thighs would be changing as I practiced walking every day, and multiple adjustments on a continuous basis would be necessary. He was concerned about the future adjustments and was saddened he would not be there to do it. But at this point Michael could not do anything about it and he said he would just have to trust the local specialist and asked me to keep him updated on the process and he will assist via email when needed.

Even though I was warned difficulties might occur in the future, my biggest joy was that I could walk without counting every minute, not having to wonder how much longer I could endure the stabbing pain. After so many days of struggle and the ongoing trial of my faith and endurance, I was able to take a deep breath and feel sincere joy, finally experiencing again the ability to walk and sit and stand. At this point though, I didn't know which was my bigger joy – my ability to walk again or having found a person with whom, together, we felt like one.

The truth is, Michael and I were falling in love with each other at light speed. We did not care that our closeness had to be kept in secret; we treasured the miracle of finding each other and that was the most important part.

Yes, I know. You might be shocked to hear this. All these years I was sure I would never disclose this. For more than seven years this has been my secret that I held from all. I kept this side of my story to myself as my most cherished love experience. At the same time, it's the part of my life which I can hardly remember without tears in my eyes. Remembering and telling this story is like reopening the deepest scars of my soul.

Why am I telling you about this now? I hesitated for a very long time. I did not want to bring this up and was pretty sure that I wouldn't ever do it. After a long time of careful consideration, I decided to tell you about a cornerstone of my story. It would not be complete without it. Without sharing this part of story, my efforts to pass on to you my message will not fulfill its purpose. My life and who I am today were greatly impacted by this experience. It is very difficult for me to remember and describe it all. But for the sake of truth, I will tell you how it all was, how I felt then and why I made the choices that I did. This story lasted for two years, and this is where it all began. I want you to read it until the very end, as it carries important lessons.

As I mentioned, by the time Michael arrived in Lithuania, no longer did I feel he was a stranger to me. After we met in Istanbul, it was much easier to talk via email. Even though Michael was a down-to-earth specialist from the first day we connected, after our meeting he was talking with me on an even more personal level rather than formal professional to patient, and I spoke to him the same way.

While prosthetics connected us in the first place and that was the major hurdle that united us and we worked on together, I don't think either of us noticed how our messages became more personal and less businesslike. It seemed like we were drawn to each other – our letters became more frequent and they were about various topics, not solely about prosthetics or trip arrangements. By emailing one another continuously, we got to know each other without realizing it. Through his messages, I got the sense that he was looking forward to my emails daily just as I was looking forward to his. Reading his letters and writing him became an important part of my day. I noticed how he felt exactly the same. Through daily emails, in half a year we became so attached that we worried about each other's well-being if one of us did not reply the next day.

Michael was very tactful expressing his feelings; yet through his messages, I sensed that in addition to working on prosthetics his interest to see me again was beyond that. I had to admit to myself that I felt the same way.

I knew I would want to see him again, even if he wouldn't be helping me with prosthetic legs. At times I would have a question mark in my mind: Where is this going? Especially I wondered about it when he wrote that in order to express how he felt, he wanted to tell me he was invited to give a lecture in Chicago at the same time he wanted to go to Lithuania. And he chose to go to Lithuania. He said he was very excited about going to Chicago and doing the presentation, but now he was much more excited to go to Lithuania, and see me again.

I was surprised that Michael would make such a choice. Yet I was thrilled. In the back of my mind I questioned what it was supposed to mean, but then I stopped myself from drawing any conclusions and suggested to him to go to Chicago and then from there travel to Lithuania. Despite noticing our attachment, I did not allow myself to dwell on my insights and questions; I was dismissing it all, patiently waiting for Michael to arrive.

When he came to our home – with family – and us being together all the time in the prosthetic rehab center, it united us. Since we both stayed at the same center, when busy days of workshops and training would come to the end, Michael and I would meet again for tea and conversation until late night. Our continuous emails laid the foundation for our closeness, and now when we were physically together, we could hardly stand to be apart. We couldn't wait for the business of the day to come to an end, so we could meet and spend time together away from everyone else. Challenges of the day and our open conversations about many of life's aspects drew us so much closer.

In fact, the more we talked, the more we noticed how we had the same standards for work, friendships and relationships; and that we had the same values and appreciated many of the same things in life. Michael said he was not used to having people sincerely caring for how he felt, or what his interests and values were. I truly did. The more we talked, the more we found common experiences and values, and it seemed like there was no end to it.

There was a moment when I glanced at him, and saw him gazing at me with such deep admiration and love. No matter how much I was telling myself "no," I couldn't help myself – I felt the same. We looked at each other's eyes slightly smiling, and without saying a word we fully understood how there was a special bond between us that neither of us could deny or reject. We both felt the same – we cared for each other on a much deeper level than just prosthetics.

And then the first kiss, and the first "I love you" made our inner bond undeniable and inescapable. We had reached a turning point from which there was no return. To be as honest with you as I have been about everything else, I didn't want to go back. It became a need, not a choice. The relationship became one both mental and physical, and instead of "specialist and patient" we became intimate in only the way deeply connected lovers can. We both knew we had entered a new phase of our relationship.

Our feelings and our mutually shared desire to have each other in our lives swept away all concerns about age difference, specialist-patient status or worldwide distance. Even though we knew the risk and how others might get hurt, the intensity of our feelings seemed to trump that reasoning and overshadow any objections. We both wondered who would have thought how this was possible, two people from across the world, different cultures, different ages and completely different worlds, coming together as one and all starting with a short email.

I shared with Michael that when I first saw him at the hotel in Istanbul, when we met for the very first time, I instantly felt peace inside. And deep in my soul I felt the words, "Finally, finally we meet." For some reason, I felt like I already knew him very well and that I'd known him for a very long time. I had never felt that way before with anyone. I dismissed it. Yet everything evolved in a way that, suddenly, here we were, in another country and together again, sharing our deepest feelings with each other. It seemed like we were those two single pieces of a puzzle that, perfectly united, completed each other.

The only thing was that Michael was not really a "free" puzzle piece. He had a wife. Her name was Margaret. It was cause for concern – one that did not make me feel at ease. Michael said his decision to help was not related to our personal relationship in the first place, and that it wouldn't be affected by it in the future. He decided he was going to help me until my dream was fulfilled, and he was ready to do whatever it took to make that happen. He said there was nothing he needed from me; simply by being in his life had already made him happy. After our very open, very frank conversation about everything that concerned us, we decided to hold on to each other for as long as we could.

I knew it was a risky path to take. It was wrong in the sight of the Lord. I had already faced the outcome of making wrong choices. Besides, I always had a firm standard to never stand between a husband and a wife. But then, seeing how our feelings and desire to have each other were like flames in a wildfire, I started contemplating on his explanations for his unfulfilled marriage and his strong feelings toward me.

I tried to find an explanation for such an unexpected turn in our relationship, and to find justification for all that had happened and was happening, hoping that the Lord saw our lives, knew our hearts, and how we felt about each other. I quenched my uneasy feeling by reasoning that the Lord is love and He understands. It was hard to overstep my standards, and yet I realized that it was too late to remind myself of this standard; I did not even notice when Michael became much more than just a specialist, and now I was unable to reject his love and my own feelings.

I've never had a man with whom I could feel like he was part of me. The term "soul mate" might sound much like a cliché, but that's how it felt. No matter how much I tried to remind myself that he was my specialist, Michael was way more than that. Even though there was a gap between our ages, it was totally unnoticeable for us. Besides our inner connectedness, the physical attraction between us was unquenchable. Michael was a handsome, vigorous, physically fit man, and looked much younger than other men of comparable age. On the other hand, Michael could not take his eyes off me, kept repeating how beautiful I was, and how much he appreciated me. When I thanked him for coming into my life, for showering me with his loving care and doing all he was doing, he would interrupt me saying that it was him who was receiving so much and thanked me for being in his life. I don't know if he realized how he lit my life, and that his love and our shared connection breathed life into my existence.

For the first time since the accident I sincerely felt happy I was alive. I was grateful to be alive to experience those precious feelings blooming inside me like a wild flower in the sunrise. His words still remain in my heart when he looked at me deeply and quietly said, "Inga, where have you been all my life? Please, never go away."

And I, gazing back at his loving eyes, fully understood how this was who I had been waiting for. And I didn't want to leave him, either. It was forbidden love; it became our secret. Behind the prosthetics, we lived an undisclosed side of the story, which made our lives much more fulfilling.

By the time two weeks came to an end, neither of us wanted to separate. It was hard to bear the thought that we would be a world apart. Michael promised that we would meet again somewhere soon. There were a lot of questions and a lot of unknowns. But now I felt much more secure. Since we had to keep our secret, we had only each other to talk to about our relationship, our feelings and fears. Now our emails became like the air – necessary to breathe. While it was so difficult to be apart, we still felt together and decided to focus on the beauty of our bond and what had to be done to reach the ultimate goal of walking again. We agreed to take one step at a time, and see where the events would lead.

After we saw Michael off, back to America, I went back to the Orthopedic Center to stay for some time, so I could fully improve my walking skills and get prostheses adjusted as needed. I renewed my intensive training of walking, ascending and descending stairs and practicing sitting down and standing up by myself.

It was hard to believe that I was back again, walking in the same hallways, but now there was a major difference – no longer was I suffering and I was able to sit down to rest when I needed. Since I did not feel any pain walking, every day I was increasing the length of time of wearing prostheses.

But just as Michael had warned me, soon my prostheses became uncomfortable. My local prosthetist tried to adjust them, but no matter what he did made no difference. In fact, it was getting worse. I again went back to where I was before I met Michael, I walked enduring the pain and then bandage and treat the wounds from where the sockets cut into me.

Michael and I stayed in touch via email while I was at the center and I was sharing with him my progress on a daily basis. When Michael started receiving news of my pain and disappointment, he was concerned and rather frustrated that he could not be there to fix it. He tried to help my local prosthetist by emailing directions on how to fix the problem, but it was in vain. Simas was frustrated; he knew Michael's theory, but practically he could not fix the problem.

One day I woke up with a blister right on the scars of my thigh. In order to prevent worse issues, the wisest thing was to stop wearing the prostheses. Knowing how this was going to take some time, I left the center and came back home to Vilnius to let the wound heal. My prostheses were not being improved, so I could not walk comfortably no matter how much Michael tried to relay his suggestions to the local specialist. My news that I got blisters and had to stop walking really upset Michael.

"Okay, enough," he said. "Inga, let's talk about your visa, money and airline tickets to the United States. We tried our first plan, but it didn't work. Let's have you come to California now and I will make them for you myself."

Preparing for My Trip to America

Michael was frustrated that I was in pain again and was not able to walk. He said this would not have been the case had he adjusted those legs, and now he wanted to make sure this would not happen again. Michael said that in Istanbul he was not really sure about my skills, but after he saw me walking and performing complex activities in the Orthopedic Center, he had absolutely no doubts I could walk and do anything I desired to do. He was excited about my progress in such a short time, he said he couldn't wait to make comfortable legs for me and see me walking.

We talked about this option before but now, after receiving his invitation to come to California, it took me a moment to grasp what was going on. Making the arrangements for my trip and a several month stay was a big challenge, and we left that option as a last resort. After reading his invitation, I knew Michael was not joking. I also knew he was serious about my prostheses. Watching how much we had accomplished in those two weeks during his visit, we knew together we could make the impossible possible yet again. And we couldn't wait to see each other.

Chills would go up my spine just thinking about traveling all the way to California and have Michael make me legs. Michael had already shown what he could do, and I trusted he would make my legs perfect. Since he left Lithuania, Michael had been emailing that he was thinking about my legs and had already secured some parts if it turned out that I would actually travel to the states. And now it looked like I was coming indeed. I could barely hold myself from shouting out loud, thanking God heartily. Along with the excitement, Michael's invitation brought many questions at the same time.

"What about the cost? Prostheses are expensive. We don't have money to pay even partial cost for them. What about a visa? And where am I going to get the money for the trip?"

The biggest obstacle was financial. Our family didn't have the money to cover the cost of prostheses, nor there was money for the roundtrip tickets much less the expenses to stay in California.

In response to my concerns, Michael responded that he would make my prostheses as a donation and I shouldn't worry about it at all. He also told me that if money became a challenge to obtain an airline ticket, that he would gladly help with that as well. My astonishment and gratitude for making prostheses as a gift were beyond measure. I still remember how I held my breath not knowing how to respond to express my gratitude for everything he had done, and was doing for me. It felt like my guardian angel had been sent to fulfill the impossible.

I thanked him for everything, but told him we would take care of the ticket cost. I had no idea where we would get the money for the ticket and other expenses, but my conscience didn't allow me to have Michael cover the ticket cost, in addition to the costs associated with my new prostheses.

My family at first was shocked by my news about Michael inviting me to come to the United States. They were in wonder as to how a person, who had met me only twice, would offer such an enormous gift of time, money and craftsmanship. Even though they were not aware of our secret, after this visit Michael no longer was a stranger to them. My family came to love him and he felt the same way about them. They were touched by Michael's generosity and good will. My mom kept saying she wished she could speak English to be able to express her gratitude to Michael. His gesture to my parents meant more than just making prostheses. Michael was fulfilling something that was the only reason what I lived for since I was brought back home without my legs.

They watched me all this time relentlessly trying to break through the brick wall of obstacles. Mom shared with me that the most heartbreaking was to watch me suffer as I took those timid steps and yet courageously claiming there was a day when I would walk again and even dance, while seeing specialists standing aside ironically smiling.

Yet mom and dad supported me because they saw how the idea of me walking with prostheses was the only thing that kept me from giving up, and they didn't dare to try and stop me. But now, since Michael had become part of all our lives, they saw this dream was really possible. Michael was fulfilling my faith, which kept me breathing all that time. This trip was much further than my first one, but my parents trusted Michael and they were okay with letting me go across the globe alone. Along with the excitement there were numerous questions, but together we all agreed to tackle them one at a time.

While my family was figuring out the trip's finances, Michael and I began discussing my six month stay via email, and all the arrangement details and upcoming work fitting me with prostheses during my visit. We knew there were enormous challenges ahead both for work and personal reasons that had to be kept secret. But one of the most beautiful things Michael and I had in our relationship was open communication. We knew we could talk about anything, any concerns or fears, and we could resolve anything and always come to an agreement. We talked daily, discussing every aspect of our personal relationship and the challenges we were about to face. It was hard to imagine being there, with his wife around every day.

In one of his messages Michael wrote, "Inga, I know how you feel about me, but I know you don't like to have two faces. I want you to know that I will help you and I want you here and I will love you, even if you decide that you cannot have two faces and can only be friends. I will help you no matter what."

Michael remembered our conversations concerning how much contempt I felt for hypocrites who show a different face than what they really are at times. He ensured me again that he would help me no matter what.

At this point, however, we could not see how we could be just friends. Finding ourselves helpless against our feelings, we agreed to do everything necessary to be discreet about our personal relationship while doing our professional work, just so we could be together. We knew it might not be easy, but we felt that our close bond made us so much stronger, and we knew that together we could accomplish anything. After discussing our major concerns, we continued planning the trip and our time together in the land of sunshine. For my family, the greatest challenge was to secure enough funding for my ticket and other expenses for my stay. Since this endeavor was way beyond our financial means, I brought this before the Lord, asking Him to help. A few days later, my dad came into my room and handed me the phone saying, "Some journalist is asking for you."

"A journalist? Again?" I gave a non-verbal cue that my focus was on other matters which demanded my attention, and that I didn't want to be distracted by another interview. But my dad was holding the phone, giving me a facial hint that there was no other way but to talk, because he told the journalist I was home.

The call was from a leading nationwide magazine *Miss*, targeted for young women but popular among all ages. The journalist who was calling asked me to give an interview for the section that publishes inspirational stories. Before I got a chance to say, "Thank you, but –," the journalist continued her proposal by asking, "Do you need anything at this time, Inga?"

"What do you mean do I need anything?"

She explained that at the end of these articles they write how readers can help the person interviewed, whatever it may be.

"Me? Do I need anything?" There was nothing I really needed and just as I was about to say "no thank you," a thought came to mind, "What is your biggest concern at this time?" Suddenly I was enlightened. It was perfect timing for this journalist to call and ask this question!

"As a matter of fact, I do," I answered with slight laughter. "I need money."

"Who doesn't need that?" the journalist replied laughing as well.

"No no," I said. "There is a reason why I need it. Let me explain."

I shared my story and while I was talking, I got the sense that she was listening and becoming interested. I continued, sharing how the American specialist was inviting me to come to California to get prostheses made specifically for me, but how our family didn't have the money to cover the expenses.

"Wow, that's a very interesting story, Inga!" she responded. "I would be happy to write the article and at the end, we'll ask people to send donations to your account to help you with the trip."

"What a perfect coincidence," smiling, I said to God thankfully. "Right at this time, when I am getting ready for the trip and questioning how I am going to get the finances, a journalist calls me for an interview with the intention of providing support. Only you, Lord, could arrange things like that!"

In a few days I did the interview and not long after, the magazine was published. As soon as it came out, money began pouring into my account. This interview was another update on my journey, and when the nation read the article about me not giving up and finding a way to fulfill my long-sought dream to walk again, people were greatly inspired and generously sent me financial support. Every day I marveled how supportive and generous people were – my bank account was filling up with contributions every single day.

And that was just the beginning. In several days I got a call from another journalist who worked for a newspaper that was focused more on business people and the government. She said she read the article and was inspired to write an article in their newspaper, so that I could reach out to business people. Soon another publication came out and I began receiving even more generous support. Every day I was astounded by what was happening – my bank account was filling up with contributions not just daily, but hourly. In addition, my parents told me that some of my relatives made financial gifts as well.

Very soon the major concern was wiped out. We had more than enough money to pay for the airfare and expenses for my visit to America. As though the hand of the Lord hadn't helped enough already, to my surprise, a woman called me and thanked me deeply for sharing my story. She said it inspired her greatly and as a "thank you," she invited me to her clothing store and asked me to pick whatever I liked for my journey as her gift to me. Words cannot ever express the depth of my gratitude to those who read my story and contributed to help defray the cost of traveling from Lithuania to America.

In the meantime, Michael was making arrangements for my stay. He secured the parts for my prostheses and was coming up with ideas as to how I could put them on with one hand. He also connected with a physical therapist, who agreed to work with me on a donation basis as well, once my prostheses were made and I was comfortably able to wear them. Michael was also able to secure a discount for me at the wheelchair accessible Deluxe Room at the Flamingo Resort, one of the nicest hotels in the city.

Michael then wrote a letter to the U.S. Embassy on my behalf, requesting permission for me to enter the United States for medical reasons. And on that early morning I was one of only three people who received a visa that day. My friend Gintautas, who worked for Lithuanian Airlines, arranged a most convenient flight (at a much-reduced price), with only one stop in Amsterdam. It seemed like I didn't really have to put much effort into what at first seemed like an enormous challenge. Yet every day, one piece of the puzzle was adding to another, and soon we had a very beautiful picture – every obstacle was out of the way and everything was arranged for my trip to California. Michael and I were very excited about meeting again soon. It seemed like the time apart brought us even closer and we were counting every day until we saw each other again.

Part 2 ~ My Trip to America. My Dream to Walk Becomes My Reality

As the previous New Year's Eve was spent in prayer and hope for a miracle, this Christmas and New Year's season was filled with the sheer joy of living that miracle. I was astounded by the changes I'd experienced in one year. My action guided by inspiration opened the doors to opportunity. After many months of personal trials of endurance and faith, I had a specialist who believed in my vision just as I did, and he was committed to making my dream come true.

"How is this possible?" I kept asking myself. The changes were so mind-boggling that at times I had to pinch myself to believe it was all true. So many days, weeks and months were spent in prayer hoping for the impossible. And now, my impossible dream was about to be fulfilled. My life was about to turn around.

After I got the visa, my family and I started preparation for my big trip. All I thought about was traveling to the land of sunshine, seeing Michael again, and fulfilling my dream to walk. Michael and I were constantly emailing one another, discussing the arrangements of my stay, my trip's ultimate goal, and our ideas and intentions as to how we were going to achieve all we'd agreed upon. We both could hardly contain our excitement.

Michael said he was telling everyone about me and his new undertaking. He also took it upon himself to fundraise for the cost of my hotel and other expenses during the visit. Every day he would give me news of his fundraising ideas, the latest arrangements he had made for my stay, and about my prostheses. He kept saying he wanted to prepare every detail perfectly to make sure that I was staying at the best hotel, and had everything I needed for an unforgettable time in California.

We were very well aware that a lot of work and quite a few challenges were ahead. Yet, we agreed together make every effort to turn the impossible into possible. Michael said he would do whatever it took to see me walking comfortably and be fully independent as I desired to be. And I was fully determined to train hard and do everything on my part to attain my long-awaited dream. We were a team, fully devoted to the vision we both had.

February 2, 2003 was the day that opened a new chapter of my journey. I was on my way to America to meet my dream. After countless days and months of being imprisoned at home, I was about to break free. I had absolutely no doubts Michael would make perfect legs for me, and I was ready to work hard. I was confident that I was going to return home fully ready to start my new life. On top of all that, I was so thrilled that I was traveling to California, the land which I could never even have dreamed of visiting! I couldn't wait to see San Francisco and the part of the world so famous for its beauty and pleasant weather all year round.

My trip seemed long but I enjoyed it. While listening to my favorite music, I analyzed the sequence of events, wondering how it all could come together in such an amazing way. How could it be that just recently I was dying and later was helplessly confined to a bed, and now I was flying by myself across the globe? Just last year my life seemed to be in such deep hopelessness that I thought only God's miracle could pull me out of that pit, and now I was living that miracle – in a divine way I got connected with an American specialist and now I was on my way to receive comfortable prostheses!

I couldn't really grasp the concept that soon I would be walking again. It would unlock the doors to the fulfilling and dynamic life I'd dreamed about. How was it possible to write a letter to some stranger in another continent, and to have it turn out that he was planning to travel to my part of the world? And if that weren't enough –he was willing to help me from the first day we met? I remember, during Michael's visit to Vilnius, I asked him what made him answer and invite me to Istanbul. And he said, "I don't know. I just wanted to."

And then came the trip itself. From the invitation to the ways in which all the trip arrangements were so precisely arranged, one has to stand in awe of the Lord's mysterious ways, making one person's dream a reality. There was no question in my mind (nor is there now) that the Lord had blessed me. I was experiencing the unexplainable.

On top of all, what an unexpected turn had happened. Some American stranger becomes the closest person in my life, who brought back my love for life, joy in my heart, and hope for my future. Daily ongoing emails and instant messaging conversations made us much closer and our invisible bond much stronger; it felt like we were right here with each other even though physically we were a world apart. His daily letters and actions for my well-being showered me with love that I never had in any of my previous relationships. His desire to have me in his life, his care and total devotion was breathtaking.

I must admit quite candidly that my feelings for Michael and my desire to be with him rapidly grew into complete devotion to him. I wanted to do everything I possibly could to be there for him and make his life fulfilling no matter what discomfort I would encounter or confrontation I was to face.

After an eleven hour flight our airplane was about to land at San Francisco International. My exhaustion disappeared once I saw, through the little round window, the blue waters of Pacific Ocean and the famous craggy California coastline.

"California! I am about to land in a dreamland!" I could hardly contain my excitement. Trying to grasp that I was not dreaming, I looked at the television monitor and among the data I saw, outside it was 18° Celsius (65° F). It was hard to comprehend that the weather was May-like (in Lithuania) in the month of February. It felt like my heart was about to jump out of my chest from the thought that in minutes, I would see Michael.

I will never forget the moment when I came out of the airport: the warm wind gently touched my face; right in front of me, on the horizon, I saw bright blue clear sky, all kinds of flowering trees, including palm trees, and I glanced to the right and there was Michael standing with a gorgeous bouquet of flowers. It was so good to be in his arms again.

He helped me with the luggage and we got into his car to get out of the airport. As we drove, sharing our news and my travel experiences, I admired rolling green hills, exotic manicured trees, colorful blossoming flowers and more. My mind was in overdrive. It really did feel like I had landed in a different world. On my way to the airport I had been dressed in a fur coat, freezing my nose off, and in the blink of an eye, I got out of the plane in summer weather.

It was a sunny, beautiful day and I could hardly believe that all I was experiencing was not a dream. While chatting with Michael, in a moment I saw the grand, elegant buildings. It was the City of San Francisco.

I had seen this stunning view only on television and online, and now I was looking at it with my own eyes. The magnificent Golden Gate Bridge, surrounded by the ocean and rocks. Stunning views of San Francisco and the exotic nature totally captivated me. I immediately fell in love with

California. And I knew that San Francisco would always be my top favorite city.

After coffee, fueling me with the energy to keep my brain and body awake (since there was a ten hour difference from my homeland, it was midnight for my body), we drove to the hotel where Michael arranged for a six month stay. Friendly staff welcomed me and gave us the key to my room. I could not believe how this elegant and luxurious place was to be my new home for an entire half-year.

In a moment, another surprise took my breath away. When we entered my room, on the coffee table, there was a basket with colorful balloons, filled with a variety of snacks, drinks and sweets. I looked at the attached card and found a lovely note from Kathryn, welcoming me to the land of the sunshine. Before I left Lithuania, she wrote me a very beautiful and encouraging email stating that she was looking forward to meeting.

Kathryn learned about me in the same mysterious way as all my events seemed to happen. She was the mother of Michael's patient, Vanessa. Michael told me that he was so excited about our meeting in Istanbul and our new endeavor that he shared the story with nearly everyone he met, even his patients. Vanessa was one of the patients Michael was working with at that time, and she got to hear the news that I was coming to get fitted for new legs. Vanessa, after hearing that I was Lithuanian, was astounded. Her mother's genealogical roots were Lithuanian. She knew Kathryn was making an effort studying her family's roots and wanted to know more about the country. Vanessa immediately told Kathryn the news, and that's when I received their warm and welcoming letter right before I departed. Then Kathryn found out what room was booked for me and made this delightful surprise for me. Then, later in the evening, Kathryn and her husband made another surprise by stopping by at the hotel to welcome me.

The following few days were filled with new surprises and exciting experiences, just as on the day of my arrival. Since my first days in America turned out to be the weekend (and Michael did not have to work), they were filled with meeting new people and sightseeing.

On the day after my arrival, Michael first introduced me to Margaret, his wife. I had no idea what my meeting with her would be like but to my surprise, it was a great pleasure. As soon as they both came into my room, she hugged me and very warmly welcomed me. She seemed to be as full of energy and joy as was Michael. Margaret was very sweet and seemed to be just as excited about the endeavor as we were.

It was awkward. I had never been in that kind of position. It was not easy to look into her eyes knowing the hidden side to the story. But I liked her a lot, just as Michael told me I would. It didn't take me long to realize Margaret was a very smart woman. She also seemed to be someone you could totally count on. And she was a lot of fun; it was very easy to be with her.

After a moment of thought, my reality check with my conscience, I had to dismiss my inner conflict. I couldn't bear the awareness of our double life. I knew this was what I would have to face and I had to find a way to deal with it. Per our mutual agreement, Michael and I acted as though nothing secret was going on. For her and anyone else we naturally showed only one side of the story. After a short acquaintance, they invited me to join them for breakfast, and then they prepared a surprise for afterwards.

After the breakfast, they drove me the Armstrong Redwood National Park. After walking in the park among those gigantic incredible trees that were hundreds of years, even a thousand years of age, my second surprise brought me both awe and tears of joy.

I had the opportunity of watching the sunset standing on the cliff looking at the magnificent Pacific Ocean. The sky was constantly changing its bright colors as the sun made its way down into the ocean. What a stunningly gorgeous view. My life since the tragedy went through my mind in a flash. After the horrifying turn and three years of complete hopelessness and hardship, here I was, across the globe from my home in California, gazing on the breathtaking views of the Pacific Ocean. It was peaceful and yet, powerful and constantly changing. And every way I looked into the horizon, I saw no limits.

I thought to myself, "Such is the journey of life. Any circumstance can change and the possibilities in life have no limits when you put the effort into obtaining what you set your mind to. When I was confined to a bed, totally helpless, who could have ever thought that several years later I would travel across the globe by myself and would be watching the sunset on the coast of the Pacific? The plans of the Lord are not ours. If I could just tell the world how important it is to never give up! I wish I could tell them that their lives could truly change if they just break through the times of hardship and never stop pursuing their dream."

I was so grateful to my Heavenly Father for His astonishing plan and provision for me. And now that the Lord brought me here, I knew He would bless me to finally fulfill my aspiration. There was only one thing that raised a question – the secret that Michael and I had. How was it going to affect everything? While gazing on the sunset, I spoke to the Lord in my mind, contemplating and pleading with Him for His understanding. I was grateful to the Lord for Michael and for the miracle He blessed me with, but that one detail, the hidden side of the story, was simply not right.

I didn't know how I was going to deal with the triangle I found myself involved with. How was I going to look into Margaret's eyes on a daily basis while having a love affair with her husband? Even though my relationship with Michael was way beyond a playful "love affair" to me, it did not change the fact. I couldn't stand even thinking about it. Only remembering conversations with Michael about his marriage helped me to reason and justify the choices I made. Michael would never bad mouth his wife, which I highly respected. But hearing stories and thoughts about his marriage, and how strongly he wanted me to be in his life, gave me comfort, and I reasoned that maybe I was not doing the wrong thing after all. Furthermore, our feelings and bond were so strong that I just didn't see how I could possibly break that. At times, it felt like the reason we breathed in life was because we had each other. And the reason we were able to take upon ourselves such an endeavor, and face the emotional and physical challenges, was because we had each other.

It's as simple as that. Our beautiful connection found us in such an extraordinary way, connecting through a simple email. Our vision and our faith that we together could implement a vision made the endeavor exciting and achievable. Together we felt fulfilled. Together we felt strong. I couldn't see how to stop it. There was no turning back. After contemplating what the right thing to do was and what was actually going on and what we felt, I knew I was not ready to make any changes. So I didn't. I dismissed my conflicting thoughts and feelings, pleading with the Lord for His compassion and understanding. I decided to act as if nothing hidden were happening between us.

On the second day, Michael arranged a surprise dinner with Vanessa and Kathryn. Vanessa lost her leg in a motorcycle accident and was comfortably walking with a prosthesis that Michael had made for her. I was surprised. Looking at her, I couldn't tell she had an artificial leg. The sockets were made precisely according to her body shape so that she could wear tight pants, where the edges of the sockets were not visible, like I used to have.

Vanessa encouraged me even more, telling me I was only a step away from walking again and, yes, that Michael would make it look good in addition to the comfort. Dinner with Michael and his wife, Kathryn and her husband and Vanessa was very pleasant. But speaking American and my exhaustion due to the drastic time change made it difficult for me to understand what they were talking about. I knew, however, that I had met my new friends in California.

I was overwhelmed from being in a completely different environment and being able to hear and speak only in a foreign language. If that weren't enough, becoming used to a different time zone turned my life upside down. I guess my biggest initial shock was realizing that my excellent grades in the English language meant zero in this country. I could not understand what people were saying to me. American English was much different than what I knew, and it didn't take long to admit how this would be my fourth language to tackle. I could understand only Michael, because he managed somehow to speak in a way that I understood. I was glad he was always there, and he ended up being my interpreter.

After a weekend filled with excitement and surprises, there was Monday, the day that I have been waiting for. Michael would begin to build my prostheses. Early in the morning he picked me up from the hotel and brought me to his office, introducing me to his staff. To my pleasant surprise, everyone was very warm and welcoming. I hardly understood anything they were saying and had to keep asking them to repeat themselves, but I felt welcome. I was always loved by my family and friends, but it was unusual for me to have strangers be so friendly, even when they didn't know me. And on that day Michael did measurements for my new sockets and began fabricating my new legs.

Prior my arrival, Michael connected with Gabija Jonaitis, leader of Lithuanian-American Community, Los Angeles Chapter. She invited us to come to their upcoming fundraiser event and I was scheduled to be a guest speaker. And so the first weekend of my visit, Michael and I drove to Los Angeles, and I had no idea that California was that big. I thought San Francisco and Disneyland were not that far away from one another. I didn't realize it was about a 6-8 hour drive from my hotel there to the fundraiser. Michael and I enjoyed meeting Gabija as she graciously welcomed us and showed us our assigned table. Fancy and delicate decorations throughout the room gave me a hint, this was an upscale, elegant event. My assumptions were confirmed when I observed formally dressed guests greeting each other and having conversations in a variety of languages. I overheard some of them speak in Lithuanian, and some were struggling with it. Here I assumed the majority of the guests were Lithuanians who had lived in the United States for a very long time.

When I was introduced to speak, positioning myself at the center to face the crowd, it felt like my heart was about to stop. The eyes of several hundred people were attentively directed towards me. Some of them felt my pain, exerting signs of compassion, and some were eagerly waiting to hear what I had to say. It was my first time speaking in front of the group.

I looked at Michael. His eyes comforted me. Having him by my side gave me courage. Looking at him I could hear in my mind, "You can do this, Inga. You can do it." After a moment, I pulled myself together. I remembered why I was standing there in front of those beautiful people. There was a message I had to convey and I remained focused. Previous interviews with my Lithuanian journalists had been good practice sharing my story, so I already knew what to say.

Hoping that I could touch people and inspire them, I began sharing my story. As I spoke, looking at the audience reaction, I could tell many hearts were touched. I saw some people wiping away their tears. After dinner and the event's program, people came up to me, sharing their admiration and handing to envelopes with their contribution, wishing me their best to return to Lithuania with my dream to walk again being fulfilled.

After the event, Gabija said guests were exceptionally generous that night and that the fundraiser was very successful. Quite a few guests provided financial support for my stay, and the Lithuanian-American community also committed to join Michael in providing some financial support to finish the project successfully.

Afterwards we stayed the rest of the weekend in Los Angeles, which turned out to be a memorable getaway. After being separated by the worldwide distance and challenged by Michael juggling his work, his wife and me, now we could be together twenty-four hours a day and not worry about anything. We went sightseeing around magnificent Los Angeles and enjoyed the beautiful paradise-like Santa Monica, and the world renowned Venice Beach, an extraordinary and entertaining beach that is unlike any other beach I had ever seen.

It was the perfect weekend, as we didn't have to worry about anything and could enjoy the freedom of being together, doing whatever we pleased. We wished how the weekend would never end; yet regardless of our desires, we had to come home. But we were excited about working on my prostheses.

And besides, it was just the beginning of my visit and we knew we had many more days ahead together.

While feeling happy to have the love relationship I always dreamed of, the guilt silently began strangling me. Margaret was generous, caring and good to me. I couldn't live with myself knowing what I was doing. I was living in a lie doing a horrible thing behind her back. After sleepless nights pondering my choices and all aspects of the relationship, I decided to stop everything that Michael and I had to hide. I couldn't lie to her and continue going against my personal standards and my faith.

When one early morning Michael stopped at the hotel to see me on his way to work (as he did daily), I shared with him how I felt about this double life and the heavy burden of pretending. I was torn apart between my deep love and connection with him, and disgusted for our actions hiding who I really was to Michael.

As Michael listened, his excitement gradually turned into a sadness that I had never witnessed in him. Yet he did not confront me and listened very attentively. Then, he quietly said how he fully understood. We both knew what we would have to face, and it was his biggest concern. Michael said he was very sad, having to cut short our newly born relationship, which made us so alive and fulfilled, but he wasn't going to force me to do anything I didn't feel comfortable doing.

He looked into my eyes and said, "Inga, as difficult as it is for me, I will respect your decision. I will still love you and will do everything I can to fulfill your dream to walk, no matter what decision you make for our relationship, just as I told you months ago."

Then, he walked away and disappeared behind the closed hotel door. He went to the office to continue building my prostheses as though nothing had come between us. After he left, I took a deep breath, but instead of easiness, I felt emptiness. It felt like the joy of life and fulfillment I got to experience had deserted me altogether. I lost my only treasure, the one who made my life worth living.

The next few days turned out to be completely opposite from what I had expected before my conversation with Michael. Instead of peace I felt tormented. While I knew I had done the right thing, without Michael I felt empty and miserable like never before. All I could think of were memories of our time in Lithuania, and the daily emails at least to exchange a few words, and his efforts to keep his promises and total commitment; and our desire to meet again, and the conversations how we were ready for anything just so we could be together. We counted the days and hours until we could see each other, and so eagerly we anticipated our time together in California.

And now what?

A day not talking with Michael and not seeing him seemed to be the longest day I could remember. After a long sleepless night, meeting the sunrise was a heavy burden. Another day like this? I waited for Michael's phone call. But my phone was silent. No longer was my morning lit up with him opening the doors and storming into the room bursting with excitement and joy, greeting me with a kiss for another beautiful day. It felt lonely and empty. Even though I knew he was working on my prostheses – my long-awaited dream – without him it seemed like nothing made sense anymore. All I could think of was my longing for him.

Michael's desire to love me and have me by his side fueled me with love for life. I was never loved by anybody like I was loved by him. Remembering his attentive care, affection and his expressed feelings and intentions, it seemed like besides his love for work, I was the reason why he lived – his major focus was my happiness, my prostheses and our relationship. While receiving prostheses was all I was aiming for in the beginning and dreamed about since the day I began a new life, I realized that at this point this was no longer my most important thing. No longer was I excited about receiving prostheses if there was no Michael by my side.

I faced the fact again. Michael had become significantly more than a prosthetic specialist. Remembering his expressed feelings, conveying how he desired to have me in his life, and how eagerly he was anticipating my arrival, I knew he must have felt as empty as I. Remembering how tormenting the previous day was, I knew I could not live another day without him. No matter how much inner conflict I had about my relationship with a married man, I found no strength to reject the beautiful connection had come into my life in such an extraordinary way.

After my relentless battle with my inner conflict, contemplating and carefully thinking through everything, I called him. As soon as Michael heard about my feelings, he said he would be right over. Before I realized what was going on, Michael was already there. He stormed into my room and ran to me, and tightly squeezed me in his arms.

"I am so happy that you called, Inga!" He kissed me and held me in his arms tight. "I was afraid of losing you. You have no idea how much I love you. Thank you. Thank you for calling and saying what you said."

I felt complete and secure being in his arms once again. I told him that I loved him too and that I could not break us apart. We admitted that we didn't want to lose what we so cherished. Any challenges for our relationship paled in comparison to the cost of losing what we had together. We agreed again to nourish our union and go through the challenges together. We agreed to talk openly about everything and all our concerns, supporting each other as we went.

The Work Begins

In a matter of days my prostheses were ready. The irony was that my first steps with them were made on the day I lost my legs – February 12 – the third anniversary of the tragic accident. Deep within my tears of joy and sadness were all mixed. Michael and his staff members comforted me, trying to cheer me up and reassuring me that I would definitely walk again.

Since the crash, on that day, I would always be in tears. I was reliving the horror and the loss and I couldn't get away from it all. After a moment dealing with my emotions, I pulled myself together, bringing myself back to the current day. In a moment, I was able to step out of my emotions and see that I was living such a miracle now. I was in California having my impossible dream fulfilled – I was going to walk again. Why would I go back to the tragedy and grief about the loss? I decided I needed to stop dwelling on the loss on my anniversary date, just as I did on a daily basis. It was time to focus on the beautiful changes that were happening. I made the decision to no longer relive that tragedy. A new journey had begun, and all I was experiencing now was so thrilling and delightful. Now I had the opportunity to begin with an entirely new perspective.

After some time of being alone outside the office, I calmed down and decided to not think about what was lost, but rather to see and focus on the blessing I was receiving today. Since then we began working on our big impossible project. While I was staying at the prosthetic facility in Lithuania, I kept saying to myself and others, "Oh how I wish I could put them on by myself, stand up and walk." What seemed a simple thing to do for many, to me was the biggest dream and an enormous challenge.

Michael said we were going to achieve much more than that. Our goal was to have me comfortably wearing prostheses all day long and being able to do activities that were needed on a daily basis: to put prostheses on independently, to comfortably walk indoors and out, to sit down on any height of chair and stand up, to ascend and descend stairs, to ascend and descend curbs, and to get in and get out of cars whether they were low-riding sports cars or sport utility vehicles.

To my activity wish list Michael added one more. He wanted me to learn to get up from the floor independently in case I ever fell. I shared with him the incident when my dad and I went outside to the school's stadium to practice walking for my come-back to the airport, and due to an uneven path, I fell upon the cemented pathway. It was the scariest experience I ever had wearing prostheses; it was a miracle I did not get injured. My dad had to lift me up and help me sit down in the wheelchair to come home. What if I had been alone? After hearing the story, Michael wanted to make sure I knew how to get up by myself.

Since my ultimate aspiration was to be fully independent, that meant I had to learn to do all those activities without any assistance – a very ambitious goal to be achieved in six months. But Michael and I had the same vision and the mindset about attaining it. Even though it seemed impossible to have me do all those activities independently, we knew there must be a way and we were determined to find solutions. We knew how there was a great deal of hard, continuous work ahead and we were ready for it. We agreed to do our best, to work together so we could reach every single goal we had set.

After my sockets were made and the prostheses were built, the arduous work began. These were the most intensive six months I had ever experienced since I began aiming to walk again. The level of training at the Orthopedic Center in Lithuania could not be even compared to the work in California. Every day, without an exception, I would get up at 6:00 AM to get ready and afterwards, Michael would pick me up to go with him to the office. The rest of the day was spent strenuously exerting my entire body, practicing and developing my skills. As my thighs were changing, and I felt discomfort wearing prostheses, Michael was right there to make the necessary adjustments, and then I would continue my training. It took a while to get used to new standards – instead of being told to endure pain, now I was urged to notify Michael immediately when I felt any discomfort.

No longer was my walking experience a test of how long I could endure physical pain. Now my time spent wearing prostheses was exciting and pleasant, something I was eagerly looking forward to continuing. If it was a test, it was the one for my physical stamina. Walking and even standing still required a lot of energy; by the afternoon I was totally drained.

The more comfortable I felt wearing prostheses, the more work was added to my daily schedule. Michael challenged me every time to do extra to increase the time wearing prostheses. Soon he suggested that we start practicing outside. It was very new to me. Even though I practiced walking in the nearby stadium with my dad, it was not the same: Dad was right there with me, guarding me just in case. I remember how much I dreamed of being able to walk outside by myself. And it had remained a dream. Yet now here it was being fulfilled – making step after step, having no fear or doubts, comfortably walking out of his office. Now I could visit technicians at the workshop and watch how they made my legs.

I loved the uplifting atmosphere at Michael's office. They all seemed to me like a team-family. Cheerful greetings at the reception, guys' laughter in the workshop, happy, smiling patients leaving the office were things I witnessed on a daily basis. It was always a pleasure to go to Michael's office and spend the day there. While practicing walking, I would visit staff and talk to them, which was practice for my English skills at the same time.

After several weeks Michael challenged me to face one of my biggest challenges – to get into a car. He had already gotten me to sit in his sport utility vehicle, which had higher built seats than a regular vehicle. But my challenge was to learn get into a regular height car. One day, as his wife parked her car in the front parking lot, Michael playfully asked me to get into the car using the technique he showed me. I was a little hesitant at first, but then my desire to learn and fulfill my dream took over. While he and his wife were standing aside watching over me, using Michael's directions I managed to sit down in the vehicle's front seat and then stepped out of the car. "Yay! Inga, you did it!" Their loud shouts could be heard all across the parking lot.

I guess if there were any people walking by, they must have thought some event of major importance had just happened. There was no end to the loud shouts of congratulations for learning new activity, which at one point seemed so impossible. It was a victory for me. I wished my dad could have seen it. He was the one who had struggled so much helping me stand up. I wished my friends had seen it; in fact I wished everyone who told me I would never be able to do it, had been able to see it.

Living a victory. My dream to get into a car turned into reality.

That day my surprises continued when I learned that instead of going home, Michael and his wife were planning a trip to Yosemite National Park to spend the weekend in the mountains. We were to leave right after they closed the office for the day. Michael took my prostheses and put them in the car without a question, stating that he would teach me to walk outside in the mountains. We arrived close to midnight when it was dark, and I could not see the surroundings.

Early morning, when Margaret opened the door, the view took my breath away. Right in front of me there were the most beautiful mountains I had ever seen. Everywhere I looked, I was surrounded by the gorgeous mountains. The beauty of those gigantic and perfectly sculpted rocks changed in their magnificent colors as the sun rose.

"What a stunning landscape!" I said, standing in awe, feeling shivers all over my body from a clear sense of God's might. "Lord, how is it possible to create such beauty?"

"Oh, this is just the beginning, Inga," Michael said. "Let me show you something special. But first, let's put the legs on." He was not going to waste any time. He took out my prostheses and said confidently, "Now is the time for a new challenge."

Challenged by Michael, for the first time I walked outside in a place I was unfamiliar with and which was not evenly set as the stadium path or Michael's office parking lot. At best, the terrain was uneven. This time, walking outside was a different experience. I walked not for solely training purposes, but we went for a walk to enjoy the incredible views of Yosemite waterfalls and the surrounding mountains. Many times I stood there looking at the Lord's creation speechless, unable to find the words to express my astonishment. That weekend, we got to tour one of the most beautiful national parks in the country, observing the stunning views of Yosemite Falls, El Capitan and the surrounding landscape, and on top of all that we got to rejoice in another milestone of my personal progress.

Practice of overcoming of fear. Walking outside for the first time.

Practicing to walk again while enjoying incredible views. Half Dome, Yosemite National Park.

After a restful and enjoyable weekend among the majestic Creator's art, we were ready to continue working on our project. Seeing that my prostheses got to the point of complete comfort, and the fact I felt more confident wearing them, Michael said it was time to move my training to a new level.

He introduced me to Edward Thompson, a physical therapist. Edward and Michael connected prior my arrival and he agreed to work with me pro-bono just as Michael had. We became a team of three. Edward was one of those people who won my respect and friendship immediately. He was a very pleasant man and I learned quickly that he knew his job very well. Since then, I began traveling to his office three times a week for physical therapy sessions.

It was time for me to learn advanced skills, and Edward was going to train me, teaching me different activities with exercises how to hold a steady balance and make steps correctly, sit down and stand up at ease from any chair-height, ascend and descend stairs, and every activity that would be necessary on a daily basis. I enjoyed my sessions with Edward. He made trainings productive and fun at the same time, coming up with various fun exercises for me to learn new activities and practice them. While we were chatting, and laughing from challenging exercises Edward set me up with, trainings were really intense. They required courage, stepping out of my comfort zone and enormous concentration.

Often after my hour and a half trainings I was soaking wet, and I would return to the hotel from his office feeling totally wiped out. After lunch I would collapse in bed until dinner time. On other days, Michael would take me to his own office to practice my skills there. On those days, training was even more intense, since I was wearing prostheses for many more hours at a time, which meant that "training" lasted for as long as I would wear them.

Everything I had to do demanded concentration, courage and physical exertion. Even standing was not equal to resting because it required intense muscle work and well-developed balance skills; at times standing still was more challenging than walking.

In between appointments with his patients, Michael worked with me either by teaching me to develop skills from my newly learned activities, showing me techniques for new activities or adjusting my prostheses when needed. He was a good teacher just as Edward was, and somehow he knew how to challenge me in a way that I would conquer my fears.

Ascending and especially descending a curb was the most difficult and scariest thing. In order to descend a curb, I had to have excellent balance skills and a precisely calculated distance and angle between me and my cane. Since I was fully leaning on the cane when descending the curb, the slightest wrong move could end in a traumatic fall. It was so scary that I would be standing on the edge of the sidewalk looking down with my palms soaking from paralyzing fear, and would not make the slightest move to step down for a long time. Michael was my cheerleader exclaiming, "You can do it!" He repeatedly encouraged me, showing time and again how much he believed in me. In his eyes, I could accomplish anything I set my mind to.

Conquering my fears and descending the curb was my biggest victory. We were like children rejoicing and congratulating each other with one more victory. Edward, Michael and I quickly became a strong team. They would check in with each other to discuss my progress and the desired outcome, and for ways to succeed in every goal that I had. Since my physical condition was unusual and made it very complicated to perform simple activities that "normal" people take for granted, they came up with ideas for various exercises and unique ways to perform those activities. Edward focused on the indoor activities like taking steps, sitting down, standing up and balance skills, while Michael trained me to walk outside, climb stairs, step over curbs, and the process of getting in and out of cars.

Due to the intense and strenuous daily workouts, I began losing weight. Every week Michael had to make sockets smaller and then constantly adjust the prostheses. With that, we began facing new difficulties on an ongoing basis. It was hard to fit me. Sometimes due to the physical changes in my body we encountered some serious issues, and battling them was not easy. Some of these issues made us feel like we were stuck at square one. Nevertheless, Michael worked tirelessly to make adjustments, making sure that I didn't feel any discomfort and felt secure wearing them.

Soon Michael said that a local service club had donated a new set of R-80 knees for me, which had the feature of allowing a person to sit down in a way that people normally sit down. Being able to sit down independently had been one of my biggest dreams. The knees that I had were also made by the Ottobock Company in Germany, and they made my walking secure on uneven surfaces, but I was unable to sit down. I learned only when Michael showed me a special technique, which was very challenging at times when I had to sit on a low-height chair.

The new knees were supposed to make it easier to sit down. Upon receiving the new parts, a new round of training had begun: I had to re-learn all the activities from scratch, since newly built prostheses functioned in an entirely different way. Receiving new parts was a blessing and at the same time a huge challenge, which tested my patience and determination. It was hard to learn a new way of sitting and walking on an uneven surface, and so once again, daily repetitive exercises became my daily routine.

Even before I came to California, I knew I was going to have to work hard to succeed, and I was prepared for that. But I could never imagine how much work it was going to be. Since I was visiting for a limited time, we wanted to make certain we used every single day to the utmost to fulfill the purpose of my trip. The ultimate goal, to walk in total comfort, and being able to perform every activity that was necessary on a daily basis while wearing prostheses all day long, required daily intense work and absolute discipline. We basically had no days off.

Michael would take the prostheses home, even on weekends, and we worked on my strenuous routine no matter what day of the week it was. Big portions of the weekends were Michael in the shop making adjustments and me sitting down and standing up countless times on a variety of chairs, walking on carpet inside and a variety of surfaces outside, getting into and out of the car, and going to various places. I again tasted the high cost of success: relentless perseverance and hard work.

There were days when all I wanted to do was rest. Not only was my body exhausted, but my relationship with Michael was never far from my conscious mind. And even though I wanted to skip the training and simply relax, my wishes were not even a consideration. I have to admit that at the Ortho Center the test of my endurance was a light rehearsal compared to the physical program I signed up for in California. Even though I no longer had to deal with pain, my physical and emotional endurance were being tested each day. Relentless effort and unwavering determination were imperative to accomplish what I aspired.

Each day, it seemed, the work was increasing and new challenges were arising and the amount of work was far beyond what I thought I could take. Often, I would return to hotel so exhausted that I could hardly comprehend the content of email messages written to me in my own native language by my family and friends. Often, I felt so physically drained that in the morning I did not have the strength to take the covers off. From repetitive exercises sitting down and standing, ascending and descending stairs (which fully involved my right arm to perform those activities), my right shoulder got so overworked and started hurting so badly that in the morning I barely could lift a cup of coffee to my lips.

Only the sense of responsibility and knowing why it was important for me to keep training, gave me the endurance to get myself out of bed and continue with that day's challenges.

What's more, Michael's complete devotion inspired me greatly. He kept saying that he truly believed I could walk and he did everything possible to make sure I was comfortable and secure walking with prostheses. He spent literally hundreds (if not thousands) of hours in fitting, adjusting and training me so that I could perform various activities. Watching how much he loved what he did and how much effort he put into my prostheses was very compelling.

Our relationship kept us unbreakable when challenging issues made our ultimate goal look like a too high of a hurdle to overcome. I had faith in Michael. He had faith in me. We always supported each other. Not once did we say any words of reproach when something did not work right. When either of us had difficulty handling a task, the words "I know you can do it, I believe in you" was our way of communicating. I kept reaffirming that I didn't only believe he could fix any problem and make prostheses comfortable, but I knew he could. Michael ignited in me the inspiration and belief in the impossible when I would start questioning if I really could do it. Michael was stronger than me.

He became my rock. He would always encourage me if I was doubtful. He would bring out the courage in me when I was afraid. When I did not succeed, he would always gently and calmly say, "Try again," and he would stand by me until I succeeded. And then, he would rejoice with me every single time I succeeded, as if it was his own biggest accomplishment, as well. My success was his success. My success was our success. We both couldn't wait to celebrate the day when all our goals were accomplished.

Often we would talk about my return to Lithuania. We were dreaming what it would look like to be able to get out of my home and go wherever I wanted. What it would feel like to be able to leave home with my friends, get into their vehicle and go somewhere. And this time, I would be standing and walking again, leaving my wheelchair at home. I shared with him my secret dream of being able to meet my parents at the airport walking, and not in a wheelchair. Oh how I wished to hug my mom standing!

And then, being even more inspired by the dream, we would dive back into our daily routine of focused, arduous work to be fully ready to make our dreams become a reality. I think the only thing that held us from going insane from the daily, ongoing, enormous amount of work and stress were the rest and distractions we shared after work hours or on the weekends when we didn't work.

Michael always had ideas about down time, or even already arranged plan, for the evening after we completed a laborious work day. Often our evenings included dinner, either at a restaurant or at his home, going to San Francisco, or enjoying the evening relaxing in the Jacuzzi at the hotel where I was staying. Sometimes we went to concerts, and other times we went out for the evening and met some of his friends or family.

Soon after my arrival Michael introduced me to his parents who, after hearing his stories about his "Lithuanian challenge," wanted to meet me personally. His parents gained my respect very quickly. Watching how caring and respectful they were to each other was such a delight. They got to love me from the first day and from that point on, they would invite me to join them when they invited Michael and his wife for a family dinner.

I especially enjoyed evenings when we could go to Michael's house and finally loosen up from work mode. Michael would often cook his favorite dinner of grilled salmon with corn and salad, and we would spend the evening together doing whatever he would come up with, and then late evening he would bring me back to hotel. Our evenings were both relaxing and entertaining. For the most part, we spent all of our free time together; very rarely would we spend evenings or weekends separately.

"What about his wife?"

It's a legitimate question. I saw her nearly every day, since Michael had me with him basically all the time. Often the three of us would do things together after work or on the weekends. No, it wasn't easy. In fact, it was the hardest aspect of my trip. The truth is that I really liked her and enjoyed spending time with her. She was very thoughtful of my needs and a genuinely caring person. I felt pain for her that she was being lied to. I struggled with my inner self, watching her to be so generous and sweet to me, not knowing that her husband and I had a different story. I hated what I was doing. And I could not think of the pain she would suffer if she learned the truth.

But because there was no other choice and it seemed like there was no turning back, I had to deal with my double role as a patient and a lover. The only thing helping me to numb the inner conflict was Michael's explanation about his marriage and his true feelings. I believed everything he said, and I saw his pain, and I wanted to give him what he was missing and seeking.

It was a delight to see his liveliness and what a difference it made for him when he felt loved, cared for, important and respected. His loving and joyous eyes, always smiling with an exuberance and excitement for life, would always make my day. He used to say that he would show his love with his actions and not just his words. He would repeatedly say how strongly he loved me and treasured me, thanking me for being in his life, and that he didn't know how he could live without me if he had to. I felt exactly the same.

Observing him, often times he acted as if he was trapped with no way out, and he treasured me as if I was the only breath of fresh air for him. When we would talk about the triangle we found ourselves in, he explained to me why he could not divorce his wife, but he would reassure me that he would love me and be there for me no matter what. He kept asking me not to disappear from his life, because he didn't know how he could live without me. By finding ways to justify my choice, I hoped my Lord understood me and His commandments could be molded for this situation, since this case was not ordinary.

With that I overstepped my moral standards so I could live another day knowing that I had him and he had me by his side. I decided to be there for him and with him without thinking about the future or the possible consequences of our "you and I" story. Just as Michael and I agreed, I continued acting in a way that revealed only one side of the story.

The only relief came when he would come to the hotel in the morning or bring me back in the evening, or times when the two of us would drive together to San Francisco for the evening, or had any other getaway that he could arrange. He always made an effort to arrange circumstances for us to be together and to go away, time after time.

One of those short getaways remains unforgettable up to this day, when he fulfilled another dream. Michael and I left town and drove to another Lithuanian-American Community event. We were dressed well and I was wearing my new legs. While we had our break-free getaway for few days, Michael was training me to get used to going out wearing prostheses rather than in the wheelchair. I used to practice activities like getting into the vehicle, walking on uneven surfaces or on carpet, and sitting down or standing up. It was all part of my training. But it was beyond my comfort zone to go out in public wearing legs; for some reason, wearing prostheses in public always made me nervous. And I'll tell you why.

It was hard, challenging work, requiring enormous concentration and physical exertion to perform activities that others take for granted, and I was anxious having to perform in an environment that was unknown. Knowing that people were watching was paralyzing. Michael was trying to break that fear, and he began arranging trips to places like the coffee shop, leaving the wheelchair at home.

Michael loved coffee, and he enjoyed going out to one particular coffee shop in town. He began suggesting that I wear my new legs when we go out. In his wisdom, he knew he could teach processes and techniques in a sterile, classroom-like atmosphere, but the real world was entirely different. I had to learn how to adapt to the environment in which I found myself the best I could, whether it was a nearby coffee shop or a formal, black-tie, Lithuanian-American function. He wanted to not only change the way I walked, but he wanted to change my point of view about wearing my prosthetic legs. And this was a big event. He wanted me to show up without my wheelchair. After so many days of hard, continuous work, I finally had the opportunity to use all those skills and appear in public wearing my prostheses.

After being welcomed by the hosts and some of the guests, we had a glass of champagne – it was our celebration. I was able to attend an event wearing my prostheses. No wheelchair. While rejoicing in our mutual achievement, with the first notes of the music, Michael put his glass of champagne down, gently took mine out of my hand, and reached out his hand to me.

"Inga, let's go to dance."

I couldn't believe what he was up to! His playful look revealed he was ready for an outrageous adventure. Just the idea that I would have to move while many would be watching was paralyzing.

"What? Dance? I can't do it, Michael. Not yet."

I tried to convince him that it was a bad idea. But Michael, as always, knew what to do and how to speak with me. And in a moment I found myself on the dance floor with him moving according to the rhythm. It was one of the scariest things I had to do and yet, this one dance became a precious gem adding to my lifetime experiences. Prior to the crash I always loved dancing; losing the ability to dance was something I could barely handle. And now here I was, dancing again, with the one who had made it possible.

Michael somehow knew how to make the time we spent together memorable. He and I always had a delightful time together no matter where we were or what we did. And after the distractions we knew had to come to an end, we would dive in back into the work that would lead to the ultimate goal.

Progress

My progress was rapid and successful. One day Michael surprised me again. He went to the shop and in a moment brought my prostheses.

"Here they are, Inga. I want you to try these."

He was enthusiastic and yet, thoughtful. I looked at them closely and noticed some changes. Michael saw a question mark in my eyes. He explained that the changes I saw on my prostheses were made for me to be able to put them on by myself with one hand. And then he demonstrated. Michael first put them on himself to show how it worked. I stood up and to our mutual amazement, the prostheses were holding tightly. Then he took them off and handed all the component parts to me.

"Try it yourself now," he said, being thoughtful and eagerly waiting to see how I would handle fastening them by myself using his newly invented system.

I did exactly what I saw him doing a few minutes earlier. I put the silicon liner on my thighs, which Michael modified to attach to the sockets. Then I put on the prostheses, which also had been modified to fasten liners to the sockets. In a moment, which seemed like the blink of an eye, using his newly invented system I fastened my prostheses to my body. I stood up – by myself – and they felt completely comfortable and tightly attached to my body. I took a few steps and the prostheses held tight. Then I lifted each leg up higher to swing them back and forth, took a few more steps, and they were still attached to my body tight.

"It works! I cannot believe this, Michael. Yes, they are holding on tightly!" Then I came to the realization that I had again done what I was told was impossible: I put them on by myself, and I did it with only one hand. "You did the impossible, Michael. You made another impossible dream come true!"

I didn't realize how loudly my voice carried. There I was, barely holding my tears and flabbergasted by another one of Michael's gifts. I didn't know what to do, so I tightly hugged him. "How did you come up with this? It's even easier for me to put them on with one hand than for another person to do it with two hands," I marveled.

Michael shared that he could not sleep at night; he'd been thinking about various ideas he could use to make it possible for me to put them on with one hand. Suddenly, an idea came and soon he knew exactly what to do. Following his vision, he manufactured the necessary attachments to the liners and prostheses before saying anything to me; he wanted to make it a surprise. I can hardly find words to describe the thrill when I found out. The most complicated procedure had become the easiest one of all. I was able to put on my prostheses quickly and easily by myself; no longer was I dependent on anyone for walking.

This was it; the last challenge was resolved and that made my dream complete. As time went by, we all felt the sheer joy of watching how the impossible had become reality. Day by day I continuously trained for new activities that I was told at the Rehab Center, I would never be able to perform. Now I found myself able to put my prostheses on alone with one hand without any difficulty; I walked without suffering pain or discomfort and was able to wear them for many hours every day. I could sit down and stand up independently; I could ascend and descend stairs; I was able to walk outside and handle uneven surface or curbs; and I was able to get into and out of cars without assistance. I was even able to perform Michael's added activity, to lower myself and lay down on the floor and then independently get back up. Now I knew how to get back up in case I would ever fall. With every day, I was getting stronger and more confident.

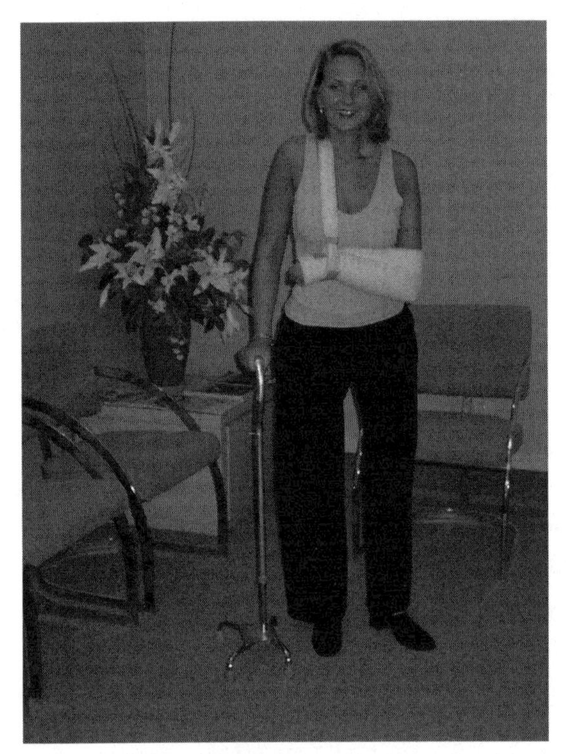

Standing again.

Saying goodbye to the Pacific. My dream has been accomplished.

At the end of my trip, when it seemed like we reached the target, all three of us were surprised by the unexpected. Michael, Edward and I were at Edward's office working on some advanced exercises when I felt a pulsating, enormous pain in the bottom of my left leg that hit like a lightning bolt. It had never happened before, and in looking at the sockets, my leg was not even hitting the socket. A mysterious problem had materialized and none of us had a clue as to its cause. We were wrapping up the project, thinking about returning to Lithuania, and here suddenly I started having a major issue that threatened to ruin all our efforts.

The pain was so strong, I was not able to walk at all. The problem was bewildering. I was in a total shock. After multiple adjustments to my existing sockets, Michael did the recast again and rebuilt prostheses from scratch. To our surprise, newly made casts and any kind of adjustments were in vain. Time after time, the pain returned with a vengeance. Michael predicted this might be because of some physical changes in my body again, but he continued trying to find a solution by adjusting my prostheses. After continuous attempts, Michael found a way for me to be comfortable.

But the problem did not go away though. The pulsating pain would return periodically, and only by fastening prostheses in a particular angle we were able to eliminate it. The mysterious pain that was demolishing my dream raised a question. As in the old days, after I would close the Business Lounge and self-reflect, I again analyzed my life and the decisions I'd been making. I wondered if this problem was the consequence of losing my blessing. Deep down at the core of my being, I knew my relationship with Michael was sinful before the Lord. After all, I knew that what I was doing was wrong and that made me feel uneasy to the point of wondering, "Am I losing the Lord's blessing?"

But then, I would dismiss the thought by reminding myself of all the reasons why I was making my choices and my justifications for why they were not wrong. I rationalized that I knew how the Lord was compassionate, and because of our circumstances, He would show grace over us. After all Michael and I had been through and how well we handled everything, watching how our connection made us simply inseparable and devoted to each other, I did not see how it could possibly be not blessed by God. I pushed away my questioning and focused on the victory I did have.

The Beginning of the End

After six months of strenuous daily work, my prostheses were finished and I had reached every single goal we had set for ourselves. I was able to walk comfortably, perform major daily activities, and I was able to wear prostheses all day. And as July was fast approaching, Michael and I started planning details for our trip back to Europe. He was planning to go back to Lithuania with me. I never expected him to return with me, but he had another surprise for me.

Within a few months of my arrival, Michael told me that he had been thinking about my dream to walk up to my parents at the airport and hug them, standing, and not from a wheelchair. He thought of how I would be able to do it and said it would be too difficult to manage alone; he decided to fly back to Lithuania with me and help to fulfill this dream.

Then, he laid out the plan. It would be too complicated and uncomfortable to endure a ten hour flight wearing prostheses, but it could be manageable for a second, much shorter flight. My dream would be possible if we put on prostheses at the airport where we had a connecting flight.

"But first, we need to practice this before we do this in Europe," Michael said, sharing his strategic plan. "Since we don't know how your thighs will handle the pressure in the air being in the tight socket, we need to test it. The best way is to actually fly somewhere. My birthday is coming up so why don't we fly to Las Vegas to celebrate? This way, we will have the opportunity to get on the flight and try them on. Besides, I've always wanted to show you Vegas."

Michael again surprised me. I felt grateful for how he was going beyond and above the call of duty to fulfill my desires. But I had no idea how he was going to explain this to his family. His children were coming home for his birthday, so how was he going to explain why he was leaving for Las Vegas?

To my concerns for his family's reaction he said not to worry. He would take care of it and we all were going to fly there for the weekend. So, Michael organized the weekend trip to Las Vegas for me and the family and we got to try our plan and visit this unforgettable city. Flying wearing prostheses went smoothly, and that determined the final plan. Michael was going to fly back to Europe with me and I was going to walk into the Arrival Hall to make my dream come true.

When we were planning our trip, we were thinking through every detail of how to make this happen. Michael also connected with Orthopedic Center in Lithuania where it all began, and offered his continuing training while he was visiting Lithuania. Michael wanted to show the final result of our project and teach them how it was accomplished, so they could advance their techniques and provide good care for their patients. He also wanted to make certain the specialists and doctors at the center were updated on all the new developments to be able to handle my prosthetic needs in his absence. He wanted to show them, step by step, what to do in case anything happened, and make certain they had the skills to make any needed corrections.

As my visit was coming to the end, Margaret and Michael organized a goodbye party for me at their home. They invited Edward and his family, and many other friends of whom I got to meet during my visit. A local professional photographer, surprised us with the book that she published about my story, illustrated with pictures of my progress reaching my dream. Dorothy was thrilled about the story, and she decided to capture the journey through her photos. For several months she was like my paparazzi, taking pictures of everything I did to reach my goal. What a surprise gift that was! That day Michael's house was filled with people, congratulations, laughter and stories of our aims for the results we had. After hearing our stories, many were inspired, seeing the finality of me all dressed up, looking so different standing and walking, so different from when they saw me in a wheelchair when I first arrived.

After sharing the joy with everyone and saying goodbyes, we began getting ready for the trip back to Lithuania. After Michael connected with Orthopedic Center in Lithuania, we were scheduled to visit their center to showcase the results of our project, and Michael was asked to teach there again for a week. Since we were very tired from intense six months of work, we needed a vacation, and so Michael planned to visit in Lithuania for three weeks. One week for the center and two weeks for our rest together and with my family.

Even though I came to California for a temporary visit, I admit it was difficult to leave. I realized that I had fallen in love with this beautiful land of sunshine. The Americans I met, strangers at first, became dear to my heart. Michael's family and staff, Kathryn's family, Edward and many others – it was sad to separate myself from them. It was sad to leave my Flamingo Hotel, which had become like my home. I was thankful to the manager and staff who were so good to me during my stay. I knew

California would remain in my heart and memory for the rest of my life. After all, this was where my biggest dream was fulfilled. This is where I got to spend my most beautiful and memorable moments, which I knew I would cherish for the rest of my life.

On the other hand, I was so longing for my family, my friends and my home city, Vilnius. I couldn't wait to return and hug them tightly and tell them how much I loved them and thank them again for everything; for being my hands and my legs when I was helpless, for not trying to stop me but fighting this battle with me when no one else believed in what I was aiming for. And now, I was so eager to show them that the impossible got to be fulfilled! And, they're the big reason why I was celebrating the victory.

The flight from San Francisco to Amsterdam was long and yet, smooth and comfortable. As always, we enjoyed being away, just two of us. During the flight, there was a lot of silence between us, which was so unusual. I could sense we both felt a little uneasy. I was not sure whether we were simply overtired, or we both were in our worlds thinking over things that concerned us.

I think for the first time we did not talk about nor shared our concerns. I don't even know if talking about them would have made us feel easier. I knew many of those concerns about our relationship, my prostheses, his marriage or what we were going to do after he returns to the United States, had no answers nor did they have solutions. In three weeks we were going to separate. And then what?

To continue living worlds away again – just the thought was too difficult to bear. While Michael was affectionate and caring, I saw he was deep in his thought and I wanted to give him space. So, for the most part we flew in silence, holding hands. Just like he and I used to do to manage our challenging circumstances before, I decided to see and appreciate all the beautiful things that we had now.

And I had a lot for which to be thankful. Michael was right here by my side, flying back with me. And we would have three weeks together. And I was returning home having my impossible dream fulfilled. A new life was ahead of me. I was about to meet with ultimate victory, establishing a new and independent and fulfilling life.

In Amsterdam, just as Michael planned, during a short layover, he helped me put on my prostheses. On the second flight to Vilnius, I flew wearing my new legs. As always, before landing, my heart started racing. Soon I would see my parents, my brother and Renata – my people. After we got out of the airplane and got our luggage, I was ready to see them. To my surprise, I saw dad coming up to me. The security people knew dad and me, and because of this exceptional event, they let him enter the zone while the rest of my family remained in the Arrival Hall. It was so good to see him.

"Dad!" I exclaimed smiling, barely holding my tears. "Didn't I tell you that it was possible, that I would get this done no matter what?"

"Well," he replied, hugging me tightly. "It's because you have my character."

Dad was always there to help me fulfill my dream. He had never tried to stop me nor did he ever deny me help. While training at home, every day through struggle (yet with lots of parental patience), he would put on my prostheses and help me stand and sit. Just as mom had at the various centers I'd been to, he witnessed my efforts, my successes and failures. He saw my pain and the wounds. In spite of it all, he always supported me even in times when our joint efforts seemed to be in vain. And now, after all we'd been through, it was done. As soon as he saw I wanted to stand up from the wheelchair, he jumped to help me. But this time I said, "You no longer have to do it dad. Watch me."

And right in front of him I independently stood without any struggle. His reaction was priceless. From now on he knew, memories of what standing up were like would remain like a bad dream.

I couldn't wait to see my mom and brother, and I started walking towards the Arrival Hall. As I went I looked up, and among the crowd I saw my beautiful mom, in tears looking at me speechless. To see me beautifully dressed, walking up to her was the last thing she could have ever expected.

"Inga! Daughter!" Holding a beautiful bouquet of flowers she immediately ran to me, and tightly hugged me.

"I did it mom! See? It was possible. I got this done in spite of it all. Thank you for everything, mom."

Barely holding back my tears I held her tightly. She was crying, unable to say a word. But her tears said it all. She was the one who witnessed my very first ten steps wearing prostheses. She was the one who saw my emotional agony and my efforts to fight through my discouragement and hopelessness. She witnessed my ongoing struggle, bruises and wounds. But, despite realizing that my dream to walk was nearly impossible, just like my dad she never tried to convince me to let go of my dream. She saw how much faith I had in my goal, and she was always there for me no matter what. And now we both were holding each other. And both of us were standing.

Soon I noticed my brother, Renata and a group of my friends, who came to welcome me back. We all hugged each other and this time, I could hug them all standing. It was a victorious return home. For the first time my parents witnessed me independently getting into a vehicle, entering the house by ascending those ten steps and stepping into my own home, while my empty folded wheelchair was pushed few steps away from me. While I was away, with my dad's coordination, a local non-profit organization for people with disabilities built the ramp in the entrance of our building and installed a handrail from the right side (which I was so grateful for because I needed the handrail from the right side to be able to ascend stairs).

Returning home. Walking again.

These stairs prevented me from leaving my home.
Now, they no longer were an obstacle.

Walking out of the elevator; in a moment
I will walk in to my home.

It felt so good to cross the doorstep of our home. Finally, I was back home. Unlike the last time I entered after my prolonged absence, this return was filled with joy and ongoing conversation despite the jet lag and exhaustion. Mom as always had prepared a delicious lunch and all of us shared a meal, with Michael again with us. My parents were so shocked and astonished by seeing me walking without suffering and standing up at ease that they didn't even know what to say or where to begin asking questions.

But Michael and I agreed that no matter how much we tried to tell stories of the hard work and ongoing challenges, that it would be impossible to convey the reality of what it took to attain this. I don't think we even needed to tell them; they somehow knew. While I was back in California, my mom mailed a birthday card, which brought me to tears as it contained the gem that I found in this journey. In the greeting card, she wrote a quote from the former U.S. President Calvin Coolidge:

"Nothing in this world can take the place of persistence. Talent will not; nothing is more common than unsuccessful men with talent. Genius will not; unrewarded genius is almost a proverb. Education will not; the world is full of educated derelicts. Persistence and determination alone are omnipotent."

The first several days we rested and visited downtown Vilnius City to walk around and show Michael more of tourist's favorite places. Again, unlike the previous time, this time my return to my beloved home city was entirely different – for the first time since my life had a dramatic turn. I got to walk again in those narrow historical streets of the Old Town and see my gorgeous city from the perspective of a standing height.

Before the accident, I looked at the city from the perspective of 5'6" eyesight. After the loss of my legs, I was forced into the confinement of a wheelchair; and since then, I had to look up to look people in their eyes and see their smiles. I know that normally people don't even realize this, nor did I, until I was forced to see the world from a sitting position. The world looks a lot different from when you sit as opposed to when you stand. Matters had changed.

"Yes," I thought. "The 'Old Inga' has returned."

No more wheelchairs! Finally, I could independently go out, get into a car and go to the city.

With my parents, first trip to the city of Vilnius wearing prostheses.

My parents and I are enjoying coffee with ice cream in Vilnius.

Visiting the Trakai island castle.

Those days we relaxed after the trip, went to the city for sightseeing and met some of my friends. After a short visit in Vilnius, Michael and I drove to the Orthopedic Center for a week, as was scheduled. Again we were warmly welcomed, except this time the second guest room at the center's hotel was given to me. It was good to return there as a guest, not a patient.

That week at the center was scheduled for us to showcase the result of our project, and then demonstrate Michael's hands-on training to local specialists fitting patients with comfortable prostheses. During the opening of Michael's training, the room was filled with doctors and specialists. Among the group, there was my favorite team, Dr. Anna, former prosthetic specialist Simas, physical therapist Erikas, and Benas (in charge of making arrangements for Michael's seminar). This time I was not in stretchy sport shorts and a t-shirt like they'd seen before, but dressed up nicely with black suit-slacks and a top. And I was comfortably walking and standing, sitting down and standing up at ease, being totally independent. The most important was that I was doing it without pain.

I knew everyone was paying close attention. The image of what they remembered then and what they saw now was completely different. I looked at each of their eyes, those who worked with me when I was a patient. I felt gratitude for their efforts. And it was a great satisfaction to show them I was able to do everything that I wanted. While Michael was telling them about the techniques he applied to make my sockets and steps that were taken to teach me perform various activities independently, I was interpreting him and was practically showcasing some of those activities. And Michael's slideshow of pictures showed me performing every single thing that they told me I would never be able to do.

The week at the center passed by quickly. Even though it was not a vacation spot with spectacular views or beaches, it was the ideal getaway week. Simply to be able to be together without any concerns was all that mattered. That week ended my story with that center, and the closure of it was far beyond what I anticipated. On our last night the center staff invited us for a goodbye dinner at a restaurant in the city. Midway through our celebration, Michael whispered, "Inga, let's go to dance."

I looked at him quite surprised, as his idea was another unexpected turn. This time I gladly accepted his invitation and without telling anyone what we were about to do, we excused ourselves. Our move got their attention and they quietly followed us, trying to understand what we were doing. As Michael stood by me, I independently stood up and we walked to the dance floor. Then, he put his one hand on my waist, took my right hand, and we began dancing. Michael and I looked into each other's eyes and smiled. I knew what he was doing. He was fulfilling another, final dream of mine. Without saying a word, we understood this was a fulfillment of my vow that I kept repeating over the years, that I would not only walk, but I would even dance and they would see it.

It was a rocky road to my dream. But after all, I did reach it. And now, everyone saw me dancing, wearing my prostheses, with the man who had made it all possible, and whom I loved with all my essence. In his eyes, I saw the kind of love that to this day brings tears to my eyes. Michael was both sweet and romantic, yet cautiously professional because so many of the center's eyes were watching. For us it was the victory dance, one that together we had worked so hard to achieve. Yet underlying it was the sadness that for all the fun and happiness, we both knew that in two short weeks we may never see one another again. My tears of victory were bittersweet because I could not imagine a future without Michael.

With that night, my dream to walk came to a full completion, a victorious and romantic closure. Every single one of my aspirations were accomplished. How could I have known that my desire to walk again would lead to such a beautiful journey? And little did I know how this journey would become my love story, the one for which I'd been waiting for so many years.

The next two weeks we had only fun ahead. Upon our return to Vilnius, my parents planned out a week in the resorts near the Baltic Sea. That week was another beautiful week, where we had no work, no to-do list; only rest and fun, exploring the most famous places in Palanga, and visiting the dunes of Nida. Many of my relatives and friends met Michael during this time. It was truly a great time, a time Michael said he would cherish.

Sunset tradition at the Baltic Sea, Palanga.

I am so thankful to my father, who made every effort to help me fulfill my dream.

My girlfriend Renata and I celebrating achievement of the impossible. Our friendship remained unbreakable despite enormous trials.

Time went by in a flash. Michael and I had a hard time coming to the realization that we were about to be separated once again. After being with him daily and having gone through so much, I couldn't see how we could be apart. Michael felt the same. But being positive and optimistic as always, he comforted me that we would see each other again, somewhere, somehow. After all, now he has established connections with the Lithuanian-American Community both in the states and in Lithuania; he would be returning to visit me. But the scariest part of my future was unknown.

After our goodbye dinner at the television tower restaurant in Vilnius, the next day Michael left to return to America. To the world that he had before he met me. I had to go back to my world. Separation with Michael was heartbreaking. What was next? The question made me restless. After all, now my impossible dream had been fulfilled, the life that I dreamed of for so long and worked so hard to achieve. After breaking through the stumbling blocks and changing my circumstances, I knew that many of the answers for what was next depended on me.

12

Breakthrough Formula

Dear Valdas,

I'm sorry that I disappeared for a while. Since my promotion to the Public Relations position, all I've been thinking about is how to perform my new duties successfully and meet the expectations of those who trusted that I would do well in this job. It is a different position from what I was doing before, and I need to learn everything that needs to be done.

One of my new duties is to organize fundraising events, and this is what I had to do immediately after I stepped into the role. I didn't have any event planning experience, nor have I ever solicited sponsorship funds or donations, so I had to learn quite a bit. My goal was to improve the results compared to a previous year's event, so I had to come up with new ideas to make it happen. It took a lot of effort and hard work and on Thursday, June 14, 2007, our organization had its annual fundraiser gala event, where we presented the Independent Living Legacy award to the Mayor of the city. It was my first event and it was a success. Our guests were impressed and everyone enjoyed their evening. As part of the event's program, I was one of the speakers. I spoke about the accident and the breaking point in my life, and by sharing my experience, I showed what a life changing impact the mayor and my organization's efforts can have in making this city wheelchair accessible.

As you well remember, my first three years following the accident, I was imprisoned by the walls of my room due to inaccessible housing, streets, building entrances, etc. Yet here in California, I can live actively despite my physical limitations. Now I finally can say that "I don't exist. I live." Everyone was very touched. Our executive director was very pleased with my presentation, and the mayor and many other guests approached me afterwards to extend their appreciation.

It felt good to see the fruit of my strenuous efforts. I worked very hard to organize the event, and it was a great satisfaction to see that after all, people enjoyed a beautiful and meaningful event. In addition, after the event the executive director announced at a staff meeting that it was the first event in the agency's history which resulted in no loss of money. It was such a big accomplishment to me.

It was a lot of hard work, often skipping lunch and working at home after work (no one really knew that I was working at home after work), but it taught me some very important lessons. It showed me once again that any desired goal can be successfully achieved, even if in the beginning you may have no idea how you are going to accomplish it. You can achieve whatever you want, if you are truly determined and committed to your outcome, do whatever it takes to achieve the desired result, and believe in your success.

And with this letter, I want to reveal what empowered me not to give up and break through those times when my vision and goals seemed too high of a mountain to climb. This is one of the things for which I am most grateful today. You may wonder why I feel so much gratitude for it. It's because I would not have the life that I do today if it weren't for the gems I share in this letter.

I lost count of how many times I met hopelessness face to face and questioned how I could possibly go on. So many times, it seemed that all my efforts were in vain. So many times, I was tempted to let go and stop pursuing my aim. Despair and potential failure repeatedly were staring right at me with their cold look, watching my next move. Oh, how glad I am that I made choices to not give up but to continue my pursuit! I pursued my goals despite the contrary circumstances that were against me. It's because I learned *how to break through* those times then that I get to live my miracle today. For many years, I just naturally kept on going despite any obstacles, and now, after I got acquainted with teachings of some successful entrepreneurs, speakers and authors, I noticed the same actions, patterns and attributes.

Let's face it, when you set your intentions to achieve something great, you will face obstacles. You can count on them; they will definitely show up. The reality is that you will have to conquer the resistance before you reach your success. The greater the vision and loftier your goals, the greater the resistance and obstacles you will meet. It is your responsibility to decide who is going to have a breakdown versus who is going to win. In other words, your ultimate outcome will greatly depend on you and how you deal with these obstacles.

And that's what I want to talk to you about this time – how to keep on going when it feels like you can't continue on anymore, and how to break through, so you reach your destination in spite of stumbling blocks placed in your way. I want to pass on to you what I have learned over the years of handling challenges and conquering obstacles, so you are equipped to face them with courage and knowledge how to break through and how to keep on going, no matter what.

I can't even describe how imperative it is to understand and apply what I am going to share with you. With all the knowledge I've been sharing with you, I would *not* have attained success in any of my life-changing goals if I did not do what I am going to share with you in this letter.

You may know the important aspects in achieving your goal, but you might not achieve it if you don't know how to break through the tough times. It is not a secret that when people face obstacles, many give up on the decisions and commitments they have made even though it seemed like they had the necessary training and skills.

Many give up on their dreams or making changes in their lives when the journey of achieving them seems too difficult. When I look at my life as an observer, the fact is – the only reason why I did not achieve the goals I wanted to achieve was because I left them alone in the midst of my pursuit, and the only reason I did achieve my other goals was because I did not give up on them, no matter how tough it was.

In both cases I had a vision and high work standards, but only some of my goals were achieved. What made my results different? What determined the outcome was how I handled stumbling blocks and the hopelessness when it showed up in my way. Every significant goal I set for myself had enormous challenges and obstacles that made my goals nearly impossible to attain. And, it's because I successfully handled such difficulties and never gave up that I reached my dream and I get to live my miracle today.

I know you are going through hardship now, and you might come to the point where you will be asking yourself how to keep going. Or you might contemplate giving in to challenging circumstances that face you, saying "forget it" to your aspirations. I am here to tell you, the only way to achieve and enjoy your goal is to break through the difficulties. I know I can tell you countless times, "Don't give up" or, "You can do it," but I feel like they would be but mere motivational slogans if I didn't give you the nuts and bolts as to how to not give up. In this part of our journey together, I want to pass on to you another priceless gem, but before I go into my explanation in depth, I have few questions for you:

- Are you ready to pay the price for the success that you want?
- Are you ready to do whatever it takes to achieve your desired outcome?
- Are you ready to keep going when the going gets tough?

I want you to ponder these questions and honestly answer them. Most likely you will face situations that will require such answers, and they will determine whether you will win or lose.

Many get excited about their new goals, and having strong intentions to reach them they do get it done. At the same time, there are many who get excited about their new intentions but don't achieve any of their goals, even though they were very sincere about their intention at the moment when they made that decision.

I missed many of my goals and did not attain what I had claimed to achieve when I was actively involved in the direct sales business. I did achieve other goals in that same business and in other areas of my life, which were very challenging and some of them seemed nearly impossible. I have had the sweet taste of success and I have had the bitter taste of missed goals. So why do we attain some goals and some of them we never reach? Why is it that some people achieve big goals and thus make a significant impact in the world while others don't? While there are many reasons why the goal might not be achieved, one of them – and it's a very common one – is making wrong choices when matters get tough.

It is not easy to do the work when arrows of life's troubles are hitting you and there is a strong temptation to drop this additional challenge that you have facing you. It is very hard to continue doing the work when the excitement, which was there at the moment of the decision, has gone. It requires courage and faith to get to work when ahead of you there are obstacles that seem too big of a mountain to move. The journey of the pursuit gets to be tough when those challenges seem so difficult to bear. It is hard to continue doing the work when your strenuous efforts are not paying off and you start questioning whether your aim is actually achievable. It requires enormous discipline to continue doing the hard work when discouragement is all you feel and motivation fades away like a fog.

It is much easier to let it all go, right? It certainly is, but that's when giving up and failure arrives. Moments of difficulty become critical and often decisive because for the most part, subsequent events are going to depend on how we handled the difficulty. Our future circumstances will depend directly on the choices we are going to make during that difficult time. So what can possibly motivate your perseverance when the going gets rough?

1. It's a Choice

I will start with the first key, which may seem invisible at first, but plays an incredibly significant role in our lives. When I look back, I see how there was always a fine line between continuing my life in misery, blaming unfortunate events or other people, as opposed to attaining a fully engaged and meaningful life.

There is a difference between entrepreneurs who became highly productive and those who could not achieve the results they dreamed about. There is a difference between those who achieve extraordinary results in life despite their struggles, losses and hardships and those who are miserable even though they have everything they need to lead a fulfilling life.

What was that fine line that made such a big difference in my personal experience? What can determine which direction our lives will take after adversity strikes us or when difficulties and overwhelming distractions take place in our lives? It all comes down to a choice. It's a choice whether we are going to show up stronger than those difficulties or anything that interferes with our intention.

All of us have difficulties in our lives, and each of us handles them differently. While we are going through some hardships, we don't always think about what's far ahead, because we are focused on the moment and how we feel at that time. Often we make conscious and unconscious decisions in order to get away from pain as soon as possible, regardless of its subsequent impact later on. But the fact is that our choice – what we are going to do during the difficult times – whether we are going to allow that hardship to sweep away our decision to pursue our aim or we are going to push through and continue our pursuit, will determine our ultimate result.

There is always a choice to step into the victim's role and blame somebody else for our broken destiny or failure to achieve our goal. At the same time, there is a choice to accept the responsibility for our current circumstances, be determined to make a change and take action to improve the situation. There is always a choice to take an easier route that does not require effort and discipline, and there is also a choice of diligent and relentless work. Both of these choices have different paths, and both will bring you to totally different destinations. There is always a choice to let it go when it seems too difficult to bear, but there is also choice to continue on in spite of it all. Again, these two choices have completely different outcomes. We have a choice to focus on how tough and laborious it is, but we also can keep our eyes on the horizon where our destination is and choose to keep going toward it no matter what. We have a choice to say, "This is it; I am facing the block I cannot get through; this cannot be done." Another choice – use this obstacle as a turning point and find another way. There is a choice to adopt the belief that nothing can be changed and go along with whatever circumstances arise, justifying it by saying "That's just life" or "I guess it's just my fate." Right beside us, there is another choice, belief that there must be a way, and with God's help I will be able to bring a change and improve my circumstances regardless of how bad they are. Now take your troublesome situation and apply these options of choices. Would you agree that in the long run those different choices will affect your circumstances differently?

Every time you face a difficult situation, there are always two choices that are waiting for you. It's like a crossroad - these two choices are going to take you on different paths, and each of those choices will bring you to totally different destinations. It is very important to:

- Always keep in mind where you are going, what is your ultimate vision, and
- Respond to a hardship or obstacle in such a way that will support you in achieving your ultimate goal and not jeopardize you in your pursuit.

"Sure, I would like to make the right choice, but how can I make it?" you might ask. "How do I make that step forward when I can't do it anymore? I feel tired, frustrated, disappointed, and at times don't want to get out of my bed and do anything. How do I continue?" Yes, I know. It is very hard to think about things that you need to do when you don't want another morning to come. This feeling is familiar to me. But there is a way. I am going to share it with you as we move along. For now, please know that while you are going through a hardship, it is best to not allow your emotions to determine your decisions about your ultimate goal. Have a rule for yourself that you are going to move forward relentlessly regardless of how you feel, despite obstacles and hardships that you may meet along your way.

2. Understanding Where Your Focus Must Be

While we're going through hardship, normally we don't think about what's far ahead because we are focused on what's going on at the moment, how we feel at that time. Would you agree that naturally we think about the problem, often focused on analyzing how difficult it is rather on our ultimate destination?

But the fact is that it is imperative to keep our destination in mind at all times. How many times have you heard sayings like, "I got bombarded by so many problems that I didn't have the energy to continue," or, "The challenges I encountered were too much to bear," or, "I got so tired that I just couldn't do this anymore." And you find out that they gave up on something they were just recently passionate about. There might be different reasons why they gave up on their pursuit, but overall it all comes to the same point: their difficulty overpowered them. For the most part – because they put so much attention to how difficult it was – more attention was paid to the challenge than on the ultimate goal. When we face any difficult situation, what will determine what's next is:

- How you are going to look at the situation (choosing the perspective),
- What you are going to focus on, and,
- What you are going to do about it.

I believe putting your focus on the wrong aspect of the situation is one of the fastest roads toward failure. It's very easy to give up when you focus on the obstacle or difficulty you are facing. Why? I am sure you have noticed in your life – the more you think about the bad situation and how difficult and painful it is, the worse it seems. Negative thoughts become more and more dominant and darker, and your problem snowballs into something bigger and more challenging. It reaches the point to where it seems unresolvable and you might say to yourself, "I can't do this." And here you are, you have arrived to a different destination that you first intended to.

We all want to get away from pain, and when the pursuit of our goal comes to the point when difficulties and challenges seem unresolvable, it is easier to drop it. When our mind is focused on the problems related to our goal, we will make unconscious and even conscious decisions to give up in order to get away from the pain as soon as possible.

For a moment, we might feel relief because the burden we carried is lifted from our shoulders and we won't feel that pain anymore. But there is a price to pay – the vision that we were so passionate about did not come to life. I've lived through it myself and watched people giving up. When I analyzed myself in the cases when I did reach my impossible goals, the interesting thing was that I never dwelled on how hard and painful it was for me to get there. Instead, my eyes were always on the ultimate outcome. My mindset was - I must overcome the obstacle, so I could continue moving forward toward my destination.

Imagine a race with hurdles. When an athlete runs close to the hurdle (obstacle), he jumps over it and continues to run. When he gets close to the next hurdle – he overcomes this as well and races until he reaches the finish line. The interesting thing is that while the runner sees every hurdle ahead, his eyes are not on the next hurdle, but where the finish line is. His focus is the destination, not obstacles on the way. I know this because I used to be an athletic runner when I was teenager. We were taught not to focus on the hurdle, but always to focus ahead where the race was ending. Why? Focusing on the hurdle most of the time resulted in the failure to overcome it, and the chances of winning were reduced. The major focus was the final destination; hurdles were just obstacles along the way which we needed to overcome and continue on running no matter what, until we reached the finish line.

That's the mindset I had when aiming for my goal. My eyes were set on my ultimate goal where I was going, and difficulties were something I needed to overcome, so I could continue my race until I reach my final destination. Obstacles are there to be overcome, and not something that could stop me.

When I trained to walk with prostheses, I didn't think of the pain. Instead I remained focused on the ultimate outcome: being able to walk independently. Now I know that if I had focused on the pain, no way would I have reached my goal. You called that "nonsense" and suggested I find a different strategy for life, because you saw what an insane hardship it was for me to walk. I didn't see it that way. While I was making steps, my mind and vision was far away into the future seeing my goal achieved. My focus was on the training that I must perform daily to attain that goal rather than on the hardship it takes to get there.

When I was in the process of establishing my new life in the United States, I did not think on how heart-wrenching it was to be separated from you and our parents, nor did I ever focus on how demanding and arduous an endeavor it was. My eyes were set on the horizon that had the gorgeous, colorful sunrise of my new life. My focus was on the actions I needed to take and goals that needed to be accomplished in order to meet my sunrise. Now I see that I unconsciously had the same thought pattern every time:

- During difficult times, I never focused on hardships, no matter how difficult or painful they were.
- My mental eyes were always directed toward my final destination.
- The immediate focus was on the work I had to do to attain my goal.

It's one of the most important key points in self-management that played a major role in my ability to break through the obstacles or handle hardships when it felt unbearable.

While you are going through a rough time, make every effort to keep in mind where you are going and focus on the activity you must do to keep moving forward. Do not dwell on anything that would pull down your determination. Rather, look up and in your mind look at the horizon. In faith, see what is going to change, where you are going to be in your life once you reach that destination. Stumbling blocks are mere hurdles that need to be overcome, that's all. It might hinder you, but it can't stop you. The only thing that can stop you is you.

Maybe for a moment you will need to focus on that challenge, but the only reason why you would allow yourself to focus on it is to see what you need to do to resolve it, so you could keep going forward. But while you are working on resolving it, do not forget why you are on this journey in the first place. Always keep your sight on the horizon and focus on what you have to do.

3. Show Your Resolve, Commitment and Relentless Action

Most of the time it is quite exciting when we decide to reach a new goal or to make a difference in someone's life. The thrill and enthusiasm about potential achievement motivate us to take action and we "start the ball rolling." The excitement, however, often passes away like a wave in the ocean. And then life takes its course and a variety of difficulties and obstacles show up greeting us with ironic smile. And that's when the trial comes, which will test us and our intentions. The dangers of a detour and even giving up on the goal will be right there even if we might be very serious and determined about our intention.

How many times have you or I decided to change something in our lives and yet it did not get accomplished? How many times have you heard people making New Year's resolutions and then after a month or so, their resolution no longer carried any value? Many of us get to the point where we feel drained, disappointed and discouraged to continue working on something.

The truth is that we must be wholeheartedly committed if we want to achieve anything and especially if we aim to implement a lofty vision. You can absolutely count on obstacles to appear. Therefore, you must equip yourself so they will have no power over you, your decisions and your choices.

Once I read an interesting idea: "God gives the food to the birds and animals, but He doesn't deliver it into their nests." And when you think of it, it's up to the bird to fly out of its comfortable nest and find food. It's the animal who needs to search and persevere, finding what to eat for themselves and their young ones. And some of them need to fight before they can satisfy their hunger or provide for their families. It's the same with us – we must make an effort to obtain what we want. In addition to expecting the Lord's blessing, we are very much responsible for our part and how much effort we apply. That's how it was in my experience. All the blessings I have in my life today did not land on my lap only because I believed and did nothing more. The Lord arranged opportunities for me, and I would get out of my comfort zone by faith and make an arduous effort to attain the vision that I had received. And the Lord has blessed me abundantly.

One of the things that contributed to the achievement of goals I set for myself was the will and non-negotiable determination to make it happen. Honestly, I don't think I would have ever achieved my victory of walking with prostheses or establishing my life in California If I was not as determined. I might create an image to others that it was not all that difficult, since I don't really talk about the difficulties. I will tell you the truth – no, it was not easy. However, my commitment to the outcome I was pursuing was way more important than any troubles, hardships or discomfort I had to deal with.

To be honest, shivers go through my body when I remember those years, when I was training to walk with artificial legs made in Lithuania. At times it was scary to even look at my own thighs, bruised and covered with sores and even open wounds. So many times it was painful to have my thighs touch each other when sitting and lying down or, even have a blanket on top of me. Nevertheless, I would put the medicine and the bandages on the sores, and would train again. I know many did not understand me.

Many were wondering how much longer it would take to realize this was not achievable. There were many moments when I would secretly ask myself how I was ever going to go to work or anywhere else while suffering such horrible pain. Yet my faith that I would still walk again did not allow me to give up and I was ready to do whatever I could to attain it. My resolve to walk again no matter what and my commitment to that goal was what made me get up in the morning and develop my walking skills, not negotiating with the price of stabbing pain and physical exhaustion. I refused to listen to people's advice to quit my pursuit, did not conform to their opinions and did not obey my mood or daily "want and don't want." It was my total commitment that pushed me beyond the hardship and fueled my determination to train every single day.

When Michael and I started working on my prostheses, our shared resolve to implement my vision was steadfast. Even before I arrived, we had absolutely no doubts that it would get done. Michael committed himself to do everything possible for his part, and I committed to do the same. We knew it would not be easy, so we had a mutual agreement to work together relentlessly. Looking back and remembering the difficulties we faced, what got us through was our complete commitment.

There were times when Michael encountered serious challenges to fit me due to my physical changes or figuring out the way for me to be able to fasten my prostheses with one hand. Finding the solution to each problem was more important to him than the amount of work and time it was costing him. I watched Michael working evenings after work hours and weekends; he would not stop talking and thinking about my prostheses. Michael's determination was unbreakable and he would not stop until he found a solution. I was the same way.

There were no questions "if" I would be able to perform the activity that I wanted to be able to perform. I was determined to do it. There were times when the fear I faced was so paralyzing that even my palms would sweat and I couldn't move. So many times I would question my ambition; it would have been much easier and safer not to pursue my aspirations. Yet the resolve to make it happen pushed me through the paralyzing fear and physical exhaustion.

I tried over and over again until I finally got to perform the activity I aimed for. We worked every single day including weekends, without exception, constantly reminding ourselves that having me comfortably walking and able to perform necessary activities was the only way I would return back home.

The aim of establishing my independent life in California required unshakable resolve and relentlessness as well. When I look back, what empowered me greatly were determination and a certain mindset – the same as my decision to walk with prostheses, the decision to establish my independent life in the land of sunshine was so strong that in my mind there was no "I will try" or "Let's see *if* this is possible." I arrived having faith as though I already had accomplished that. In my mindset, there was no other alternative and the only question left for me was *how* I could make that happen.

Difficulties and obstacles were ahead of me every time I aimed to implement my aspiration. But my determination and commitment pushed me forward, and those who were helping me through were inspired by my determination to succeed. While I was in the process of attaining my independence, the commitment I had made to myself and to the Lord got me through the hardships and those times when I thought, "Enough is enough."

I've never told you this, but once I even checked my finances with the intention of going home to take a break. I was at the point where I felt I couldn't stand another day of my experience and I was a moment away from purchasing a ticket to escape it all. The only thing that stopped me was my commitment to my ultimate vision. I decided to stay, numb my dissatisfaction and tiredness, and push through the struggle. I continued working, continued persevering until I attained my desired results.

Obstacles, challenges and problems will show up at your doorstep because they are a part of life. Don't be surprised by them. Don't fear and don't panic when they show up. Instead, equip yourself to meet them in such a way that they won't be able to sink your ship. At times life's troubles and other important matters of life will appear like roaring waves in a storm. It will look nearly impossible to sail forward. It is hard to continue doing the work when it gets painful and tough, or when problems are bombarding you. But these troubles will not be able to win if you persist. It's your resolve to reach that destination that will get you through. Don't leave any other options for yourself but to implement your goals. Instead of saying, "I will try," change it to, "I will get this done."

To *try* is to be in a state of mind where you allow the possibility of not making it happen. Resolve makes your decision non-negotiable. Once the excitement passes away like a beautiful wave, your ocean will be still and wherever you look – it's all the same view; it will seem like your ship is not moving, no matter how much effort you make to reach the shore.

It's hard to continue doing the work when no visible or tangible changes are happening, right? The path toward your destination might get lonely, difficult and endless. You will have days when relaxing, sleeping longer in the morning, or spending time with friends or family will look much more inviting and pleasant than doing the hard work. You might want to allow yourself to take it easy and not try so hard. There will be many temptations to drop your goal. But, the commitment will keep you on the path.

There is a big difference when you merely want something and when you are committed to achieving it. I will take a simple example: When you spend your time with your son, do you wish he would be comfortable and have a good time with you or are you committed to make sure all his needs are met and he enjoys his vacation with you? Can you feel the difference how your inner intention changes when you are committed?

When a ship gets into the ocean, for the most part the captain does not see the shore. Yet does he stop because he doesn't see the shore right away?

No. He knows where he's going and he knows he will reach that shore as long as he moves forward. The only way his ship will reach the shore is if he consistently moves forward, whether the ocean is still or it encounters a storm. Think the same way about reaching your own shore. It's the relentless work that will bring you to your destination. It's your daily choices and work repeated over time that will bring you the result. Consistent action toward achieving your goal is imperative. If a captain won't move his ship consistently, what would happen? His ship will either stand still or break and go under if the storm hits. Exactly the same way you will either stand still and never reach your goal, or you will lose your determination, passion and vision, and finally will give up on your dream and never reach your shore. In any situation, we can see that it's the consistent work at all times is what gets us to reach a goal.

Be committed to your final outcome which you are aiming for, and not to your expectations of how the process will go. Does this sound confusing? Well, think through this with me: if a person is ready to drop his goal because of difficulty he's experiencing while attaining the goal, so what is he really committed to? Apparently, he is committed to his comfort, but not to his goal. If he is ready to quit when it becomes tough, then his commitment appears to be conditional, right? The commitment to your goal is when you don't care what your journey is going to feel like – you will get there no matter what. Resolve, commitment and relentless work were always the answers to breaking through and reaching a successful finish.

And it's not only in my story. If you would do a little research about those who faced struggle and yet attained successful results, basically you will hear the same. You can find these attributes as a "secret to success."

It is not really a secret. It is the reality of what it takes to have a breakthrough and attain your goal. It became a secret to success because many already have forgotten that it takes commitment and relentlessness to attain a desired result. We live in a "microwave world" where many services are given to us quickly with comfort and without much effort. While I am glad to live in this age when we can get many things that way, I want to pass on to you what has not changed with our modern world – know that attaining successful results require hard work.

It will require your resilience. It will demand your relentlessness. It will require you disregard your "wants and don't wants" and require that you persevere. And this is what separates champions from losers. Winners are the ones who take action even when they don't feel like it. Only those who keep on going and push through the hardships reach their destination with a victory.

What Makes the Resolve and Commitment Unbreakable?

While resolve and commitment are imperative attributes of success, it is not a secret that many commitments end up being broken or left aside and then forgotten. Believe it not, I know very well the taste of "I can't do this anymore." I have thought that even when I was so determined to reach my goals. But I would always remember my ultimate goal and, as a result, I remained on my path persistently aiming for what seemed like I couldn't do. There was something that held my resolve together and strengthened my commitment every time I felt I couldn't take anymore the hardship.

1. Faith that It Can Be Done

Do you believe that it can be done? Don't rush to answer. I am not asking you to answer this as a cliché. Be honest with yourself. Do you really believe that what you aim for is possible? Do you believe that you can do this? Will you believe it can be done if the world around you claims that you are out of your mind to think that you can do this? Are you going to stick to your belief and be unflinching in your decision no matter how hopeless your pursuit might get? If people, who are far more competent in some areas than you are, come to you and say, "You are crazy, this cannot be done," will you believe that you can do this anyway? Are you going to hold on to your belief, if the journey will feel endless and you won't see your destination no matter how many steps you take?

The reason I am asking you these types of questions is because you will need faith in order to reach your finish line. When you think of it, a person would never take any project unless he believes in a successful result, right? You would not have started any projects in life or be involved in any of your business ventures if you had not believed in your successful outcome, would you? On the other hand, you did not even get into any activities, which you did not believe in.

The reason I am asking you these types of questions is because you will need *unshakable* faith in order to reach your finish line. This is very important. Would you make a strenuous effort and deny your own comfort and your needs for something that you don't believe is going to work? That's why it is so important to have this settled. Faith is what holds it all together. You begin something because you believe in what you are doing and you believe you will attain the desired outcome. You will persevere only as long as you believe in what you do. When you face trials in the midst of your pursuit, faith in your successful result will hold you steadfast and you will keep your commitment to complete your task.

The reason I put faith as number one is because faith is what held me together all these years. Many times it was the only thing that was left to me for hope for. Faith that with God's help somehow I would realize my vision/dream/goal was the only thing that carried me through the times of despair and hopelessness. When, after countless hours of strenuous work I did not see how I could possibly attain the results I was aiming for, I continued working because I believed success was possible. When I heard numerous opinions that what I was aiming for was impossible, I held on to my decision because regardless of their opinions I had faith this could be done.

I don't know if I had the tenacity to pursue my dream to establish my life in America if I did not have faith that the Lord was going to bless me in my aim and if I did not believe this was possible. My faith gave birth to my resolve and it was unbreakable. My strong determination and ongoing tenacity to pursue my goals came particularly from this one gem – you have to have faith that it can be done.

If you will not believe in your heart that what you are aiming for is going to happen, your ship might break when the storm hits you. You must have unbreakable faith that what you set your mind to reach is really attainable for you. When problems and hardships will show up, motivation and emotional excitement will fade away very quickly. But faith will carry you through. If you meet challenges that will try to destroy all you've worked on and facts before you validate that you need to quit – faith will strengthen you and will carry you through. Even your resolve and commitment might be shaken when challenges are enormous, but if you have unshakable faith in what you do and that it can be done – your resolve and commitment will not be broken by anyone or anything, because faith will carry you through.

2. The Power of "Your Why" and "What's the Cost?"

Would you jump into a raging ocean just to have fun with the waves when it's windy and the water is freezing? I assume not. And, would you jump if your son was drowning in front of your eyes? You know the answer. You'd jump not even doubting about it.

It's the reason why you'd have to do it that would make such a difference in your action.

Many say to me that I have strong willpower. While I have some, the truth is that it is not really willpower that got me through the hardest times. Have you noticed in my earlier writing that when I was sharing with you about my decision to attain any of my big goals, I always mentioned why I was driven to do it and why I was so determined to reach my goal? When I felt exhausted and was questioning my ambition, I would always go back and ask myself these questions:

- Why I started it in the first place.
- Why it was important to continue my pursuit.
- What it's going to cost me if I fail.

When the reason why it is important for you to achieve the goal is important and compelling enough, you will do whatever it takes to achieve it.

When I decided to increase the level of my independence, the desire to be self-sufficient again and live my life to the fullest was simply unquenchable. When I was making my first attempts to do something by myself and struggled with it, I would always hold my vision in my mind. Even though my idea required relentless perseverance, I knew why I was making those efforts. Knowing why I needed to work motivated me to make continuous attempts until I found my way. At the same time, I was escaping from the alternative – giving in to my traumatic injuries meant remaining helpless.

The cost of not trying would have left me being dependent on someone else for every little thing. I was ready to pay the price of the relentless perseverance. The crash had placed me in unthinkable circumstances, and I knew that I would remain in them if I was not going to do something about it. I couldn't tolerate the thought of spending my life being labeled as disabled within the four walls of my home. My arduous efforts were a high price to pay, but the cost of spending the remaining years of my life isolated from my world seemed to be a much higher cost.

When my strenuous work training to walk seemed to be endless and the pain hardly bearable, I always kept in mind my vision of freedom – going out and leading the lifestyle I'd had before. I knew why I was doing it. When I looked at my sores and swollen thighs, I would tell myself that this was the cost of my dream. There is always a cost for everything in life.

Another cost that was to be paid if I fail to achieve my dream was the immeasurable pain of being forced to live an imprisoned, lonely and purposeless life. Keeping in mind my dream and what's at stake fueled my determination every time my commitment faltered. I would remind myself daily where I was going and what would be the cost of not reaching my destination.

When I was in the United States making my first steps toward establishing the final stages of my ultimate vision, my mental sight was always directed forward where my dream was. Even though my immigration was quite smooth compared to other stories I've heard, still there were times when it seemed I could no longer tolerate my experience and I felt so tired.

Many times I wished I was home with all of you. In fact, as I mentioned earlier, there was one time when I was seriously checking my finances and the flights back to Europe to get away. You know what stopped me? I asked myself one question – what is it going to really cost me if I leave? That moment I fully saw that the expensive airfare cost was going to look like pennies if I made that step. The choice to run away from the hardship could have cost me beyond what I could possibly handle. What's at stake? My life was. I was already on my way toward full independence and the life that I so dreamed about; was I going to trade it with what I escaped from only because it was hard to deal with something? Sure, temporary comfort of being with my family in a home where I grew up would have healed my wounds. But then what?

The other side of the coin was the consequence of losing the opportunity. The pain of regret would have been unbearable. And it would have stayed for the remainder of my life. So, after having long, mental discussions with myself about why it was imperative to attain my goal to establish my life in California, and what would be the cost of my choice if I quit the battle, I decided to pull myself together and stick to my commitment.

You have to be ready for the hardships and equip yourself to meet them in a way that you come out of each battle as a winner. Challenges tend to show up in a way that scare us and make us think that they are stronger. Just like fear is powerful only as long as you allow it to dominate your thoughts, challenges seem like that until you start eliminating those obstacles, one-by-one and get them out of your way until you fully demolish them by your courage and relentless efforts.

When you are attacked by problems and challenges that make you question your pursuit, hold on to your faith not allowing for even a shadow of doubt. When your journey gets to be tiring and you feel like you can't go on anymore, always remember why you are on the journey in the first place. Remember your vision. Why is it important for you to continue? Why is it imperative that you successfully achieve it? If the reason why you are doing it is strong enough, you will get it done no matter what it takes to get it done.

And what's going to happen if you give up? What will it cost you if you won't make that happen? Now you are paying the price of your patience, efforts and hard work, and yes, it is a high price to pay. Yes, there is a cost to attain big goals. But the fact is, there is a cost to every choice we make. Giving up on your goal will have its cost, too.

Our ultimate destination depends on which price we are willing to pay – the price of our strenuous efforts or the unbearable price of regret. While you may be annoyed by the amount of effort it takes to attain success, consider carefully what it is going to cost you if you don't achieve your goal. Which path are you willing to take?

Remember, you make your own choice about what you are going to do during the difficult time. Your choice is critical. Most likely it will determine whether you will succeed or fail. There is always a choice to take an easier route, or step into the victim's role and justify that your vision cannot be achieved for whatever convenient reason you can justify. At the same time, there is a choice to accept the responsibility for your current circumstances, resolve to make a change, and be fully committed to your outcome, having faith that you are going to succeed.

Lay a firm foundation for yourself that you will always make a choice that will align with your purpose. You will always make a choice to overcome and do the best you can in any circumstances. Resolve to give life to your intention and be wholeheartedly committed to your decision. Make the non-negotiable decision that you will never give up, no matter what it takes for you to take another step. When you face some tough situation, don't rush to do anything based on an automatic reaction. A lot of times we simply react, making unconscious choices based on our habitual mental or emotional patterns. Stop. Think about the situation in the big picture.

Remember where you are headed. What is your ultimate destination? Why is it important for you to get there? What's at stake? Before you make any decision, keep in mind your destination and ask yourself, "Where will the choice I am going to make now take me ultimately?"

One of the lessons I've learned is that success is not mere luck, even though many have adopted this belief. Success comes as a result of resilience, perseverance and relentless, hard work. Those who have achieved success in any area will tell you that it's the result of their relentless perseverance and conquering every obstacle that tried to hinder them. Hardships are just a part of the whole picture. Knowing how to respond to them and knowing how to overcome obstacles will have you come out of the battle as a winner. Remember:

- It's your resolve that will be your driving force to make this happen no matter what.
- It's your commitment that will keep you going and will bring you further.
- It's the non-negotiable consistent, relentless action that will deliver results.

This golden trio will establish the ladder to ascend your highest mountain. And,

- It's knowing "Your Why" and "What's at Stake" that will keep those ladders unbreakable.
- It's your unshakable faith that will be the rock solid ground for you at all times. It will inspire you, strengthen and encourage you to keep ascending that ladder until you reach the top. It will hold you and everything together.

Well, now you know. This is what's behind my achievement of insurmountable goals. This is the formula for a breakthrough that I've learned through experience and which never failed me. This is why I was able to breakthrough, overcome and achieve. Think about it. Apply it in your life. Meet those hardships with courage, because now you know what will defeat them.

Remember, the only one who can stop you is you.

Love you much, till the next time,
Inga

13

My Decision to Build My Life in California

Dear Brother,

Now I will tell you about a very special time which, once again, changed the course of my life. When after the accident, watching its consequences, and questioning how I was going to live from that point forward, none of us could've ever imagined that my life would turn so incredibly. Just like my Lord spoke to me through His Word telling me that He was going to restore my life, that's exactly what happened. In this letter, I will share with you where that miracle started. This was the time when I paid attention to the signs through which the Lord my God communicated with me, directing my steps toward my life's recovery. That time frame was like a blind man walking into the unknown.

During this time the Lord continued teaching me to hear His words, to have strong faith and rely on Him. It was not easy and a bit scary, but I sincerely believed and stepped out of my comfort zone, and through faith made that step forward. Today, as you know, I live in this unbelievably beautiful place of the planet where I am very happy. I am living my dream. During this time I learned very valuable lessons. It's amazing how our lives can change if we:

- Pay attention to the signs and messages which God sends into our lives.

- Listen and do what God tells us to do while totally being confident in Him.
- Remain steadfast in our determination to achieve goals and work until we achieve it.

After returning home from my trip to the United States having achieved my dream goal, for a while I was in euphoria. Finally I was able to do what used to be my great dream – I was able to independently put on my prosthetic legs, stand up and walk. I was able to perform activities which before were impossible. Usually for a person these were natural daily activities and nobody really thinks, "Oh great, I can stand up; I can walk; I can climb stairs." I know I was one of those who never thought about it and didn't really appreciate it when I could. Now each time I walked up a step, sat down and stood up independently, I was as happy as a little child.

For a while I shared my victory and happiness with family, friends and acquaintances. Many were impressed, supportive and happy for me. I got support and congratulations from people who didn't know me personally. Again I was asked to give more interviews for some local television programs. I didn't really want to appear on television again, but it seemed a good opportunity to bring closure to the story that many followed, and to thank the generous people who sent their financial support. I was grateful to those who sent their financial assistance because they opened the doors of opportunity for me. And I wanted to thank them for all the support and love they gave to me, a complete stranger.

And now, my relentless strive to achieve my desire to walk again reached its culmination. I was so happy that I could go out and visit friends, and to go to church to thank my God for His goodness and His blessings. Of course, walking with artificial legs was a much different experience than walking with real legs. It wasn't easy. Nevertheless, there was no end to my sheer joy that I was able independently to go downstairs, walk out of our house, get into the car and go with my friends to various places. Finally, I experienced what I had desired for so long.

Do you know the very first place Renata and I went for lunch? It was the same Pizza restaurant/bar where Dalius and I were on the night that was pivotal to both of us. When she and I were discussing where we could go for lunch, Renata immediately said she knew a very nice place in the downtown area that had the most delicious avocado salads she had ever tried. Then I heard hesitation in her voice. After I asked her what it was all about, she said this was probably not a good idea because the restaurant she had in mind was the last place Dalius and I visited before our lives ended. I responded that actually, I would love to go. My appearance in that place will be a victory. I lost my both legs after I left that restaurant, and now I would walk in again, because I did not give up and got my legs back regardless. Indeed, it felt great to revisit the place which played such a crucial part in my destiny.

Upon entering, I had no special feelings or particular memories, but I could see the table where we sat that night. In my memory, only a few moments remained from our party that night. The last thing I could vividly remember was the moment I walked out of the restaurant and was approaching his car. What happened next I could not recall. It seemed that everything had been wiped out from my memory. For a moment, my mind was captured by the last memories of my previous life. Shivers of horror pierced me through. I decided to push away all my thoughts about it. It was in the past and the events of that night cannot be brought back to change them.

I was alive. I didn't give up. I fought and I won. I came back to this place with courage, looking into fate's eye and saying that I wasn't afraid and that nothing could stop me. I got my legs back and I would live my life how I chose, not how the tragedy tried to dictate.

Renata and I were enjoying our avocado salad lunch and shared our stories that happened while I was in the U.S. I was looking at her and thought to myself how happy I was. My dream came true! I could go out with my friend again and have lunch in the city, share our experiences and stories just as we used to do. I was so longing for it.

As I look back, I believe this was the time when I began thinking about what helped me achieve that which seemed impossible. I thanked God with all my heart for everything. The way events had evolved had been absolutely incredible. It seemed like some invisible force had brought certain people into my life, creating favorable circumstances. Everything fell into place with such perfect timing and precision.

I was astonished watching what was happening. I could not then and still cannot find any other explanation than this was God's answer to my prayers. It was His provision. Then, of course it was Michael's and other people's help. He and many people reached out their hands to me, and each of them played a big part in why I succeeded. And it was ongoing, disciplined hard work. Without a doubt, I would not have attained my successful result without resolve, perseverance and relentless striving to achieve the goal.

But I wanted to see what was deeper, what was behind the scenes. I wanted to know what was beyond all the work and help that I received. How had I managed to accomplish all this? I began analyzing myself and all I experienced. What came to mind was that I had a very strong desire for what I was aiming for. I did not *want* to walk, it was a *burning desire* to walk. It was far more than a simple wish or thought that "it would be nice to walk again." I refused to hear anything that contradicted my intention to fulfill it. I was determined and there could be no discussions about not accomplishing it.

Also, I worked very hard. I did not spare myself or my energy. I worked every day. I trained without any debates whether I liked it or not, whether I wanted it or not, whether I was in the mood or not. I would tell myself that I must train and there would be no questions about laziness or reluctance. Of course, there were days when I did not want to get out of bed and generally didn't want to see anybody or do anything. But I always kept in mind my dream and I knew that I could not fulfill it if I allowed myself to be lazy or comply with my mood swings or reluctance to work. I would pull myself together and continued working with diligence. Without continuous persistent work I would not have learned to take steps, to maintain my balance or perform any other activities. I worked hard and did everything possible to achieve results.

The essential part, the core that was holding it all together, was the belief that I would achieve this goal. My driving force was my dream and strong desire to fulfill it, and what gave me strength to break through and did not let me give up was my faith. My belief that I would walk was so strong that I knew I would. I did not allow any doubts to sow seeds in my mind. When any doubts would come, I would immediately push them away. I believed that I would walk and I would repeat to myself over and over, "I not only believe, but I know that I will."

What's more, I did not give any attention to the opinions of others that my desire was simply not possible or that all my hard work was meaningless, or that I had better find a different life strategy or that I'd have to live in a different way and accept it. I got to watch many different reactions and hear a myriad of doubts about accomplishing my desire, but I did not pay any attention to them. I believed that this was possible and I was ready to prove it to everyone. When my efforts seemed to be in vain, my faith that it could be done pushed me through. My decision to walk and my belief in success was unshakable. When I felt disappointed and had no inner strength to move on, prayer, faith and love of my closest people would lift me again. Step by step, I continued striving to fulfill my dream, believing I would succeed in spite of it all. Finally I came to the conclusion that we could achieve anything we wanted, if we truly desire it, if we did whatever it took to achieve our goal, firmly believing in our success.

So What Now?

As time went by, the excitement of victory began to fade. It seemed that something was not quite right. Something was missing. Something was not the way I envisioned. My daily life was not the way I thought it would be when I was able to walk again. My mornings began with no plans for the day. I didn't have to go anywhere, nor did I have anything to aspire to. No longer there was there joy or this wonderful feeling of victory after overcoming obstacles. There were no challenges that made me push and go beyond what I thought I could do. I would get up in the morning, make my coffee, and get on the computer. I would check my email to read Michael's letter and then – I didn't know what to do with the rest of the day.

In California, I got used to the fast pace of life. Every day was a new day with a purpose. Every morning would begin with my intention to get closer to my goal, and I was fueled with anticipation and excitement. Each day was like a new gift, which surprised me every time I got to unwrap it. I was constantly aiming for a goal and had daily progress. Upon my return from America, I was occupied for a while but then, after it all settled down, suddenly there was nothing to aim for.

No purpose. No intention. No anticipation. Nothing to look forward to.

I did not need to rush anyplace. I did not need to get ready to go anywhere. I wanted to put on my prostheses, stand up and walk. But I did not need to go anywhere. It didn't make any sense to put them on and walk in my apartment back and forth from one room to another.

That's not why I wanted them. Walking back and forth in my apartment was not the purpose for why I wanted my legs back and why others had worked so hard for me and I worked so hard. I looked at my new legs standing there in the corner and thought to myself, "Well, I have them. So what now?"

I felt empty inside. I began analyzing myself and my life, trying to understand why I felt this way even though I had finally achieved my dream. After I looked deeper within, I realized that what gave me more joy was not the result itself when you achieve it, but its pursuit. The real value in achieving a goal wasn't the feeling of success when you attain it. The greatest value of achieving an aspiration was what you learned and who you became in the process of achieving. It's the progress and personal growth that made me feel alive. My life seemed more interesting and exciting when I had goals to pursue, when I had a reason to get up with the sunrise and begin my day. It felt as if someone had opened my eyes and I was finally able to see - after I achieved one goal, I must find another one, and this is the way to move forward in life. And so I had to find another goal.

Since ultimately my vision was to gain full independence, I needed to set the next goal that would bring my life further to this aspiration. I remembered my inner dialogue with myself at my aunt's, when I decided to conquer my depression. I wanted to be active and useful, to connect with people and lead a lifestyle as I had in the pre-accident past. Walking again was the key to opening the doors of that kind of life. After obtaining the key, now I had to open the door to create what I desired. Working at the Business Lounge was not an option anymore, due to the fast pace of work and my physical limitations. Knowing what it would take to fulfill my duties, I knew even walking with comfortable prosthetic legs would not meet the requirements to perform. I needed to find something different. To be honest, by that time I was missing California.

I didn't tell you this nor did I talk about it with our parents, but a few months after my return to our homeland, I started longing for the land of sunshine; I was longing for everything I experienced. I missed the uplifting atmosphere, joy and laughter with Michael and other people. And I was longing for Michael; I was longing for everything about us. But my longing went beyond missing him. I missed the daily sun and the crystal clear blue sky; I missed the ever-changing landscapes; and I missed having a daily purpose, anticipating new goals and achievements.

I felt freedom in California. There were no obstacles or challenges to go out and do whatever we had planned. Even though I had never thought of living there, I began to think it would be a fantastic place to build a new life. From the perspective of a person born in Lithuania who has experienced so many bitter cold winters, it seemed to be summer all year long in California, whether or not it was the northern or southern part of the state. Cold winters would not be a problem anymore.

More importantly, the environment in California was highly accessible for people in wheelchairs; I would not have any obstacles using public transportation, entering buildings or moving around the city whether I was wearing my prosthetic legs or using a wheelchair. I knew, California was a place where I could be completely independent.

But these were dreams. Quite frankly, it didn't seem realistic. How would I live there alone? At home I had my family and friends, without whom I simply did not see myself. And so I had to push such thoughts away.

I got on the Internet to look for colleges in Vilnius. I called Vilnius Pedagogical University where I hoped to study English. Yet I heard that it was not handicap accessible, that every day I would have to overcome stairs to enter the building. Built in 1935, and like many historical buildings in Vilnius, it hadn't been remodeled to accommodate wheelchairs. The building had neither accessible bathrooms nor an elevator that would allow me to get to my classes. I don't remember the other schools I researched, but after reaching out to several I felt I would see a stop sign wherever I looked.

"I don't really have access to any school that I want," I said. "And the same issue is going to occur with work. I will face the accessibility issue everywhere I go. Instead of seeing the doors open for me, I will hit a brick wall everywhere I hope to go. Something's not right with this picture."

I caught myself thinking that I didn't have what I thought I would have. I thought prostheses would give me the possibility to live a full, active lifestyle as I had before the car accident. Of course I was able to get out of the house; I could even get into the car and leave. Yet I had to face the fact that even though I was able to do these things, it wasn't the same as I anticipated.

Walking with prostheses in my physical condition was challenging, and I had to have at least a somewhat accessible environment; at least stairs had to have a handrail on the right side for ascending. I soon learned how the environment in the city was not even close to what it was in most American cities.

Besides, in Vilnius I couldn't simply visit people all the time. And I wanted to work. I wanted to be useful and helpful. I wanted to have a purpose, to do things that were meaningful. But now the question was whether I would be able to go to my studies or even work, continually overcoming obstacles due to the lack of accessibility.

I was advised to look into other studies or work from home, but I immediately refused; it wasn't why I aspired to obtain comfortable prostheses. Michael did not work so hard for me to put these prostheses in the corner and work from home. And studying or working from home was not what I was aiming for.

I fulfilled my dream, we all shared the joy, and now it was the time for real truth. I saw that even having comfortable prostheses was not going to open the doors for an active lifestyle in Vilnius. My conclusion was reaffirmed when the weather cooled and the first snow covered the ground. I wanted to try and walk on the snow and I went out to see how it was going to work. Quickly I found that it was not only difficult, but very dangerous. My legs would slide, it made me unstable, and I could fall at any second with no control over the outcome. My cane, the only protection and tool for stability, was also unstable on slick surfaces, and it fully pulled my security away from me. To take steps and hold my balance was nearly impossible.

Although I had never let the fear of falling and other obstacles stop me, this time I had to admit and accept that to walk independently in the winter was going to be far too dangerous. I told my father how this would be the first and the last time that I would walk outside in the snow. This meant that for about four to five months of the year, I would be restricted to our home; only this time, by something which I had absolutely no control over: the Lithuanian winter weather.

It was difficult to accept, but I realized that obtaining prosthetic legs fulfilled my aspirations only partially; it didn't really open the doors of the life that I envisioned and was aiming for. I had finally gotten comfortable prosthetic legs, but due to the inaccessible environment and the climate, I was not able to use them whenever I wanted.

I started feeling uneasy. After such a wonderful time in California, and after all the work and so many heartbreaks and victories, and after so many tears of joy when accomplishing a new activity wearing prostheses, I again found myself among four walls, with no opportunities to move forward in life. I found myself imprisoned by my home again. At one time, I was offered a job from home to do the search on the Internet. I agreed because I wanted to have at least some kind of occupation, but it only reaffirmed that working from home was not what I was aiming for.

Watching how I was slowly but surely reverting to a dull existence, my feelings of discontent began to stir eagerness within me, to do something with my life. I knew that I could not continue my life like I'd been living. I needed a change.

The idea of going back to California wouldn't leave me alone. More and more did I long for the land which I had fallen in love with from the very first day. People's outlook about life and their attitudes about people with disabilities were different, and the environment was so accessible. The streets, transportation, entrances into buildings, bathrooms and just about everything else were accessible for people with disabilities. I never had any obstacles whether I moved in a wheelchair or wore artificial legs. And the sun! I so missed California's bright blue sky and always present sun.

Yet moving seemed too high of a leap that I didn't dare speak to anyone about it. I imagined living across the globe from my family and friends. It was impossible. I couldn't even think of it. Furthermore, questions as to where I would live and how I would survive alone were too overwhelming. Once again I pushed the idea away. But I couldn't find any peace within.

At daytime, I couldn't really do anything because whatever I did, I felt there was something different that I was supposed to be doing. At night I could not fall asleep due to the endless thoughts about my life and which direction I should take to move forward. I was flustered and didn't know what to do. I was both mentally and physically stagnant.

I started looking for the answer in the prayer. I asked the Lord to direct me which way I should move forward in life, because I was torn apart and couldn't handle the ongoing restlessness anymore.

As it's written in the Bible, *"Ask, and it will be given to you; seek, and you will find; knock, and it will be opened to you." (Matthew 7:7).* Little did I know that soon, I would receive my answer.

At the Crossroads

One day, I was getting ready to visit some friends at my favorite rehab place, the Valakupių Rehabilitation Center. I called the taxi. I was absolutely thrilled that I independently was able to put on my artificial legs, got dressed, walked out of the house and got into the cab to go where I needed to go.

On the way, the driver and I talk about something insignificant, and then somehow our conversation turned serious. We ended up conversing about success, what was necessary to achieve a goal, even that which seems impossible. The conversation made me think again about what made it possible for me to achieve my goals that at one time seemed almost impossible. The driver asked me if I liked to read. I answered that I was not patient enough to sit for hours and read. I did some while I was in bed in the hospital but naturally, I was more into action rather than sitting in the same place doing the same thing.

He continued by asking if I had ever read *The Greatest Mystery in the World* (1997) by Og Mandino. I answered "no" and we continued our conversation, which I must admit deeply interested me. In fact, the subject had been lingering in my thoughts lately, as I had been contemplating my next life move. When we arrived to my destination, he escorted me into the building and then asked me to wait for him. He returned in few minutes, holding something in his hands. When he came up to me, he reached out his hand, giving me the little book, as though it was an invaluable jewel.

"Inga, this is for you," he said smiling. "And I hope next year to see *your* book in our bookstores."

Then he made a facial expression to make sure I understood what my next important goal was to accomplish. After saying goodbye, I stayed there speechless for a few minutes, holding the little book. I looked at the title – *The Greatest Mystery in the World* – realizing it was the book we were talking about. Looking at its pages, I could tell it had been through a number of hands. I paid close attention to his manner in handing me the book and it seemed, he was passing on to me a treasure. For some reason the little book intrigued me, and that was a feeling I had never felt before about any other book. His request to see my book in the bookstores was quite an unusual idea. In fact, the way he had spoken, it sounded more like he had been challenging me to write a book.

"Me? Write a book? Who am I to write a book?"

I questioned his challenge since I never even considered doing it. But his words seeped into my heart. I was mesmerized by the conversation with the driver and the way he handed me what he considered a precious treasure; and I couldn't wait to get home and read that book. When I returned home, without talking to the parents or even having dinner, I immediately went to bed and began examining my gift saying to myself, "The Greatest Mystery in the World? Why did I meet this particular driver, have quite an out-of-the-ordinary conversation, and then, he hands me this? But there are no coincidences, not like this."

While still being a bit puzzled, I opened the book and began to read.

I found myself reading page after page. I could not stop. It captured my attention so strongly that I did not want to do anything else but read this book. It began with an intriguing story and soon I understood the title. The book taught wisdom about what it took to achieve success and have a purposeful fulfilling life. I was absolutely astonished. It was giving me the answer to the question that I so intensively had been thinking about since lunch downtown with my best friend - what was behind the successful achievement of my dream, and what enabled me to achieve such challenging goals, something considered impossible by so many people.

It turns out that I had been using the universal principles of success without even knowing it. I read page after page, stunned; it seemed like I saw myself in every chapter. As I was reading, in my mind I kept saying, "Yes, that's exactly how I was thinking. That's the attitude I had; I had a clear vision of my desire. I did not give up and I firmly believed. I was completely focused and persevered to achieve my goals."

I learned that my attitude, my way of thinking, the vision and my actions had been exactly the same as what the book taught about what it takes to achieve success. The more I read, the more it seemed as though the book was alive, and that it was speaking to me. Every chapter, every paragraph spoke to me. I wanted to learn as soon as possible everything that was written in this book. In addition to learning what stood behind my achieved success, it showed me what I needed to do next to improve my life. I was especially touched by the chapter on opportunity, learning how it is that every one of us is given an opportunity, yet when it comes, we must act on it without waiting or hesitating, otherwise it will pass and never come back to us again. It urged to remember that four things do not come back: the spoken word, the past life, the sped arrow and the neglected opportunity.

I knew I had to pay close attention to the wisdom laid out in this chapter. It felt as though a divine voice was telling me that my destiny was in my own hands, not in the hands of circumstances over which I had no control. I stood at the crossroads. I could either continue living in misery, restricted by my circumstances, or I could use the opportunity to return to California and take action to change my life.

The author called the book the Hand of God, and now I felt that the Lord was reaching His hand out to me, answering my prayer by putting this book into my hands, which showed me the direction I needed to take. This book opened my eyes; it was time for me to take the initiative and change my life conditions that I was not happy about. I could not wait any longer. My family, Michael and many others have helped me as much as they could. Now was the time for me to step up and create the life I desired. Now it's up to me. I must use the opportunity to change my life.

Earlier in the year I visited the place where I knew I could be independent: California. I knew some people there, so I wouldn't be completely alone. I had to go back and put all my efforts into re-establishing myself. I knew that in California I could live independently and have an active and interesting life despite my injuries. I already had a glimpse of it during my visit, and I knew my life would be transformed if I resided in the land of sunshine.

There was no way I could continue spending my days in my room, occasionally having the chance to go to some rehab center or some camp for those with disabilities. Yes, my physical condition had changed due to the multiple injuries and yes, I couldn't perform certain activities, but I am a living human being. I have feelings and a clear mind. I wanted to live a full and active life in spite of it all. No matter how much I loved you and our parents, and no matter how difficult it was to even think about me living so far away from all of you, I just could not see how I would be able to live in Vilnius the way I desired. I knew I must be willing to pay the price, be courageous and change it all.

Interesting and strange was the fact that inside I felt the urge to make a decision right then and there. I felt that the longer I hesitated, the more time I would waste, missing my once-in-a-lifetime opportunity. Time was moving forward without waiting, so I had to use it wisely.

It seemed to me that I was standing on the crossroads of my life, and the decision I would make then would determine the path for the rest of my life. I had two choices: to use the opportunity, take the initiative, and return to California to change my life; or to stay in Lithuania in my comfort zone and go with the flow. Between these choices an inner conflict formed.

Going to California meant heading into the unknown without any security or guarantees, all the while risking my family's savings, but it would open the possibility of creating the life I desired. The second choice meant living a secure and comfortable life with my family and friends, but then I would pass the chance to create and live an independent life, and continue living being restricted and limited by my circumstances, with no opportunities to be active and helpful. I would live a dull existence as a disabled person in a society that looks upon the disabled with condescending attitude as though they are an inconvenience to them.

Which path should I choose? The path of the unknown, but with the opportunity to change my life? Or the path of security and comfort, but with no chance to fulfill the life my Lord had set out for me by letting me live following the accident? To tell you the truth it was scary. Struggling with the decision was scary because returning to California meant going into the total unknown.

In California I had no place to live, nor did I have the money to rent an apartment. And then came the other things like food, utilities and furniture. I didn't have a job, nor did I have the University education to get a good job. I didn't even have the legal right to live or work in the United States. And I had no legs. My left arm was still paralyzed, so out of all four limbs I had only one arm that I could use to do the activities I needed. How would I accomplish household activities? How was I going to move around the city alone in a manual wheelchair? All this time I had my family taking care of me. How was I going to do these things from across the globe, alone?

In comparison, it felt good and comfortable and safe being at home. My family and friends were always there with me. Mom and dad or you would always make sure that I didn't have to worry about anything. But sitting at home all the time was a waste of time, especially without any occupation. I couldn't tolerate such an aimless and meaningless way of life. Now that I knew there was a place and a way for me to live a full meaningful life, it became unbearable to watch how my days were going by in such an empty and wasted way. I didn't want to be a shut-in and I refused to be treated like a disabled person.

And so I couldn't find peace because I didn't know what to do, but I knew *The Greatest Mystery in the World* had been placed into my hands to direct me towards the path I needed to take to move forward. I received it right when I asked the Lord to direct me and show me what I should do with my life. The book appeared in my life to encourage me to take the initiative, to create the life I desired rather than waiting for life to get better by itself somehow. Now was the time to make a decision.

But I felt so lost from all my various thoughts, doubts, questions, assumptions and feelings that I just didn't know which choice would be the right one. Finally, I decided to bring this before my Lord in my prayer, and ask Him to tell me clearly what I should do. I didn't even know whether those thoughts about California and desire to return were inspired by Him or just my own emotions. I was mixed up and I needed to hear from my Lord.

One evening after prayer, after asking the Lord to speak to me through His Word, and give me an answer if this was Him directing me, I opened the Bible. Once again, I opened it believing that I would be led to a passage telling me exactly what God wanted to say. The Old Testament unfolded before me, and without even choosing any particular verse, I began reading:

> *"For the Lord your God is bringing you into a good land—a land with brooks, streams, and deep springs gushing out into the valleys and hills; a land with wheat and barley, vines and fig trees, pomegranates, olive oil and honey; a land where bread will not be scarce and you will lack nothing; a land where the rocks are iron and you can dig copper out of the hills. When you have eaten and are satisfied, praise the Lord your God for the good land he has given you. Be careful that you do not forget the Lord your God, failing to observe his commands, his laws and his decrees that I am giving you this day. Otherwise, when you eat and are satisfied, when you build fine houses and settle down, and when your herds and flocks grow large and your silver and gold increase and all you have is multiplied, then your heart will become proud and you will forget the Lord your God, who brought you out of Egypt, out of the land of slavery. He led you through the vast and dreadful wilderness, that thirsty and waterless land, with its venomous snakes and scorpions. He brought you water out of hard rock. He gave you manna to eat in the wilderness, something your ancestors had never known, to humble and test you so that in the end it might go well with you. You may say to yourself, 'My power and the strength of my hands have produced this wealth for me.' But remember the Lord your God, for it is he who gives you the ability to produce wealth, and so confirms his covenant, which he swore to your ancestors, as it is today. If you ever forget the Lord your God and follow other gods and worship and bow down to them, I testify against you today that you will surely be destroyed. Like the nations the Lord destroyed*

> *before you, so you will be destroyed for not obeying the Lord your God." (Deuteronomy 8: 7-19 NIV)*

While reading those words, I felt an unexplainable force from these verses. It seemed like those words were alive and talked to me. I had a clear insight that the Lord put me onto this path and that it was He who was directing me to return to California to rebuild my life. He would provide and would bless me abundantly. But I was cautioned to be obedient, and not get distant from Him by not following His commandments. I was astounded. Like the supernatural feeling when I read the passage through which the Lord spoke to me about restoring my life, now I felt the same. I knew the Lord was speaking to me again through His word. I had not read this chapter before and had no idea what was written when I began reading it. How could this be that I opened this chapter and started reading from this verse which answered my inquiry after praying and sharing my questions and doubts with the Lord?

I knew it was not a coincidence. Even though this was not the suggested way to read the Bible, I walked in faith searching to hear from my God, and I believed the Lord was speaking to me according to the level of my faith and understanding. I read again Deuteronomy 8. And read it again. I felt very clearly that this chapter had been the answer to my prayers and concern for my thoughts as to whether or not I should move to California.

In the morning I woke feeling very good and easy. I remembered what I had read the previous night and noticed that I was no longer restless. I felt at peace knowing that the Lord my God had spoken to and directed me. Now it was up to me. I had to make the decision. I had to choose action, to move to California, or no action, to stay at home. I felt much better and easier after I got the answer as to what I had to do to change my life.

However, now I had numerous questions of *how* I was going to do it. I had no idea how this would be possible. After all, I had absolutely no means or resources to establish myself in California, one of the most expensive states in the country. Besides, I would be going to America alone, and who would be there with me if something bad happens? I trusted Michael would help, and I knew people whom I'd met and who loved me, and probably they would help. But they had their own lives and I couldn't be there with me all the time to take care of my needs.

All day long I thought about it, but I didn't talk to anyone. I felt that I had to make the decision on my own, so that I wouldn't be influenced by anybody's opinions. In the evening, alone in my room, I again prayed about my uncertainty and concerns regarding the unknown. After prayer I picked up the Bible believing that I would find an answer. Again I opened my Bible and started reading from where I opened it:

> *"Fear not, for I am with you; Be not dismayed, for I am your God. I will strengthen you, Yes, I will help you, I will uphold you with My righteous right hand." (Isaiah 41:10)*

I can't describe how I felt at the moment. To say that I was shocked is not enough. I felt that the Lord was directing me with divine encouragement not to fear, to take that step and move. At the same time, I felt indescribable inner peace. It was the kind of peace that surpasses human understanding. It was strange and difficult to grasp how this was possible as I faced the challenges of travelling alone across the globe, away from my family, to establish a new life without the means nor the resources to do it.

Despite my realistic thinking, I felt at peace. My mind and my heart were battling, and I decided to follow what I felt peaceful about, and by faith I put my confidence in my Lord. I believed God would take care of all my questions and concerns; I simply placed my life in His hands. And I knew I was safe. As I was thinking about it all, holding my Bible, I opened up yet another verse:

> *"I will both lie down in peace, and sleep; for You alone, O Lord, make me dwell in safety." (Psalm 4:8)*

With that peace of mind I fell asleep.

My Decision

In the morning, I got up in a good mood and realized, thoughts about returning to California were filling me with serenity and joy. That was the last sign that helped me finally make my decision. Although it seemed unrealistic to accomplish what I had in mind, I decided to listen to the inner voice and walk in faith. Even though I was aware that I had no means or guarantees, with no idea as to how I was going to survive on my own there, what mattered was that I finally had direction; I saw where God was leading me. And if I received His promise to bless me and protect me, then what should I be afraid of? God has authority over all circumstances, and if He said that He would help, then it meant opportunities would arise, and that He would send people who would help, and that everything was going to work out successfully. This was another time, when I had completely – with all my heart and my mind – by faith rely on the Lord. Without hesitating any longer, I went to the family room and told everyone about my decision. Of course, to the parents the news was shocking.

"What do you mean, you are going to live in America?" they asked. "How are you going to live there alone, Inga?"

I could see how they were caught off guard. I couldn't say how I was going to do it, because I did not know. But then I shared my heart with them, explaining that I could no longer sit at home restrained without the opportunity to create a fulfilling life. I was yearning for a fulfilling, meaningful life, and in Vilnius living conditions kept me restrained. Every day I was heartbroken watching how days were passing by, and as they passed, my life was going nowhere.

I wanted to live a full, active life again. I wanted to study, work and be helpful to others. I wanted to be able to get out of my home whenever I wanted to. I wanted to build relationships with my friends and be connected with new people. I wanted to travel and see the world. I simply wanted to live as everyone else did.

During my stay in California, I recognized how the non-winter-like climate, the equal opportunities, and the accessibility for people with disabilities would allow me to live independently. Public transportation was equipped for wheelchairs, streets had curb cuts, buildings had accessible entrances, services were high quality, people were very friendly and helpful, and I certainly wouldn't be alone. Apart from Michael, I knew other Americans, so I wouldn't be alone if something happened or if I needed help.

I honestly told them I had no idea how my idea was possible, but the only way for me to know about the possibilities was when I am physically there and actually see how this could be done. I would never know by sitting at home. I had to travel back, to see if I could start studies in some college, find a job, and step by step find a way to establish myself.

I was fully aware it would not be easy and I would face many challenges, but I still wanted to try. And if I didn't succeed for whatever reason, then at least I would know that I really tried everything I could. I did not sit idly and wait until someone else would come along and make my life better. I would not be able to forgive myself for missing the opportunity only because I was afraid of the unknown and had no courage to leave a comfortable and secure life.

After the conversation, I saw that concerns had subsided. As well, the parents trusted Michael and knew that I had met new friends in America, and that I would not be there totally alone. So, they supported me in my decision.

I could see the relief in your eyes after I told you I wanted to move. You always believed it would've been much better and easier for me to live there. I saw in your eyes how this time you were happy about my choice, and you believed in my success. I was so very happy to have your support even though this plan was crazier than flying to Turkey to meet with an American prosthetic specialist whom I'd never met.

When shared my decision with friends about moving, everybody supported me because America was considered a dreamland. While I was making the announcement about my new goal, usually it was accompanied by, "My next goal is virtually impossible as a flight to the Moon, but I will try anyway."

Perhaps I was the only person who realized in what unknown and challenging position I was putting myself into. But what they didn't know was how faith took me to this decision and faith would sustain me once I got there. Of course, I couldn't wait to tell Michael. We'd been continuing our email correspondence since he had left. Since we had achieved the impossible once already, I knew Michael would be the one to say, "You can do anything," and would cheer me up on my new venture.

To my surprise, he wrote a very nice, but not very encouraging letter. I cannot remember exactly how he put his thoughts and concerns, but suggested that I should think twice if I really wanted to do it. In essence, he could hardly see me living in California alone. He was worried about me being separated from my loving family and friends. He tried to explain that I would be taken care of, comfortable and safe living at home with my family. I wouldn't have any concerns or troubles, which would be totally opposite if I were to move. Besides, it would be very challenging for our relationship because of Margaret. If I stayed at home, he could travel to Europe for business to visit and we would avoid any trouble in that particular matter.

But I had already made my decision; nothing could stop me, even if it was Michael, whose opinion I greatly valued and respected. I responded, explaining my motives as I explained them to my family. After reading what I had to say, Michael agreed with me that, indeed, it would be easier for me to live in California because of the climate and accessibility. Only he was concerned about obtaining legal resident status. In addition, the cost of living was one of the most expensive in the country, and he couldn't imagine how I would be able to rent an apartment and survive having no formal education and no job. Michael said he was afraid that he no longer could guarantee that my dream would come true, and I would be very disappointed when reality set in.

I told him that I understood everything and that I wasn't going to argue, but in spite of the obstacles, I wanted at least to try. There must be a way and I was ready to work hard and do everything I could to make it happen. Michael said he would not be able to give me as much time and efforts as he did previously, but he would help in any way he could. He wanted to make sure I fully understood that this time he could not promise anything, and that there were absolutely no guarantees I would succeed. It was enough for me. All I wanted him to say was, "Okay." I didn't need reassurances. Nor did I require any guarantees; it was obvious there were none. I just wanted to use my opportunity and try.

From other Americans I got various opinions. Most of them were very happy about the idea. I received support and encouragement because they thought California was the ideal place. Margaret, among others, was concerned and repeated the same issues, but I didn't have any answers.

But it made me feel good to receive support from some American friends, although there were no promises to help me. I didn't blame them because they had their own families, jobs, businesses and their own problems to deal with. Besides, I did not want to load my challenges onto their shoulders. For me the most important thing was to have at least their emotional support, so as a stranger I wouldn't feel completely alone in a foreign country. And I would have someone to ask for help, should that become necessary.

I again found myself in a position where I could not rely on family, money (we simply didn't have any), or favorable opportunities from others. I did have friends who loved me and were very supportive, and I believed they wouldn't leave me alone if I were in trouble. However, there was no one and nothing to rely on. Even Michael, who would always encourage me and empower me to be unstoppable in my aspiration to walk, was doubtful about my new aim. I was left to rely only on God and to trust in His promises. I believed that if He told me I should not fear and go – He would create opportunities, would send people to help me and circumstances were going to be in my favor. I knew that everything was going to be alright.

I would be less than forthcoming if I said that I didn't have second thoughts: "What if nothing works out and I have to go back to Lithuania? What if something happens to me?"

Of course such thoughts came to mind more than once. And the more I focused on questions of potential failure, the scarier it felt to take that step. But finally, I made the decision to not be afraid and instead trust God with everything. I replaced fear with faith. Maybe it might sound like another cliché slogan, but I truly did that. When doubtful thoughts came, consuming me with fear, I would immediately stop entertaining that thought and replace it with, "Since the Lord directed me and promised me, everything is going to be well."

And in the worst case, I would come back to Lithuania, but at least then I would know that I tried, that I took the risk and did everything I could to improve my life. But I would regret it for the rest of my life if I hadn't even tried.

So, after all the sleepless nights and thoughts about the uncertainties before me, I made the decision to do everything possible to fulfill my dream. I was determined to put all my efforts, and ready to pay any price of my work and strength to achieve my next goal. Now, I know that it's possible to achieve even that which seems impossible.

Quite frankly, I spoke that I was going "to try" to establish myself in America, but my mindset was different. In truth, I was not going "to try" it. I was going to do it. I did not leave any alternative to myself. I was very well aware that I would not be able to live in Vilnius the way I desired, so I just could not allow myself to not achieve my aim.

Establishing myself in California was the goal that I had to achieve and there could be no turning back. I would look for ways as to how I could start my life, and I would not give up until I made it happen. I remembered my thoughts about what was beyond my successful result of my first goal, and I repeated to myself, "You can achieve anything you want, if you truly desire it; work hard and do whatever it takes to achieve your goal and believe in your success."

So, my dear brother, that is how I made the decision to return to California to rebuild my life. I think you remember that time; it was a very difficult time. My journey to the United States required absolute trust in the power of God. And my faith in the Lord and confidence in Him did not fail me. The Holy Scriptures states: those who trust in the Lord will not be put to shame.

> *For the Scripture says, "Whoever believes on Him will not be put to shame." (Romans 10:11)*

> *"Then you will know that I am the Lord, for they shall not be ashamed who wait for Me." (Isaiah 49:23)*

From my personal experience, I can testify it is true. I sincerely encourage you to believe in your heart and your mind that the Lord your God has authority over all and we all receive according to our faith. As we believe we receive.

As you see, it was not that easy to leave everything and step into the unknown trusting God, while the facts were showing me bluntly this was simply not possible. But because I have chosen to trust my God's promise despite the 'realistic facts', I received a blessing. One of the greatest gems I would like to pass on to you is this – have total, unshakable faith in the Lord your God. He has control over all your circumstances.

I really don't know which direction your life will take, but I believe (and I also want *you* to firmly believe) that all together will work out in your favor. Just fear not and do not worry.

Always remember that we all receive according to our faith.

Another important thing I want to note, in addition to my faith I was determined to work hard and do everything I could possibly do to achieve my goal. I was ready and willing to do any job and put in any amount of work. No goal and no dream can come true without our actions. We live in a physical world, and nothing will happen if we are not willing to work for it. The Lord will open the opportunity and create circumstances in our favor, but then we must use the given opportunity and do the work to attain results. Our actions and work are inseparable from what we have and what results we will have in the future.

Of course, many people have helped me, and I will always be grateful to them. I don't know how I would have been able to achieve my dream without the help and assistance from others. And that in itself is a miracle when God stretches His hand to us through other people. It was absolutely amazing to see how all of a sudden some people appeared in my life and helped me. But we can't relax and think that other people will do it all for you. You must work with a strong determination and persistence until you achieve your goal.

One of the most important lessons that I've learned is to observe and pay close attention to the signs through which the Lord communicates with us. Often people think that God is somewhere there in heaven and He can't (or won't) speak to us. But God speaks. God is the spirit and speaks to us in various ways. It may be circumstances that occur in your daily life, various opportunities that seem to present themselves, meeting other people who are willing to help you, through the Bible, nature, and other books. The Lord speaks to us in many ways. Only we have to pay attention to what He says as well as how it's said. And believe.

It is difficult even to imagine what my life would be like today if I had thought that the little book passed on to me by a taxi driver, and the Bible verses I read after the prayers were just a coincidence, and dismissed the inspiration.

On this note I will finish my letter to you.

I love you and wish you strength. Remember, there is a reason for everything. Pay attention, what the Lord is trying to tell *you*?

Take care, and, till next time.

Inga

14

My Second Trip to California

Dear Valdas,

You have heard me saying repeatedly that with God all things are possible, even though it may seem you face an insurmountable challenge. As I continue sharing my heart and story with you, now I will tell you my experience and you will see when I say this, I am not saying it as a cliché. As you read below, you will see it for yourself. May it inspire you and sparkle a hope in your heart. Your situation can transform as well. Only believe, and do what you have to do.

After I made my decision to return to California, I felt as though the heavy burden of search and indecisiveness had been taken off my shoulders. Restlessness was gone. There were questions, many unknown and unresolved matters ahead, but at least I knew where I was headed, what my next goal was, and what I needed to do. Michael and I began discussing our next steps.

Michael had established good friendship with local professionals and one of the Lithuanian-American Communities in California, and was asked to travel again to Lithuania to give lectures to the local medical and prosthetic specialists. My story created a big buzz in the industry in our country, and our team's success had made a significant impact. We agreed that in April Michael would arrive in Lithuania with Edward, my physical therapist, to conduct the lectures. And then on May 2, I would return to California with them.

While I was eagerly waiting to start my new life, I treasured every day with my family. I came to the realization that I had no idea when I would see them again. My way of escaping the anxiety of leaving was making that step based on faith. I had the positive mindset and expectation that I would succeed in fulfilling my ultimate vision, and that I would see my family again soon. So, instead of dwelling on the concerns and fear of the unknown, I put all my focus on what I could do to implement my new challenges.

Since I was halfway across the world, and I didn't have any answers to my questions, I began researching the resources that I would need for when I arrived in the USA. I spent countless hours from morning till night searching and collecting information of resources, where I could receive immigration assistance, along with housing, education, employment opportunities, services for people with disabilities, and services for immigrants. And I was impressed by the resources I found. But while it seemed promising, most of my questions could not be resolved by sitting at the computer. I had to get to California to figure out my options in person.

When Michael and Edward arrived, I was ready to open a new page of my life. But before that, we had quite an intensive program for two weeks in three cities in Lithuania. They were scheduled to give lectures on prosthetics and physical therapy in a variety of hospitals and rehabilitation centers. During the work I would assist them as an interpreter and show model for how to perform various activities wearing prostheses.

Their first lecture was scheduled at one of Lithuania's largest hospitals, in the Children's Orthopedic Department. While visiting Vilnius, I arranged a separate visit to the Valukupių Rehabilitation Center. After Vilnius, we were taken to the city of Utena to continue with the work. There Michael made a set of prostheses for a little boy, who was missing both of his legs and arms. I knew many had benefitted from their expertise, but I thought for this boy, it was all so very worth it. His parents reached out to me when they got to know my story, and I was glad that Michael felt compelled to help this family when I shared their struggles with him. It was rewarding to know that now this boy would be able to walk. It was heartbreaking to imagine what this boy would have to face in the future, but knowing the determination of his parents, I trusted he would be a fighter just as they were.

At the same time, our endeavor was like a pleasant vacation as we were welcomed with some exclusive pampering at the Finnish Sauna and Spa and Russian Bathhouse at one of the local specialist's dacha. After a five day visit in Utena, we drove to the Orthopedic Center where my "walking again" story had begun. Michael prepared a lecture according to the center's needs and Edward taught the local specialists techniques that were new to them.

These were very productive weeks but at the same time, we had fun. I was thrilled to see what my decision to not give up and a strong commitment to walk again had grown into. The three of us were proud of what we had accomplished and were happy to pass on that knowledge. At times we joked that Michael, Edward and I were like the three musketeers from the famous Dumas novel.

In between our business trips and lectures, I coordinated our leisure time. It was a pleasure showing them around Vilnius City, the gorgeous forests and lakes, its castles from the fourteenth century, and showcasing a variety of genuine Lithuanian dishes and other cultural aspects. Michael and Edward both appreciated greatly the sightseeing and the culture, the food and the drink.

On May 1, the night before our trip to the United States, the three of us with my family went to downtown Vilnius City to watch the celebration of Lithuania joining the European Union. It was a very festive and spectacular evening as the country was opening a new page of its history, the same as I was opening mine. Finally, on May 2, 2004, I breached the threshold of my life's crossroads. I relinquished my comfort zone for the unknown, onto a path I believed would propel my life to the next level.

Early that morning our home was a hive of activity getting ready for the trip, my parents assisting us the whole time. As we prepared for the long trip, in the midst of our jokes and laughter, the nervousness we felt was like the "elephant in the room." Individual and collective feelings were palpable. In each of their eyes I could see the anxiety.

My first visit had been with a clear purpose and a plan, a definite time frame under the supervision of professionals. As opposed to that well-planned journey, this time my family was letting me go across the Atlantic Ocean for an indefinite period of time, with no clue as to where I would settle or what I would do when I got there. This time my aspirations were mine alone, and I was heading into the total unknown. Edward was very supportive; he thought it was a great idea because it would be much easier to live. Michael agreed with Edward, only he was thinking more as to how it would be possible. He was concerned. He wasn't sure, and he said with sparse encouragement, "I have no idea how you're going to make it."

Michael said he would help with what he could, but suggested to me and my family to be ready for anything, implying that I might have to return home.

The trip to the airport was probably the longest I had ever taken. I'd never had so many mixed feelings as I had that morning. Looking through the window at my gorgeous home city in the sunrise, I thought about the step that I was about to make. I was leaving behind all that I cherished, all that gave me comfort and security, going somewhere across the globe to face the biggest challenge I'd ever had to face. I was pulling myself away from my family and my friends for an undetermined period. And for several weeks, my father asked me time and again if I was sure I wanted to take this endeavor upon myself. Each time I replied firmly, "Absolutely, without a doubt."

Even afterwards he told me, "Inga, I want you to know that you can change your mind at the very last minute. Mom and I would feel much more at peace if you didn't go. We worry about you. And if you do go, and at some point decide you want to come back, please don't hesitate. This is your home and we always will be happy to have you here. We will be here for you no matter what."

I knew I still had time to rethink my decision until I boarded the plane. It was so heartbreaking to leave my family, my people; it was the only thing that could possibly hold me back. While visiting California the first time and falling in love with the country, I didn't even consider the idea of leaving my homeland for the same reason – my family and friends were too important and I couldn't see myself without them. But I got to the point to where I had to make that choice. I could not continue my life only to be reminded of my loss on a daily basis, as I was constantly facing accessibility issues wherever I went. Never-ending obstacles conveyed to me that no longer was I a person of full value.

It was very hard to separate myself from my friends, who had remained faithful to me and were by my side after the crash, and with whom I had formed such a strong bond. But life did not stop with the crash. Life continued and they would move on, marrying and having their own families, developing their careers and fulfilling their own goals. They would move on creating the lives they desired. But where would I be if I continued without making any changes?

I could not even think of remaining in the position I was in. But I knew nothing's going to change if I did not make that change. A better life was not going to just show up at my doorstep if I just sit there expecting it to change 'somehow' hoping that Lady Luck might decide to visit me. I needed to take charge of my own circumstances and intentionally change them. If I wanted my life to be other than it was, then I needed to make choices that would bring that transformation. As heartbreaking as it was to separate myself from that which I cherished the most, I realized that my life was not going to be different if I was not willing to leave my current world.

I was standing at the crossroads where I had to make a choice which would literally define my destiny. I knew I could change my decision at any time and stay home and take a chance away from any risks. I also knew that by doing this I would be taking a chance away from myself to resurrect to a new life. Who knows if I would ever have that opportunity again, if I don't use it now? The little book of wisdom said four things do not come back, and one of them is the missed opportunity. And this one I didn't want to miss.

As we approached the airport, after my internal struggle, I assured myself that this was the right decision. This was my chance to get out of the cage where I had been locked up for four years. At this point, I wasn't afraid of the new and the unknown. I was afraid to stay where I was. Even though the unknown did not give me comfort, I chose not to fear; I decided to have faith that I would succeed in establishing my life in the land of sunshine, just as the Lord has promised.

The fact that I had no idea how I was going to implement it was only one detail of the whole picture that I saw. And that detail was not a determining factor. The determining factor was God's will for my life and His direction, not my personal circumstances. And if God opened that door of opportunity for me and I was ready to put all my effort into this, then I didn't need any guarantees in advance. The Lord's direction and His promise replaced any guarantee. I already had experienced how the impossible could become very possible. When the Lord gives you the opportunity, He will give you all the required 'tools,' including: favorable circumstances, people to help you, and the blessing in all your efforts to make your opportunity fruitful. And what's needed from me was my obedience to the Lord and to do my part by working hard and making the best out of what I had. I believed I was opening the door into my life's transformation.

After an emotional goodbye with my family, Edward, Michael and I went through security and Duty Free Shop saying farewell to my former co-workers. It was good to be at the airport; the people I had met there and the experiences I had at the Business Lounge made those few years extraordinary, the most beautiful years I ever had. But I had to leave this place with no way of returning back.

After I got on the airplane, I felt a little easier. It was hard watching our mother, the strenuous effort she exerted to hold on to her conviction that she was doing the right thing by letting me go. I saw she was heartbroken to have me go alone, so far away, not knowing when she would see me again. It was too hard to say goodbye to dad and you. I gazed through the window. I knew in the Departure Hall you were still there to see me off.

"Leaving everything behind is such a high price to pay," I sighed.

But like you and mom and dad, I comforted myself that it was the right step for a better future, and that our separation was only temporary. Shortly after, I heard my cell phone; it was a text message from you, brother. I still remember that moment very well. You wrote how you felt heaviness in your heart, how you felt empty having me leave so far away. You asked me to be careful and wished me success. I wanted to run out of the airplane and hug you one more time; I wished I could pass on the peace and confidence that I had, to reassure you that I would be alright. I knew you were very supportive of my move to America, but at the same time you were concerned about letting your little sister go. Up to that time you were always there to protect me and take care of me; it was hard for you to let me go across the globe alone. Through tears I responded to your text, asking you to take care of yourself and our parents, and I tried to comfort you by stating there was no need to worry.

After the flight attendant notification told us to turn off our cell phones, I turned mine off and looked at Michael and Edward to see how they were doing. They both had shared some of the brightest memories from this extraordinary trip and repeatedly said how much they enjoyed Lithuania. Now we were looking forward to returning to the land of sunshine. Michael and Edward were returning to their homes and their families, and I was going to meet with my new life.

As the airplane took off, I took a deep breath and closed my eyes asking God to bless the trip and guard us from all evil. I said I believed that He was directing me and I trusted that He would bless me, just as He promised through His word. In my mind once again I said goodbye to the people I loved as well as to my homeland, telling them that I loved them very much, and that I would be back to see them, but only after conquering my impossible goal.

I looked at Edward and Michael. Michael was dozing off. These two weeks were quite intense. I knew Michael was happy about the work we had done, as we accomplished quite a lot in each city. To me, the most touching and memorable experience was watching how he changed little boy's life right before my eyes.

Edward was somewhere in his thoughts; this was his first trip for this kind of project. He was thrilled about visiting my home country and the work we'd accomplished. It was his first visit to Lithuania, and from what he has shared, this was the first time he was so far away from his family for such a long time. He was bringing back home lots of beautiful memories and gifts to his wife and his little girls. I knew he couldn't wait to see them.

I put on my headset with my favorite music and drowned myself in my thoughts. The last several years appeared in my mind like an overview. What an amazing journey. The first three years since the crash were continuously filled with anguish, horror from the sudden, drastic changes to my body, my struggles and fear of unknown. In spite of that, my decision to not give up and continuous perseverance delivered its fruit, and now everything had changed so beautifully. Observing my path and how I changed in the process, I realized that going through the pain and despair actually benefited me. I learned some of life's greatest lessons, which I would not have learned otherwise.

Dark despair taught me to have unshakable faith, which can literally turn things around in an incredible way. My hope, despite hardship, developed endurance. Pain and disappointments developed a tough character to withstand hardships. With that, it made me more compassionate than I ever was before. The impossibility of my desire revealed to me the power of relentless perseverance, which can make you break through any obstacles and conquer any challenges you face.

Continuous struggles and hardships showed me that the decision to never give up always wins in the end. So many times I felt I couldn't go on pursuing my goal. And it would have been so much easier to let it all go and take the easier route. But then, there is no way I would be living this miracle had I given up.

I felt like I'd gone through a time frame, which taught me some very valuable lessons that I needed to learn. Tough circumstances shaped some character traits in me that needed to be developed. Unbreakable determination, non-negotiable discipline, tireless persistence, relentlessness, unshakable faith and optimism were developed in me particularly through those difficulties.

Now, as I was looking back, it was hard to believe I really went through that. It was like an endless desert. The only thing that got me through that arid desert was my faith and constant effort to move forward. I was left with no way to improve my life, but to hope for a miracle. I was so glad that I chose to hold on to my hope, believing that there must be a way and that the Lord was going to bring this agony to the end. And then, a miracle really happened. I would not have gone through all of this the way I did if not for my God, who comforted me, gave me patience and strengthened me all the way. I was amazed how Lord led me all the way and pulled me out of desperate circumstances when I could see no end in sight.

And now, I believed my God was bringing my life to a whole new level. I remembered those events that spoke with me about taking this step, and the night when after my prayer I read Deuteronomy, the 8th Chapter. I felt just exactly that - my God was bringing me out of the desert where I experienced hopelessness, pain and struggle and brought me into the good land, where I would be able to restore my life, and again be independent, self-sufficient and lead a dynamic, meaningful life.

And although I'd been told more than once how difficult it would be to establish myself in California, I didn't care. I put my trust in God, not what people said. Thinking realistically about my aspirations was paralyzing, so I decided to push such thoughts away, looking through the eyes of faith. Since the Lord had directed me, it meant He was going to create favorable circumstances. He would send people to help and everything was going to work out. Why would I listen to the concerns and be dismayed, if I had the promise from the Lord God? When God opens the doors, who is going to close them?

My Return to the Land of Sunshine

The long flight was exhausting, but my heart trembled with excitement when the pilot announced we were approaching San Francisco, welcoming everyone to the United States. Adrenalin pushed away my fatigue seeing the Pacific Coast. As we descended and the landing gear touched the ground, it felt as though right that moment I was opening a new page in my life journey. I did not know what was going to be written into this new page of my life, but I knew it was going to be extraordinary. I knew the pen was in my hand, and it was up to me what kind of story was going to be written in the next chapter of my life's story.

I was so happy to be back! Gorgeous San Francisco, with its majestic Golden Gate and the stunning views of the city; the sunshine, the ocean, the beautiful rolling hills, and the vineyards and palm trees were so missed during the long months since I'd been gone!

"Yes, this is where I want to be," I thought. "I want to continue my life's journey in this beautiful land."

Observing the beautiful scenery, I felt like I was returning home. I knew it would take few days to settle down and get used to the new time zone, but I couldn't wait to start reviewing my options. Michael arranged for me the same discount I had previously at the Flamingo Hotel, in exactly the same room where I stayed on my first trip, and that took care of the most important need that had to be resolved right away: I had a place to stay. But I could not live at the hotel forever. I needed to find a permanent place. But how was I going to pay for it?

I didn't know yet. I had saved up enough money to live for several months, and Michael said there was still some money left from my last trip that was raised by the Lithuanian-Americans, but it wouldn't last forever. And Social Security from my home country was not enough; I needed to work to support myself. But where would I find a job? I didn't know yet.

I had gathered information about various organizations that help with career and employment opportunities, but first I had to resolve my status, because my visa did not permit me to work in the country. I had a tourist visa, which meant that I couldn't live and work in the United States.

As I was thinking about it all, realistically my desire to live in California was an enormous challenge. In addition to the issues I faced, I didn't know how I was going to move around in the city in a manual wheelchair, operating it with one hand, taking care of meal preparations with one hand, and doing my shopping or any household activities by myself. I had to admit, it was a beautiful dream that I had, but my goal was far beyond my reach. I smiled to myself thinking that I had broken my own record of challenging myself.

Before I went to sleep, I went out to the balcony to take a breath of fresh air and reflect on the latest events. It was warm outside, so quiet and relaxing. I gazed on the palm trees, and the crystal blue water in the pool, with its hot tub so closely nearby. It brought fond memories and I was glad to be back. I was so grateful to the Flamingo manager, Patricia, for agreeing to let me stay at the highly discounted price. She was always very nice to me and she was very supportive of my aspirations. Welcoming hotel's staff and my stay in the same room made me feel even more like I was at home. Now the weather and the wheelchair access would not be obstacles. I could go to school, I could work, and I could be as active as I desired. For countless days and nights I envisioned what would be the perfect place to live, and here I was; I had arrived. I was far from my homeland, but I felt like I belonged in California and I didn't want to leave at all. I wanted it to be my home.

The first few days I reconnected with my new "old friends" whom I'd met during my first visit. I was cordially welcomed back, and I received positive responses about my intentions. No one told me it was impossible; it was only a matter of finding a way. I smiled in my mind, hearing those kinds of responses. Finding ways how to manage things on a daily basis having no legs and only one functional arm, was my strategy, which made me self-sufficient after all. That's exactly the mindset I had now - it was not a question "If" it was possible, but "How to" make it possible. Seeing a welcoming and positive response from my American friends gave me both hope and encouragement.

After settling in I began working on my goals. I prayed asking God to give me the inspirations and insights of where I needed to go and what I needed to do. I asked Him to arrange circumstances in a way that would lead me the way I needed to go according to His will and send me the right people, who would help me along the way. Being in the position that I was, I needed to work on several tasks at the same time. My priority was to find a permanent home and clarifying how I could get legal resident status; without it I could not get a job nor could I live in the country. I looked through my resources and chose which organizations to go to first to seek for the assistance.

I was very blessed to have my American friends. They loved me and not only willingly assisted me with giving me rides to where I needed to go and helped with my daily needs (that I was not able to do on my own), but they went out of their way to make sure I had everything I needed. They assisted me every step of the way. Even friends of my friends helped me with rides to some of the organizations and immigration law offices.

In a few days, Michael drove me to a place known as an Independent Living Center (ILC), a place that provides services for people with disabilities. I wanted to ask for their assistance in finding a non-hotel place to live. I was glad Michael was with me to help. I still had difficulty understanding Americans and I doubted I would have understood the American English without him. (I was joking that during my first trip, I was spoiled by having friends making it easy for me to understand them, and now I was in the real world where nobody was making language accommodations.) During my visit, I learned that I could receive their services even if I was not a legal resident, and that brought a great relief to me. We were asked to come back the following week for Orientation, which was the first step I'd take in receiving the services I needed.

A few days later, in the very first week after I arrived, I received my first miracle. I got a phone call from Edward and his first words were, "Inga, you won't believe this."

In a moment, I found out news which were really unbelievable. He said that just a day ago unexpectedly he received a phone call from someone representing Medtronic Company, who said the company would like to donate an electric wheelchair to Edward's company, so that he would donate to someone who needs it. Edward said he couldn't believe it. Without a doubt, he knew this wheelchair was destined for me, and he called right away to tell me the news.

I have to admit that moving around in a manual wheelchair, pushing myself with one hand, was very difficult, and one of the questions I had on my list was how I was going to move around by myself. And here it was. While electric wheelchairs cost thousands of dollars and there was no way I could buy it, I received one as a gift the very first week I arrived! It took me a while to get used to it, but the electric wheelchair increased my independence greatly. It enabled me to get around the city independently, go shopping, and anywhere I needed to go. My first big challenge had been solved within my first week.

Now I needed to use the resources that I had to tackle a time-sensitive goal: changing my legal resident status and finding a home. On Monday May 10, I went back to the ILC. This time, Michael brought me and then left me alone to go back to work. I was a bit timid being alone, especially when it came to finding out important information when I could barely understand the language.

I received a lot of information about housing in the city and the county, and brought home a packet outlining various resources. The only thing was that I had such a hard time understanding what the presenter was speaking about, so that after the presentation I had no idea as to what would be the next step in my situation. I made an appointment to discuss my case.

On the next day, Michael's friend Albert drove me to another ILC in Berkeley to see what kind of help I could get there. Another friend of Michael came from San Francisco to meet us as well. They both became my advocates, making sure that I received all the necessary information. The counselor was very nice and helpful; she said their center could definitely help me with a variety of resources, if only I could reside in Alameda County. What was particularly helpful – the counselor provided me with resources on where I could find information about immigration.

My visit to the center was really promising, but I needed to find a place to live in Berkeley or at least near it. Living in Berkeley seemed to be a great start; Berkeley was known as an international city as there was located one of the best, most well-respected universities in the world. What's more, since Michael and I knew some local Lithuanian-Americans there, we visited some who lived in the area. While having a fun time enjoying delicious appetizers and local wine and sharing our latest stories, we discussed my goal. I was recommended first of all to obtain all necessary personal documents because without them, I could go no further. Without solving my legal status, I could not live in the country, could not get a job, nor would I get medical care. Without being a legal resident (or having some form of immigration status), it was extremely challenging to become a student, considering the high fees for international students. Kristina and her boyfriend, whom Michael and I visited that night in Berkeley, welcomed me and invited me to stay at their home and comforted me that we would figure out solutions to any challenges. If so many people could move to the United States, so could I. Their place was not wheelchair accessible however, which presented an issue, but they said it wouldn't be a problem; they'd make it accessible. At the end of our visit, it was decided that I would move into their home in Berkeley.

On our way back home, Michael and I discussed the options. I was excited about living in a bigger city and having more opportunities, although it was a bit scary to be far away from him. Michael said he would visit me, so we would see each other, and that he would help when needed. But this was a great opportunity, and I shouldn't pass it.

I was new to the area, so I had to trust Michael, who knew better. I liked the city, I liked the people who welcomed me to stay with them plus, my excitement was overflowing from thinking about my new life. By contrast, when I examined how I felt in my spirit about this step, to my surprise I did not feel comfortable. There was no inner peace. While keeping in mind the Berkeley option, I decided to continue looking at other options.

I set my intention to check all opportunities, to see everything without making any rash decisions. I went back to the ILC to meet with Arlene, their housing coordinator. She seemed inspired by my story and willing to help. She was very resourceful and gave me a lot of suggestions, including steps I needed to take to find a permanent residence. She assured me that knowing three languages and having the skills and work experience that I had, it would not be a problem for me to find work. I simply had to be a legal resident of the United States. Again I faced the same barrier, which seemed to show up every time I talked about living here or wanting answers about my goals.

Michael drove me back to Berkeley to meet the immigration counselor to find out all the information I would need about this subject. The visit did not give me much encouragement. Every option to receive legal residency status was not applicable to me. I was suggested to apply for "asylum" as my justification due to my physical disability, but that meant I would not be able to return home to Lithuania to see my family for seven years. This thought was unbearable.

Thus informed, I returned home to the hotel discouraged. I was facing a serious obstacle, which seemed an unmovable mountain. The math was simple: without addressing my legal status, I wouldn't be able to live in California, and there was no way I would have agreed to stay illegally.

After meeting with people, visiting organizations, and especially talking with an immigration counselor, I realized this was not going to be easy. My aim to walk with prostheses was nothing in comparison. This time my goals involved other people, another country's systems, and the most challenging hurdle was directly related to the federal law. Had I known that only I was the key to my success, I would not have been as dismayed, because I already knew that through consistent and relentless work one can achieve anything. But how was I going to deal with this one?

I couldn't think of returning to Europe. It felt so good to be back in the land of sunshine; I felt so comfortable, as if I were home. This was the place where I felt alive. I felt respected and valued despite my physical challenges. This was the place where I knew I could lead a life which I dreamed about and envisioned. I was not even homesick; I already had it set in my mind that I wasn't going to see my family for a long time. I was happy to be back in this land and I did not look back. I was so enjoying the daily sun and bright blue sky; I was so happy to be in an uplifting atmosphere. I was thrilled that I was able to go out and have days packed with things to do. I had a purpose and a goal to aim for. Every night I was already looking forward to the next day, when I could work on creating my new life.

I did not have any idea how I was going to deal with this particular barrier. But what I did know was that I couldn't back off from my objective. There was no turning back. I decided to work on other goals, believing that when the time came, I would get the solution I needed to become a legal resident. But aiming for several complex goals simultaneously and receiving so much information about them was overwhelming. It was difficult to recognize the best solution, which decisions were right.

Not knowing what choices were the best, I began praying in a specific way. I asked the Lord to direct me by blessing and giving me the arrangements to that which needed to take place in my life and not opening the doors to those options that were wrong and destroying that which was not of His will. I prayed for Him to arrange circumstances in a way that would lead me the way I needed to go according to His will.

In a few days, Michael called to tell me that due to unknown reasons, Kristina cancelled her offer to have me stay at her home in Berkeley. All plans related to Berkeley were suddenly terminated. This was quite unexpected, to say the very least.

I felt lost. It seemed like Berkeley had been the spot to start my journey, and that the people were so excited about their offer. How could it all suddenly change? As I was thinking, I realized that I had prayed for God to not give the blessing to those options that were wrong. I had asked Him to destroy that which was not what I was supposed to do, and arrange what was right. I thought, "Looks like this is the answer to my prayer, isn't it."

For some reason, I guess it meant it wasn't the right option for me, that this cancellation was for the better. I believed everything was in God's control and therefore, it was part of the plan. Having remembered my prayer, I smiled to myself. My faith gave me comfort for the latest turn of events. And I was glad that Kristina didn't wait to tell me. It was better to find out sooner, before I moved out of the Flamingo Hotel.

Since the door to opportunity in Berkeley was closed, it meant I had to look for a place to live all over again following local ILC's advice. I knew I could not rent on my own because I had limited financial resources. I could not get a job because legally, I didn't have permission, and I knew that changing my legal status was the biggest obstacle of all. Wherever I looked, it felt like I hit a brick wall.

To strengthen myself and get back the inspiration and enthusiasm I needed, I again looked at it all through the eyes of faith. I had to hold on to the belief that God would not leave me, and that was the only thing that strengthened my hope. I wrote in my diary, "He blessed me from the very beginning; He will not abandon me halfway." Then at some point in time, my perspective changed: confusion and frustration turned into curiosity. Since I put my confidence in God's promise, I grew curious to learn how the Lord would lead the way. I looked at the future with anticipation and a smile, wondering, "So what is it that the Lord has prepared for me?"

I continued working on the housing question. Time was ticking and with every day I had less time to stay at the hotel at the discounted price. By the end of May I still did not have a place to live, so I asked hotel's manager to extend the discounted price for one more month. She was not sure if she could do that and said she needed to talk to her boss. I made another appointment with the Housing Coordinator at the ILC. While we were discussing my need for a place with a roommate, suddenly I saw a woman in a wheelchair rolling into the office. She looked straight at me and said, "Are you looking for a place to live? Soon I will have an available room, and I would be happy to offer it to you. My house is wheelchair accessible and has all the accommodations."

"Who is this woman? Where did she come from?"

I was caught by such a delightful surprise. Up to this day I have no idea how she found out about my situation and why she was willing to accept me in her home, even though she didn't know me. I sat there astonished. I learned that her name was Nancy, gratefully accepted her offer, and we set the date to visit her home to see if it would work. On the agreed day, Michael and his wife drove me to her house to check the place out. It was a wheelchair accessible home in a good neighborhood. I looked at my room and around the house and I liked it. I liked that she had a pool, which meant I could continue my sun-pampering times getting my California tan as I did at the Flamingo.

Nancy seemed a nice and caring person, and willing to help. She had a severe disability, and looking into her eyes I could see that she knew the taste of pain. We left her house so excited! One of my first major goals was about to happen. And, this place to live was so much better than Berkeley. So, it turned out that yes, the Berkeley option being canceled was truly for the better. Now, since my immediate goal of finding a residence was resolved, I decided to tackle the legal obstacle.

I wanted to learn about college enrollment. Kathryn drove me to the local college, which I'd heard was one of the top 100 community colleges in the nation. However, I faced sad news: the tuition for an international student was more than I could possibly afford, and I didn't qualify for any international scholarships. The admissions counselor told me it would have been entirely different position had I been a California resident; then tuition would be radically reduced. Again, I faced the same barrier – my legal status.

It was the barrier that prevented me from moving forward. Kathryn made an appointment with an attorney whom she knew and brought me to her to discuss this matter in detail. To my deep disappointment, I was told facts that were not favorable. The first option presented was asylum, but I immediately knew that I wouldn't be able to see my family for seven years.

My second option was really no option at all: marrying an American citizen; I did not want to get married just to change my immigration status while having no relationship. The only one I would have married was Michael. My heart totally belonged to him and I refused to even consider this option.

The option of becoming a student to get a student visa was not one I could use either. While I was in Lithuania, I spent countless hours searching for the way to become an international student, but for the schools and programs I was interested in, I did not find a scholarship program that would pay full tuition. What's more, there was no way I could possibly afford the cost of that tuition.

The only option left was to find a company, which would employ me for the position that would qualify for the immigration process and would be willing to go through the process on my behalf in order for me to receive legal residency status. I had no idea where to find such a company. What company and what position could I possibly find that would require my unique skills?

Looking at the legal aspect was very discouraging. It seemed like it made no sense to work on anything else if I could not obtain the right to live and work in the United States. Everything else could be achievable, but I could not change federal law. Still, I could not see myself dropping everything and leaving. I started talking with everyone I knew about finding a company which would want to hire me and go through the Immigration process on my behalf.

Discouragement was like a shadow, reminding me that I was facing a giant obstacle. At this point, only faith in the impossible gave me hope and optimism, regardless of the facts that were shutting me down. Every day I kept in mind what I read in the scriptures when asking God how I could possibly establish myself in California. Through His word I received Lord's promise that He would guide me and help me, and indeed, from the very first day of my arrival I saw God's blessings and arrangements for my needs in His incredible way.

I stayed at a gorgeous resort in an Executive King room with all accommodations at a 75% discount; my American friends willingly helped me, giving me rides and assisting me with whatever was needed; I was showered with various resources that showed me which doors I needed to open to attain my aspiration (which I would not have gotten if I stayed in Lithuania). And several days after my arrival, I received a state-of-the-art electric wheelchair as a gift.

In all that time, I did not meet even one person who would want to harm or hurt me, except for one funny experience. After being at the ILC for their orientation, Michael could not leave work to bring me back, so he called a taxi. The driver figured out that I was not local and so he basically gave me a tour of the city, telling about his adventure stories along the way (which I couldn't understand). The ride increased the fare to an amount that nearly gave Michael a heart attack. He was not amused, though, of course, he took it upon himself to pay the bill.

The month of June began showering me with better news. The Flamingo Hotel extended my stay at the discounted price until the first of July, and then I planned to move to Nancy's home when she confirmed that the room was available. Then my biggest miracle greeted me right around my birthday - the solution to my biggest obstacle presented itself as the perfect gift.

Michael called me and with a sheer excitement asked me when I could see him. From his voice I guessed that he had something important to tell me.

When we met, Michael said that over the years he had been dreaming of creating a non-profit organization to help people who had similar disabilities to mine. Over the past year he had been particularly inspired watching me recover my life after the devastating event, and had been thinking even more how great it would be if there was a company that would help people to re-claim their lives after life changing events. He said he has been thinking hard how to help me stay in the country. Since I needed to have a specific job for the immigration process, he thought this was a perfect time to establish the organization he had been thinking about and hire me, and then we would go through the Immigration process.

He shared his vision with me and the organization's mission and its functions. My need for a specific job position to meet immigration requirements was a perfect match because one of the major positions in the company required a person with the unique expertise and skills that I had. The combination of my experience and my skills was exactly what was needed for that position. He asked me what I thought about it.

What did I think about it? I thought it was fantastic!

Then he asked if I would be interested in taking the position. It was the position in company's development, which involved fundraising, planning, developing and coordinating projects, public speaking for fundraising, and coordinating activities to achieve the company's purpose. In addition, the position involved my disability expertise and the ability to coach others as to how to deal with catastrophic loss and then claiming personal independence back.

I just could not believe what I heard was true!

As I was hearing his vision, I was already falling in love with the company and its mission. He had never told me about these kinds of plans, but listening to him, I could see he had thought about everything and was very serious about the goal. He had his heart set on it and was eager to get started. I asked him if he was sure he wanted to do this, and he said he had absolutely no doubts about it. This company would bring great benefits to many people; he would fulfill his aspiration to have an organization to help others and, this would be a perfect job opportunity to me, which I needed, opening the doors for me to stay in America after all.

I was fascinated by his idea, and cheerfully agreed to take the offered position to work with him to fulfill the organization's mission. Michael said he was going to go ahead and start the process of legally establishing the organization.

I was so astonished by the news that I kept asking myself could this be really true - the unbreakable obstacle which was the most important piece of the puzzle was being placed to complete the picture! It was a miracle!

Now my doors were fully opened. Michael's news gave me the green light to go full speed establishing my new life. I was thrilled not only about the obstacle being removed, but also I was very excited about the work itself. The more I thought about it, the more passionate I was about the organization's mission and purpose. I saw this position to be promising because it was an opportunity for me to grow and contribute to others. After experiencing my own life breaking down after the devastating event, and then rising up from the ruins to a new life, gave birth to my compassion and desire to help others do the same. I had become compassionate about the struggles and losses of others. And after crawling through the endless desert of despair and reaching the living waters, I felt like I wanted to shout out to the world not to give up, no matter how bad it may seem, because through perseverance and unshakable faith there *is* a way back to life. And I fully trusted Michael would do a great job establishing the company.

The one thing that concerned me was how Margaret was going to respond. We would be spending more time together; we would be traveling together; and I suspected that it might create conflict. What if she complains and raises a storm about the company and us working together?

It was not just an ordinary job opportunity – my future depended on it. But Michael said not to worry about her; he would work it out and he reassured me that this was what he wanted to do and nothing was going to prevent him from making it happen. I had already witnessed countless times that Michael always would find ways to achieve what he wanted, and this was one of those times when he seemed absolutely confident he was going to follow through on his decision.

After talking about our fears and concerns, I was confident in his commitment to lead me through the immigration process. Michael, as always, remained my rock, showing me once again that I could lean on him. We were excited about the opportunity. We shared a beautiful vision of the company's future and were thrilled about the wonderful impact it would make on people's lives. I fell in love with the company before it was even established. It felt like every strand of my being belonged to the company and I was fully dedicated to make it successful.

Then in the middle of June, Nancy called and said that the plans for having me move in to her house had suddenly changed. "But," she continued, "I have a friend, who is looking for a roommate. Would you be open to look at another place?"

"Hmm," I thought. "Again a sudden change?"

An unexpected turn again made me question what was going on. But then I remembered my prayer and said to myself that everything was in God's control. I continuously prayed about everything and believed all would go the way it needed to go. If this was how circumstances changed, it meant there was a reason. I decided to trust in God. I told Nancy that I agreed to consider the offer.

Michael assisted me with meeting this person looking for a roommate. The three of us met for lunch and we had a wonderful time sharing a little bit about ourselves. Bruce was an older man on staff at the ILC. He seemed a very intelligent and nice person and I felt comfortable being his roommate.

"He is an angel," Michael said on our way to see the house. It'd been a rocky road finding a place to live with a nice roommate, and here I met Bruce, who seemed to be caring and kind, and he worked at the organization that was the primary resource for people with disabilities in the region. This was one of those cases when it seemed too good to be true.

Bruce's home rental was very cute, located in a nice neighborhood nearly downtown, not too far away from Michael's office. It looked accessible enough; the only thing needed was an entrance ramp. Michael said it wouldn't be a problem, that it could be easily built. Even though I had another unexpected change, it was not for the worse. Bruce seemed a very kind man, the house was nice, and my rental share was affordable. After checking everything thoroughly, we agreed that I would move into the house and share the rent.

On June 26, at the end of my second month following my arrival, I moved from the Flamingo Hotel and into a home. It was not big but I was happy – I had a place to live. Michael and his staff technician Ronald built a ramp for me; Michael and Margaret had some extra furniture they didn't need so they gave it to me.

Soon I had access to the house and I had my room nicely arranged with necessary pieces of dark, cherry colored, Victorian style furniture. It was a small room which had a twin bed, a nightstand, a large dresser with mirror, and a table for my computer.

Full of enthusiasm, I cleaned all the windows, the walk-in closet, washed the floor, and I bought flowers to make it more home-like. How I wished family could see this – I was creating my own space, taking care of my household duties as if I had no physical challenges! I could easily go in and out of the house and had access to everything. Michael printed some of the photos from his trip to Grand Canyon. He put them in frames and hung them on the walls. My new home looked even better!

It was not a place with fancy accommodations as the hotel had been, but I was happy with everything because it was *my* room, not a hotel. It had a backyard with lots of flowers, a little garden, and some fruit trees. Being raised in a city, I was not interested in gardening, but I liked that I had a place to go out to spend time in the sun. It did not have a pool or palm trees as Flamingo had, but that didn't matter. I had a place to stay. And that meant my first check-mark was complete; I had met my first big goal toward my big beautiful dream.

After continuous effort, everything started coming together: I had a place to live; I had an electric wheelchair, which enabled me to go to places independently; Michael started the process of founding the non-profit organization, which was solving my legal residency status and providing me with work for a continuous source of income. Now I could work on other goals, figuring out my other independent living matters. I enjoyed taking care of the household. Since Bruce worked at the ILC and was well-informed about various services, he advised that maybe a little later I could get a personal caregiver, who could come help me with what I needed. I politely neglected the offer, because I wanted to do it all myself. The past three years I suffered, not being able to do things around the house and now, with all the accessibility, was I going to have someone do it for me?

I was going to take my independence back in everything. The will and the joy of being able to do it all again outweighed the challenge. As a matter of fact, taking care of the household was not all that complicated. I only had to do it in a different way. Each time I faced some task, I asked myself how I could manage with one hand in a wheelchair, instead of seeing my physical limitation as an unsolvable obstacle. I kept remembering myself in the prosthetic facility in Lithuania, when I had to make a sandwich with one hand: there was no other option but to find a way. It was like a challenging game; I had fun figuring out the solutions. The most challenging was cooking, and still that was probably because I did not like to cook, not because I couldn't. Since it was hard to cut vegetables with one hand, Michael made a special cutting board for me with nails to hold the vegetable, and that was my special accommodation.

While Michael worked towards founding the company, I began researching non-profit organizations to learn how they functioned. Not to waste my time, I decided to go to school to take some classes to equip myself with necessary knowledge. For that, I needed to figure out where the school was and how to use available public transportation to get to and from independently. Margaret helped me figure out the local public transportation. And since it was all so new, she took time to take rides on the bus, to help me figure out the accessibility, the routes, and the local bus system in general.

I will never forget the first day I was able to get out of the house independently, get on the bus, and go anywhere that I wanted. It was a dream-come-true moment. Just several months ago it seemed unrealistic. I knew that for many, it might not be understandable how a daily routine like leaving the house and using the bus could be a dream come true, but for me it was. Having a chance to be outside only several times a year had been the worst part of my life for the past three and a half years. A breath of fresh air was such a gift. I couldn't stand to be carried out, or have no access to the places and buildings I wanted to go. I felt strong resentment about going out. It would make me face the fact over and again that I was no longer the same; I was permanently different. The lack of access was like a statement that I was less than everyone else and therefore I couldn't have or enjoy the things that others could. It was so painful to me that I was ready to spend the entire year without going out, just so I could avoid that emotional pain. With nature's awakening in spring, warm sunny summers, colorful and rainy autumns, white gorgeous winters were spent within the four walls of my room. Holidays were spent at home alone, away from the joy and fun of friends and gatherings.

So many days I dreamed how life-changing it would be if I could get out of the house by myself, not having a need for someone to carry me down or up the stairs, and now I did! So many times I envisioned how liberating it would be if I could get out and get into public transportation without obstacles, and now I could! The city buses had special wheelchair accommodations and all drivers were so nice and helpful.

When I faced obstacles getting into a building due to stairs, every time I dreamed how great it would be if I could get into any store and any building I wanted, and now I could. I left home, used a public bus, and went into a shopping center I wanted to visit and had access to any services I wanted. That day will always remain in my memory as the day of the beginning of my freedom.

Soon I found a free local school for adults. At the beginning I signed up for English classes to learn the language and take computer classes to learn

MS Access. I was eager to take those classes. While Michael was working on establishing the company, I was determined to gain the knowledge and skills that were necessary to perform my duties. I promised that he would not be disappointed. I would learn the American English language quickly and gain any other knowledge necessary to do an outstanding job.

I was a little anxious about school, due to the language barrier, but my feelings turned around when I attended my first classes. It didn't take long to see that my English skills exceeded necessary levels. Yet I attended them because my English was not "American English" and I wanted to understand people fluently. The teachers were supportive, nice and understanding. My classmates were from all over the world, and we all had a hard time understanding American. We learned together. My experience in an American school brought me much joy and confidence. I loved my classes and was happy to have the activity that would move me forward.

By the third month of my stay, everything started coming together like in giant crossword puzzle. With every day, I was getting closer to my vision. Gradually I started feeling like myself again, like I was a person of value. I had access to things that I wanted. All those years I had to experience the lack of equality because in my culture people didn't accept people in wheelchairs as an equal part of the community. That went all the way back to the time of the Soviet Union, and it was taking a long time for the culture to change. In California I felt respected, regardless of the fact that I had to use a wheelchair. People were welcoming and friendly wherever I went. Even strangers would smile and greet me, some waved, wishing me a good day, so different from what I was used to. I did not feel lonely even if I was alone in the city.

I was becoming more and more independent. One day, I looked at my new life at a glance and realized that I had achieved my dream. My daily life had become exactly what several years before seemed impossible. And even my biggest obstacle that seemed to be unbreakable had its solution as well – I had a way to get my legal residency status and obtain the right to live and work in the United States. And it wasn't just a job, it was a passion; a fulfilling career opportunity. I knew I would put all my efforts into it and would do my best to ensure success for the company.

At the end of July we had our first team meeting, where we discussed our mission, each member's role, and the plan for the future. I got to work on my assigned tasks immediately after I returned home. I continued researching non-profit management and development. Every morning I would start with joy and excitement, expecting another miraculous day, and I would end with gratitude to my Lord, for how He had arranged situations and circumstances which led to these opportunities, meeting the right people and solving various challenges in absolutely incredible ways.

I was astonished, how everything had come together, even if it seemed unattainable. When I made the decision to implement my long-awaited vision, I had absolutely nothing to make it happen, and now, my dream was becoming my life. All the questions had their answers, like puzzle pieces coming together to create a beautiful picture. I met my goals one after another, and by achieving them I grew closer to my ultimate goal, my biggest dream: To live an independent and active life in the most gorgeous sunny State of California in the United States of America.

As you see, brother, every obstacle was met by a solution, no matter how big those stumbling blocks were. When there is Lord's will for something, He will help you to make it happen even if it seems impossible at first. The Lord provides.

But there was one thing that made me restless at times: my secret relationship with Michael. It would make me question the future and it bothered me. But I didn't make any changes, failing to realize that my choices would come with a price.

That's for now.

Be well, I will speak with you very soon.

Inga

15

Lesson for Life

Dear Valdas,

I know this time is as unforgettable for you as it is for me. There is much that you still don't know. I will continue being open and honest with you just as I have been so far, telling you my story. In this letter, I want to pass on one of the most important lessons I had to learn on my own. Learn from me.

Hugs,
Inga

* * *

It was another gorgeous sunny morning. Being thrilled watching how another impossible dream was coming true, I was getting ready to go to school to my American English class. The overall day had been scheduled to accomplish a variety of tasks for both school and the non-profit. I was excited about finally bringing my stay in the United States to the next level. My new life started having its first heartbeats and I couldn't wait to nurture it with my diligent work. I always knew my life was going to blossom again, and here it was! It was unfolding before my eyes.

In the midst of my morning rush, preparing a cup of coffee and getting myself ready to go out, I received a call from Michael. Usually we would talk in the morning to check in and discuss the upcoming day. This time however, after an unusually cold greeting, I heard his formal voice.

"Inga. Everybody knows everything."

"What are you talking about?" I replied. "Everybody knows what?"

"Inga, Margaret and everyone in the family knows *everything*," he quietly repeated. I instantly understood. I'd never heard Michael so scared.

"What? How?" The terror of the news electrified my body like lightning.

"Yes," he continued. "Last night I came home and found them waiting for me. Margaret asked me directly if I had an affair with you. And I said, 'Yes.'"

"Why did you do that?" I asked, utterly shocked. "Why now?"

"I couldn't lie to her anymore, Inga. I can't see you anymore, nor can I talk to you. I can't work on your prostheses, and we can't work together on the organization anymore."

"What do you mean we can't talk or work anymore? What are you saying, Michael? You want me to be out of your life?"

"No!" he cried.

"But Michael," I said. "Do you realize what you are saying? You are breaking everything and the opportunity for me to stay in the United States. I will have to go back home."

"No! Don't go back!" I heard devastation in his voice.

"You say you don't want me to be out of your life and you don't want me to leave, but what you are doing will force me to! Don't you understand?"

Michael was quiet. Based on how he was speaking, I knew he couldn't really talk. I had never heard him speak to me in such a frightened and formal voice. I could not recognize my Michael.

"Michael, it's not you who I am talking to right now."

"Yes, I know," he replied. "But I have to do this if we want to survive."

We were both quiet. Then I asked, "What about my prostheses, Michael? You know I have this issue with my left leg. I can't walk. What am I supposed to do now?"

"I am not the only prosthetist in the world," he said coldly. "I did everything I could. You will find another prosthetist."

"And what about my immigration process?" I asked back. "What's going to happen with all that we were working on together, Michael?"

"I don't know, Inga," he responded, hurrying. "I have to go. I will call you later." And he quickly hung up.

My body went numb. Still holding my cell phone in hand, I sat there paralyzed, trying to grasp what had just happened. What I heard was a bolt of lightning from a cloudless sky.

"What? He told his wife and family all about us?"

The comprehension of what had just happened hit me like another lightning bolt. My heart was thumping loudly, diminishing the surrounding world. I couldn't see anything; I only felt my heartbeat and Michael's voice in my mind saying, "Everybody knows everything. Everybody knows everything."

"Oh Margaret… She feels so hurt. She trusted me and she helped me, and I betrayed her in such a despicable way. Why? Why did I allow this?" Now I couldn't see the room through my tears. Just a thought of how much pain Margaret was going through after learning the truth was crushing. I was so disgusted with myself.

"And Michael? Is he really going to choose to stay with Margaret? But he cried right here in front of me, saying how much he loved me, and that wished he didn't have to return to the house but stay with me! He kept telling me how trapped he felt in his marriage, how can he choose to stay with her?

"He continues to lie to her! And what if he does stay with her? Oh, I can't imagine my life without Michael... I love him with all my essence. There is no Inga without Michael. And what about my legal residency? I surrendered the most important obstacle into his hands, and now he says that we cannot work on it anymore? All the questions of me establishing a new life in California had been resolved. And now what?" A series of thoughts went through my mind in a flash. A thought of what's next was terrifying.

Still, I turned around to look in the mirror, so I could continue getting ready for school. I was committed to completing the program and I knew I had to go to class no matter what. I didn't want to disappoint Michael; I promised him that I would learn American English and attain the skills necessary to do the work and make the company successful.

"Be strong, keep going," I kept telling myself, the teardrops falling. Feeling on the verge of collapsing, I tried to hold myself together. I picked up my makeup tools to finish what I was doing.

"I must go. Everything will be alright," I reminded myself of my commitment, trying to convince myself that all would be fine; Michael would not stay without me. That's what he was repeatedly saying to me all that time.

I looked in the mirror and paused. In my eyes I saw nothing but fear and anguish.

"It's over, isn't it?" Looking at my own eyes, at the core of my being, I realized there was no point for me to go to school. It's all over. I was losing him. And, my beautiful new world – my impossible dream – was breaking like shattering glass. I knew from that point forward my entire life would not be the same.

Realizing what Michael's phone call really meant was devastating. Tossing all my makeup tools onto the floor, I burst into tears uncontrollably. Totally alone, in shock and unknown, I sat in the middle of the room, with tears of heartache and guilt streaming down my face, wondering what's going to happen now.

The thought of Margaret's pain stabbed me like a knife. It was the only time when I knowingly betrayed someone and I couldn't stand the thought that I was a part of it all. I wanted to talk to her. I grabbed my cell and found her in my contacts. I stared at her name in my list but I couldn't dial the number. I knew I was the last person she wanted to hear from. I held the cell phone in my hand, through tears begging her to forgive me. My love and respect for her, my feelings toward her husband, the memories of his efforts for our relationship, and his words that were forever imprinted in my heart, tore me apart. I could not forgive myself and yet, I was so deeply in love with her husband. As I was convinced he was in love with me, too.

For the first time ever, I hated myself. I could not forgive myself for leading a double life. All that time I so hated having to look into her eyes, knowing how devastated she would be if she learned the truth. And now she knew. How I wished I could run to his parents, whom I so highly respected and say, "I am so sorry." How I wished to say "Please forgive me" to my new American friends, who accepted me, trusted me and loved me, having no idea what Michael and I were hiding behind our 'legs story' and a mask of being 'good friends'.

"Why did I allow our friendship to develop into a deep romantic relationship? Why didn't I stop him? Why didn't I stop myself? Why does Margaret have to go through this? Why did I allow myself to get into the affair with him?" Feeling gut-wrenching regret I kept asking myself questions for which there were no answers.

My self-hatred for how I betrayed these people and my love for Michael tore me apart. As much as I hated what I had done, I had to admit that it could not have happened differently. The only way for us not to have fallen in love was for us to have never been friends in the first place. Just the thought of not having him in my life anymore was simply unbearable. I couldn't see myself living if Michael wasn't in my life.

"But Lord," I protested, "he and I are so connected, and we love each other. Why does he have to be with her if he kept telling me he wanted to do otherwise? You know it all, Father, and all this time, You were blessing us and everything we worked on! Why does it have to end like this? My God, what is going on here?"

I cried out for God to speak to me. I could not understand what was going on. I fully realized that my life was breaking down again. This time, I was totally alone. There was nobody I could call and talk to; it was the part of my life that had been hidden from everyone. The only person I could openly talk to was Michael.

In complete despair, I took the Bible, crying for the Lord to speak to me. I was desperate to hear from the Lord, who I believed had the power over everything that was going on and I needed to hear from Him. Feeling scared and perplexed, I opened the Holy Scriptures begging my Lord to speak to me. I didn't know what I should open to read. So, I just opened it, having faith that the Lord would speak to me through His word. Barely seeing the letters through tears, I started reading the verse that my eyes were directed at:

> *"These things you have done, and I kept silent; you thought that I was altogether like you." (Psalm 50:21)*

These words pierced my whole essence like electricity. I sensed an unusual feeling. It felt like the words were alive. I *knew* the Lord was speaking to me through these words. But unlike other times, instead of His promises and encouragement, I sensed the voice was serious and strict. I immediately stopped crying. I stopped questioning. For a second I could not even take a breath. It felt like someone shook me, and I'd been awakened from a deep long dream.

"No way. It can't be true," I thought. "Father? So, all this time you didn't agree? But everything was going so well? I thought that if You didn't stop me, it meant that You were supporting us and everything we were working on. I thought you understood us and that you were blessing us!"

I sat there in silence in complete shock. It seemed like someone had taken off the veil from my face, and I saw that reality was far different than what I had been seeing. Through the veil of my created justifications I saw one thing, though I was deceiving myself by seeking for ways to justify my actions, thinking that God's commandments could be flexible for my situation, that the Lord agreed with my choices because He was a loving God who understood me. Since I saw His blessings everywhere I went, with success in everything I was aiming for, I thought that God was blessing everything that was going on and that's why He kept silent.

What a shock it was to realize that the fact that I had success in everything I was aiming for and everything was going so well for me did not mean that my choices were right before the Lord God. My Heavenly Father was blessing me because He is patient and graceful. He was silent not because He agreed with what I was doing. He kept His silence because He was patiently waiting, giving me more time to realize what I was doing and stop my transgressions against His commandments.

I remember, though, feeling restless about my double life. At times I would catch myself wondering if God was going to stop this. But then I would push such thoughts away, reminding myself of the rationalizations that I created for my comfort. Seeing that the Lord was not stopping me and seeing His blessings in all that I did, I continued without making any changes. And now, the cards were all on the table. It was stopped. I faced the moment of truth. I had taken for granted God's given opportunity, His patience and grace. I kept doing what was forbidden by His commandments, justifying my actions in order to subdue the awareness of what would be the right thing to do. I turned His blessing into a sin, which was an abomination in the sight of God. And so He closed that door. I knew it was over.

It felt as though the regret of my choices tore me apart. So many times I had the chance to make it right and I ruined it all on my own. Everything would have been different had I been obedient to the Lord, had I made choices that were right before God. Now I had lost my blessing. The regret was so tormenting that I just didn't know what to do with myself to escape it.

I begged God for another chance; one more chance to stand at the crossroads when I had a decision to make; one more chance to be given that opportunity so I could make the right choice. But it seemed like heaven was shut down. There was no way to have that chance again.

Michael and I had made choices which delivered severe consequences. I can still hear the joke he made, "You play – you pay." At that time, we were laughing about it, but our joke became a painful reality for the both of us. We paid a very high price.

Have you ever experienced the hardship that caused you such immense pain that it seemed like it would choke you and you just couldn't say a word about it? Or you didn't even know *what* to say because no words would be able to describe your feelings?

That's what it felt like for me for many years. It hurt so much that I couldn't speak about it, nor could I think about it at all. The only way to move on was to numb myself and live as though Michael never existed, as if I'd never had this experience. I mentally deleted this period of my life from my daily awareness. I forbade myself even to remember him and this time, because I simply could not endure the pain of losing him and losing my blessing.

To be honest, I can hardly see the letters through tears as I am writing this to you, Valdas. I did not cry this much after losing my legs. Truth be told, the pain from this experience was worse than what I had to go through after the accident. I can't describe the mental devastation, what it really felt like. It's been seven years since, and it hasn't gone away.

I have kept this side of the story to myself all these years. I've shared my story many times to individuals and publicly for the media, or in front of an audience. But I shared my story only partially because I wanted to protect Michael from the story going public. Besides, memories of it caused such anguish in my heart that I just couldn't even think of it. So, I only shared what the Lord had done, the blessings I had before it was all destroyed. But, as I mentioned in my earlier letter, this part of my life is a cornerstone of my story and I won't be able to bring my message to you fully if I keep this story secret.

The reason why I decided to disclose it is because I wanted to share with you the lesson that so greatly impacted my life. I want you to learn from me, so you don't have to repeat the same mistakes in your life, so that you don't have to go through the heartache and trials as I did. This experience changed the course of my life and changed me as a person. Some lessons and experiences become dull after a while, and we even forget them. However, this lesson was imprinted onto my heart and my awareness for the rest of my life.

The lesson is about how we are capable of lying to ourselves so we can justify our choices and actions, even though deep inside we *know* what the real truth is. We are so sly that when we really want something that is not right, we start seeking all kinds of ways to justify why it's OK to do what we want to do. Consciously or unconsciously, we can convince ourselves in such a powerful way that we start seeing things that we want to see, but not the truth. It is scary, because we might end up making ourselves truly believe in things that we want to believe in, and *not* see the real picture and what the *real* truth is.

By looking for ways how we can justify that which is not right, we are simply deceiving ourselves. The truth remains the truth, and the facts remain the facts, whether we are successful in painting the picture we want to see or not. For the time being we might enjoy that which we wanted so badly. We might even get used to that nagging feeling of inner discomfort and not notice it any more. Finding comfort in our justification and reasoning, we may end up sincerely believing that our choice is not wrong and even see it as a blessing. But the fact of the truth does not change. While finding comfort in justifying our wrong choices, in the end we lose the game either way. Facing the truth can bring an enormous amount of pain and confusion, or we might end up living in the trap of a lie that we set up for ourselves.

If we were honest enough with ourselves and had the courage to accept even that which we don't like, we would save ourselves from many mistakes, disappointments and the devastating consequences of our choices.

This experience has shown me again how loving and forgiving God is. His grace is beyond our understanding. We might get distant from Him by our thoughts; we might go against Him by actions that contradict His commands; but He always stays the same: righteous, loving and forgiving. He is a faithful God, regardless of who we are. He is a strict and righteous God, yet His grace and love are beyond measure. He teaches us as a father teaches his son, and some of his lessons are not pleasant and even painful. But then, the Lord forgives everything, wipes our tears, and surrounds us with His unconditional love. He can cause wounds by teaching us, and He is the one who heals the wounds and restores our hearts completely. He is always ready to give us another chance to straighten our ways. He is the same God yesterday, today and eternally. He never changes. He does not turn away from those who sincerely seek Him. He never leaves those, who come to Him with the honest heart. He always comes in time to make an impact in our lives. He is never late, and provides help, support and consolation when it's needed. He is able to renew and restore even that which seems to us totally devastating and unrecoverable.

It was one the most difficult and painful lessons I've had, which again turned my life into a certain direction. The result of my choice almost killed me inside: this was the first and the only time in my life when I wanted to give up. I felt I had no strength anymore and I didn't even want to fight for my life. Everything was meaningless if Michael wasn't there. All I wanted was just simply to be left alone and let life be whatever it would be. I did not feel so broken inside even after I realized that I lost my both legs and my arm. I had a big shock from the accident's consequences, but I always had the strength to strive and the strength to move on. This time, I did not even want to.

The results of my choices were absolutely devastating and it totally broke me inside. It was a miracle that I did not stop and kept going on. It was the second crash in my life. The first crash was the car accident, which almost killed me physically and spiritually. The second one nearly killed me emotionally and I almost gave up on life.

Both of those crashes were the result of the choices that I made earlier. Both times I knew what I was doing was wrong, but kept doing it. And both times those choices led me to total destruction.

This time though, the emotional pain was beyond comparison to any anguish I had gone through before, because it involved unspeakable heartbreaking betrayal. I betrayed people who dearly loved me, trusted me and helped me. I was leading a double life while they sincerely accepted me in their lives. At the same time, I myself was betrayed by the person who continuously assured me of his love and unconditional trustworthiness, and then abruptly forsook me in order to save his well-being in life.

You might say, "But you knew he was married...what were you thinking?"

Yes. I knew. If he didn't have a wife, I knew I would agree to be with this man for the rest of my life. He told me many times various reasons why he could not break up his marriage, assuring me that he would continue loving me and doing everything in his power to make me happy. I knew we did not have any future together, but I could not break our bond. I could not leave him when I was witnessing how much effort Michael put into our relationship and my well-being, and repeatedly said how he could not see his life without me. It seemed like he would be devastated if I disappeared from his life, and so I continued being there for him because I loved Michael and wanted him to be happy. And, I could not even imagine myself with another man and I did not even consider that option.

I knew it would be a big storm if our secret got revealed, but I did not care much who would think what. I was ready to confront you or anybody else to stand up for my love. After some unsuccessful previous relationships, I would question whether it was actually realistic to have the kind of relationship that I wanted. Now I found that it was possible. I wished I could share with the world how wonderful it was to have mutual feelings of love, a strong inner connection and unquenchable physical passion, to share the same values and be able to laugh and cry, to work and play, to share joy and sadness, share excitement and frustration, concerns and victories and disappointments together.

It was my dream to be able to have mutual absolute trust, to talk openly and share the deepest feelings or thoughts with my partner, knowing that the closest person to you will always be there to listen and have an open, honest conversation with you. And we had it.

I was there for him at all times to listen, understand and support him, and to show love no matter what; and he did the same. We were best friends. We knew we would support each other and could count on each other no matter what the circumstances were. My deep desire was to have a relationship with no games, twists or dishonesty, and here it was. Our relationship was like a gem to me, which I cared for, protected and treasured.

By sharing my story how it all began, you can see the fine line that I overstepped. I sought for ways to justify the relationship. I started doubting if that truth which I knew could not be compromised. I started questioning whether the Lord's commandments and my personal standards could be flexible depending on the situation. I allowed myself to think in the way that gave me comfort (and permission) to do what I was doing. I found ways to explain to myself why I was not doing the wrong thing. Eventually, I managed to convince myself that I was actually doing a good thing by making the person happy whom I loved with all my heart and soul. And when I thought of God's commandments, I also sought for the compromise. I made myself think that God saw our hearts and knew the situation, and that because He was a loving God, He understood.

I had a constant battle within for a long time. With time, however, I did quench that voice. Eventually I convinced myself that to have this relationship was not a bad thing, but actually opposite; it was meant for us to meet, so that we could be together.

Once again, I repeated the same mistake that I did prior to the accident – I knew the truth, but then I found a way to justify my choices and actions, and then kept doing what I was doing. In the beginning of relationship, I had a strong battle within, but eventually it ceased. I gave in and convinced myself that God understood me because He saw why I was taking that path. Both times God was patiently waiting. He was patient and graceful to give me time to stop. But I did not. I kept doing what I wanted, while justifying my actions in various ways. Finally, God stopped me both times before it went too far. And this time, it hurt so much more.

I hated myself for what I had done; it was so tormenting that I wished I could get rid of myself. For months I couldn't find rest. Sleep wouldn't come. The pain that I felt, knowing that I betrayed those who loved and trusted me was far stronger than the pain of being betrayed myself. I could not forgive myself for bringing so much pain and disappointment to those who had believed in me, those who sincerely accepted me and loved me without question. All that time I absolutely hated to look into their eyes knowing that which was hidden from them. I knew it would devastate them if they knew the truth. And now, they did.

I so wished I could look into their eyes and speak with them, but I knew they'd had enough and did not want to hear from me. There was nothing I could say that would ease their disappointment, but still I did not want to leave their lives without apologizing and saying goodbye.

I emailed Margaret, as well as Michael's mother. This was my last message to them. My betrayal was simply unspeakable, no matter what I would have said could possibly make them feel better about me or the situation. The act was done; words couldn't bring relief.

At the same time, I felt betrayed and abandoned by the person from whom all of this I least expected. I so sincerely trusted in Michael's love and trustworthiness that I could not even consider this could possibly happen. To be honest, besides you, Valdas and our parents, I never trusted anyone as I trusted him. I had more confidence in Michael than in anybody else, even myself. I was absolutely sure about his reliability and I surrendered my future into his hands without a shadow of a doubt.

However, one day, suddenly and totally unexpectedly, I was left behind by the same person who I was confident would never hurt or betray me. The person, whom I thought I knew well, was acting in a way that totally contradicted his own words and actions I witnessed for a very long time. It seemed like someone totally changed Michael.

I kept recalling the night before the morning of his last phone call and I could not understand which Michael was the real one. That last night we had a very long and difficult conversation about the burden of our double life. We felt we could not be apart, but neither could we be together. He said he could not end the marriage and bring so much pain to his family. Nor could I live in a lie any longer.

We did try to stop the romance a few times and continue working on the company as friends, because he shared with me that it had been very difficult for him at home. Michael felt badly about what he was doing to his wife, because he was giving me so much attention and time that it was creating problems. Our relationship had gone too far for us to be able to hide it, and we both agreed that this had to stop.

But our efforts were in vain. And I was afraid of losing him. After all that we shared and experienced I loved Michael way beyond my ability simply to throw it all out and overnight become solely business partners. Our relationship had gone too far to suddenly shut it all down and act as though nothing had happened. In addition, I couldn't stand lying to people whom I dearly loved and respected. I absolutely hated living the lies and having a secret hurtful to many. The truth was the biggest thing that I wanted. I told him I could no longer do this and that he needed to finally tell his wife the truth.

"Inga," he said, on his knees in front of me with his eyes full of tears. "You have no idea how much I love you and care about you. I showed you my love with all I've done, in every email, in everything I've done for you each day. I love you so much, and your well-being is all I think about. But I cannot break my family. I will love you and will always be there for you, do you hear me? I will do whatever I can to help you and make you happy. I want you to be happy."

He was trying to explain it and convince me to not make any drastic changes in what we had. He couldn't understand that it wasn't what he could give me or do for me that would make me happy. I loved him, not what he could give me. I wanted to be with him and not hide anymore. Not pretend anymore. I was tired of watching how Margaret was being lied to. I was tired of being his mistress. If he was so unfulfilled in his marriage as he said, why not stop the masquerade and bring out the truth.

We were both crying. We put ourselves in a position that was like a dead end. We had no way to resolve it, yet it was hard to continue the way we had been. After many hours of intense and emotional conversation, we both felt drained and tired. It was about two in the morning when we realized how late it was. Yet we did not see any way to resolve the situation. He kissed me goodbye, smiled, and quietly said he would see me the next day. Sadly smiling, we gazed at each other. I felt such a deep, inner connection with those sad, warm, loving, eyes that I couldn't see myself breaking this bond. I knew that I would continue to be there for him no matter what, without thinking of where it could lead.

On the next day, he called me to say that his wife and family learned the truth about us, and that this was the last time we talked. Then, he completely disappeared from my life as though he'd never even existed. He just simply cut it off. It felt like somebody tore me apart alive and took half of me away, leaving me wounded and bleeding. It hurt.

All the love that we had, the care for each other and our common values, our deep, open conversations and special moments, our business opportunity together and the vision of our future helping others, all were torn apart and thrown into a trash bag with one phone call. I could not believe that he simply threw everything away. His act of abruptly disappearing out of my life totally contradicted himself and all that I heard from him and experienced.

I was confused what the truth was and I refused to believe the fact looking at me, straight into my eyes. While being in total shock that he was capable of making a cold, cut-off like that, I defended him before others, trying to explain the situation he was in. I was holding on to our strong bond and memories of how much he valued me in his life.

And I waited for him. I re-read all his letters, remembering all he'd said and did and I did not want to believe that he was capable of removing me from his life, after all. I did not want to believe that this was really the end. Every day I kept waiting for him to walk into my driveway or call me. But every day looked the same. Dead silence. There was no Michael in my life anymore. At times it seemed to me I would go insane. We had been like one; we always shared our intentions, thoughts and feelings and suddenly, without warning or explanation, he vanished from my life.

I totally shut down. I did not sleep, did not eat, did not go anywhere. It seemed like my life had come to a complete stop. I cried and cried and cried, waiting for Michael to return. Memories of how he would go out of his way, so we could spend time together and his words about how much he loved me and how important it was for him to have me in his life, raised the question whether he was going to stand up for what we had built together or not. I was waiting for him to stand up for it and to stand up for me.

All of a sudden, my life turned into a dark, abandoned, empty, purposeless, agonizing existence. Nothing made sense anymore. My world was all around him. He was my world. I did not even notice how Michael had become more important than the reason why I left my loving family behind. It was him, his happiness and our relationship that became the essential part of my life.

I completely stopped everything I was working on after that phone call. I dropped out of school. I stopped exercising. I stopped researching additional resources that would help me to establish my life in California. Of course, I did not do anything for the company as Michael played the key role establishing it.

I stopped walking as well. For some unknown reason, the sharp pain in my left leg, which showed up at the end of my first trip, began increasing while wearing my prosthesis. It was getting stronger and more excruciating to the point where it made it totally impossible for me to walk. Michael tried to make adjustments, but I felt the sharp pain regardless. But now Michael was no longer there to work with me. I made several appointments at his office. When I went there, other specialists tried to solve the issue, but neither of them made any improvement. The specialists were perplexed, finding no other explanation but a possible medical issue. While I did not want to accept this as a possible cause, I was recommended to have x-rays and check the medical condition of my remaining left thigh.

My dream of walking again was now falling apart as well. But at this point, I didn't even want to walk. I didn't have the inner nor the mental strength to endure the strenuous efforts of walking, nor was I strong enough physically to do it after sleepless nights and not eating. I pushed away the dream that carried me through the toughest times, when I did not see the purpose for why I was left alive. Up to this point I'd been moving forward in life very steadily, regardless of any difficulties and obstacles. I handled all the hits and bounced back every single time. Now, I was not able to get back up. I was no longer able to make a single step forward.

I was only thankful for the people who were there and helped me to deal with this unexpected explosion in my life. I was thankful for my roommate, who spent hours and hours listening and talking with me. Bruce was there with me at all times, comforting me, giving me hope that things might change. My friends Kathryn and Vanessa picked me up and carried me through the hardest times.

Vanessa was the first person I called and she was immediately right there. Her mother, Kathryn, called as well, as soon as she learned the news. They would call me every day and talk for a long time to provide comfort and support. I called a couple of more friends to tell them I needed to talk to them, and asked them come visit me. Totally devastated, in tears I revealed that which was hidden from them and asked each of them to forgive me for not being honest. Each was caught by the surprise when they heard the news, but I received their understanding and support. Neither I nor Michael had been judged but rather, just the opposite. They said they hoped Michael would come to his senses, connect with me and do the right thing. With every conversation, I felt relief.

In the midst of all this drama, there was one beautiful thing for which I was so grateful: I now felt free. It felt like someone had lifted heavy weights from my shoulders of which, I had been carrying for too long. It felt good to know that I could be open and honest, and look into the eyes of my friends knowing that I did not have to lie any more. I did not have to pretend any more. There was nothing I had to hide. I could be who I was without having to keep secrets. I felt my spirit saying, "Finally, it's over."

While trying to manage my vulnerable emotional state, I had to figure out what I was going to do next to resolve my legal status. The non-profit organization Michael was establishing had been the only way to remain in the country. I had been counting on him to resolve this barrier and now, all of it was up in the air. I didn't know what was next, and the person who played a major role in this story had cut off all communication, leaving me in shock and the unknown.

My visa was valid for only three more months, which meant I had to either find another way to get legal residency or leave the country. I did not have an employment opportunity anymore, which would work for Immigration. Other options did not work for me, and by no means was I going to stay in the country illegally.

There was nothing else I could do to secure my stay. The only one thing that was left were the memories of Michael's desire to help; turning his promises into reality was my last hope that he would at least follow through on his promise for my employment for the immigration process. I'd seen Michael follow through on every promise and decision he had made, in spite of his difficulties, and I wanted to believe that this time he would do the same. Every day was ticking by and I waited, in my mind begging for him to connect with me. After several days, Bruce picked up the ringing phone and, showing a big surprise, handed me the phone.

"Inga, it's Michael."

"Finally he called. I trusted that he would," feeling a relief I took a deep breath. My heart began thumping. I couldn't wait to hear his voice, to have him share with me what was happening, just like he always used to. I eagerly picked up the phone. I heard the voice that was so dear and familiar to the deepest core of my soul. However, Michael was unrecognizable. It seemed like he'd completely changed. He merely called to give me the final confirmation that we could not work together any longer on the company. As an answer to my question as to what I was supposed to do for my legal residency status, he stated, "You can find another way, Inga. You are strong. I know you can do it. I believe in you." And then he hung up.

With those last words and then sudden silence on the other end, something died within me. I did not cry. I did not have any more tears left.

"Another way? What way? He knows very well there is no other way."

After hearing the sentence that shattered my last hope, I sat there gazing, feeling both emptiness and complete hopelessness. I couldn't believe this was actually happening. My most meaningful and loving relationship, with my only opportunity to bring myself back to life, was crashed.

"And now what? What am I going to do?"

I can't remember thinking or yelling those words. But I knew then I had been betrayed. Every tiny fraction of my being screamed out in despair as I was watching how my life again was shattering into thousands of pieces and I was absolutely powerless to do anything about it. One day it seemed like I was living a dream, and the next day my life suddenly transformed into a nightmare. Once again, just like the car that had robbed me of my body, everything in my life was gone overnight.

Unstoppable

Having Michael end everything so abruptly, leaving me all alone wounded and bleeding, totally broke me. And now, it was the final blow as my last hope was taken from me. Up until this conversation, the only thing that kept me from drowning was the chance that I was holding onto – his promise to help me no matter what. He had the keys to unlock the last doors of what seemed to be an unmovable obstacle. I used to say that there was always a way. No longer could I say it because I saw none.

I used to always withstand the most hopeless times, relentlessly breaking through any obstacles and steadily moving forward regardless of pain or difficulty. Now I no longer felt the same. My relentlessness was gone. I felt like I could no longer continue. My desire to move forward and push myself was gone. I did not want to do anything to fix or improve my circumstances. I did not want to inspire anyone. I did not see myself being strong. In fact, I did not even want to be strong anymore. I couldn't understand why people allowed themselves to hurt me, thinking "She could handle it with no problem, since she's strong anyway."

The fact that I overcame my obstacles did not mean I was made of iron, someone who could take one hit after another and not feel any pain. I was the same human being, who has feelings, who wants to love and be loved, who can be strong and weak. I did get tired, and now I felt tired. I simply didn't want to do anything anymore. I wanted it all to stop. This was too much.

Another sleepless night came. My thoughts about what had happened and the unknown kept me awake until sunrise. I got up early, made a cup of coffee, and decided to go outside. The night before, Bruce had bought me a lawn chair so I could lay down and enjoy the sun; he knew how much I loved catching a tan. It was thoughtful of him. I think he wanted me at least to get out of the house and spend some time in the fresh air. I took my cup of coffee and went out to show that I appreciated his efforts. I sat down to watch the beginning of a new day and took a deep breath of fresh, crisp, morning air.

It was so good to be outside. Only now I realized it was the first time in two weeks of endless crying and sleepless nights in tears, I came out to be outside. I knew it would be a beautiful sunny morning. Within me however, there was a complete darkness. I've never felt so broken and in such pitch-dark despair. It was so difficult to believe that this was truly happening. Up to this moment everything had gone so well and it seemed like I was just about to soar. Even though everything that I envisioned and aimed for seemed unrealistic, I once again saw how with God the impossible could become possible. Every day I was astonished, watching how my biggest impossible dream was unfolding. And now what? Now I was looking at the ruins of my precious new life.

I wanted to hope that matters would turn around. Deep inside though, I knew that God closed that door and nothing was going to change. I felt that behind the events there was a stronger power working. Nobody can close a door that God opens, and likewise nobody can open a door if God closes it. Everything is in His power and deep inside I knew that it was over.

I called to my Lord in my prayer but it seemed like I was left alone to think about my choices and the consequences they caused.

"Lord, I ruined your blessing with my own hands," I said apologetically, feeling gut- wrenching regret and dark emptiness. I cried for what I had done. I was shocked by how easy it was to bring destruction simply by making wrong choices. This would never have happened if Michael and I hadn't crossed that boundary between specialist and patient. Everything had been coming together like a huge puzzle, and my life was turning into a beautiful picture. There was only one puzzle piece left to be placed to complete the picture. I was one step away. And my one wrong choice ruined it all.

A series of thoughts and questions to myself kept bombarding me. I had no answers to any of them. I felt perplexed and could not understand what the right thing to do in this situation was. I knew that Michael's decision to save his marriage seemed honorable; in a way I respected his choice to save his marriage. Yet, it was hard for me to understand him. He was doing the exact opposite from what he had been telling me of what he wished, and now I was mixed up what his truth was. He used to say he wanted to do the right thing. Is it the right thing to please others while lying to them?

Is it the right thing to do, to promise not to step back from a commitment, reassuring others that you're going to follow through no matter what, and then break that same promise? I had asked him time and again to think carefully, to see if he was ready to have a company together, considering that his wife might not like the fact of us working together. And here he promised that he would not step back, even if it created trouble at home. Yet he dropped everything and vanished. Was this the right thing to do? I think it was the first time I sincerely argued with the Lord. I kept asking God, "What is the right thing to do? Break the commandment and stop lying? Or follow the commandment but continue living the lie?"

I did not find my answers and I did not understand many things. What I did know was that there was more to the show behind all these events. That night, after Michael left at two in the morning, feeling fully exhausted and drained from our conversation, in my prayers I cried out, "I cannot do this anymore. Lord, please help me and You bring us both closure. I cannot endure this anymore."

That same night the Lord answered my prayer, and in the morning I received it. I had asked the Lord God to direct my path the way I needed to go according to His will, and in my spirit I knew that everything came to a stop because my Heavenly Father put the stop to it. I lived in adultery and apparently, the living God was not going to agree with it and bless that which was an abomination in His sight, no matter how much I was able to justify it.

It was hard for me to understand why the Lord was so radical about certain things. But I trusted that behind each commandment there was a reason. If I didn't understand some of His commandments, it did not mean that I didn't have to follow them. If I didn't agree with or didn't know the spiritual laws, it didn't mean they were not working in my life. The spiritual laws, just as any federal law, have the power and they work whether we are aware of them or not, like them or not, and whether we agree with them or not. One of the spiritual laws, that sooner or later everyone reaps what they sow, just happened in my life. Now I was reaping the destruction from what I had sowed.

I felt reverence before the Lord God. I knew He is a loving God, but again I saw that He's a righteous God and I can't take His word and the spiritual laws superficially. Deep within I knew this chapter of my life had come to an end. I had to learn my lesson of my thoughts, my choices and actions. I had to learn my lesson and move on.

"But God, how can I move on?" I asked. "I don't have strength anymore. I can't do it anymore, Lord. I can't take these hits anymore. I simply don't want anything anymore."

In my mind I kept talking to my Heavenly Father through tears, watching how the first morning sunlight was trying to break through the thick leaves of a large old oak tree. I tried to imagine my life without Michael and I couldn't see myself without him. I did not want anything if he was not there. I wished I could be at home now with my family and cross off this part of my life as though it never happened. Better yet, I wished I would disappear at all, so that I would not be able to feel.

"How are you doing this morning?" It was Bruce approaching. He did not find me inside and went out to look for me. "Are you alright?" He came up to me and looked at me attentively.

"I don't know, my friend," I replied. "I just don't know. I feel like I am done. I am watching how my new life and all my hard work to make it happen are crashing into pieces, and I can't do anything to stop it. Nor do I have the strength to pick up the pieces and put them back together.

Michael's words and actions have killed me inside. I can't do it anymore Bruce."

"Well, don't worry so much," Bruce positively responded. "Things might change."

"What is going to change, Bruce? It's all over with Michael, and with him the opportunity is taken away from me as well. I have attained my independence on a daily basis, but I can't bend federal law. I figured out ways to be self-sufficient, I can go out, use public transportation and go to school, I can shop or do whatever I need to do. I did everything that depended on me, but I can't win against my immigration obstacle, because the law is the law and I can't change it. By no means am I going to stay here illegally. The only opportunity I had is destroyed. And now, I don't really have much time nor do I have the resources to find another one. I am facing the facts. I will have to leave the United States and that means that my new life and absolutely everything that I've attained so far is going to be thrown out the window."

"Look, Inga," Bruce said. "It's a big emotional drama now and everything is put on hold. Michael is going to call you soon when the storm calms down and you guys will continue working again on your organization and the mission you both had."

"No, Bruce," I insisted. "He is not coming back. And we won't work together any more. It's all over. I do not see any other way to improve my circumstances. I have no strength any more to push it. I am tired, very tired. I'm going home and I'm going to let everything go. I need to be alone. I need a break."

"What?" Bruce looked at me with an expression showing more than a little concern. "What are you talking about?"

"Bruce, I am exhausted. I feel drained. I can't push it anymore. I am so tired to constantly go against the stream and keep fighting. All these days, months and years I kept pushing and pushing and pushing. All this time I kept hearing my goals to either walk or be fully independent were impossible, and yet, I went against all the odds to try to find ways to attain them. I worked on my goals, no matter how impossible and crazy it seemed. And then, when I would finally attain my impossible goal in spite of it all – I had to watch it all shattered. Still, I picked myself up each time and continued moving forward. And now, when I thought I had finally found a way to bring myself back to life and I was about to complete my one last step – I find myself watching it happen again. It's all breaking down and I can't do anything about it.

"I had to give up everything in order to come here and aim for my goal and I did. I agreed to pay the highest price – leaving my family and my whole world behind me – in order to try and attain an independent, full life. I left absolutely everything behind and traveled across the globe to a land that is unknown to me even though there was absolutely no evidence that I might succeed. And why? Because I had faith this was my chance for life. I gave it my all, because I sincerely trusted it could be done.

"I put so much effort in everything I did and was ready to go above and beyond working hard because I believed it could be done. I knew that it's hard work that brings results. And I never questioned whether I would have to work hard.

"I fully surrendered to Michael my most important and biggest obstacle, because I so sincerely trusted him and relied on him. I mean I trusted him with all my heart and soul. When he suggested the establishment of the company and us working together on it, I asked him to think carefully if he really wanted to go ahead with his idea, because I assumed this might create problems for him at home and I needed to make sure he would follow through because my future depended on it.

"I asked him about it time and again if he was sure about what he was planning to do. He promised me, not to step back no matter what. I dropped looking into any other possibilities, fully relying on him. And what did he do?

"I was only one step away. And he simply terminated everything saying icily, 'You can find another way,' when he perfectly knew there was no other way.

"No longer can I endure obstacle after obstacle, heartbreak after heartbreak. I can't do it anymore. I think I'm going to leave and be done with it all. I don't have the strength anymore. I can't push it anymore."

Bruce looked straight into my eyes. "Inga, you can't give up. Look how much you have achieved already. You've been through excruciating pain and loss. You overcame your adversity from the accident. You overcame all your obstacles and successfully reached all your goals. Look how far you've come! Now what, you are going to stop? Give up? Are you really going to allow this to break you? People like you don't give up."

He turned around and left, and in few minutes, returned holding a book in his hands. "Take it and read a little. You are one of them. You are unstoppable. You must fight for your life, Inga."

Bruce wished me a good day and to stay strong and left to go to work. I remained in my lawn chair, holding the book in my hand. Bruce's words were resounding in my mind, "You can't stop. People like you don't give up. You are unstoppable."

While fatigue, anguish and disappointment were all I felt, I kept hearing Bruce's words in my mind over and over and over. I knew myself. I had always fought for my life. Up to this day I never said out loud that 'I am giving up.' Never even once have I allowed myself to even think of that. I wished I could bring myself together and tell myself that I was going to keep my eyes up and move on no matter what. But I could not. I found absolutely no strength within to keep on going. I felt so drained from never-ending pain, tears and sleepless nights. I felt empty. I felt wounded and vulnerable.

I took the book in my hand and read the summary. It was a book of inspirational stories, how people overcame adversities. And Bruce's words kept repeating in my mind, "You are one of them. You are unstoppable. You must fight for your life, Inga."

I thought back over the past several years. I never allowed any kind of pain to make me say, "I can't do this anymore." Absolutely nothing and nobody could possibly make me admit that it couldn't be done. Like a ship under full sail I kept going, breaking through the roaring waves. Always. No matter how devastated or heartbroken I was, I always kept moving forward. Bruce knew me well enough to say those words. He was right; nothing could stop me until this day and I couldn't give up now.

As I was reflecting on my previous ways of being, somewhere deep inside I had a tiny flame letting me know that I was still alive. In the back of my mind I knew I would not be able to give up. I knew I could not allow myself to give up if I was serious about rebuilding my life. Giving up was definitely not going to make my life better. In fact, it would do exactly the opposite. On top of that, I wouldn't be able to live with myself knowing that I was the one who made the decision to stop. However, at this moment this was just awareness about myself. I felt absolutely no strength or even desire to do anything to improve my situation. Nothing could possibly make me feel better and improve my life if Michael was no longer in it. Somehow, everything came back to Michael.

I started reading the book. The inspirational stories were about the endurance, resilience, faith and outcomes when the heroes of these stories relentlessly pushed through their times of hopelessness. Reading was like a breath of fresh air. That tiny flame of resilience was trying to break through my exhaustion and disappointment. My hope still wanted to hold on as smoldering embers among the cold coals. "Maybe there is still a way?"

As I saw the sun come up, I hoped that one day my life would see the sunlight as well. My last hope was the Lord my God. He is the God of Abraham, Isaac and Jacob and He is Almighty. He is my Heavenly Father, who loves me unconditionally, and I hoped He was going to show me a way out of this dead end. I knew I had to close this page and not look back.

Bruce suggested that I go to the ILC to volunteer, to get something to do and get at least a little bit distracted from what was going on. I was thankful for his efforts to give me comfort and take care of my well-being. I did not want to go anywhere, though. I saw myself working only with Michael and particularly for the company he had established and I did not want to do anything else. I refused to go anywhere with anybody. I still was waiting. Every day I hoped that I would see Michael in my driveway or at least hear from him.

On the third week since the breaking point, Kathryn called me and said she needed my help to choose some outfit for her. Normally I refused to go anywhere, but since she said she needed my help, I agreed to go. We went to the mall but instead of looking for outfits for women, she went straight to where they had more youthful clothing. She started picking up the outfit that was a smaller size and I knew she could not wear. I got confused and asked for whom she wanted to pick the outfit.

"Do you like it?" She looked at me and smiled, letting me know for whom she wanted to pick the outfit. "What do you think about these tops? Take it, and go ahead and try it."

After numerous days and nights of tears and misery, she brought a smile back to me. I could not believe how she tricked me and came up with an idea to get me out of the house! I felt cared for and loved. That day she showered me with gifts and later took me out for dinner. It was the first time in three weeks since I'd been out of the house, the first distraction from all that drama. It was good to feel valued and important. Since that day, Kathryn called every single day to check-up on me and take me out of the house. A lot of times, the dinner at her home was my breakfast. I'd totally lost my appetite and I wouldn't eat. She knew I needed love and care more than anything, and she was there for me. She asked me to pass on to my mom that she should not worry. My mom and I were writing emails every single day. I didn't have a way to speak to her, as phone calls overseas were expensive, and there were no video chats online yet.

Hearing my mom's voice was a treasure, and now I needed her the most. Like when I was hospitalized after the crash, she was like my angel, daily sending me love and support. It was hard even to imagine what she was going through seeing her child again being broken and devastated, and not being able to be there to help. I promised her to write her every day to give her the updates on how I was doing. After hearing that Kathryn was there with me and taking care of me, my mom cried, feeling grateful to Kathryn for everything. She felt easier knowing that I was not alone.

Kathryn and her husband took me under their wing. After she was done with her real estate business or duties helping her husband with his law practice, Kathryn would take me to her house, where all of us had dinner, shared heartfelt conversations or watched movies. She would spend a lot of time with me, buy me gifts, take me out to dinners and spoil me every way she could possibly think of to make me feel loved and cared for.

Her daughter Vanessa and I developed a close friendship as well. She called me daily and spent hours listening and talking with me. Vanessa and I were very different and yet, we shared common values. I was fascinated by her style of wearing dreads and her active participation in the local Renaissance Faire. We shared the same challenges, as she had also lost her leg in a motorcycle accident. I appreciated watching how independent and strong she was and how she managed to enjoy life despite any difficulties she was forced to face. I also appreciated her wisdom and insights about life. She helped me look at the situation from a different perspective and also helped me to work through the anguish I was going through during that time. Often times, Vanessa would come over and take me downtown, so I would be around people. Being out and around others distracted me quite a bit. It was good for me to interrupt my constant thinking about what had happened. I felt unconditional love, warmth and support from them.

Slowly I started feeling more like myself. More and more I found myself enjoying my day. I again had interest in going places, meeting with others and having an active day. Kathryn and Vanessa carried me through this most difficult time. I don't know how I would've gotten through if they hadn't been by my side. They became family. Since then, I call Kathryn my American Mom and her family my American Family.

After some time, Bruce encouraged me again to come to his work as a volunteer. He thought I would add a great value to the agency, and this, too, would distract me. By that time, I felt a little bit better, and I thought I wouldn't mind that at all. No longer could I stand sitting at home all day long. I was so tired from constant dwelling about Michael and all that had happened, but there was no way to hide from it. I needed to find something to occupy my mind by some activity. I thought this would be a good start for me to learn working in this country. I needed to practice my American language skills and learn what I needed to learn about American culture and life in this country.

I accepted Bruce's encouragement and went with him to his work place to volunteer. Executive Director of the organization pleasantly welcomed me and wished me to enjoy my time volunteering at the agency. I met some other staff members, who were very nice to me and welcomed me as well. Especially I felt welcomed by Bruce's co-worker Nancy. What a surprise it was to find out that Bruce was sharing his office with the same woman, who first offered me a place to stay at her house – and then she introduced me to Bruce.

From the very first day, Nancy took me under her wing. She found some office tasks for me to do to assist her. I didn't mind helping. In fact, I was very happy to do so, because I was fascinated by her. She was the first person who truly inspired me. Here she was, fully paralyzed and yet, working like everybody else and doing so much for the community. Soon I learned that she was a great inspiration to many.

Ten years previous, Nancy had developed Guillain-Barré Syndrome, which left her paralyzed up to the point that she was not able to speak or breath without assistance. After countless procedures, she was able to breath with the help of Montgomery Trach transplanted into her body. It was painful to watch how every breath she took had to be made through this effort. It made me speechless watching how a person, who could hardly breathe and speak, and who also was fully paralyzed, was an advocate for the rights of people with disabilities, and was helping other disabled people become independent.

I was fascinated watching how she managed to type on the computer or handle papers while her hands were paralyzed. She could move them only from her shoulders and elbows, but the palms of her hands and her fingers remained paralyzed since the day she got that syndrome. Watching Nancy, I again realized how fortunate I was to have one hand working fully. "If she can do so much having no working hands, then I can do anything having a fully functioning hand."

I was not rushing to volunteer for more serious tasks. As I still had trouble with American English, I did not feel confident because I did not fully understand people, did not know the office administration systems and regulations, or how things functioned in this country. Only later I revealed to her that I had a quite extensive experience managing office duties, since I worked at the Personnel Department at the Vilnius International Airport assisting and managing the paperwork of hundreds of employees, and managed airport's archive. I appreciated having the opportunity to do some work in this country, meeting people and having at least some activity. Yet it was difficult for me to be there. While I was given the simplest tasks, memories of me working in the Airport's Personnel Department, managing the Airport's archive, working in the Business Lounge, helping coordinating Michael's and Don's trip in Lithuania and assisting them with their lectures, were constantly on my mind.

It was made worse knowing what I was supposed do in the position created for me at Michael's company. It was like my shadow and I could not get rid of the feeling that it wasn't how everything should be, that all of this was wrong. I kept repeating in my mind that this wasn't where I needed to be and that it wasn't what I needed to be doing. It was so heartbreaking to be in some other company, performing these simple tasks, when I knew what I was really supposed to be doing.

Nevertheless, there was nothing I could possibly change. Michael was gone. The company was gone, too, as far as my involvement was concerned. I had to face a different reality whether I liked it or not. It was so heartbreaking that I sometimes could hardly hold myself from crying right there at the office. But then, what could I possibly explain to them why I was in tears? So, I would swallow the anguish and continued acting as if there was nothing wrong in my life.

Opportunity?

Day by day the drama and turmoil began to subside. No longer was I at home crying. At times, I would go with Bruce to his office to get distracted. Oftentimes, I did not want to go, but I intentionally went against my feelings because I knew I had to make steps forward. Sitting at home dwelling on Michael was not going to let me move on, and so I forced myself to go to places and meet people.

In addition to spending time with Kathryn and Vanessa, I ended up going to the church with Tammy, the wonderful receptionist from Michael's office. She was the first person I met when I came to his office. Her sheer excitement meeting me and showering me with her compliments remains in my memory. What a surprise it was to learn that she was a Christian. After opening up to her with the truth and getting rid of the shackles of lies, I asked her to bring me to her church and now, I had someone to talk to about the Lord, to discuss the biblical matters that I was so perplexed about.

As days were passing by, the gut-wrenching anguish subsided, but it was replaced by emptiness. Without Michael I felt lonely and empty, no matter what I did. I started giving up the idea that he would show up. My pain and disappointment were turning into anger. However, the clock was ticking and I knew I had to hold myself together and think about my future.

One evening, I heard a knock on my bedroom door. Bruce, as always, was checking up on me, "What are you doing?

"Eh...Nothing."

"Inga," he said. "You have very high potential, and you can realize it here in the United States. I see how much you want to live in California, and I don't want to see you going back to Europe if you can't live there as you want to. I want to help you. I will marry you, so that you can stay here in the United States."

"What?" I exclaimed. I was caught by surprise. "Get married? Are you serious? I can't do that. Plus, I don't have the money to compensate you. It's a big responsibility."

"Inga," he responded. "I'm not doing this for money. I want to help, that's all. I can't watch you suffering like this anymore. You don't have to answer that now. But think about it."

Bruce got emotional as he reached out his hand to me to catapult me out of this despair. Just like before, he left me with something to think about. Bruce's offer was like another unexpected bolt of lightning from the sky.

"Opportunity?" I thought. My first feeling was a spark of hope. "Yes, opportunity. This could be a way to turn around the situation I am in. But this is not right. And yet, at this point, it's the only and the last chance for me to rebuild my life." I was so mixed up and lost that I didn't know how I should treat this offer or what I should do next.

I realized that it was a serious decision which would determine my future. It was scary to decide immediately because I was not sure which decision was right. I experienced how one wrong decision broke my biggest dream and greatly impacted my future. Once again I was standing at the crossroads, and depending on my decision, my life would go in one direction or the other. I didn't feel in the right emotional state to make that kind of a decision, and I wished I didn't have to. But I didn't have much time left. With every day I was getting closer to my visa's expiration.

My sleepless nights continued. It looked like an opportunity to change my life and this was my last and only chance. But I did not like that idea. I had a very strange feeling. It wasn't right again because I would be breaking the law. If it got out that it was a sham marriage, I would be deported from the United States with no chance for ever coming back.

And then I faced the critical part of my decision: I did not want to tie myself into a marriage with a man with whom I had no actual relationship, a man who would not really be my husband; he would become my husband in name only. Deep inside I felt like something bad would happen if I took that step. On the other hand, logically and realistically thinking, this opportunity was the only door left: A person who became my friend, who supported me in my most difficult times, and who was very caring and considerate, offered his help to stay in the country, who did not want to accept any monetary compensation for his selfless act. He was opening the doors to America for me, which had just been slammed in my face.

I was sick to my stomach imagining myself returned to a purposeless existence, watching how the most fruitful years of my life would pass me by in my room, day by day, year after year. Again, to see the sun and the rain only through the windows for months? Again, not have a chance to be outside and take a deep breath of fresh air? Again, to spend day and night among the four walls of my room, imprisoned at my home? Again, not to be able to enjoy anything in life, unable to connect with the people I love, unable to be valuable to and for others, unable to have any work and any activity for all year round? Would the television and the Internet be my only window to the world and to the joys of life? Would I have to read and watch about the successes of other people, with no opportunity to grow, to work and succeed on my own? Again, will I have to start my day much later so that I have less hours in the day, so I would not have to feel my bleak presence and total hopelessness?

My desire was to live a complete and dynamic life and I could do that in California. Here I could live like every normal person does. Here I would be able to go out whenever I wanted and go wherever I wanted without having those accessibility issues! I would be able to meet people anywhere I wanted and enjoy my time with them. Here I could go to work and bring value to others and succeed. I could travel and enjoy my life just as other people do. This is where my life was supposed to continue and be restored. All I needed to do was go to the court, sign the appropriate marriage papers and go through the immigration process as Bruce's wife.

After a month of thinking about it daily, I weighed my options and despite a big, heavy feeling in my heart, I finally agreed to take that step. It was my last chance and I couldn't pass it by. I considered, after all, that maybe I was given another chance to mend the situation and continue on towards my dream. Maybe I hadn't lost my blessing and this was another opportunity. We chose the date and began announcing to my closest friends about the upcoming marriage.

While I was preparing for that step, two strong feelings came into conflict: hatred for marriage idea and the fear of rejecting it. Day and night I was tormented by feelings of uncertainty about what I was getting ready to do. During the day, I could not focus on doing anything. At night, I would go to bed feeling exhausted, but could not stop my mind from thinking and considering all my options. I couldn't fall asleep until the sunrise. Anxiety and the feeling that I was again doing the wrong thing haunted me and would not leave me. The fear of losing the opportunity to stay in the states paralyzed me from changing my plans and buying my ticket back to Europe. I was afraid to leave. I was afraid that I would never come back to the land of sunshine if I left now.

One evening came when I understood something that changed the course of my plans. Vanessa was visiting and we were sitting outside enjoying the warm evening, talking about the latest events in our lives. I shared with her the options I was facing and the inner conflict about the choice I was planning to make. After listening carefully she looked at me peacefully and said, "Inga. Never make your decisions based on fear. Fear is your enemy. Do that which makes you feel peaceful."

At that moment those words like arrows of light breaking through the invisible strongholds of my fear, doubt and logical thinking, reached the deepest core of my heart. "You are so right my friend," I replied. "Why didn't I think of that before? So many times have I made my best decisions guided by my intuitive feelings, not by logic. You are so right! That which is from God brings peace and joy, not fear and anxiety."

That night, before I went to bed, I prayed. I asked Father God to give me a sign showing me what I needed to do. In addition to not knowing which decision was better for me, I was so lost and mixed up in my own feelings that I didn't even distinguish which option I felt more peaceful about. I asked Him to show me in the morning which path I should take by clearly giving me peace. That would point me in the right direction of the decision He wanted me to make. If I felt disturbed or anxiety-filled, I would know the decision was wrong and is against His will for me.

I started the next morning with the intention of calling upon my Lord to ask Him for His guidance as to what I should do. I believed that through prayer, I would have an answer. As I prayed, asking the Lord to direct me, I thought about the marriage. Immediately I felt a very strong uneasiness deep inside. I had the feeling of danger, as though I would jeopardize myself and later I would face even more despair than I was facing now. I knew that Bruce was not a bad person, but for some reason it was such a strong disturbing feeling that I immediately knew it was a clear warning that I would be making a big mistake if I took that step.

Then I thought about my second option, going back home to Lithuania. To my astonishment, the disturbing feelings I'd had cleared up in a moment, and I felt peace within. I even felt joy and easiness deep in my spirit. Due to my drama and stormy emotions lately, the feeling of calmness was like a stranger who unexpectedly showed up. I fully grasped that this feeling of peace was supernaturally given to me just as I had asked in my prayer. I missed that incredible feeling so much! I had no doubts it was given to me as a sign of what option I was supposed to choose. Right that moment I knew what I was going to do next. I had no doubts. I needed to cancel my marriage plans and go home to Lithuania.

For a second, logic got my attention. This step was totally opposite of what I desired so strongly. If I left the United States now, I might never come back and I might not have another opportunity. But I knew that such a clear and strong intuitive feeling was the sign that I had asked for the night before, and I had to trust in it. I had to have complete trust that such a radical and clear difference in my feelings was the answer that I had asked the Lord to give me. I felt a clear answer from Him and that's the choice I needed to make, regardless of logic.

I was longing to be at home with my family. I was broken and vulnerable and I needed to feel safe, loved and wanted. I missed them so much. I wanted to be with people who I knew would never ever reject me or betray me, no matter what mistakes I may have made. At that moment, it felt to me that even the walls of my room would heal me. I had no idea what would happen once I returned to Lithuania, and what I was going to do once I arrived there. I had absolutely no idea how my circumstances could possibly be improved or restored once I left this country.

To be honest, though, I did not even want to think about it. I felt so tired and wounded and I didn't care what was going to happen next. Love and warmth were all I needed at the time. Even though it was scary to see that I was going to make a choice that totally contradicted my vision and my goal, I knew that at this time, I again needed to make a step of faith. I had to stand strong in my faith that my life was in my God's hands. He led me through the endless deserts and storms, and He already has shown me how He can create new opportunities and pull me out of despair. I needed to trust Him and I decided to surrender myself, my feelings, my desires, my plans, my future and absolutely everything to God, who blessed me and protected me all these years. That was my first time I brought my plans before the Lord and consulted with Him.

> *"Trust in the Lord with all your heart, and lean not on your own understanding; in all your ways acknowledge Him, and He shall direct your paths." (Proverbs 3: 5-6)*

And, just like it's written in Holy Scriptures, once I brought my plans before the Lord, He answered my question and directed my path. That same day I cancelled the marriage plans and called friends who had been notified. I called Kathryn and told her about the changes. She was very surprised about my decision, but she supported me. She agreed I needed to go home to be with my family and recover emotionally. She said my marriage decision could wait until I was not as emotional and could think more clearly. When I called my mom to ask if I could come back home, she was crying with me and kept repeating, "Of course Inga, come back home. I can't imagine how you can be there alone, all by yourself. Come back."

My dad said the same thing that it would be better if I came home, and asked me not to worry saying, "Inga, as a family, together we have gone through so much. We supported each other throughout the toughest times, and we will simply continue living as we did before. Do not worry about anything. We love you very much. Pack your luggage and come home. It's not the same here without you. We need you here, please come home."

When Bruce got home from work, I told him I had cancelled all our plans and that I was leaving. He was very surprised. He looked attentively and asked if I was sure about what I was doing. I said that I wanted to go home and think about it. I might come back in several months, and then we'd see what was next.

Kathryn decided to fly with me. She wanted to meet her Lithuanian relatives for the first time, and to support me on my way back as well as to meet my parents. We bought the airline tickets and got ready for our trip to Europe.

Saying Goodbye to the Land of Sunshine

Early in the morning, while driving to San Francisco International Airport, I was gazing through the window. I so adored those palm trees. Other bright, colorful trees and vineyards spread over the hills like a beautiful carpet knitted by the Creator. Everything seemed so dear and lovely. I cherished California's beauty. I was looking at the scenery I loved so much and wondered whether this was the last time I was able to admire its exceptional beauty.

My heart was torn, losing my love, my new friends and California, what I already had accepted as my new homeland. I had fallen in love with the land of sunshine from the very first day; it was the place where I wanted to continue my life's journey. When I arrived to California the second time, I felt like I'd returned home. Now I was on my way to the airport with a one-way ticket.

"Father God," I cried inside. "Why do I have to leave? I know I made a mistake, but I don't want to leave this land. Why do I have to go away?"

For the second time, I had lost absolutely everything that I dreamed about and worked so hard to make come true. Two of my biggest dreams crashed soon after they became my reality. My prosthetic legs were again standing in the corner of my room without any use. Since neither Michael nor any other prosthetic specialists found any possible way to make my socket comfortable, they suggested that I check in with a doctor to see if there was any medical issue that could be the possible cause of that excruciating pain.

And I had lost my opportunity to establish myself in California, where I could continue my life being independent again. I was going back to where I was before I even contacted Michael: I did not have prosthetic legs that

I could walk with, and I was going back to sad existence among the four walls. I felt betrayed and abandoned by someone whom I trusted with all my heart and had trusted with my life. I lost the person who I loved and to whom I had devoted myself. And I felt miserable for what I had done to Michael's wife and the people who sincerely trusted me and loved me. I was leaving my dreamland wounded, betrayed, miserable and empty. And there was nothing I could do to get away from it.

I missed everyone in Lithuania and couldn't wait to hug everyone. At the same time, I didn't want to go back to that which I tried to escape from. Until the last minute, I hoped for the phone call which could change it all. I waited for that one phone call as we drove to the airport, while we were checking-in our luggage and going through the processes to get to our gate. I got onto the airplane and yet, I still waited for the miracle.

"I wonder," I thought, "if you are aware that I am leaving the country? Are you really going to let me go like that, Michael?" Gazing upon the airport activity through the airplane's little window, in my mind I spoke with him. I didn't want to turn off my cell phone. Up to the last minute I hoped to hear my phone ringing. I knew I would change my plans all over again and would arrange to get out of the airplane if I just heard Michael's voice. But my phone was quiet. Then I saw the sign that cell phones must be turned off. I had to let it go. I shut down my last hope and put it into my bag. No longer would I need my American cell phone.

When the airplane took off, it felt as if someone ripped my heart apart. It was hard to breath. Now I understood what people meant by saying, "It hurts your soul." I saw through the window the land of sunshine dissipating further and further into the distance. I looked at the monitor showing the route of the airplane, across the United States, back to Europe, crossing the Atlantic Ocean. I was really leaving. The tiny icon of the airplane and the picture of the globe map on the monitor started fading away. Tears started uncontrollably rolling down my cheeks. I was not able to hold the pain within any more. Kathryn, sitting next to me, understood everything. But there was nothing she could promise that would give me comfort or give me hope. She took my hand and squeezed it, letting me know that she was there, letting me know she felt my pain.

I turned on my CD player and with those first notes, I closed my eyes. I wanted to disappear from all the passengers and flight attendants. I did not want to drink or eat anything, nor did I want to see anybody. I wanted to understand why everything had to happen the way it did.

It was a long eleven hour flight, and again I had a lot of time to think. This time however, I was not envisioning my future, nor was I setting goals. I reflected on how my choices had impacted the sequence of events, and how they destroyed the beauty God had brought into my life. My Lord was patiently waiting for me to stop, and because of his grace, He was silent for quite a long time, giving me more time to wake up from the lie that I set up for myself. God allowed the consequences to play out. A moment came to my memory, when a few days after our secret exploded, I opened the Bible and the first thing my eyes saw was a verse I'd underlined a long time ago:

> *"Know then in your heart that as a man disciplines his son, so the Lord your God disciplines you. Observe the commands of the Lord your God, walking in obedience to him and revering him." (Deuteronomy 8: 5-6)*

And at this time, I did feel like a child disciplined by his father, my Heavenly Father. It was as if a father warns his child not to play with fire because it's dangerous, but the child wouldn't listen, and would play close to the flame, only to get burned, anyway. That child was me. I did not listen to my Father, who warned me that if I started playing with fire, I would get hurt if I didn't stay away from it. Scripture warns us so many times about adultery. But I chose not to take the warning. And as a result, I suffered. I could not blame anyone but myself. I knew I got what I deserved for my actions.

I was shocked to realize what a huge, life-changing impact our choices can cause. That one wrong decision had ruined such a wonderful opportunity. I made those choices based on whatever I wanted at the time. But what I didn't think about was that those same decisions had the power to impact my future. While I was carelessly making certain choices and decisions, I did not realize that they created subsequent events and circumstances, and thus, directed my destiny. Decisions that seemed to be not that important and did not make a big difference at the time, over time they delivered their fruit.

The accident was an important lesson for me to learn about me making choices even knowing they were wrong. But apparently, I had not learned my lesson. The lesson showed up again in my life. And again, I didn't pass the test. I could have been employed by now and had a fulfilling career, implementing my ultimate plan for living an independent, active, lifestyle in the states. Instead, I was in an airplane leaving America feeling lost, miserable, wounded and vulnerable as never before. No longer did I want to aspire for anything. In fact, there was nothing that I wanted. And I did not have the strength to pick myself up and continue on. At this point, all I wanted was to shut myself in my room and simply be. During hours and hours of flying I could not fall asleep, and did not want to eat. I turned on some banal movie to get away from myself, but while I was looking at the screen, my mind was in my world. I closed my eyes and tried at the very least to relax my eyes and my body.

After a tiring and what seemed endless flight, we landed in Frankfurt to change planes for a connecting flight to Vilnius. Now I was halfway around the globe and thousands of miles away from all the drama. In a way I felt easier, as this was an entirely different environment and atmosphere. Only now I realized how much I missed Europe. On the other hand, it was even more painful to be torn so far apart from Michael and my new world.

Kathryn and I both were very tired after the long flight, and the time change added its own challenge to stay awake during the daytime. After a little walk in Frankfurt's airport and some coffee, we boarded our second airplane. After getting a little distraction from my painful reflections, I felt I could no longer dwell on them anymore. I didn't know how to handle the pain.

I continued talking to God in my mind, asking why these lessons had to be so painful and what I was supposed to do now. As a response to my thought, a verse came to my mind; I quickly took my Bible and found that verse:

> *"And have you completely forgotten this word of encouragement that addresses you as a father addresses his son? It says, 'My son, do not make light of the Lord's discipline, and do not lose heart when he rebukes you, because the Lord disciplines the one he loves, and he chastens everyone he accepts as his son.' Endure hardship as discipline; God is treating you as his children. For what children are not disciplined by their father? If you are not disciplined—and everyone undergoes discipline—then you are not legitimate, not true sons and daughters at all. Moreover, we have all had human fathers who disciplined us and we respected them for it. How much more should we*

> *submit to the Father of spirits and live! They disciplined us for a little while as they thought best; but God disciplines us for our good, in order that we may share in his holiness. No discipline seems pleasant at the time, but painful. Later on, however, it produces a harvest of righteousness and peace for those who have been trained by it." (Hebrews 12-5:7 NIV)*

I smiled in my mind as that was exactly how it felt. I remember my mother saying, "If I say *no*, then it means, 'No.'" And if I wouldn't listen, she would discipline me. Now I felt the same as I did when I was a little girl. I understood that if God says "no," it means "No."

There cannot be any, "Well, maybe He understands because He is a loving God." He is a loving God and yet, He is a just and righteous God. If it's not right, there cannot be any way to justify it. You simply do not go there. I realized that obedience to the Lord was vital to my own well-being.

As I was contemplating, peace filled my heart and my mind. It was a similar feeling to the peace which I felt that morning in prayer, asking God to direct me. Deep within, I had an awareness that everything was going to be alright. Somehow I perceived that I needed to put my hope and my trust in my Lord, who has the power over all circumstances. I had to completely surrender myself and my situation to Him and trust Him, just as I always had from the day when I woke up in the ICU.

I had absolutely no idea what I was going to do when I returned to Vilnius. My major goals were ruined. Everything was ruined. But I knew that God was all powerful. I had seen His mighty hand, how He could create circumstances in my favor when I could not even imagine the possibility. I knew that God had the power to heal my inner wounds and turn around my circumstances. And this was my last hope. Again I was in the situation when I simply did not have anybody or anything to count on. Lately I had been fully counting on Michael. In fact, only now I realized that I put more confidence and trust in him than in the Lord. No longer was Michael in my life. Now I had again only God to count on. I had to hold onto my faith regardless of how desperate my situation was. Instead of dwelling on how ruined and hopeless everything was, I needed to trust that the Lord could perform a miracle, and that He could change even that which seemed completely ruined.

I believed there was a reason why He encouraged me to go to America to build my life, giving me promises of a blessed and abundant life in the land that He had led me to. And I know I destroyed His initial plan. I made a mistake. Yet I believed the Lord would give me another chance. If it was His will that I would live in California, I believed He would create another opportunity that would take me back. I didn't know how it could possibly happen, but I knew it would, if it was His will. I was very emotional but interestingly, deep inside, I had a firm awareness that everything was going to turn out well. I would have another chance.

I opened my eyes to look at the clock. The airplane was approaching my home country. I missed Lithuania. I was longing for Vilnius all this time, and it was good to know I would finally see my gorgeous city again. Just thinking that in one hour I would see my family and friends made my heart tremble. I couldn't wait to hug everyone. I was so wounded that the thought of being with the people whom I loved, and who loved me, was so very comforting and healing. I closed my eyes again, chose my favorite song, and drowned myself in its familiar sounds. Now I was curious what was going to happen next.

16

Rising Above it

Hi Valdas,

I wanted to write about something I believe is very important. Would you agree that we certainly have wonderful things in life that we love and are thankful for? However, sometimes various events, people or situations show up in our lives and overshadow our joy and feelings for how really blessed we are. I think you'll agree that it's hard to feel gratitude when we have roaring storms around us, isn't it?

There was a time in my life when I realized that in addition to God's blessing, my experience greatly depended on how well I managed myself. My biggest eye opener, and probably one of the most significant, was when I realized that my experience about one or another event depended upon how I choose to look at it.

In one of my letters to you, I talked about how our perspective determines our response and, ultimately, affects the decisions we make about what we are going to do next. The actual event is a plain fact; your perspective will give color, feelings and emotions to that event.

When you think of it, what causes you to feel excited or angry? Is it the situation itself or what you think about that situation? Let's take a simple example: When we would get sick as children, how did we feel about it and how did our parents feel? I remember you and I were always excited about catching a cold because to us it meant a vacation from school. We would relax at home, watch television in bed, and not worry about anything. Our focus was on the fact that we didn't have to go to classes or do homework, rather than on feeling sick or doing what the doctor said to get well. On the other hand, how did mom feel about the situation? Was she as excited? Of course not, because it meant a totally different thing for her. It caused pain watching her children not feeling well and additional trouble making sure she took a good care of their health and their needs. It wasn't until later, when we became adults, that getting sick stopped being fun for us because it meant restrictions. We could not go out and do the things we were used to and that we needed to do.

Think about it. It's the same situation, but with many different responses and different feelings. And of course, our feelings changed the older we got. As we see, one situation can bring about different reactions, depending on how we look at the situation and what our focus is.

This simple example shows that the situation is merely a fact, nothing more. It's how you look at it and what you think that makes you react in a certain way.

Another big eye opener for me was when I realized that nobody could make me feel angry or frustrated unless I allowed it. How many times did you feel angry because someone said or did something to you? Often times we react automatically, and usually we put the blame on the person who said or did something that made us feel a certain way.

I invite you to look more deeply and see how you can change your response and overall experience. People and situations cannot make you feel any particular way. It is your response that makes you feel a particular way. Nobody can make you angry and frustrated unless you allow yourself to be put in that angry inner state. How? By thinking about it in a certain way.

I know, it might be hard to accept it.

Walk with me through this. As I was analyzing myself the other day, I saw that in order to get angry, we go through three stages: Let's say a person did something to us:

- First we think about what has been said or done.
- As we dwell on what was said or done, we start feeling certain emotions, depending on how we look at the situation and what meaning we give to the actual event. The more we think about it, the stronger our emotions enter into the picture. Our emotions will depend on how we perceive that situation.
- Finally we draw conclusions and come to a decision on what we are going to do. Usually, when we choose the perspective that does not support us, the perception of what occurred will make us feel

rejected, angry, not loved, frustrated, ignored, left out, belittled or lacking in self-esteem. And it all began with what was said or done.

Once I broke it down like that, it helped me to understand how I could control or at least impact my outcome – by consciously choosing my initial response to the situation. You cannot control other people, but you always can control your response, and that's actually more powerful than trying to make others act the way you want them to act.

Let's say your girlfriend didn't answer the phone and hasn't called you back, even if you've left voicemail and text messages. More than half of the day passed since you tried to reach her; your anxiety level is getting higher and higher. You start thinking her lack of response is a loud message to you. She should call you back or at least send you a short text message as soon as she can. Probably she's ignoring you and you are not that important for her to take the time to respond. This means that she disrespects you and does not take you seriously.

What's happening is your perspective gave you the meaning that hurts you and very quickly your emotions escalate. What conclusions and decisions are you going to make with this perception?

What if before you automatically go into the cycle that will make you feel in a negative way, you stop yourself at the moment when you will be at the point of choosing your perspective about the situation. It is the very first step as soon as the situation occurs. How about a perspective that you both respect each other without a doubt and due to busy schedules and unexpected situations at work, you two cannot always connect? Let's look at a few reasons she may not be answering her phone:

- She's super busy and can't take personal calls when she's on deadline.
- She left her phone at home.
- She forgot to charge it.
- She left her charger in your car (or at home).
- Her phone is not close by her.
- Her phone is on mute.
- She changed purses and left her cell in her other purse.

Her not answering the phone might mean a number of things, so why not decide to wait until you actually talk to her and find out what the reason was? Before your emotions escalate, choose the perspective that will support you.

As you know, we meet various people at certain times in our lives and every one of them has their reasons for why they say what they say and do what they do. You don't know these reasons until you get to know them, and a lot of times their behavior might be totally unrelated to you. Every human being has values and human needs. After a lot of reading and researching, I found the tool I believe is accurate and explains why people do what they do. They are called the "6 Human Needs" by Anthony Robbins:

- Certainty
- Variety
- Significance
- Love and Connection
- Growth
- Contribution

Every individual has them; only priorities are different for each person. A person will do whatever it takes to fulfill his or her top two needs. People try to fulfill their own needs consciously or unconsciously, and everyone finds different ways to fulfill them. Some people will strive to achieve great success or will do a lot of good work for others in order to feel significant, and some people will put others down or harm someone weaker than they are to fulfill the same need.

I have personally met people, who continuously put others down, while exalting themselves. They think that this way they will show how "cool" they are (and fulfilling their need to feel important, significant), not understanding that they are only showing how desperately insecure they are about themselves. They cannot feel significant and good about themselves in other ways, so they try to laugh at somebody and put them down so they can feel important and better about themselves.

Would I be upset with such a person? Not at all. Instead of anger, I would feel pity for that person because they feel so insignificant that they choose such a pathetic way to fulfill their needs so as to look important or better than anyone else.

This is an example how you understanding why the person treats you poorly helps you to respond appropriately and in a way that empowers you. Before you take anything personally, try to see the true reason why the person acts the way he does. Remember, everyone tries to fulfill their needs, and understanding their needs will help you respond in a healthy way.

Understanding and fulfilling another person's needs might turn an unpleasant situation (or even potential conflict) into resolution, mutual understanding and, perhaps friendship. If a person tries to hurt you intentionally, you can take a different approach.

The storm of negative emotions starts when we put our attention to what has been said or done and start thinking about it. Someone said something offensive to you, then you really hear those words and start analyzing them. You feel hurt and offended. The more you think about it, the worse you feel. Then you decide what to do about it. Usually we react and say something back or hold it within while being tormented by negative emotions, or feeling insecure. The point I'm making is: Where does it lead?

What if you don't dwell on what has been said and don't even pay any attention to it? The person said something, so what? Let it fly right by you. Why would you care about the words that were said to you out of anger, jealousy or with the intention to hurt you? You know who you are. You know what you are capable of. You know your value, your intentions and your achievements. If people choose to do or say things to you or about you, it's their choice and let them have it. Let them wallow in their miserable intention to hurt you and their insecurity about themselves. As far as you're concerned, just move on. Let those words stay with them, not with you. Your inner peace and joy are much more important than who said something to you or about you. Once you learn not to even respond to things that have been said and maintain your inner tranquility and stability, you will see how much easier life will be for you.

I speak from personal experience. Once in my life I had a relationship with a person, who out of the anger and jealousy tried to snap at me by making rude and abusive comments. It offended me and hurt my feelings. Then I realized that I was in charge of how I feel. Nobody can make me feel bad if I don't allow those behaviors affect me. So I stopped my negative reaction (which usually led to even deeper, more bitter arguments), and started responding by simply ignoring those vain attempts to offend me. I cared more about my inner peace and protected it by not getting engaged in a conversation that would lead me into conflict. It was quite fun, actually, to watch how that person noticed my different response and tried to bombard me with even more attempts to irritate and bully me. But it was all to no avail.

I got hold of something that gave me a full control over my negative automatic reaction and my emotions – it is a full understanding that nobody and nothing can make me frustrated, upset or angry unless I allow it to happen. My feelings are created by my thoughts, and I am in full control of what I think about.

You can manage how you feel by choosing what you think. You can make yourself angry by thinking about things that make you angry and make yourself feel uplifted by choosing to think what's good in your life.

Here's an example: I am sure you experienced numerous times when you wake up in the morning, and you feel peaceful and good. But then, when you are fully awake and remember some negative situation from the day before, your joy disappears. Then you start analyzing it and slowly but surely you start feeling irritated and your happiness disappears by degrees. It's what many people call a "bad mood." And you remain in a bad mood as long as you keep your mind focused on your bad situation.

Then, let's say you have some unexpected pleasant surprise. What happens then? You immediately get excited and happy, right? A pleasant surprise creates positive feelings and you feel great because this surprise took your focus away from the bad situation and shifted it to a pleasant one. Here is the trick: you will feel great as long as you stay focused on the pleasant surprise and the beautiful experience it has created for you. But as soon as you go back into analyzing and thinking about that bad situation that you were thinking about in the morning, you will go back into your bad mood. It is you who directs the ship of your emotions and overall inner state, not circumstances.

Have you paid attention when you start dwelling on a bad, painful situation, the dark thoughts expand and grow? First you get irritated. Then you get angry and nervous. And finally, you develop such anger that you can't even sit still. The fact is, the more you think about that, the worse you feel. Maybe in reality nothing is really going on, and maybe those people already forgot what they said and didn't even mean to hurt you. But you still keep thinking about it and make it worse. And you make it worse only for yourself. Please understand that dwelling on those thoughts is not going to change your actual situation, but you only torture yourself. Stop doing that to yourself.

Do you remember my letter to you about depression? You can't get depressed if you focus on things that make you excited and content with where you are in life. You give the direction to how you feel by choosing what you focus on, what you think about most of the time. Of course, there are times when we might not see any light and not even hope to see the light. It's hard to be positive when we are in difficult circumstances and have difficult problems or if we are in pain. But we still can be in charge of how we feel.

You know what helped me to hold on during my most difficult times? I focused on the beautiful that I had and what I was grateful for. And I never lost hope that things would get better. When I was barely holding myself from literally crying out loud from pain after the surgeries or anguish I felt for my loss, that's exactly what I did to hold myself together. In my mind I was thanking God for saving my life, for my family, for friends who did not desert me, for the love and care that I was surrounded with. I felt gratitude for what I had and hope is what helped me to endure the times when I couldn't see an end to despair and pain.

I found that gratitude is the best way to change how you feel, to focus on what you want to create in your life, and to create enthusiasm for the future. You may ask, "How can you feel grateful if you are surrounded by so many problems and circumstances with no positive solution in sight?"

In reality, you have so much to be grateful for. But you will not notice it if you are going to be focused on what's not good in your life. I know it seems like you have only bad things happening in your life right now, and there is no way you can find something to be grateful for. But you must relax, take a deep breath, and think for a moment about what you can be grateful for. Here are some simple things:

- You are healthy. You have all parts of your body and you function well. How would you feel if you lost a leg or an arm or more? By now you are very well aware that it can happen to anyone anytime; nobody can be sure about their tomorrow.
- You have family that loves you and cares about you. What would your life be like if you lost me and our parents, and you were lonely in this world?
- You have friends who love and care about you.
- You have your little son, who loves you more than anything in the world, and he loves you unconditionally.

- Many times you could have gotten into a horrible car crash, but you survived and were not even injured. You wouldn't want to be in my position, would you?
- And what about hardships, bad people you have met in your life, dangers you have faced, and somehow by divine miracle you did not have any life-changing impact from it all.

There is a lot that I don't know about your experiences, but you know all those situations that could have impacted your life in a bad way. You know them all. You have what you can be grateful for. You just have difficult circumstances, that's all. The question is what you focus on.

I want to share with you a very interesting experience that made a major shift in my life. I remember very well this special moment. It was like a turning point in my life. At the time, I recently moved to the United States. I lived in the beautiful land of sunshine, California, but I felt very unhappy. Everything in my life seemed dreary, cold and dark. I did not feel happy nor was I even pleased with my life. I was on the bus going home from work. I did not want to go home. I did not want to see anyone and I did not want to do anything. I just felt empty and sad. As I was looking through the window, black thoughts were bombarding my mind. I did not see even one reason why I could feel happy or at least at ease.

I caught myself feeling this way and asked, "How did I get to this? How in the world I got myself to the point that I feel so unhappy?"

Suddenly, I felt this quiet gentle voice within me saying, "Rise above it. Rise above all your problems and what you are not happy about. Inga, look at how much good you have in your life! But you don't see it because you are focused on what doesn't go the way you want it to go and you are constantly thinking about what you are not happy about. Rise above all you are not happy about. Rise above your dissatisfaction and look how much good you have in your life."

In my mind I envisioned myself going up and leaving behind all that made me unhappy. I left behind my dissatisfaction, my daily routine, household and job duties, concerns, problems and worries. As I left it all below, here above it felt so good and bright. I felt at ease. I looked at the horizon and saw success, happiness, joy and the victories of my goals yet to be achieved. I was so longing for the sheer joy and contentment. I was so longing for the thrill of anticipation and excitement of moving forward and achieving the goals that were getting me closer to my ultimate vision.

The victory was ahead of me waiting for me to reach it, but I stopped moving toward it. Just a while ago I had so many goals that I wanted to achieve. I was striving for excellence every time I did something. I had such a wonderful vision for the life I wanted to create. But I lost my sight of the vision because I switched my focus to what was right in front of me, to the facts of today's reality. I focused on the parts of my life that made me irritated, unhappy and annoyed. I was constantly thinking about that, which made me unhappy instead of what I have achieved and what made my life fulfilling and beautiful.

I focused on what was not working. I knew I needed to switch my focus back to my vision. I needed to rise above all that made me so unhappy, to leave it all behind and move towards my dream. I had to walk in faith – I had to visualize my dream to be achieved. I needed to shift my focus. I had to choose to think about what I wanted and how I could realize it.

This was the day when my depressed inner state turned around. It seemed like someone opened my eyes and I saw what I didn't see before – my life was amazing and I had so much in my life. All of a sudden I saw how much good I had in my life. I came to America knowing only one person and now I had so many wonderful people in my life. When I decided to move, I had nothing except my suitcase, few friends and my dream, and now I live in this absolutely gorgeous spot. I move around independently, work, travel and enjoy my life as I did prior the accident. When I decided to establish myself in California, I said to my family and friends, "This goal is almost as impossible as a flight to the moon, but I am going to try it anyway." And I landed. I lived my dream, which had seemed so out of reach. My life is a miracle!

I did not see how much good I had only because I focused on what was wrong in my life. I made the decision not to dwell on the things I was unhappy about. I had too many good things happening in my life to waste my time and my emotions on negative things. I decided to focus on how much beauty there was. I finally recognized all I have achieved and what I was yet to accomplish. You see, it was a conscious decision to manage my own mind of what I paid attention to, what I focused on and what I was mostly thinking about.

If there were situations that I was not happy about, instead of sitting there complaining or being drowned in dissatisfaction, I was looking for ways to improve my circumstances, so I didn't have to feel that way anymore. And I did not even bother myself thinking about some things that irritated me.

That was a new beginning for me. In my mind I kept the vision of the life I wanted to create, consistently worked on my goals, and by achieving one goal after another, I improved my life conditions and my circumstances. Today I live my vision. Of course, life had and still has its low moments and unexpected surprises, but I always remember what that quiet voice gently told me. And today I want to pass that message to you:

Rise above it, don't look what's in front of you. Rise above it and look ahead. See the vision of the life you want to create and move towards it; I did it, and you can too.

Love you, take care, and till the next time,
Inga

17

My Second Chance

Dear Valdas,

I know your situation seems broken to the point of devastation. You tell me that you can't see any light in this dark dessert. Devastated, you are looking at the ruins of your life and are asking yourself, "And now what?"

After the storm the sun comes out. Hold on to the hope. How? By faith.

As you now know, I looked at the ruins of my nearly established new life. There was no way to bring back life to that which seemed destroyed. I did not see any way. But the Lord makes a way when there is none.

Just hold on. Break through this time and you will see your sunrise. May my further journey brings you hope. Do not let your hope desert you.

Love you.
Inga

****

Greeting my family was the best thing that had happened to me in the past several months. It was comforting to hug them and be wrapped around with their love. It was not as exciting to return home as it was from my first trip, but it was good to be with my family and in an environment that was so familiar and comforting and welcoming.

I did not cry. It hurt too much to even cry. After months of ongoing stress, sleepless nights and storms of emotions, I felt exhausted both emotionally and physically. I just wanted to go back home, have my

Mom's prepared meal and go to bed. I wanted to hide from everyone and everything. I needed to be alone.

Neither my parents nor did my brother rush to ask me about everything that happened. (And for that I will be eternally grateful. I wasn't in the space emotionally to share with them the details about what happened). I knew each of them saw that I was not my normal self. They knew I was hurt and I saw how they made an effort to not bring up even more pain by digging into my soul with their questions and making me relive the past several months. Mom only said that I'd lost quite a lot of weight and looked very tired.

My mom's prepared meal was the best meal I had for the past six months. Even meals at the fanciest restaurants were nothing like her home-cooked meals. It was good to see my dearest people and be at home. It felt as though even the walls comforted me. Finally, after so many sleepless nights and stress I was able to relax. We had a late lunch all together and talked about many things, except about my situation in the United States.

I talked to my family later, after they saw I had rested a bit and was coming back to my senses. I don't think I had ever seen my brother so upset with someone as he was then. He was determined to fly to California and find Michael. It took quite an effort for me and our parents to talk him out of it. What Michael and I did was not right in the first place, and at this point the best thing to do was to let everything go. No conversations were going to fix anything.

The parents were not upset with me nor did they judge me. They could see why I could have fallen in love with Michael. They said watching how he went above and beyond fulfilling my dream to walk and even beyond that, raised the question in their minds, "How come he does all of that for her?" Mom said that others could see that our comfort level with each other was way beyond patient/client status, but they were reluctant to question the relationship. They were afraid to learn that their insights were not misleading them. Sometimes finding out the truth is so scary that we are willing to close our eyes, not face it. My mother said, validating her fears, "I was afraid there was much more than we had been told."

Learning how everything little by little was coming together, and how everything had been utterly destroyed, raised my family's bewilderment as to how it was possible for Michael to have cut everything off, after all he had done and the experiences that we all together shared. While my parents did not support our secret relationship, they also could not comprehend how it was possible to shower one with love and devotion and then end it like it had been. Mom said the only thing she was grateful for was Kathryn. She was so thankful to her that she was there for me and helped me to endure the drama. Seeing me so heartbroken left both parents deeply grief-stricken. And, my father and mom had many questions for Michael.

Without voicing it, we all felt the emptiness; hope and even the smallest anticipation of anything good had deserted us altogether. None of us knew what to do. Once again, hopelessness ironically stared at us. This time no longer could I enthusiastically say, "There must be a way."

I did not call many of my friends, as normally I would have done. I did not want to talk to anybody. I knew talking with anyone would raise the question, "How was your trip?" I didn't know how I was going to explain my return home; after all, it all seemed to have been working out for me there in the United States.

While I was on my way to Europe, my father quickly connected with my surgeon and arranged an appointment to see what the problem was with my left leg. The pain in the bottom of my left leg was unendurable while wearing prostheses, and I had to find out if there was a physical problem with my leg. After I rested from my trip, the following Monday we went to the hospital and had x-rays taken to see what was happening with my bone. In a few days, my surgeon called to say that I had a bone spur on my left leg. Nobody could explain how my bone developed a spur, but I knew I had to take care of it if I ever wanted to walk again. I had to go to the hospital for the surgery to remove the spur. It was scheduled a week after I arrived home.

I did not have any emotions about that. After six surgeries or so, I was used to them. It was nothing compared to the emotional pain I was feeling. I felt depression like a shadow, a predator constantly watching how to devour me. Thoughts of losing my new, long awaited, life when I was just a step away from establishing it, caused me anguish and hopelessness I could not bear. Having been in that lifeless pit before, I knew that all I needed to do was keep remembering and dwelling on what had happened and I would take a dive into that same quicksand again. Only now I would be even more depressed than I was ever before. So, I knew I had to get my mind busy with something else just so I would not think about my recent experience.

To my surprise, the week until I had to go to the hospital, ended up to be scheduled so fully with meetings with people, that I did not even have time to think about myself. I didn't even have to make an effort to get away from my personal matters, because every day my friends called me saying they wanted to see me, and every day – throughout the entire day – I would spend my time with them. I was deeply sad and I did not really want to talk to anyone, but I was happy to see my friends, whom I had not seen for a long time. I met them regardless of whether I felt like it or not. I kept my experiences inside and did not show anyone how I truly felt. I did not want any questions asked, and did not want to explain myself or anything related to my personal relationship with Michael. Interestingly, nobody was bothering me with too many questions about why I had to return.

When our conversation would come to a point of why I came back, I told them that there was no way for me to obtain legal residency rights (which was the truth, only without giving in-depth details), and our conversation somehow would move on from that point. Nobody asked questions that would make me think of Michael and what happened.

Another interesting thing I noticed: this time the intensity and frequency of meeting friends was much increased, compared to my first return. After my first return from California, I did see a lot of friends, but this time the dynamics were radically different – I would receive phone calls every single day from a variety of friends. Nearly all of them wanted to meet. Every day for the entire week I had people coming to visit, and I ended up busy from morning till night. This lasted until the day I had to go to the hospital for surgery to remove the bone spur. It made me wonder. It seemed as if some invisible hand was playing a chess game, making arrangements in such a way that I was constantly with someone with never any time to be alone with my own thoughts.

After a week I had to go to the hospital for a surgery. At the hospital, neither Michael nor what had happened were on my mind. The only time I thought about my situation was when I re-evaluated my earlier choices and decisions. Now I could look at it all more objectively. I saw what a huge impact our choices can make in our lives, and how careful we must be in making them.

Every day I talked with the Lord in prayer. I understood my lesson. It was a lesson for the rest of my life. I asked Him to arrange a way to return me to America if that was His will. I had no doubt it was the Lord who sent me there the first time and had created the opportunity for me. I knew I destroyed it by my disobedience. But I hoped maybe I could get one more chance. Bruce's offer to arrange a marriage of convenience was still open, which I could use, but then my new life would be built on a lie again and I did not want to do that. I did not want to consider it as an opportunity. Before I left California, I did tell Bruce that I might come back to see if I could find another way to obtain legal residency status in the country. But at this point, all doors were shut and I had no idea how to break through that barrier.

However, in the midst of hopelessness something inside did not allow me to give up on God's promise to bless me establishing my life in California. I trusted my Heavenly Father and was holding on to my hope. He is God who has control over everything, and I knew He could turn my situation around. The Lord already showed me how He can turn the impossible into possible, and I knew He could do it again. I have learned my lesson and, I pleaded with the Lord to give me another chance if it was still His will that I would reside in California.

The surgery went well and my surgeon said it was good that I agreed to the surgery because it was a serious problem. My recovery began smoothly and I would have come home in several days. But little did I know what was ahead. Overnight my smooth healing turned into an extremely painful and complicated healing process. Due to a medical nurse's mistake, internal bleeding began in the leg that was operated upon. My leg was swollen to twice its normal size, and changing into black-purplish color. The pain was excruciating.

I was given morphine every day to release me from the pain, but even morphine didn't help. I could barely keep myself from screaming. The only one thing I had was prayer. I asked Jesus to help me cope because it was beyond what I could endure. And it did not end there. I noticed I felt unusual weakness all the time and that I had strong migraines. But I thought it was because of surgery and related issues, so I didn't inform anyone about it. Then one morning a nurse stormed into my room with a terrified look on her face and said there was a serious problem: the hemoglobin in my blood had become so low that I could die at any moment. In a moment, a group of doctors rushed into my room, in a hurry to set up the process to perform a blood transfusion. Later I was told that normally people do not survive from this measure of low hemoglobin; if they had not checked my blood that morning and found what they did, I would have been dead in a few days or less. I could not believe what was happening in my life. Again, I was on the verge of life and death? I thanked my Lord that

He did not allow them to miss the problem and I profusely thanked Him for saving my life once again.

The healing process after the surgery, the medical error and my low hemoglobin count was long and complicated. I was in constant, excruciating pain, and even strong pain killers did not help. It was a never ending torture.

While I was going through that tormenting process, I was longing for California's beauty and for my friends. More and more I felt how much I loved that land and the people I met there. It was agonizing to know how all the puzzle pieces that came into my life so beautifully had been scattered. I knew there was a dreary existence ahead of me among the walls of my home, and I could not stand even thought of it. I believed God had a purpose for me, and every day I asked the Lord to give me another chance.

After two weeks I was finally home. I was exhausted both physically and mentally. I did not have any feelings about anything. At times, it seemed that something was blocked inside of me, and I felt no emotion about anything. There was no desire to fight for myself any more. I felt totally depleted of my strength.

I knew however, if I asked my Lord to give me strength, He would. Remembering those very first few months after my crash when I would ask Jesus to give me strength to live another day, and I received it each time, I knew what to do. Memories of how the Lord would pick me up after each time I fell, encouraged me to seek for strength in Him, who was faithful no matter what mistakes I have done. I began praying, asking a Living God to give me the endurance to get through. Also, I prayed for God to fix the situation I got myself into.

I emailed my California friends, sharing the reason why I couldn't walk and what my surgical process entailed. Right away I received a response from my close friend Nicole, who said she, too, had missed me, and she shared some of her news. Nicole worked at Michael's office and we hit it off on my very first visit. I will never forget how she tried to talk to me and I kept asking her to repeat herself or say things in a simpler way because I could not understand her. Often we filled Michael's office with our loud laughter. She and her husband were very sorry for the drama I endured, and they were sympathetic for the both of us. Nicole and I became very close and she and her husband wished I could have stayed in California. And now, we continued our friendship via email. At the end of her email, she said, "By the way, my husband and I told our friend Frank about you, and he is very interested in getting to know you. So I gave him your email and you can expect his letter in a few days. I hope that's okay with you."

"Oh, my, Nicole, you gave him my email," I thought, laughing in my mind. I knew she would laugh with me if she had been by my side. "So, it's already done and it doesn't matter if I'm okay with it or not!"

In a few days I received an email from Frank. It was a long and beautiful letter. He shared with me that he also had experienced the accident that resulted him losing his right arm and a leg as well, but he dealt with the loss and recovered his life successfully despite all of that. He said he was very impressed from what Nicole had told him about me and said he would like to get to know me. I had to admit, Frank's letter was quite impressive. He seemed intelligent and strong. Most of all, I liked his attitude – he did not allow his loss to break him down.

In a few days we exchanged photos. In addition to his beautiful letters that revealed his politeness, maturity and attitude of not giving up, he was an attractive, pleasant looking man. After he saw my picture, Frank immediately wrote back saying he really liked me and would love to meet me in person. I told him that I was planning to go back to California, perhaps some time in February, but first I had to wait until my leg healed. I said for now we could stay in touch via email. I was really not in a rush to meet any other men who liked me. I was so heartbroken and still deeply in love, so much so that I could not even think of developing any kind of romantic relationship with another man. At this point, I wanted to be left alone. I knew, however, I had to shut down the past and move on.

Michael was gone and he would not be back. The Lord shut that door and I had to forget everything related to him. I had to leave behind the past two years and be open to new people, to new and different opportunities. I kept wondering whether this was the Lord giving me a new blessing in my new acquaintance, Frank, who had absolutely nothing to do with my previous, personal life drama. He seemed to be a very pleasant man, and it would be unfair to him if I refused his friendship because of my issues. So I decided to continue to stay in touch with him.

Meanwhile, my days continued being filled with ongoing visits, just like before the surgery. The mystery continued of someone playing a chess game of not allowing me to be alone with my own thoughts. I would receive phone calls every single day from a variety of people, beginning with my faithful friends to acquaintances who barely knew me. And they wanted to come see me. So, I continued meeting with people every single day. My mom rejoiced saying our home had become alive again, filled with nice people and loud laughter.

I noticed one especially interesting thing: mostly I was visited by people, who said that they needed my help. Honestly, I didn't feel like giving hope to anyone or inspiring anyone because I was on the edge of giving in myself. After my heartbreak and recent agonizing stay in the hospital, I had little encouragement for others. I had neither the strength nor the will to be a helper. I just wanted to be left alone.

For some reason the people visiting me were sharing their struggles and were eager to see me to get inspired and encouraged. Some of them came to me as though I were their guru, their last hope to inspire them, to say that everything was going to be alright, to coach them on how to deal with their situation, how to move on. I was especially surprised by someone who opened up, sharing that she had attempted suicide due to her disappointment in her boyfriend. Praise be to God that her attempt did not work, but now she did not know how to continue living. She couldn't see her life without him. I thought, "If she only knew how well I know what it feels like. And the Lord brought her to me, so that I would help her. Lord? You do have a sense of humor, don't you?"

I was so deeply touched by hers and other people's stories that my heart started beating with a sincere desire to help them. So, I pushed aside my own deep sadness, tiredness and pain, and focused on them – how to help them. I was trying to feel their pain and their struggle to understand them. And then I would point out their strong character traits and brainstorm with them, throwing out ideas that they could do to improve their situations. In order to give them hope and inspiration, I would share with them my own experiences about how desperate circumstances turned into opportunities. I would strongly encourage them to not give up, but keep moving forward, no matter what was going on and no matter how bad their circumstances seemed at the time.

To my big surprise, after each visit like that I began noticing a change within me – by pushing away my own pain and focusing on how I could help others, I felt stronger myself. It felt as though I was breathing in life each time I helped another person. I began feeling how at the core of my being I was slowly recovering. After I said goodbye to the visitor, who felt so much better than he or she arrived to see me, I felt fulfilled inside. What's even more interesting, I had sparkles of hope for my own situation. I myself was inspired to resist sadness and discouragement, encouraged to continue fighting for my life. Strength and desire began to pulsate once again. I knew I could not give up.

"I will not allow him or any crash to stop me," I began saying to myself, as though it were my mantra. My determination was rising from the ashes of destruction. Bruce's words went through my mind, "You can't give up, Inga. You are one of them. You are unstoppable." Now I could identify with Bruce's words. I knew that I would fight for my life for as long as I was alive.

I was going to break through my pain and deep disappointment. And then, get up and move on creating the vision that I had, fulfilling God's purpose for my life. By faith I put my trust for the future and confidence in my Lord, who was my rock and who can do the impossible. Every day I was praying for new hope, for another chance and strength to move on.

I began feeling my strength was being renewed. I was ready to rise from those ruins and fly out into a new horizon.

> *"But those who hope in the Lord will renew their strength. They will soar on wings like eagles; they will run and not grow weary, they will walk and not be faint." (Isaiah 40:31 NIV)*

One day I finally understood what was happening behind the scenes of my daily routine and all these ongoing visits with my friends: before the hospital, the Lord was sending me people daily throughout the day, so I didn't have to stay alone or even have time to think about my second trip to California. God was protecting me to from getting into another bout of deep depression and despair.

And then the Lord was sending me people who needed help; and by focusing on how I could help others, I was getting inspired and stronger myself. I would receive so much joy when I saw the sparkles of hope in their eyes, or when I heard that now they were not going to give up, that they felt inspired and stronger, that they now knew how to cope with their challenges. The fact that I was able to help someone made my day! I began seeing hope from my own devastation and I felt eager once again to continue my journey.

This period taught me a big lesson: when you feel depressed - go help someone who needs your help. Shift your focus *away from **you***, and assist those who need help. Your own misery will end when you help those in need.

I was clearly noticing the shift that was happening within me: I was slowly recovering from my emotional pain and, in addition to that, I started becoming more intrigued by my new acquaintance, Frank.

Soon Frank began stating on an ongoing basis how strongly he wanted to meet me. I would respond that I was still going through a healing process and couldn't travel quite yet. The more we exchanged letters, the more often I read in his email about his strong desire to meet me as soon as possible. One night, after my friends left, I saw his email again saying that he couldn't wait to meet me, and with a smile I responded, "I can't come right now. But if you are so anxious to meet me, then why don't you come yourself! Come to Lithuania, and then maybe we will go back to California together."

After sending that email I went to sleep, since it was after midnight. The next day I found Frank's message saying that he was planning to take me out to dinner in various restaurants and show me some beautiful places, but traveling to Europe sounded fun to him and he's willing to come to Lithuania and escort me back to California.

His response caught me by surprise. I didn't even know how to react to his message. I didn't really expect him to come all the way across the globe for few days; nobody would do that, and that's why I said it in jest as a joke. But since I had already invited him and he was willing to come, I could not say that I was not really expecting him to do just that. But I liked that he seemed to be as spontaneous and as amenable to travel as I was.

The way circumstances were taking a new direction surprised me greatly - my new American acquaintance was ready to travel to my homeland and escort me back to the land of sunshine. I noticed that the shift in my circumstances was again beyond my control, as though the mysterious chess game continued.

"Lord? Are you bringing me back to California? Is this my second chance?" The mystery of how circumstances were changing raised many questions. But I decided not to rush to conclusions, and to continue praying, and to remain open to new opportunities. I went to another room and told my parents about it. They were shocked and surprised and they laughed at the same time, saying that one day they might get a heart attack from all of my surprises. I tried to comfort them saying that Frank and I have mutual friends who would not have connected me if he were a bad person.

My parents were quite surprised that the man, who didn't know me and had never met me, would travel such a distance, but they were willing to accept a mysterious guest, and said they would feel easier if I had someone with me traveling back to California. Especially after complications from the surgery, they would be comforted knowing that I had assistance while traveling. After my breakup with Michael, they thought it would be good for me to have a friend by my side. I emailed Frank confirming my invitation. Since then, my foggy intentions to return were taking shape. The thought of returning to California filled me with joy. I felt I could take a deep breath; I knew my journey continued.

After a few months of virtual communication, Frank and I met at the Vilnius Airport. It was quite strange meeting the person I had been in contact with daily via the Internet. Frank seemed to be a very nice person and my family liked him as did I. He seemed to be a trustworthy and strong man. We toured Lithuania for three days and then we left for America, stopping in Amsterdam, Netherlands for a few days. We enjoyed each other's company and we had a wonderful time. Staying in Amsterdam was a lot of fun. It was cold and rainy, but we had a great time touring the gorgeous city, looking at the breathtaking architecture, cruising in the canals and exploring the downtown. And most of all, we got along very well.

Behind all that was happening, I knew it wasn't coincidence. I saw how polite, attentive and caring Frank was; a true gentleman in every sense of the word. Various unexpected situations during the trip showed me that I could rely on Frank and feel secure with him. I watched how Frank was making sure all our travel details were arranged, how my every need was met, and to make certain I was warm and comfortable. I was treated like a princess. He conducted himself in a very respectful manner, keeping appropriate boundaries, and that impressed me even more. When we arrived in California, on our way from the airport, Frank took me to the Spinnaker, a restaurant on the water in the Bay Area, with a spectacular view of San Francisco and the Golden Gate Bridge, ending our return journey on a very memorable note.

From the first day we arrived, Frank and I started dating. He treated me in a very respectful manner, and took me sightseeing to the most gorgeous I've ever seen. His care and attention were healing me. I was honest with Frank and told him my story. He despised the man and said he would be there for me to help me forget everything. He knew my aspirations and he was well aware of my situation, needing that one puzzle piece to replace Michael's created company for my legal establishment in the country. Knowing how broken-hearted I was, Frank did everything he could to help me forget my experience with Michael and make my life brighter. I started feeling like the pieces of a broken mirror were starting to be put back together.

I returned to reside at the same house with my roommate Bruce. While I was dating Frank, I went back to Bruce's work at the Disability Services & Legal Center, local ILC to continue volunteering, and was looking again for opportunities on how I could become a legal resident of the United States. I enjoyed volunteering and it was a great opportunity for me to learn and develop new skills. But to be honest, it was not what I was really eager to do. The shadow of memories of the opportunity once offered, working with Michael on an organization he was establishing, were interrupting my appreciation for the newly opened doors. So, recognizing how agonizing those memories made my current life and how destructive they were, I decided to put the effort to shut down anything about Michael and anything related to him. I had to move on.

I knew now it was up to me what story was going to be written in my new chapter of my new life. I was so tired from the ongoing sorrow and grief. I decided I would leave all that was burned up and, rise above it all. To a new opportunity. To a new life. And I would put all my efforts into everything I would have to do to achieve my long-awaited dream – creating an independent, meaningful and fulfilling life.

Nancy and Bruce were very good to me and I enjoyed helping them out. Gradually I became Nancy's assistant, helping her with managing documents. Since I worked at the Personnel Department at the Airport and later in charge, organizing the airport's archives, I was very familiar with paperwork and filing. What's more, I liked doing it, and I enjoyed helping Nancy. It was not easy, though. I was not familiar with the legal documents, filing system or any rules of how office duties were performed in the United States. Further, I still did not fully understand American English, and I had to ask people to speak to me in a more formal language for me to understand them. But because I wanted to learn and work efficiently, I challenged myself.

It became like a game, figuring out new things and finding ways to accomplish difficult tasks. I decided to do my best in everything I was asked to do. I used the skills I had, and when I didn't understand or didn't know how to do something, I would find out, learn it and would complete the task the way it needed to be done. I held to my standards which never failed me:

- Doing my best, whatever I had to do.
- Doing 101%, which is do more than I was asked to do.

This simple standard created a memorable day for me, which makes me smile up to this day. It was my very first bigger task, which I could accomplish independently, was to organize one staff member's desk. The desk was so messy and fully covered with papers, file folders, books, notebooks, and all kinds of minutia there was no way even to see what color the desk was. After being asked to do that task, I humbled myself and began organizing the desk.

I could not understand what many of the documents were about and how they needed to be organized. I had never seen that kind of messy, disorganized desk! There was a variety of important documents intermixed with food crumbs and sweets and old candy wrappers spread all over the desk. Being far from thrilled to perform that task, I kept thinking, "I am cleaning *my own* desk," implying that one day this was going to become my desk.

At the end of the day, as I was finishing my task, I started seeing other staff members coming into the office to see the "miracle", as they stated, each complimenting me on how nice that desk looked. Apparently, while that staff member was working there, the desk had never been in order. It made me smile that rumors reached nearly all the staff, and many of them came to look at it. And, in less than six months, it indeed became my desk.

When I finally received permission to work and live in the United States, I was hired as a Program Assistant to assist Nancy with her duties. Soon after I joined the organization, I was asked to co-lead peer-support groups, and after a year or so I was promoted to the Peer Support and Volunteer Coordinator position. It was a very exciting step. I enjoyed running those groups because I had a big desire to help and support others to go through their challenging times. Once again, I told myself that I would learn my new job duties and would do everything I could to do my job well. I put my heart into leading peer support groups and my intention for every group was to have attendees leave the group having more hope, more belief and more inspiration to improve their circumstances.

As a Volunteer Coordinator, my first challenge was to find and coordinate volunteers for the Disability Community Picnic. I think I had about fifteen volunteers that day and they did an outstanding job. The event went smoothly because we had so much help from them, and later some staff members told me that they had never seen that many Volunteers helping the agency. It was a great compliment to me and once again, I saw that my rule to do my best at all times and "go the extra mile" was resulting with success in whatever I did.

After eight months, they wanted me to take over the Public Relations position, which involved organizing their annual fundraiser, events planning and Public Relations duties. I said I had no event planning experience, and that I didn't really know how to do this type of job.

The Executive Director said, "Don't worry. You are a quick learner. You did an outstanding job finding and coordinating volunteers, and we see that you have the required skills for this position. Senior staff and our Board of Directors want you to take this position."

That was one of the happiest days! I quickly learned how to perform my new duties, where my first event resulted in being the first event in the agency's history that had no financial loss. Having this "climbing the ladder" experience, I learned something very important. It taught me the power of striving for excellence every time. By doing your best and doing more than requested, you will improve yourself, learn new skills and definitely have better results. But, as you see, the beginning was very different from what is now. I had to go through many lessons and continuously strive to grow and improve.

And now, going back in time to when I began volunteering at the organization, I was committed to it as though it was my work. After my volunteering hours, Frank would come pick me up and we would go to the coast to take a ride along the Pacific Ocean or somewhere in the wine country to see the many breathtaking views of the vineyards, and then he would take me to a dinner in a restaurant I'd never been to before. Since his father was in the restaurant business, Frank recognized and appreciated quality meals, and he would not stop spoiling me every day by taking me out to dinner.

On Valentine's Day, while I was at home, Frank came to me, holding a large bouquet of flowers and a present. After putting my flowers in a vase, I opened the present – it was a digital camera. When I opened my present, Frank said, "This is for you. I saw how much you liked driving along the coast and taking pictures with my camera, so I wanted to get this one for you. This one will work better for you to handle it with your right arm. I know a cute little town up north called Mendocino, and I want to invite you to go there for Valentine's lunch with me. It is a bit of a drive up the coast, and you can take a lot of beautiful pictures while we're driving."

This was one of the sweetest moments. It was beyond what I'd expected. I smiled and thanked him for being so attentive and thoughtful. And those gorgeous flowers! Frank was so sweet; in fact, he was bringing me flowers almost every day. He was pampering me like no one else did. I quickly got ready and we jumped into the car and left. The road on the coast up north was absolutely stunning; these were the kinds of sceneries I had previously seen only on television. While driving on the winding road on the edge of the cliff, on the right side I saw green hills and flowers, and on the left side the ocean and the magnificent rocks. We drove many hours and the most beautiful viewpoints would open up, one after another. It was a beautiful, sunny day, so it made our day even more beautiful, and I took lots and lots of pictures with my new camera.

On the way to Mendocino, we talked a lot about our various experiences, and I shared with him how much I loved the mountains. Yosemite National Park was unforgettable, and I shared with him that I did not understand people, who said they wished they could see these mountains, but would not go there only because for them a five-hour drive seemed to be an insurmountable number of hours to drive. I shared my bewilderment, "How could a five-hour drive be an obstacle to see such incredible beauty?"

Frank attentively listened. After pausing he looked at me and said, "Inga, I want to show you the mountains. Would you like to go to the mountains with me?"

"What? Mountains?"

"Yes. I know a beautiful park in Seattle where you can see mountains like you've never seen before. Would you like to go?"

"Now? Just like that?"

"Now," he smiled. "Just like that. Let's stop in Mendocino to have lunch, and then we can keep going north to the mountains."

"Why not? Let's do it!"

My spontaneous and adventurous nature agreed to the offer immediately. By now I knew Frank enough to trust him, so I was not concerned about my safety. After our Valentine's lunch on the coast in Mendocino, instead of turning south to return home, we turned north and began our journey to the mountains. When I agreed to go to the mountains with him, I did not really know where it was. I did not know that I agreed to go on a trip encompassing all of Northern California, and into Oregon and Washington states. Instead of a several-hour drive for Valentine's lunch, it ended up being a week-long trip. I was astonished by the changing landscapes and cities, large and small, that we drove through. Interestingly, Frank noticed that wherever we drove, we always had sunny, beautiful weather even though it was February, which normally has rainy weather.

We returned home to California, exhausted after hours and hours of driving, but we felt excited after such a beautiful, unforgettable, spontaneous trip. This trip showed me even more about Frank. Spending so many hours in the car and experiencing various challenges during the trip, made us closer and showed me that we together were working like a team.

After I came back home, I continued volunteering, and after a week or so, Frank offered to go on another trip. Now he suggested going along the coast south to Monterey Bay Aquarium, and then go to Yosemite National Park to see the mountains that I told him about, then move on through Gold Country to Reno, Nevada, and then come home through the city of Sacramento, the capital of California.

He knew I would agree, so we got on the road again. I am a traveler by nature, so this was much fun for me and a great opportunity to see a lot more. Frank was showing me the most beautiful scenery that I had ever seen. I could never have imagined visiting places like these and seeing such incredible beauty.

As we drove along the coast, the bright blue waters of the Pacific Ocean and rock formations unfolded as only God could have created. I kept talking to Him in my mind, "How is this possible? What is this? Just few months ago, I was in an absolutely hopeless situation with no solution, begging You to give me one more chance, to bring me back to California. And now I am back indeed, in this beautiful land of sunshine with this wonderful man, having these amazing experiences and seeing all the majesty You have created. You again did the impossible, Lord! You turned my life around from one of total despair into one of light and joy. Lord, only You could have done this. Thank you for everything, Father. Thank you!"

After visiting Monterey Bay Aquarium, we moved on to Yosemite. Here I was back again, looking at the majesty of those rock formations. Looking at them I realized how small and fragile we are as human beings. These mountains reflected the One who created us. I felt in awe before my Lord, the Creator of all. Their power and majesty just made me hold my breath. Looking at the amazing beauty surrounding me, I thought to myself, "If God created all this in such a beautiful and precise way, what is it for Him to create solutions for my problems? Everything is in His power and my life is in His hands. He will take care of me."

After a short walk in the morning we went for breakfast at the Yosemite Dining Room, one of the nicest and more well-known hotels in the park. As we were getting ready to start our breakfast, I noticed Frank was a little nervous. He looked at me and said, "Inga, I really like who you are. I've fallen in love with you. You are my beautiful, unstoppable butterfly. We've had such a great time together, and I don't want to lose you having to go back to Europe. I want you to stay here with me. Will you marry me? I don't have a ring yet, but I promise I will give all of myself to you and will help you every step of your way to help you reach all of your goals."

As I looked into his eyes, filled with hope and expectation, the last events and my experiences went through my mind in a flash. I believed Frank was the answer to my prayers. I believed God was reaching His hand to me through him. I liked Frank and loved spending time with him. I felt safe and I trusted him. I believed he replaced that one last puzzle piece which I had lost, and which I had asked the Lord to bring.

"Yes, Frank, I will."

Since that day, my life took a beautiful direction in my journey. God gave me another chance and He was unceasingly watching over me. He taught me a lesson as a father teaches his child, but then He healed my wounds, wiped my tears, and gave me another chance. After learning my lesson, I knew I wanted to live right. No more careless decisions. No more doing wrong while justifying myself. No more lies. No more pretending. I opened a new page with the intention of making the effort to live righteously before the Lord. I knew I would make mistakes, and sure, I made them, just as every human does. But at that time, something changed in my heart. I knew the Lord was watching me. I knew I couldn't take the commandments of the Lord carelessly.

Frank entering my life was one of the best things that ever happened to me. He gave himself to me, and made every effort to help me get back on my feet in life, just as he said he would when he proposed. Today we are no longer together, though. Unfortunately, that which began beautifully came to an end. I don't have the answers to many things, why they happen the way they do. There are many "why" and "what if" questions. The answers are known only to God. I may get my answers to some of these questions in the future. And maybe I won't. But nevertheless, I am sincerely grateful for everything. Beautiful experiences remain as unforgettable memories. And those hardships and moments which at the time I wished never happened – made me only stronger. What didn't break me made me only stronger. What I have learned is we must not dwell on the past, but focus on the present and look ahead, where there is a new destination, a new vision. And most importantly, we must keep going forward and not allow anything to stop us.

While going through my journey through green pastures, valleys and deserts, before me I always held my vision of what kind of life I wanted to have and, I moved strongly and consistently toward my destination. In a few years, after overcoming each hurdle, I reached another impossible goal - I am living my vision, my dream.

I am independent despite my physical limitations and I am happy. I don't just exist – I live a meaningful and fulfilling life. I reside in an absolutely gorgeous place of the planet, my beautiful land of sunshine. I am surrounded by people whom I love and who love me. Even though I had to leave all my friends behind when I moved across the globe, I met many wonderful people, who became my new true friends. They are my family. While I, my parents and my brother always long for us to be together as a family, we are close regardless of the distance. Even though being so far away from each other is a high price to pay, my family always reassures me that they are very happy I live in California, a place where I could revive my life.

Today I am fully independent and lead a dynamic lifestyle, just as I desired. In fact, my life is much more fulfilling than I ever had before and ever dreamed of. Ironically, I even travel more than I ever did prior to the accident. And, I live not only for my own pleasure, fulfilling self-ambitious goals, but today I can contribute by making a difference in other people's lives.

It took a lot of hard work to attain the life I have today. It took resilience and relentlessness. It required unshakable faith and endurance. It did take a lot of effort. But the Lord my God led me through every hardship, protected me from evil and blessed me abundantly, just as He promised me through His word, when He directed me to return to California.

None of us could even imagine that my life would turn into such a miracle. The year of 2000 was devastating for all of us in the family, but this event turned my life around not for the worse, but the better. I can sincerely say that today, even though I do not have my legs nor can I use my left arm – I am happier than I ever was before the accident. In fact, I can't even compare how much better I feel now.

In February of 2012, I thanked my God with tears of joy for the car accident and for everything that I had to go through and experience. In fact, on February 12, on the day of my accident's anniversary, I had a party and invited my dearest friends to celebrate with me. Now I celebrate that day each year; in fact, I call it my second birthday.

I can say sincerely that I have arrived. In fact, my reality exceeds my dream that I had. I love my life's journey.

Living my Dream. Goat Rock Beach, California.

Beginning of a new life. Yosemite National Park.

I could not even imagine that
I would visit the famous Las Vegas, NV.

On our way to Hollywood along the Pacific. Hwy 1, California.

With my friend Marina, Goat Rock Beach, California.

In addition to intense work planning the fundraiser, I get to enjoy my time with a friend, who came to help. With my friend Irina at the annual DSLC fundraiser "Music in the Vines".

With my friend Gillian Ortega, Mary Kay NSD. After achieving a Red Jacket Status in Mary Kay company, I was asked to speak to inspire other Mary Kay Beauty Consultants.

I will always treasure the gift of meeting my former Mary Kay Director, Trish Reuser. Lessons and wisdom she taught me will always remain the unfading light in my life. At Mary Kay Seminar, Dallas, Texas.

On my dream vacation on a Caribbean Cruise with a beautiful group of Mary Kay ladies. With my friend and current Mary Kay Director, Joni Pritchard. Joni is one of the reasons why I am so grateful to be part of this wonderful company – I got to meet her and many other women high-achievers. It was vacation of a lifetime!

With Gillian Ortega, at a meeting for Mary Kay Beauty Consultants. She's a woman of excellence, my mentor and my friend. That night, Gillian gifted me her bracelet, looked at me and said "Inga, these sparkling diamonds became so precious after they have gone through the intense pressure and high temperature. Remember, when you go through a hard time, God is bringing you through those hardships to change you, to make you as a precious diamond. There is His purpose in the hardships."

Renata and I never thought our friendship would bring us all the way to Key West, while enjoying the Caribbean Cruise.

That's my dream vacation – enjoying the beach, turquoise sea and exotic palm trees with my best friend. Cozumel, Mexico.

With my close friends Renata, Marina and Viktoras at the Golden Gate Bridge, San Francisco, California.

Birthdays a fun again. With my closest friends in California, celebrating my birthday.

Sharing my testimony how trusting in the Lord empowered me to transform my life after the crash. Golden Gate Park, San Francisco, California.

After the interview with Alex Shevchenko for the TV Program "UGOL", Sacramento, California.

Speaking at the Light of the Gospel
Church, Sacramento, California.

After my speech at the ADA 25th Anniversary
in Santa Rosa, California. Left to the right:
Matthew Brigham, Attorney at Law, Adam Brown,
Attorney at Law and Executive Director at DSLC, and
Shirley Johnson, President of the Board of Directors at DSLC.

Interview with Andrey Shapoval for the
Christian Program “Impact”.

Receiving a Champion Award, disABILITY services at the 50th Anniversary of California Human Development. In the picture from the left: Mary Biggs, Director of disABILITY Services Division at CHD and Senator Mike McGuire, Senate District 2.

After awards ceremony, holding my Champion Award, disABILITY services at the 50th Anniversary of California Human Development.
In the picture: Mary Biggs, Director of disABILITY Services Division at CHD, who nominated me to receive this award. Adam Brown, Attorney at Law and Executive Director at Disability Services & Legal Center (DSLC).

My friend Juriy Buchinskiy and I are presenting successful results of raising funds to help the person in Ukraine to obtain Bionic arm prostheses. Russian Gospel Temple, San Francisco, CA.

No friendship is a coincidence. This one, has a big purpose ahead. In the picture: Anzhelika Polyak.

Extraordinary vacation in Jamaica with Anzhelika, at Luxury Principe Bahia Resort.

Experience of a lifetime. Meeting Dolphin Susie in Jamaica.

Through my life experience I have learned – it's not what happens to us that has the power to determine our destiny, but how we perceive what happens, and then what we do about it.

18

Handling Problems

Part 1 ~ Don't Fear Your Problems. Put Your Trust in The Lord Instead

Dear Valdas,

I want to encourage you not to have fear in your heart when you face problems and difficult situations, which surely you are going to encounter as you continue your life's journey. They are just the same part of life as everything else you consider good in life. You are not going to avoid them as much as you would like.

Difficulties can play a role in our lives, and I believe we have a big influence on which role they will play. They may lead to anxiety, fear and even despair, but they can also make us stronger, strengthen our faith, and teach us to not give up. They can either break us or make us stronger, and it depends on us what kind of results we are going to have. How you are going to cope with difficulties depends on your faith, your mindset/attitude and your actions. I have learned to see a lot of good in problems. In fact, difficulties worked to my benefit. The car accident and following obstacles, challenges and pain tested me, strengthened me and molded me into the person I am today.

After the accident I was constantly surrounded by pain, difficult situations and desperate circumstances. Sometimes I could hardly endure it. At times it seemed I simply no longer had the strength to fight for myself. There were days when I felt so tired from the pain, obstacles and despair that I didn't want the next morning to come. But now as I look back – I feel grateful for everything. Those difficult times made me stronger, more determined and persistent. They taught me not to give up even when I felt couldn't take it anymore. I am thankful for all the pain that I had to go through because it developed both endurance and compassion within me. I am thankful for the circumstances that seemed totally desperate because they taught me the power of faith and how to hold on to that faith at all times, never give up and keep moving forward, no matter what.

I am thankful for the challenges because they taught me how to be unstoppable, how to push myself and go beyond what I thought I could do. The challenges I faced and desperate situations I encountered taught me something that I would not have learned by reading a book or hearing someone's story.

One of the highest values that I gained through the difficulties is that they taught me to trust and rely on God more than on any human, and thus my faith became stronger than ever before. While I was going through those difficult times facing hopeless circumstances, I saw how powerful and wonderful the Lord God is, for He brought me out of all those situations when seemed there was no way out. Particularly those toughest experiences when I found myself in absolutely hopeless situations and got out of them in incredible ways, showed me the power of faith. God is a spirit and we cannot see Him, but our faith in God and our complete trust in Him can do miracles. Faith can turn impossible into possible.

And here is one of the areas where problems can serve us: They can strengthen our faith, if we choose them to play this role for us. They can show us that the power of God can turn our difficult situation into opportunity. Now I accept each difficult situation as an opportunity to see the power of God, and experience how He arranges everything in such a way that all the details perfectly come into its place in His precise order and timing.

I know you have heard that God is almighty and there is nothing impossible for Him. And I am sure you have had encouragement to give your problems to God because He can take care of it all. But what does it mean to rely on God and give Him your problems? How is it possible to rely on someone whom you have never seen and how can you give away your problems to someone invisible?

By faith. Nobody has ever seen God, but we trust that He exists. Logically it is very hard to explain God and prove that He exists. But faith changes it all. Through faith we can get closer to God, feel His love and experience His miracles. Faith is a bridge that can connect us to God, and shows us He can turn things around and solve our challenges and difficult problems in unexplainable ways. Have you ever heard the saying, "Faith can move the mountains?" Jesus said that we could say to the mountain move and it would move if we had faith as big as a seed of a mustard.

> *"So Jesus said to them, 'Because of your unbelief; for assuredly, I say to you, if you have faith as a mustard seed, you will say to this mountain, Move from here to there, and it will move; and nothing will be impossible for you.'" (Matthew 17:20)*

I remember my pastor stating that we have to fully trust God in all situations that we encounter, give our problems to Him, and continue our life journey led by faith, not by fear. I heard it numerous times. I knew it. But I didn't really comprehend what it really meant. How I could possibly do that? And so when after my prayer, difficult situations would not get immediately solved the way I expected, I would ask, "Why didn't I get the answer that I wanted? The Scriptures say, 'Ask and it shall be given to you,' but it doesn't always work that way." Having no explanation why I didn't get the answer to my prayers, I tried to solve my issues counting on myself or whatever resources I had. The result? I again would worry, experiencing anxiety and fear thinking, "What if things would not turn out for the better?"

When it comes to solving difficult problems, people deal with them by relying on their abilities, knowledge, money, or on other people, hoping for their help and support. Although maybe in prayer they say, "God, I give it all into your hands," but after prayer they go back to their concerns and fears and try to deal with their issues relying on themselves or any resources they have.

And only when everything seems hopeless and unsolvable, people cry out to God asking for help. Then they admit that they have done all they could possibly do and neither they nor others can do anything more to improve their situation. They fully – with their hearts and their minds – hope that maybe God can arrange things in some supernatural way. I know you have heard numerous times people saying, "Well, at this point only God can help." Feeling hopeless, people start expecting for miracles to happen, as though clinging to a small branch on the edge of a cliff asking for immediate divine intervention.

That's how God taught me to fully trust Him and rely on Him – my problems and desperate circumstances taught me to trust and rely on my Lord. Today I often hear people say, "You have such deep and strong faith in God."

The main reason for it is that I have faced many hopeless situations when I was not able to do anything to improve them, and the Lord did. And when in faith – with all my essence I fully put my confidence in the Lord – these hopeless circumstances suddenly had opportunities, problems had their solutions, and I was brought out of the desert wasteland into the comfort of an oasis.

These lessons were some of the most difficult and painful ones. But today I am thankful for them, because they taught me to surrender myself and my challenges to God and expect the answer no matter how difficult situation might be. I've seen things happen in absolutely incredible ways, and I simply cannot explain it in any other way than tell you, "It was God's miracle."

For example, how the prosthetist Michael came into my life and helped me without really knowing why he did it and why he was so committed to do whatever it takes to see me walking again? As you remember, the situation was hopeless; upon my return from our local Orthopedic Center having permanent prostheses made for me, which caused enormous pain and open wounds, none of us could see what else could be done for me to fulfill my aspiration to walk wearing prosthetic legs.

Can you explain to me how in the world is it possible to write a letter to a complete stranger half a world away – some prosthetic specialist overseas – and immediately get a response and who coincidentally in a few weeks would be traveling to our part of the globe and invites me to meet him? Furthermore, he's inspired to help me immediately when he meets me and is committed to help without charging me one penny for over $40,000 prosthetic legs, for his work, his time and other expenses? Later I asked him why he responded to my letter, invited me to meet him in Istanbul and why he wanted to help me. He thought for a moment, looked at me and having no explanation he said, "I don't know. I just did."

You might say that our relationship had something to do with it. While many experiences were happening because of our personal relationship, how we got connected in the first place, and how Michael was inspired to help me, it has nothing to do with our back story. It all happened before we even crossed the boundary of a business and personal relationship. Even after we did, Michael kept saying to me that he would fulfill my wish to walk, regardless of our personal relationship. As I said, while many experiences were related to our personal relationship, connecting with him out of countless other prosthetists worldwide and his decision to help me is astonishing. And to this day I can find no other explanation as simple as, "He was the answer to my prayers."

How can I explain the journalist calling me to suggest writing an article about me, with the intention of announcing whatever need I had, right when I prayed asking my Lord to help me somehow get the funding for traveling to America?

What about Frank showing up in my life and bringing me back to California when I lost my opportunity to establish my life there? My first opportunity was destroyed and I pleaded with the Lord to arrange another way and bring me back to California. In addition, Frank was there with me at all times and put all his effort and time to make sure I was well and successful in everything I was aiming for.

How it happened that I was employed immediately after I received permission to work in the United States, even though when I was traveling to establish my life, I had absolutely no idea where I could be employed and what kind of job I could do having my challenges? Despite the unknown, I decided to trust that God would provide everything and I stepped forward in faith. And, it happened just as the Lord has promised – He provided. The Lord provided during my first attempt – Michael was inspired to establish an organization where my expertise and skills were perfect and I was needed to perform one of the main duties to fulfill the purpose of the company. And, even if my mistake of living in transgression destroyed that opportunity, my Lord did not abandon me. Once I understood my lesson, He picked me up, and provided an opportunity again.

I never had to search for a job; it came to me at the precise timing. I have a job that I love doing and I work at the company that I absolutely love and which is like my family here. I am financially independent, while having no formal degree from an American institution of higher learning. It was only later I received my certification as a professional Life Coach from the International Coach Academy, but for many years my main work had nothing to do with Life Coaching. Even though I had no guarantees and had not even opened opportunities to establish my life in this country, which might seem like a problematic situation, I was never homeless, never lost a job and I never lacked anything.

How is it possible for a permanently disabled person to go to a foreign country having no place to live, no job, and not even any clear definite plans or guarantees, and fully establish herself? Maybe for someone it may not sound that impressive, but you have seen me in the ICU without any sign of life; you have seen me barely open my eyes and not able to speak, to move or do anything by myself. You were one of those people, who, due to my physical weakness, helped me sit up from a lying position and who fed me through a straw. You know it all from the very beginning, and know that's where I started my journey. It makes me ask, "Can it be really true?"

Having said that, I want to make a note that I never had to go through those struggles that many immigrants have to experience until they get a job that they want or residence they like. One step at a time, all those details fell into place very nicely for me. Often, it felt that some invisible power handed me all I needed by arranging favorable situations when I unconsciously took some action that was necessary, came across the information that was very helpful, met people who willingly provided the needed assistance, and found friends who even went far out of their way to meet my needs.

Also, I always felt protected. I always felt safe and well. For many years I have not had any situation when somebody took advantage of me, hurt me or harmed me in any way. And when later there were people who had intentions to hurt or harm me – they were not able to. Each of those people had no success in fulfilling their intention to hurt me and they're no longer part of my life. I don't even know where they are, nor do I care to know. The Lord knows. Once, when I had a serious threat by someone (whom I accepted in my life by mistake), when I was concerned about my safety and well-being, the Lord spoke to me through Holy Scriptures:

> *"Fear not, for I am with you; Be not dismayed, for I am your God. I will strengthen you, Yes, I will help you, I will uphold you with My righteous right hand. Behold, all those who were incensed against you shall be ashamed and disgraced; They shall be as nothing, and those who strive with you shall perish. You shall seek them and not find them – Those who contended with you. Those who war against you shall be as nothing, as a nonexistent thing. For I, the Lord your God,*

will hold your right hand, Saying to you, 'Fear not, I will help you.'" (Isaiah 41: 10-13)

Trusting in God, I surrendered that person into the hands of the Living God, and asked the Lord to protect me and take care of the situation which I found myself in. Soon that person disappeared from my life, and now is truly as a nonexistent being. What's more interesting, I didn't have to do anything for these people to leave my life. I could write much more about it, and maybe I will tell you more when I see you in person. For now, I want to say – overall, nobody and nothing else is able to protect you the way the Lord God does. I did not only hear about it. I've lived it.

I have my own challenges and at the same time, I have the blessing to handle it all. My life is full of examples, when various situations got solved in unexplainable ways. Of course, we could call it "coincidence," or something similar. But I don't believe it's random coincidence or "good luck." I believe our faith creates these so-called random coincidences. Our prayer and faith are immense power, which can do the impossible. The reason my life has transformed from endless agony to a beautiful life is because I fully trusted my God, had unwavering faith at all times, and I expected the answer even when it seemed there is no way it could get better. Of course, I had to make an effort and worked hard to achieve my desire. I made an extra effort in everything I did and I will talk about it more as we go along. But it is my God, the same God as yours, who created opportunities when there were none, gave me the strength, wisdom and ability to create the life I have now. I could not have done it all otherwise.

What Does It Mean to Trust God?

What kind of faith is that which makes miracles? I never could understand that until I experienced miracles first hand. It is a certain mindset and overall inner state. This is not some superficial awareness or thoughts about some mystical being named God, who is somewhere high up there watching and maybe who could help you, while in your heart and your mind you fully rely on favorable circumstances, money, yourself, or other people. Many have this kind of faith, but it doesn't do any good, nor does it give any results or changes in their lives.

I am talking about a mindset, an inner state, when you not only believe there is a God, but also you trust in Him with the entire essence of your being. There is a big difference between "Believe there is a God" and "Trust God." Or in other words, believing that there is a God, and relying on God or counting on Him are two totally different things.

When you have someone in your life you fully trust, how does that make you feel? What is your expectation from that relationship? You feel you can always count on that person, right? It's the same with trusting your God. It's when you not only believe that there is a God, but it's when you count on Him even though you don't see Him. Would you stop counting on your most reliable friend, even though he's in a different location than you? Not at all. You know you can count on that person at any time, and even if he's not there with you – you can call him. Well, it is the same with relying on your Lord. Except in the latter case it is even better, because you know that you can pray to your God anywhere and anytime and your Lord will listen to you, and He will help you for He is faithful. And, the Lord God is almighty. He can do so much more than what your reliable friend would be able to do.

Have a clear conscious comprehension (awareness, understanding) – allowing absolutely no doubts – that our physical world is ruled by the spiritual world and the Creator of the universe, who has the authority over every spiritual power and over every circumstance, is holding you and your life in His hands. It's when you grasp the fact that all people in your life, situations and absolutely everything in your life is in God's authority. How can you know that the Lord really holds you in His hand? There is His promise, which you can count on. Jesus said He would not turn away anyone, who comes to Him.

> *"All that the Father gives Me will come to Me, and the one who comes to Me I will by no means cast out." (John 16:37)*

That means, you will not be rejected by the Lord if you come to Him. And then, once you love the Lord your God, then in your life all things work together for good. It is a mystery to me, but I am a witness that it is true.

> *"And we know that all things work together for good to those who love God, to those who are the called according to His purpose." (Romans 8:28)*

To love the Lord is not just a mere emotion for how pleased you are with God because He has done something for you. To love the Lord is to keep His commandments.

> *"He who has My commandments and keeps them, it is he who loves Me. And he who loves Me will be loved by My Father, and I will love him and manifest Myself to him. Jesus answered and said to him, 'If anyone loves Me, he will keep My word; and My Father will love him, and We will come to him and make Our home with him. He who does not love Me does not keep My words; and the word which you hear is not Mine but the Father's who sent Me.'" (John 14:21, 23, 24)*

When you keep the Lord's commandments and abide in Christ, your life will be extraordinary. You will witness your Lord manifesting in your life; you will be blessed and protected from evil. You will know that the Lord Jesus Christ – who has the supreme power in the universe – will answer your prayers, and He has control over every single detail that happens in your life.

Faith Equals Absolute Confidence

Even though your current circumstances might seem totally hopeless, you must have a strong unshakable faith that it will all resolve. I am speaking about such faith, which becomes knowledge and finally leads to absolute conviction that when you can say to yourself without any doubts, "It doesn't matter that I have no idea how it can be resolved. But I know that my God is powerful, there is nothing impossible for Him and He will take care of it all. The Lord will provide."

> *"Now faith is confidence in what we hope for and assurance about what we do not see." (Hebrews 11:1 NIV)*

The Bible defines faith as having a strong conviction about something that is yet to happen. It is not, "I hope so." It is not, "Well, maybe." Nor is it related to "If's" or how realistic our desired outcome is. It is having absolute confidence in the outcome that the Lord will prevail regardless of what the situation is or how impossible it may seem to overcome it.

As I mentioned in my other letters, I was learning to have faith through situations that made me face a pitch-dark future – there was no realistic way to change my situation, no way to improve it, or my dreams to be fulfilled. I will never forget those nights, when, after the car accident, I was alone in my room, in my bed feeling absolutely helpless and cried out to my God. I could not recover from the shock of such a drastic change happening in my life. I didn't see any light in my life, and it was scary to even think about my future. I was seeking God day and night. No longer could I run to the Church and ask people to pray for me. I was alone. In complete despair and completely broken down. Every day I cried out to my God and waited for His answer. I did not say any memorized prayers. I simply talked with the One, whom I trusted with all my heart. I would collect my thoughts and feelings and, with the absolute conviction that the Creator of the universe heard me, I simply talked to Him. I prayed every single day and continuously expected His answer. Deep inside I always believed that my life would change. I always held in my heart my meeting with the Lord in ICU, and I knew then there was a purpose for my life that He had planned for me. I was absolutely sure that I would be able to walk again and I would live a full active life in spite of my physical challenges. I had no idea how my answer would come, but I had unwavering faith that it would come. And it did come. It didn't come right away, but it came in such an amazing and incredible way, which I could not even imagine. That was the answer from my Lord.

The greatest changes and most unbelievable turns of my life occurred when I had absolutely no doubts in my heart and my mind – I trusted with all my essence – that the God who I believed in has supreme authority over the entire universe, and He will take care of my difficult situation one way or the other. I had no one to count on because there was no one, who could change my circumstances. Feeling absolutely helpless and having no power to change or improve my circumstances, I simply by faith surrendered myself to His supernatural power and expected an answer.

I didn't know when and how my answer would come, but I trusted that I would get out of the desperate place in my life that I was suddenly forced into. My faith was so strong that it turned into absolute conviction and confidence that change for the better would happen. I did not allow even a thought that it may not. Every day I waited and expected the answer to come. Here I want to stop and make a note: it is very important to expect the answer.

Expect the Answer

To merely believe and to believe with expectancy are two different things. Faith with expectancy is when you are confident you will receive the answer; it's a question of time, that's all. Since you do not know when it is going to happen, you expect it any day, any time.

Let's say you believe that some time I will come to Lithuania for a visit. But how would you feel if I told you that my airline tickets have already been purchased, and everything is ready for my trip, but I won't tell you when I am going to arrive because I want to make my visit a surprise for you? You will not only believe that I will come, but also you will expect my arrival, because I might call you any day and say, "I am at the Vilnius Airport ready to come home." Try to imagine it and see how that feels. Can you feel the difference between those two feelings when you believe and when you expect?

It is not enough to have such faith and expectancy only while you pray or you are in church. I am talking about your mindset, your inner state that defines you all the time. It is when you live having a conscious comprehension (understanding, awareness) that your life is in your God's hands, and problems that occur will be taken care of the way they need to be. I remember when, during my second trip to the United States, to see what ways were there to establish myself in this country, every morning I would think to myself, "I wonder, what God has prepared for me for this day, what is going to happen today?"

I waited and expected for something that would help me: maybe I would meet someone who would assist with some of my challenges; maybe I would learn something useful about the immigration, housing or job opportunities, maybe something would happen, which would turn my circumstances the right direction. I did not know what would happen, but I prayed, and I believed I would get the answer and I expected for. This mindset became such a daily, usual, thing for me that it turned into my natural mindset/inner state on a consistent basis.

Of course, you can't sit around and only think about God's power. You live your life and you have to work, communicate with people and think about daily responsibilities and necessary activities, right? That is why I am talking about a "living in faith mindset," when every moment – whether you're resting or at work or talking to someone – you are aware that God is watching over you and your life is under His control. You live your life as everyone else, working, studying, having a family, and pursuing your own, personal goals. Only while you do that, you observe and pay attention to what is happening around you, so you notice your answer. When you live in expectancy, your faith goes to the next level. That's exactly what kind of faith brought miracles to my life.

Be Open to All Opportunities. Trust Your God in All Circumstances. God's Ways are not Our Ways

When we are dealing with a problem and pray about it, often we think we know or at least we guess in what way the problem should be solved. Even though many prayers may sound like, "Lord, all is in Your hands, so take care of everything according to Your will," we still hold on to our expectations as to *How* we should receive His answer and *When* we should receive it. Holding on to our assumptions about how things should go may play against us.

How many times have you experienced or watched someone being disappointed in God and losing faith when circumstances did not go the way you or they had expected? Then their anxiety and stress replaces faith. And anxiety and stress from not getting an answer is the first step toward loss of faith.

Many times, my expectations were totally contrary to what Lord's will was. Through hardship I was learning to trust God that He had my life in His hands, and that there must be a reason why I was placed in certain circumstances. There were so many times that were very irritating and frustrating to me. Many times I could not understand why it was all happening. But I was learning to trust the Word of God and walk by faith and live by scripture.

> *"Commit your way to the Lord, trust also in Him, and He shall bring it to pass." (Psalm 37:5)*

"Commit your works to the Lord, and your thoughts will be established." (Proverbs 16:3)

So, since I prayed daily for the Lord to direct my path as I was learning from the Bible, I learned to trust that God was indeed leading me the way I had to go, and was watching over me. That means I deeply trusted that various circumstances – even though I did not like some of them – occurred because that was just what had to happen and all was the way He intended it to be, because my life was in God's hands and He created those circumstances to direct me onto the path I needed to take. My faith was grounded even more when, after my prayer asking the Lord to speak with me through His Word, I was led to read:

"This is what the Lord says - your Redeemer, the Holy One of Israel: 'I am the Lord your God, who teaches you what is best for you, who directs you in the way you should go.'" (Isaiah 48:17 NIV)

And what was absolutely astonishing to me, after some time I saw that exactly those circumstances, which I did not like and seemed like a huge problem, were really for the better! It was those specific set of circumstances that brought me to the realization of my ultimate dreams. God's ways to deliver me the answer on His timing were absolutely perfect. And, knowing how Lord granted me the request, I knew I wouldn't have been happy if He had answered it according to my timing and my expectations. How I thanked my God for fulfilling my request not my way, but fulfilling it His way!

That's when I paid close attention to Bible verse:

"And we know that all things work together for good to those who love God, to those who are the called according to His purpose." (Romans 8:28)

I realized that this was really true. I had no explanation how it worked out that way, but it astonished me greatly. And it still does. I want to encourage you to trust that there is a reason why you are going through certain situations and difficulties. At the present, your circumstances do not appear favorable, but after all, you do not know where they will lead you, right? Maybe they are what you really need, because they will develop some necessary character traits in you, teach you something you need to know, will connect you with people who will assist you, or will direct your life in a way which will lead you to the answer you've been waiting for.

Right now, you cannot see it because what you see is only what is actually happening at the moment. But what if you live by faith? And faith is a deeply held trust in the Lord, your God. Be confident you are going the way you need to go, and when the right time comes, the Lord will arrange everything to be solved in your favor. And, when you look back, you will see that those situations and circumstances together worked out for the benefit, as the Lord says in His word.

I learned the hard way that when things don't go the way we ask in prayer and the answers to our prayers do not happen when we expect it, it might be actually the best answer we could possibly receive. Sometimes the answer comes in a different way and different timing than we have imagined, and it is because God knows better what's best for us, not you and me. We have to trust in God's infinite knowledge. Simply trust.

> *"'For My thoughts are not your thoughts, Nor are your ways My ways,' says the Lord. 'For as the heavens are higher than the earth, so are My ways higher than your ways, and My thoughts than your thoughts.'" (Isaiah 55: 8-9)*

Keeping in mind that God's ways are not ours, be open to different opportunities. Please hear me now - I would have missed the greatest opportunities in my life if I resisted some of the circumstances and insisted the answer come my way at the time when I wanted. If I had dismissed people or an inspiration to do something or opportunities that came in to my life and had insisted on "my plans, my way," I would have missed the opportunities that God created for me, which were there to improve my life conditions, just as I had asked in my prayers. Interestingly, some of my biggest opportunities came hidden behind some simple ideas, deep desire, doubting chances, impossible challenges, and through people who seemed ordinary persons with no exceptional wealth, careers or success.

Your opportunity may be as your diamond, which you have to see in a simple piece of a coal. Did you know that diamonds really are simply carbon, which becomes a beautiful jewel under the conditions of a very high-pressure and temperature? Like that precious stone, precious opportunities might be hidden behind not very attractive ideas, behind only very slightly opened doors and behind hard relentless work. But, if we take those ideas/inspirations and diligently work to make the best of them – they will become like that precious, one-of-a-kind diamond.

I experienced that so many times, when certain circumstances seemed to me the exact opposite of what I wanted and what I asked for in my prayer. There were times when I was confused and unhappy, and would say in my prayer, "God? What are you doing? Why do You allow this situation in my life?"

There I was, scolding the Lord. It seemed to me that my life should evolve in a different way than what was happening at that time. I kept saying to God, "Couldn't you create different circumstances for me?" Because this was definitely not how I thought it should be and I did not like what was happening at all. But, realizing that my heavenly Father knows far, far better than me how everything should evolve, I would calm down and would pray again saying that I fully trusted Him. As much as I did not want to, I would accept what was happening in my life trusting that I had those situations for a reason, even though I did not see any good in them nor did I understand why I had to be put in those circumstances. And indeed, to my big surprise, later I saw that it was those people and those circumstances that I did not like, became a huge blessing to me. Thanks to all of that my life turned out the way it did and it brought me to the realization of what I asked in my prayers. If I had resisted and pushed away people and situations that were brought into my life, I would have rejected the opportunities that were graciously given to me by the Lord to fulfill my ultimate dream.

Speaking about trust and acceptance of opportunities and various circumstances, in any way I do not suggest to you to take any activity that is on your way. I am sure you understand, we are surrounded by the bad people and all kinds of opportunities that are far from good. Every choice will bring its outcome. Therefore, it is crucial to wisely choose who you spend time with and what activities you choose.

We do not know and it is not for us to judge when and how the answer should come into our lives. Everything has its reason and its time. To tell you the truth, many of the answers to my prayers did not come immediately. Some of them did. But the ones that were about some serious changes in life came after a while, and all of them involved some challenges and required faith.

I would encourage you not to fear if problems do not get solved right away. The answer is on its way, only maybe it's coming not the way you had imagined it and not when you want. It is very important to trust your God knowing that He is directing your path and is watching over you. Maybe you have to go through some difficulties for whatever reason, and I am pretty sure later you will see why you needed that, what you have learned from it and how it directed your life.

I want to stress one important thing – when I talk about giving your problems into the hands of your Creator, I am talking about your mindset and your inner state, not about remaining idle in the hope that problems will be solved by themselves somehow. Yes, there are times when we must be still and wait when the Lord opens the door and we need to obey Him. He knows what needs to happen and when it needs to happen. Many times though, we must take certain steps to solve our problems or change some circumstances. We live in a physical world, and we all have to put out effort in order to get the desired result.

Part 2 ~ Problems and Self-Management

While breaking through what seemed like never-ending barriers in my journey, one of the lessons I've learned that in addition to prayer and faith, we must do something about the situation that we are praying about. Sure, there are times when the Lord provides the answer without our input, as I have shared that with you earlier. And these times astonished me.

While at times the Lord provides help by arranging circumstances without our input or by bringing people who help us, many times it is necessary for us to put our efforts into that which we pray about.

As an answer to our prayers, the Lord might put in our hearts inspiration to do something, connect us with people who could help, or create an opportunity for us. However, if we don't use the given opportunity and don't take any action, we might be the ones who will reject the answer that was given to us. At times, we must use the opportunity and take the first step in faith and do the necessary work, which ultimately becomes the blessing that we wanted to have.

We can sit and pray, ask for help from God, but if we remain absolutely inactive, we can spend many years of our lives sitting and asking for help. For example, we can spend a long time asking Him to give us a job, but if we reject the small opportunity due to our arrogant opinion about it, or neglect it if we don't even search for new job openings, or procrastinate to make that one phone call, we might continue being unemployed and just keep asking.

We may ask the Lord to free us from depression, but if we continue constantly thinking about all the reasons why we are not happy in our lives and focus on that negativity, having the attitude, "Nothing good is going to happen anyway," we might continue our life being drowned in sadness and despair and keep asking for that answer while it is right here by your side – your own effort to manage yourself.

As I look back, my efforts were absolutely necessary for me to have that which I requested in my prayers. I wanted to be happy and enjoy my life in spite of the crash that changed my life. I asked God to change my life conditions, so I could live an active, full lifestyle in spite of my injuries. God answered my prayers by inspiring me to take action and by giving me the opportunities, so that by accepting them I could change my life conditions. It did require faith because at the time those opportunities seemed like false hopes. And realistically thinking, my vision to walk with prostheses or live independently in California seemed nearly impossible to become a reality. But I still believed that those opportunities were given to me as an answer to my prayers. I decided to use them, and obstacles that made my desire to look impossible, I accepted as challenges to myself to win the game.

I trusted that He would bless me as I would be in the process of attaining my goal. And indeed, God protected me from all evil, blessed my efforts, sent me people who helped me, blessed the results of my work, and arranged new favorable opportunities, which I used again, and this way I moved forward toward implementing my vision.

Most of the times I did not wait until the answer landed on my lap. I took the initiative, trusting that the Lord would bless my efforts. I worked hard, was constantly learning and improving my performance at the jobs I did, and I never stopped developing my skills. Today I can say that I live the way I had dreamed of and prayed about. In fact, my life is even richer with many wonderful people and experiences than I ever dreamed. But nothing simply dropped out of the sky for me. My life today is the result of my unshakable faith, my hard work, and God's blessing.

In addition to prayer and strong faith, it required boldness and determination, continuous efforts and hard work, discipline and perseverance, and tireless tenacity to move forward. It required me to use the small opportunity and work very hard to turn that opportunity into success, even if my vision seemed almost impossible to achieve. My successes showed up because I worked relentlessly, holding discipline and high standards as the criteria for myself. Some of my choices and decisions, which made an amazing life-changing impact, were not made based on facts and possibilities that seemed realistic, but based on my faith and vision that I had.

I know I would not be where I am today if I had listened to other people's negative opinions of what I should or shouldn't do, discouragements or fear of the unknown. I would not have the blessings I have today if I had given up when I faced obstacles and difficulties. I would not have had successful results if I had done my job carelessly or without making an effort to improve my performance each day. Had I not, I would still continue my existence among the four walls of my room, with only periodic visits of friends, television or the Internet connecting me with the world.

And I know that I will not stop at this point. I ask my God to make me a blessing for other people and that my life would continue improving in all areas of my life. And I know that for that to happen I will have to work hard, be disciplined and hold myself to high standards of how I use my time and how I perform any job that I do. For instance, for many years now I get up at five or six in the morning to have more hours in a day or I cancel leisure time with friends, so I have enough time to do whatever it is I need to do. In fact, that's exactly the cost of my letters to you. But I know it's worth it and I have absolutely no regrets about it.

When you pray trusting the Lord, keep in mind your answer might show up not as you expect it or when you expect it. And, it may come as an inspiration to do something, as an idea, or slightly opened door of opportunity. God will give you opportunities, but you need to open those doors and enter them. He will give you the skills and ability to perform the job, but you need to do the job. He will bless your work, but you must put every effort in managing yourself and carry out the work that must be done. I will break it down to elaborate on some aspects I believe are important when facing situations that we call "problems."

1. Hold On To Your Faith

Have you ever experienced or met someone who goes to the church and prays for a need that they have, but when you ask them about their expectations, you can see they don't really believe in their prayer. I have been that person myself and I know it's very common.

Many people ask God for help, but they do not make any effort to hold on to their faith; they don't manage their attitude, nor do anything about their situation. And if they don't get the answers they want, they come to the conclusion that God apparently didn't listen or that He didn't answer, and that overall, prayer doesn't work, without even considering that maybe God did give them the opportunity to solve their problem and did send help. But due to their inaction, negative attitude, disbelief or putting absolutely no effort to seek the answers to what they asked for, they failed to notice His help, rejecting the answers that were given to them.

We must make an effort to resist the doubts and anxiety, and hold on to faith even when circumstances seem to be hopeless. We can pray, "God, please help me, I believe there is nothing impossible to you," and feel more peaceful right after the prayer. But then, it is very easy to slip from peace back to anxiety if we do not hold on to our faith.

You are an intelligent person, and growing up I've heard you say many times that you like to look at situations realistically. That is good, without a doubt. While it is imperative to weigh the situation, realistic thinking has two sides to it. Let's stop here for a moment and look at this together. When you start thinking about your situation "realistically," you start going into in-depth thinking about it and analyzing how complicated it is. Soon, the peace that you received in the prayer will be replaced by negative feelings and anxiety, which quickly can turn into fear. Eventually, the situation may appear too complicated and it can become difficult to believe it can actually be resolved.

Meanwhile, God wants to give you help according to your prayer, but you do not hear and do not see it, because you are so concentrated on the problem and its complexity. God is trying to speak to your heart, but you cannot hear Him, because while you're realistically thinking about the problem, your heart is filled with negative feelings, fear and even panic, and it overshadows the quiet, gentle intuitive voice. God tries to speak to your consciousness, but your mind is filled with consideration of how bad it is. God is trying to help you by creating favorable opportunities, but you are too busy analyzing the problem to notice that maybe the person you met or some small opportunity that occurred were God's help sent to you. So, how are you going to see God's answer to your prayers?

Acting in this way you might miss the answers that you've been asking for. And you may pray for years asking God to send help and not receive it only because you reject the answers that were sent to you. Sure, it is wise to look at the situation the way it is. But not worse than it is. Analyzing the problem by looking at it realistically, there is a very fine line between seeing the situation the way it is factually, and seeing only that same problem's dark side. Some people manage to get into imagining the worst possible outcomes and then get frightened by their own imagination. What is the point of doing that? The reason you want to look at the situation realistically is to consider current circumstances and see what you can do to improve them, having a strong faith that you are going to manage them. Never lose the sight of your Lord.

It is absolutely essential to resist doubts and hold on to your faith, because in addition to the fact that we might reject the Lord's answer, our anxiety and disbelief actually annuls our prayer. According to Scriptures, we get our answers according to our faith. If you read the Scriptures, you will find so many stories when Jesus healed people and He would say that it was done according to their faith.

- *"Then He touched their eyes, saying, 'According to your faith let it be to you.'" (Matthew 9:29)*
- *"But Jesus turned around, and when He saw her He said, 'Be of good cheer, daughter; your faith has made you well.' And the woman was made well from that hour." (Matthew 9:22)*
- *"Then Jesus answered and said to her, 'O woman, great is your faith! Let it be to you as you desire.' And her daughter was healed from that very hour." (Matthew 15:28)*
- *"And He said to her, 'Daughter, your faith has made you well. Go in peace, and be healed of your affliction.'" (Mark 5:34)*
- *"'Go,' said Jesus. 'Your faith has healed you.' Immediately he received his sight and followed Jesus along the road." (Mark 10:52)*
- *"Then He said to the woman, 'Your faith has saved you. Go in peace.'" (Luke 7:50)*

- *"And He said to him, 'Arise, go your way. Your faith has made you well.'" (Luke 17:19)*
- *"Then Jesus said to him, 'Receive your sight; your faith has made you well.'" (Luke 18:42)*

Observing what Jesus would say to people, we can conclude that faith is absolutely essential in order to receive anything from God. Besides, the Scriptures say very directly:

> *"But when you ask, you must believe and not doubt, because the one who doubts is like a wave of the sea, blown and tossed by the wind. That person should not expect to receive anything from the Lord." (James 1: 6-7 NIV)*

It is important to understand if we doubt and hold on to mindset that our situation most likely is not going to get resolved – generally that is exactly what is going to happen. I am sure you have heard people saying, "So it did happen anyway. I was afraid it would." Or, "Oh well, that's what I thought. What else I could expect?"

According to the spiritual laws, they have received what they have expected. It turns out we can become our own worst enemies by allowing anxiety and fear to overshadow our faith. Therefore, it is very important not to give in to our doubts and fears. We must control our attitude, what we think about and what we expect.

When in your prayer you surrender your problem to God, it is imperative that when you claim you believe God is all powerful and He can help you, your inner feelings, attitude and mindset is aligned with your proclamation. Many say in their prayer, "God, I trust You can help me," but in their heart they doubt, and are filled with anxiety and fear of what might happen. The Lord says that those who doubt in their heart should not expect to receive anything. I think that is the reason why many do not receive their answers.

When you pray and ask God to help you, you must really comprehend with all your essence that now the Lord, who is almighty and has authority over everything, will take care of your problem and you do not have to be fearful about it. Our physical world is ruled by the spiritual world, and it is much more powerful than any circumstance in which you may be involved. So when you ask for help from Him who has supreme authority over the entire universe, let go all of your concerns. Stop thinking about it as a problem, and instead look for opportunities to resolve your situation. When we give our problems and concerns to God, our hearts and minds become free from negativity and fear, and can be opened to hearing and seeing God's given help.

God communicates to us through various ways. He communicates with us through the Holy Scriptures. Also, the Lord God can give us signs, speak to us through the Scriptures, thoughts, intuition, people, books, nature, and various other ways. There are many ways how the answer can arrive, however, we must make an effort to resist our doubts and negativity in order to see and hear the answer we've been given.

2. Do Not Blame Others. Accept Responsibility

Before I move on sharing some things that empowered me to handle difficulties, I want to get out of the way something that might hinder you. In fact, I consider it deadly in your pursuit to improve your situation. Have you ever felt or heard someone say, "It's not my fault. I am in this position because he or she did this to me." I am talking about blaming someone or some other set of circumstances for your problems which resulted in the situation in which you find yourself. Countless people continue their lives in misery, blaming someone or some unfortunate occurrence for their failure to achieve something or their overall unhappiness. In the event of adverse circumstances, often our first reaction is asking, "Whose fault is that?" It will be other people, certain events, the weather or anything else. We surely are going to find someone or something to blame for our circumstances. But what's the point? What is the use of assessing blame?

Yes, maybe at the moment we might feel better taking off the responsibility from ourselves. It is easier knowing, that the problem which occurred is not our fault. But does it change the situation? Does it bring a solution? Unfortunately, often finding who or what we can blame for the problem does not really solve the problem. In fact, we may waste a lot of time, energy and emotions while trying to find fault, and later discussing the motives behind their actions. Meanwhile, the problem remains a problem. We could have better used that time to find the solution or at least improve the situation, and move on.

Would you agree, if we look at it more deeply, that searching who we can blame equals looking for ways to make ourselves victims? It's hard to take it, isn't it? But consider this for a moment: by searching who you can blame, you indirectly or unconsciously admit that someone else is stronger than you, and someone else has more control and more influence in your life than yourself. You are a victim of someone else's actions.

Sure, we can always allow ourselves to drown in self-pity, collect sympathy and justify ourselves by saying that somebody else did something bad to us and that's why we gave up or we are in the situation we're in. But what's the point, who is going to benefit from it? After all, we are the ones who will suffer from it, because this "pinning the blame on someone" approach will not improve our circumstances and it certainly will not make us happier overall. In fact, the exact opposite is true: this is a straight way toward the victim mentality.

As a victim, can you do much to improve your circumstances? We all know the meaning of the word "victim." An excellent alternative word is "defeated." Do you like to be defeated? I assume not. Unless victimizing yourself is your way to get attention. That's why I believe blaming someone is self-defeating because it robs people of their dreams, their improved circumstances and emotional well-being. In addition, I believe blaming others or circumstances unconsciously makes people feel helpless because it makes them feel their fortune was or is in someone else's hands, not in theirs.

Before you feel sorry for yourself, stop and ask yourself, are those events or people who you were about to blame really stronger than you are and have more control in your life than you have? How would you feel if you accepted the responsibility for all your circumstances and said to yourself that just as you had an impact on creating the current circumstances, exactly the same way you can influence the change? Do you think that knowing how much your own decisions influence your own destiny, would make you feel more empowered to change those circumstances than blaming someone else?

I know you may feel, "What do you mean accept responsibility? It's not my fault." Yes, maybe some events that happened were not your direct responsibility. Our life is full of situations that did not depend on us, were absolutely out of our control and we could not have any influence to prevent them from happening. But wouldn't you agree that many of our circumstances are the results of our earlier made choices? Our choices and decisions have a great impact on our subsequent circumstances, one way or another.

Maybe it's not that easy to accept and agree with this, but if you stop and think about it, you will see our choices, which sometimes do not seem so special and do not make a big difference at the time, over time bring their own specific set of results or consequences.

Our decisions determine our future events and ultimately our destiny. Stop for a moment and look at your life. Remember people with whom you spent most of your time and shared a close relationship. Do you think they had any impact on your life or not? How would your life be different now had you chosen different people?

Over time, your relationships with some people cooled off, completely broke-off or got stronger. What did you contribute to those outcomes and how it affected your life later? What would be different in your life, if you had not gotten so close with some people, and relationships with others you would have cherished, would have made an effort to protect them and would not have terminated them?

How did you spend the given time to you? Have you used it to implement your desired goals, or wasted it on meaningless things? What would be different in your life today if you had spent your time toward achieving the realization of your goals or dreams?

Your attitude about sports and your discipline to exercise – how does it affect your physical appearance and your health? The results would be certainly different if you did not care about your health and physical fitness, right?

The choice that you made regarding education and engagement in various business activities had an impact on your career and financial situation later on. In what position would you be today, if earlier you had chosen different priorities and had made different decisions regarding pursuing further education and a more fulfilled professional life?

Think about the many women you had relationships with, but for some reasons ended them – how did that affect your personal life? Would you have had a different life if you had cherished some of them more and immediately ended those you knew were there for the wrong reasons and were certainly not a long-time relationship?

I am sure you had choices for all these questions, and you have made those that seemed right at the time. Those choices created certain events and circumstances later on, and ultimately, they determined where you are today in your life. We are the ones who choose with whom we associate, how we spend our time, those with whom we have close relationships, and choose to be our partner for life, if and when we create a family, choose a career path, move to a different city or even country or stay where we are.

By making those choices, we shape our destiny. By making those choices, we create our lives. I asked myself exactly the same questions, and I fully understand that my own choices led me to where I am today. If I had chosen to listen to my intuition and stopped dating Dalius, I would not have had the tragic experience in my life that impacted all of us. In fact, my life would have gone in a completely different direction. However, despite my bad intuitive feeling, I continued dating him, which turned my life into a direction, which none of us could perceive even in our darkest moments. But it happened. And it not only turned my life around, but also it greatly impacted the lives of those people dearest to me.

If on the night of February 11, I had chosen to honor mom's request to not go out, but stay home – in the morning I would have awakened in my bed at home, not in the ICU hooked up to a life support machine. On the other hand, if I had chosen to listen to other people's opinions and my fear of disappointment – I would not have traveled to Istanbul to meet Michael, who helped me realize my biggest dream of being able to walk again. If I had decided to give in to my fear of the unknown and doubts, and had chosen to continue an effortless and comfortable life with the family – today I would not live in California, enjoying a full, active and independent lifestyle in spite of my physical challenges. If I had chosen to do the right thing and not have started a relationship with a married man – my path of establishing myself in the United States, my personal life and my career would have gone in a totally different direction. If I had given into my helplessness and had not made every effort to become everything I could possibly be, I don't think I would be living independently across the globe from my home and would not enjoy life as I do today.

There can be many examples, but I think you will agree with me that our own earlier choices brought us to where we are today in our lives. And nothing stops at this point. Life goes on, and likewise, our decisions and actions that we choose today shape our future. Therefore, I would encourage you to take responsibility for where you are today in your life.

I know you might disagree with me by stating that your problems began because of another person's decisions and they were totally out of your control. Yes, there are many situations we can't control. There are some circumstances we cannot influence nor do we have the power to change them. We are powerless against nature. We cannot control other people's behavior, the economy and so on. Disasters, accidents or illness can drastically affect our lives, and unfortunately, we are powerless against many of such events. Yours, mine and the lives of many others are full of situations that did not depend on us at all.

But what's next? We continue our lives, don't we? With certain events our lives do not end. Good and bad are part of all of our lives, and regardless of what happens, we continue our life journey. The question is, which way we choose to continue that journey? And at this point, we take over the responsibility.

Which turn our life will take from the time any event happens greatly depends on whether we are going to put all our efforts into improving the situation despite the pain and any obstacles, or whether we are going to give up, blaming a person or the event that had such a great impact. It's a very fine line, which is hard to see sometimes.

Have you met people who would share their broken destiny or any unsuccessful outcomes and would say that it's someone else's fault; everything would have turned out differently if that person would not have done something or that event would not have happened? Stay with me for a moment.

Of course, some events can drastically affect our lives. I personally have experienced the event that completely changed the course of my life. Both of us have associated with people who strongly impacted our lives and sure, we could say that they are to blame for our current circumstances. But let's look at it from a different angle.

What do you think: our life depends more on the events that happen or on what we do after they happen? In order to have an easier way to explain my point and not talk about someone else, I will use my own life as an example.

When, after the accident, the first three years I lived stuck at home with no opportunity to continue a full, active lifestyle, all the blame was pointed toward the accident. My life was drastically changed due to the car accident. And if I had continued my life that way, no one would be saying anything bad about me, but they would have a very simple, clear explanation: "It's the accident's fault; it was because of that tragic event she lost almost half of her body and is forced to live this way." There would be a short statement about my life, that "the car accident broke Inga's destiny."

Thank God, today I am in a different position in life. I lead an active, meaningful and fulfilling life in a beautiful part of the world in spite of the consequences of the car accident. The same event – car accident – but with an entirely different outcome. But at this point, nobody is saying that I live such a beautiful life due to the tragic event. In this case, when there is a discussion about my current living conditions, all the focus is directed at me, and it is said that it is all because of my efforts and hard work. And I get congratulations for attaining such a transformation after the crash.

But if I would not have taken the initiative and have not made many changes in my life, I would have continued living as I did the first three years. Who would be to blame for that?

Can you see that fine line? What determined the course of my life – the event or what I did after that event?

The quality of our lives and often our destiny are determined not by the events that take place in our lives, but what we do afterwards. Is it right to blame events or someone saying that they ruined our lives, if we give in to a self-pity, and stop even trying to improve our circumstances? Can we shift the responsibility on someone else, if we see our life collapsing, but do nothing to stop the fall and not make any changes? Or, first we try to make some changes, but then with the first challenges, we drop the ball saying that it is too difficult to handle, and end up blaming the events or other people for our broken destiny.

And what if we would say to ourselves, "Yes, maybe the circumstances that occurred were beyond my control and I could not prevent them. But what happens next is entirely up to me. I will move forward in spite of any difficulties and do everything I can to improve my circumstances."

Can you feel the difference in how you feel when you say this to yourself? You can make unbelievable changes in your life if you make the decision to accept responsibility, take charge of your life and do whatever it takes to create your life the way you desire.

3. Attitude

Now that we have faith as a solid ground to stand on and have pushed aside the self-defeating thing that might have ruined your life, let's take a deep breath together.

What do we do now? First, check your perspective. Earlier I wrote you a letter about it and I will repeat myself; this is a critical concept to fully understand. Having an empowering perspective will set you up to accept difficult situations in a way that will help you make the right decisions how you are going to handle them. Having an empowering perspective also will lay the groundwork for your positive attitude.

Paying close attention to your attitude is imperative. You may ask why. Your attitude affects how you respond to problems and how you approach solutions. It's as simple as that. Your actions depend on your attitude. And as you know, most of the times our actions are necessary to change the circumstances. For example, my faith was the basis for my empowering perspective – I believed that the Lord was holding my life in His hand, and nothing in my life could or would happen unless Father allows it (Matthew 10: 29-31) and all things worked together for good. (Romans 8:28)

And when unpleasant things would happen or things would not go the way I wanted, my belief formed the perspective that there is a reason for everything that happens, and at the end all things will work out for good. Based on my faith and perspective, I had a positive attitude during difficult times which strengthened me greatly to not give up and motivated me to look for positive things in every circumstance and do everything I could to resolve the problem.

Your attitude affects so many aspects of life: it affects how you treat other people and your relationships; your attitude affects many of your decisions, your attitude affects how you approach life. I can't stress enough how important this is. People, who have the attitude that problems are too difficult for them to handle; that they are not good enough to fix situation; that nothing good awaits them; that success is luck and they are not lucky enough; that they are going to fail; that their circumstances cannot be changed or that they can't have an influence on the outcome: they don't do anything to improve their current situation. They give up and let it be the way it is, explaining their choice by saying, "What's the point of doing anything, nothing is going to get better anyway."

If you have an empowering perspective and attitude that your circumstances can be improved no matter what obstacles you face – you are definitely going to take action and you will do whatever it takes to make a change. And if you truly believe in that, you are not going to allow anyone or any obstacles to stop you. You will move toward your goal until you reach it. Watch your attitude. It determines your decision and points you toward what you are going to do about almost any situation.

4. Problem vs. Challenge

Almost every person knows the meaning of the word "problem." Usually we do not have a favorable association with this word. Difficult situations are never pleasant, and many times it means hardship or even emotional devastation for us. Naturally, we all try to avoid problems and also naturally we react negatively when we face them.

After the accident, my life was bombarded by problems and hardships on an ongoing basis. They became a daily and almost an inseparable part of my life. As you know well, after losing nearly half of my body, I had to go through enormous physical and emotional pain and face a multitude of challenging obstacles while living in Lithuania.

Upon my arrival to the United States, some of the issues were resolved right away, because here in California there is a different access for wheelchair users plus a different climate, making access to necessities as well as to the quality of life almost easy.

However, there were many other issues and difficulties that needed to be solved. Since problems became such a common thing in my life, and I was not going to allow them to stop me from becoming self-sufficient again and creating my life the way I desired it to be, I found my way to deal with them. I had to.

There were two things that helped me overcome every obstacle I encountered: my perspective and attitude. It developed a new point of view about the way I dealt with problems. First, I started seeing them as the same part of life just as joy and success, and I accepted them as naturally as all other life circumstances. Problems and difficulties are not the end of the world as at times I might have reacted, finding myself riddled with stress, anxiety and too many sleepless nights to count. They are simply unpleasant situations that I have to deal with, that's all. They are going to come into my life over and over again, because that's just part of life. My outcome for the most part depends on how I look at those situations and what I am going to do about them.

Second, I talked a lot about the perspective, how our point of view impacts our decisions and what we are going to do about the situation. I want to invite you to see another side of the problem. I have learned to see a lot of good in problems. In fact, difficulties were to my benefit. Today when I look back, I can firmly say that many difficult and even hopeless circumstances and people that I've met were only for the better, although at the time it seemed exactly the opposite. And what is most surprising, because of exactly those difficult circumstances I had the biggest and the best changes in my life. You may ask, "How can this be?"

There were many circumstances I encountered that made me frustrated, angry and hopeless, and I was saying, "Lord, where are you? Why is this happening like that?"

I was bewildered and disturbed. Having no particular changes after my prayers, I would tell myself that God doesn't make mistakes, and if He allowed this situation and my circumstances do not change despite my continuous prayers – that means I have to go through this for some reason. I would pull myself together, ask my Lord to give me strength and endurance and I would keep on going, doing the best I could in any given circumstances.

And what an astonishing surprise it was for me to see that later, it all worked together for the good. Some circumstances the Lord was not changing no matter how much I disliked it, because through it all He was changing me. Some of the toughest times have shaped resilience, perseverance, relentlessness in me. Some unpleasant and painful experiences were very valuable lessons. Occurred situations and given circumstances directed my destiny in such a way that ultimately it brought me to the fulfillment of my dream and fulfillment of God's purpose in my life. Particularly, desperate situations fired me up to take action to change those circumstances, which literally transformed my life.

Some people, with whom at first I had no special bond, later were the ones there for me when I really needed help. Thanks to them I overcame many hardships, got to meet other, equally good people, and found new opportunities that I used to improve my circumstances. And through those people who created life experiences I wished I never had, I learned to forgive, stand up for my standards and be patient. Difficulties and what seemed unendurable experiences brought up the resilience and developed endurance in me. Have you heard the saying, "What doesn't break us, makes us stronger?"

Every difficulty prepared me for future much stronger storms that I yet had to endure.

Particularly through circumstances that seemed totally hopeless, I learned to have unwavering faith and through that I saw how the Lord transforms the impossible into an opportunity. It's because of the hardships I faced along the way that now I know I can trust my God in any difficulty.

I know that He will provide help, because I witnessed His help over and over again. I did not just read or hear about it; I experienced it personally, repeatedly, over the years and thus I have more confidence in the Lord now than I ever had before the accident.

At first, my support for my perspective was my belief as I mentioned earlier. And with time, observing my life I saw that there was really a reason for everything and everything works together for the good. Thus, gradually my mindset about difficulties took a different angle - I started looking for something valuable in them. Instead of focusing on the problem itself and how difficult and painful it was, I searched for the reason for that situation and for the benefit in everything I was experiencing. I would ask myself, "What is going on behind this event? Since the Lord allowed this, then there is something in it; what am I supposed to learn from this experience? What good can I take out from all of this?"

The more value I searched in every tough situation, the more value I found. I guess we all find what we look for, right? When I started asking myself different questions, seeking for the value in a bad situation, I started seeing the value in it all. At times it would totally astonish me seeing how beneficial my hardships were.

Very soon I noticed that once I started intentionally choosing not to dwell on how bad it is, but seek the value in everything, it totally transformed my perception about difficulties. In addition, even though I was never a drama queen or a big complainer, it helped me to pull myself away from pain and fear when troubles occurred and look at the situation from a perspective that allowed me to remain in peace and make the right judgment on what I should do about it.

Having experienced time and again that all things work together for the good, I decided to turn problems to my advantage by looking for the value in them. I started seeing how beneficial problems can actually be. It was because of my desperate circumstances that I was fired up with the non-negotiable determination to change them, and eventually my life was transformed. It's because of problems and continuous stumbling blocks that I became stronger, resilient, and more persistent. It's because of those troubles and times when I did not see any hope that my faith grew and I experienced the most incredible testimonies of answered prayers. In fact, these problems and seemingly hopeless situations made my life only more interesting, because each of them has incredible testimonies of answered prayers and stories how the Lord provided His help and pulled me out of each of them. I like to say that the more difficult your situation is – the bigger opportunity there is to see incredible Lord's testimony.

Over time, my perspective about problems changed completely. When I am facing some difficulty, instead of feeling sorry for myself or complaining with growing dissatisfaction, I look for the value. I am looking to see if there is anything I need to learn from this. I watch how this situation is going to affect future events. I am waiting on the Lord to see how He's going to answer my prayers. In a few words - I am looking for what is really going on behind that difficulty.

And you know, this kind of shift of perspective about difficulties has empowered me greatly. It changed my perception about problems and my own mistakes. I was no longer consumed by pain or fear for the future, but I was curious and intrigued while standing strong in faith that no matter what was going on in my life, God was in control and so I would be fine no matter what. It shaped a specific strategy how I deal with the problems, which has gotten me through every storm of life I had to endure. As crazy as it may sound to you, over time difficulties became nothing more than a tool for me to improve myself or opportunity for the testimony of the answered prayer.

Since personal growth is very important to me, finding the lesson meant growth and improvement. I learned to appreciate my failures and mistakes. Of course it is not pleasant to make mistakes or not attain what was desired, but since the mistake was already made, then instead of dwelling on my failure I decided to extract the lesson out of it, which could benefit me later on in life. Thus my perception about mistakes was transformed as well. With time, I trained myself intentionally to choose what I see in the situation and especially what I focused on. Life became so much easier and much more interesting when I started looking at my world through a different angle.

Once I noticed that problems played a significant and beneficial role in my life journey, I began looking at problems as an opportunity; an opportunity to learn, an opportunity to develop certain character traits, an opportunity to learn, an opportunity to develop a deeper faith, an opportunity to witness another Lord's miracle and answer to my prayer, an opportunity to test myself, an opportunity to challenge myself and grow.

I know it might be very unusual for you to look at a problem as an opportunity. But I want you to try this new perspective and see how much different your life experience will become. You will view difficulties differently. You will approach them differently. And overall, your life experience will be a lot different than it was before. So, in order to get away from your natural, negative reaction when you encounter problems, I invite you to look at them as opportunities. There was a reason why they visited your life. In addition, believing the word of God, that all things work together for good to those who love God and are called according to His purpose (Romans 8:28), means that somehow this situation – even though now it seems problematic – eventually will work out for good. Believing that, ask yourself, "What good can I see in this?" For now you might not see how this situation can be possibly good for you. But since you are learning to live by faith, I invite you to take a step of faith and just trust what the Lord says in His word and trust *Him*; the Lord will not let you out of His hand and He will take care of you.

Now that you look at your problem not with a negative perception, but you see it as a situation that has its reasons and is an opportunity for you (keeping in mind that it will work out for good, after all), let's see how you can resolve it in the best possible way.

If we see our situation as a hardship, we will soon get anxious, worried, and fearful and eventually may even wind up in a panic. It is very difficult to make a wise decision being in such a state, wouldn't you agree? Let's see if a different perspective about a problem can make a difference.

How about if you look at it not as a problem that is such a hardship, but as a challenge that has a solution? What is the solution? That is going to be your challenge – find it. Take it as a personal challenge to see how well you can handle the situation. Accept the challenge to win the game.

Do you remember a game called the Rubik's Cube? Many times, in our childhood, we would turn that magic cube over and over trying to put all those colors together. It was difficult and more often than not, we couldn't win. But we still kept playing it. We understood that the point of this puzzle game was to find a way how to put all those various colors in a way that each side of the cube was a solid color. We knew that there must be a way, and we looked for it. There were days, when we'd lose our patience and give up trying to win. But on the next day, we'd again tried to solve the puzzle.

Why would we take it again and again despite how difficult it was to find that mysterious solution? It's because *we knew that there was a way* to arrange that puzzle cube in solid colors, *we were challenged* to find a way, and *we were determined* to find it. What was the outcome? Being challenged and fired up by determination, we played until we found the solution.

Pick any other challenging game that you played. Remember how you looked at it and what was your mindset then? Why would you go back to that game over and over again, and played it until you won? You did it because you knew there must be a way, right? And, it was even interesting for you to play, because you were challenged and your only goal was to win.

What if you looked at the difficult circumstances you're facing now the same way? Try to look at them the same way you looked at the game that challenged you. Remember trying to find a solution for that puzzle game. And you found it, right? Your current situation also has a way out. What is that way? I don't know. But you can find it, if you look for it with such determination and enthusiasm as you had while playing that game. Your life's difficulties are your own personal Rubik's Cube. They are given to you to find their solutions. Problems are there for you to teach you something and make you stronger, not to break you down.

To conclude, when facing a difficult situation, it is important to control our perspective about it. The situation is solely a plain fact. What kind of feelings we are going to have and what we are going to do about it greatly depends on our perspective about that fact. It is important how we interpret it to ourselves. If we look at the current situation as a Problem, focusing on how unexpected and complicated it is or imagining how bad it can get – we will feel stuck. From there, our emotions might escalate and we will be asking, "Why is this happening to me?" or "How could he/she do this to me?" or "Why can't I get out of the problems?"

These are all questions which will lead you to frustration and hopelessness. If we change our perspective and see it as another situation there for a reason and look at it as a challenge to overcome and win – our inner state and mindset will be very different about the situation. We will handle it in a much different way, because then we will be able to focus on the solution and ask ourselves different questions. And that brings me to another important key point: focusing on the solution.

5. Focus on the Solution, not on the Problem

Have you ever noticed that the more you focus on the problem and its complexity, the more difficult it seems? The more complicated it seems, the worse you feel, and eventually you don't even know what to do about it. When you choose to focus only on the problem, it is difficult to see the solution. You feel stuck and at times it might seem like it doesn't even make sense to make any effort, because you simply don't see that it can be improved. Finally, there is a temptation to just give up on it and move on.

What helped me tremendously when I was unhappy about my situation, was that I did not dwell on my dissatisfaction and thoughts about how difficult it was to live with one arm and no legs and how unhappy I was with what had occurred. When anger at my situation would begin increasing inside of me like a volcano about to erupt, I would turn that anger into determination to change the current situation. When I would get frustrated about my circumstances, I would immediately start thinking about:

- How I would like the situation to be?
- What can I do to make it the way I want it?

I would envision how I would feel when I was self-sufficient again, what my life would be like living actively and independently, and how my life experiences would change when I implemented my vision. The more I thought about what I wanted, the more my displeasure with my current position would turn into firm determination and commitment to take action.

It greatly empowered me, because it shifted my focus away from my dissatisfaction, and inspired me to change those circumstances. Instead of dwelling about how painful and difficult it was and remaining in that position, I took the initiative and made every effort to bring about change, which ultimately brought me out of those circumstances that made me so unhappy. Later I even started calling this feeling "my good anger," because then I felt the unwavering determination to change what I did not like, and as a result, I did not remain in the situation that made me depressed and dissatisfied.

At the time though, I had no idea how I could do everything with one hand and no legs. In your eyes I saw the same question – how will I live from now on? No one knew the answer nor could anyone give me any hopeful news. There were so many questions, but no answers. But I was determined to do everything I could possibly do to take care of myself without needing anybody's assistance.

I remember very well those moments, when I would think that no matter how much time or effort it would take me to do something by myself - I would do it, no matter what. I so hated my total dependence on another person, that I was determined to look for ways to be independent until I found them. In this way, I developed the mindset of seeking solutions and focusing on them, instead of dwelling on the problems. If I didn't like the situation - I always looked for ways to find solutions to improve it. My mindset was that complaining and idle dissatisfaction will not help in any way and will not improve my circumstances, so there is no point wasting my time complaining. I realized that only by looking for the solution and taking action could I change the situation. I had the invisible rule for myself: if you don't like something, change it. How? Just find a way and change it.

When I encountered obstacles due to my physical limitations, I did not accept the mindset that I was disabled, nor did I see it as a problem that prevented me from having what I want. I saw it as a challenge to overcome and find a way. And then, I immediately looked for ways to conquer the challenge. I looked for the best solution. This way, I did not get stuck thinking of how bad my life was and how helpless I was. Rather, I would search for a way to improve my situation.

Now, after a while, I can see that such mindset, by concentrating not on the problem but on its solution, strongly and consistently moved me forward. If I had looked at those situations as if they were insolvable problems and focused on how difficult it was, I know I would have been stuck and it would have taken much longer to achieve my goals. In fact, most likely I would not have reached them at all. They really seemed very complex and oftentimes it looked like there was no way to solve them in my favor. Yet instead of focusing on a specific difficulty and analyzing how complex it was, I looked for solutions until I found them.

I will give you a very simple example, which will explain what I am trying to say. I had an experience at work, when my faith and focus on the solution helped me respond to an unfavorable situation in a way that empowered me and led me out of the difficulty. One of my work duties is to organize and coordinate the annual fundraiser for the organization. It requires a good team to plan it and make it happen. One year I looked for new people to be on my committee, and I got some really wonderful people to work with. Among a group of people there were several new members, who looked like they knew the event planning specifics, who said they were willing to put forth the effort in this project, assuring me that I really could count on them. There was one of them (let's call him Mr. X) who kept repeating how excited he was to work with us, that he was fully committed to our project, and our cause would be a priority to him even if he received a job offer (he was looking for a paid job position at the time).

I asked him if he was sure he wanted to take on such a big commitment; the committee position he wanted was key to the planning process, and it was going to take time and effort. Yet finding a paid job was imperative for him at the time. But he kept reassuring me that he was hundred percent committed and our event was the priority for him. I was convinced that he would be my right-hand person for the event planning and I could count on him at any time, no matter what. Being assured I could totally rely on him, I spent a lot of time explaining to him our desired outcome and the planning process, so he could understand what had to be done and get to work.

To my surprise, one day I received a phone call from one of the two, who said that she had to take more work on another committee that she belonged to (not ours, another organization), and therefore she needed to reduce her work on our project. Because she did not want to do her job carelessly, she decided that it would be better if someone else, who could be fully committed to our project, would take over her obligations and do the job the way it needed to be done. I was very sad to hear her news, but I respected her honesty and her commitment to excellence. Her choice showed me she wanted to either do her job well or not to do it at all, and I respected that. We wished each other success and agreed to get in touch for next year's project. A few days later when I came to work, the first thing in the morning I got another surprise: among my voicemail there was a message from Mr. X saying, "Inga, I received a job offer. I am very sorry, but the job is well-paid and I can't reject it. So I wanted to let you know I can't work on your project anymore."

That was it. He just left me a voice message and disappeared. And so there I was, when the event's planning process had to speed up and the work had to be done, I faced the fact: in a short time I had lost two committee members, who assumed some very important obligations and who I thought I could count on. Needless to say, it was very unpleasant. My first reaction was total shock. "They dropped out just when the work must be done. I can't do it all by myself, so who is going to do their tasks?"

The more I thought about it, the more restless I felt. This was going to be a big trouble if those tasks were not performed, but without them, there was nobody else who could have done the job. And, the clock was ticking.

I was left with numerous tasks that all had to be completed at the same time and there was no way I could take upon myself the duties of these two people and do it all myself.

My question, "What am I going to do now?" was getting stronger and started making me feel really anxious. For a moment, the shock paralyzed me and I couldn't think clearly, and I caught myself getting stressed out. I saw that my focus on the problem was only making it worse, and I stopped myself.

I remembered that normally I seek for ways to improve the situation instead of dwelling on the problem and its complexity. My focus on those who left the project was not going to help me in any way, so why do that to myself? I needed to get things done, no matter what, and my focus on the problem and its complexity was a waste of time.

It was then I realized that instead of spending my time on the problem itself, I needed to switch my focus and seek the solutions to the problems facing me. We find what we seek. If we focus on the problem itself and analyze it from every side checking how bad it is – that is exactly what we are going to see. And if we seek for the ways and opportunities to solve the situation in the best possible way – we will find the solution. So, I calmed down and said to myself that everything is under God's control. He knows people's hearts and intentions, and maybe it is actually a good thing that they are dropping out. In fact, it is good that they withdraw now and not at the last minute prior to the event. I know God will bring other committee members, who are a better fit for this year's project. The work can't stop and I am not going to waste neither my time nor my emotions about what had happened.

I shifted my concentration towards seeking ways to improve the situation. I decided to look for new committee members. Interestingly, I felt even more determination. I said to myself that I would make this event successful regardless of the problems I had to solve, and I vowed I was going to make it even better than last year.

I again submitted the ad in the local newspaper requesting volunteers and very soon I received responses from absolutely wonderful people, who were like a gem for our Event Planning Committee. They had experience with event planning and were excited about our event and our purpose. We collaboratively worked on what had to be done, and the final result was the event was very successful. In fact, my Executive Director announced this event as, "the best fundraising event in the agency's thirty year history."

It turned out to be the best event that I had done in my five years at the agency. My eyes were filled with tears when I heard his comments. I had put so much work and heart into this project, and aside from the money raised to help those less fortunate, this was the best reward I could have received for my efforts.

Once again I learned that going that extra mile and making a personal commitment always pays off. And this situation taught me a very good lesson. There was such a fine line between the failure and success. If I had allowed myself to panic and dwelled on the fact how bad it was that these people left our project at a critical time when it was imperative to do the work – it would have greatly slowed down my work and most likely I would have failed to plan the event successfully. But because I was able to focus on the solution rather than the problem, the situation was fixed quickly, and we ended up having an outstanding result. I know this is a very easy situation, comparing to the problems that sometimes we have to face. But I wanted to illustrate my thought.

It is very important to be careful how we interpret events and what we say to ourselves, because that determines how we feel about the occurred circumstances and how we handle the situation. We can't always have a choice of what situations occur in our lives, but we always have a choice as to how we look at them, and what we do about them.

Always remember, that various circumstances have no power over you and they can't make you feel in a certain way unless you allow it. You are the one, who chooses what you think about and how you look at things. Learning to manage your own thoughts and your focus is crucial because it determines your inner state, the actions you take, and finally, your results.

When facing a difficult situation, instead of being worried or stressed out about the problem, begin immediately to focus on the solution, and make every effort to solve the problem the best way you can.

6. The Difference Between "If" and "How"

I will share with you one very important thing that has helped me to accept and deal with all my challenges that I met on my way. Many people, after learning that I live by myself and have no caregiver service, ask me in wonder how I can independently manage the household, cooking, care for myself and everything else on a daily basis with only one arm and no legs.

I know it might seem amazing, but I have the same question when I watch some other people managing difficulties with ease.

When I hear those questions, my explanation is very simple: I hated so much to be dependent on somebody else that I always looked for ways how I could do things by myself. I transformed my hatred toward my physical limitations and dependence on other people into a determination to find a way to do things myself, regardless of how difficult they might be. Maybe it will be in a different way and will take longer, but I will do it myself. I always looked for the solution no matter how difficult the circumstances were. And I found them.

When I think how I do it, it is nothing more than having a certain mindset and answering questions I ask myself when I face any challenge. The technique I use to find solutions to various challenges is by asking myself questions, which are all focused toward seeking the solutions.

I had to seek solutions to everything, up to the smallest daily tasks, because I only had one functional arm. The fact that I completely lost the use of my left arm was very painful. It seemed nearly impossible to take care of myself with one arm, especially with the added difficulty of having no legs. The first few months after the accident I would constantly ask myself,

- How am I going to take a shower?
- How am I going to put my clothes on now?
- How am I supposed to fix my hair with one hand?
- How am I going to fix meals with one hand?

The first months after the crash, my mother would assist me with all these needs, but I knew I had to find a way to take care of them by myself because I knew I couldn't keep asking for assistance for the rest of my life. I knew I must continue my life in spite of my limitations and had to find a way to take care of myself independently. Being determined to find a way to do things independently, instead of saying to myself, "I am disabled and I can't do this anymore," I would say, "Yes, I can and I will find a way to do this." I gave myself no other option but to find a way.

Now, after so many years, I see one very important detail that helped me to find ways. When I needed to do something with one hand, in my mind I did not ask myself, "Can I do this?" Instead, I asked myself, "How can I do this?" As simple as it seems, this is the key to how I am able do things independently. This is the key to how I managed many of my difficulties and overcame obstacles that made my goals look impossible.

If I had asked, "Can I?" the answer automatically would have been "No," because normally it requires two hands to make a simple meal or get dressed. When I asked myself a different question, "What is the way?" my brain had to find a different answer. It made me seek a way, and I focused on figuring out the solution.

It brings a smile to me when I remember the first time I made breakfast on my own. At the time, I was staying at the prosthetic Rehab Center by myself, because mom had to work. It was not easy of course, and at the same time it was funny when I had to slice the sandwich meat with one hand, slice the bread, apply the butter on the bread, slice tomato or cucumber, and make a sandwich. I laughed at my first attempts to make breakfast. You may think it's simple. What's the big deal about making a sandwich? Yes, it is not a big deal at all when you have two hands to do it. Try to cut all the ingredients and put them all together, and do it with one hand. It took patience and creativity. There were so many times when it seemed very difficult and annoying, and I wanted to just leave everything and simply ask a nurse for help.

But then I would stop and think, "If I get someone to do it, of course, it will be easier and I will have my breakfast faster if someone else does it. But then what? What about tomorrow? By choosing an easier route now, tomorrow I will be where I am today. I will remain dependent on somebody else."

I would calm down, take a deep breath, regain patience, and again looked for ways to solve my challenge. I looked for ways how to make that sandwich until I made it; otherwise I would have gone without having a meal.

My left hand is still paralyzed and I do not have my legs, but today I live on my own across the globe from my family, and independently take care of my needs, take care of the household matters, laundry, shopping, cooking, etc. And it's because of this simple question – facing a challenging situation I ask myself "How?" instead of "Can I?" I developed a personal character trait, that as soon as I face a difficult situation, I automatically ask myself one question, "How can I solve this to get the best outcome?"

It helped me cope with many difficulties and problems that seemed insurmountable at the time. When I first thought of living in California, my first reaction was "It's impossible!" I was thinking in terms of whether it would be realistic. The immediate answer to that question was "No." But then, when the Lord through His word directed me, and said He would be there with me and help me, the question I asked myself was phrased differently—"How can I do this, what is the way?"

When I need to prepare a meal I ask, "How can I make this with one hand?" When I need to vacuum, do laundry or any other household activity, I ask myself the question that makes me focus not on my limitation or how difficult it is, but rather points out my strengths so I can figure out the ways to do anything that needs to get done. When I had challenging goals to achieve at work, I always asked myself what was the way for me to make it happen, I found those solutions and achieved them.

When you ask yourself *if* you will be able to handle your challenges, you already accept the possibility of not being able to handle it, and I think this is the first step toward not finding your solution. While you are considering if you can solve the problem, your thoughts will be directed toward analyzing how bad the situation is and what chances you have to solve it. And if you have more minuses than pluses, the solution will seem almost impossible and you will be inclined to give up, saying that the situation is too difficult, there is nothing you can do to solve it in your favor.

Most often that is exactly how it is going to be if you focus on the problem itself, because anxiety and fear will take over your emotions, and as you know – in this inner state, the black color becomes a dominant one. But if you ask yourself, "How can I solve this problem," your mind will automatically seek potential solutions. The same problem can be addressed two ways, and depending on whether you ask, "Can I cope with this problem?" or, "How can I resolve this situation in the best possible way?" you will choose further action and ultimately your choice will deliver its results.

Trust that none of the problems are stronger than you. With God all things are possible, remember? That means, you can take and cope with any situation you have to face in your life. You just need to receive the strength from the Lord and with His help find a way. And when you have unshakable faith, a positive attitude and will ask yourself the right questions, you will definitely find it.

Every time you get into a situation that makes you feel unhappy, instead of driving yourself crazy with questions like, "Why is it so bad? Why do things like this always seem to happen to me? How long will it last?" ask yourself some simple but very important questions that will shift your mindset into possibility thinking. Ask questions that will identify what you want, the way to get there, and what you need to do to follow through. For example:

- What can you appreciate about this situation? Maybe there is something for you to learn, improve some character traits or open your eyes to something you have not seen? Or, maybe this is the opportunity for you to do something that would bring a radical change in your personal or business life? What would that be?
- Having the situation the way it is, what could change it to make it better?
- Where is the solution to this?
- If you saw this situation as a personal challenge to win the game, what is that challenge?
- Are you willing and determined to win?
- If you saw the ideal outcome from this situation, what would it be?
- What needs to happen for you to have your desired outcome?
- What possible options can you see that would make your situation better/improved/resolved?
- How can you achieve your desired result?
- If you could make the first step toward your desired outcome, what would that step be?
- What can you do today to be closer to your solution?

Our mind is like a computer. Like when computer gives you what you need depending on what command you give, our mind has the answers, and those answers will depend on what kind of questions we ask ourselves. Choose those questions wisely.

7. The Danger of the Fear of Disappointment

It's not unusual, that fear of disappointment stops people from taking action to achieve something they desire. Many do not allow themselves to expect something better because they don't want to get disappointed, hurt or rejected. In order to avoid pain, they don't even try to implement their dreams, convincing themselves that for whatever reason, nothing is going to work out anyway. In order to justify their fears and negative attitude, they call it a "realistic perspective."

In some ways it is very understandable, because most of the time disappointment is very hurtful. For some people, deep disappointment becomes a decisive moment in their lives. Therefore, a person consciously or unconsciously puts himself into the mind frame of disbelief and does not even try to change the circumstances, protecting himself from that pain. I lost count already of how many times I heard, "It is better not to even expect, than to expect something and then get disappointed."

Yes, maybe it is one of the ways to protect ourselves from disappointment, but the question is - is it the right choice? First, when you don't expect a response from the Lord, it is basically the same as if you do not have faith. If you do not expect that your problem can or will be solved, it means that you do not believe that it can be solved. In this way, we are signing a verdict to ourselves, because we receive the answer according to our faith.

> *"According to your faith will it be done to you." (Matthew 9:29)*

Second, by trying to avoid disappointment, we might miss the opportunity given to us. We wish, desire, dream and ask God to answer our prayers, but when the answer comes in the form of an opportunity, out of fear of making a mistake or getting disappointed, we might decide not use that opportunity, and in that way we might reject our answer from the Lord.

It is hard to imagine what would have happened, if out of fear of disappointment, I would have rejected Michael's offer to come to Istanbul to meet him for his evaluation of my prosthetic legs. When he responded to my email, it felt like finally somebody heard my cry for help. Hope and excitement within started breathing again. I felt pure joy and a strong desire to move forward. However, a caution and wish to protect myself from disappointment were nearby. When I was preparing for the trip to Turkey to meet Michael, I remember you telling me I was making a big mistake. You tried to tell me I should "think realistically," because "this specialist lives in a different part of the world and he won't be able to work with you anyway. Traveling to Turkey to meet him would waste the family's money and efforts."

"Well," you said to me. "He will come, look at your prosthetic legs, will give you some suggestions, and then what? Then he will go back to California, and you will stay here with your unfulfilled dreams and your hopes."

I know you talked like that in order to protect me from disappointment. You knew how strongly I desired to walk again. And you saw how heartbroken I was when my long and hard work learning to walk with artificial legs, eventually ended up being a huge disappointment. You thought my desire to walk was not possible, and you did not want me to go through a deep disappointment all over again. And indeed, the fear of disappointment was like my shadow, which whispered to me, "What if really your meeting with Michael will not give you any good results? Your new hope that lit up within you will come crashing down again. Are you sure you're ready to take another hit?"

I knew this was the answer to my prayers, and I was ready to use this opportunity despite outside opinions. Today, when I look at the entire picture, the fact is if I had listened to the fear of disappointment – I would not have met Michael, would not have come to America, and would not have realized my dream to walk again. Furthermore, I would not live in California today and would not have implemented my vision of being able to live an independent and fulfilling life. Can you imagine? One time of choosing to listen to my fears - one time - would have directed my destiny in an entirely different way.

As I am writing this, once again I very well realize that my wish to avoid the pain of disappointment could have easily rejected God's created opportunity. I would have closed the door, which opened up for me to realize my dream to walk and live a full, beautiful life. Avoidance of painful feeling might seem the right thing to do. But it can be such a big mistake, which could be crucial in determining our future.

Don't get me wrong. I am not saying that you should not consider any of the facts before you make a decision. What I am saying is simply this: think about your decision carefully before you say "No" to the opportunity, because it might be what you have been praying for.

8. Your Most Precious Commodity: Time

Have you heard a saying, "Time is Money"? We can spend it wisely or waste it in the same way as money. Having a certain amount of money, before we spend it on something unnecessary, we usually consider if we should really spend it, or, is it better to use it for some other useful thing, don't we?

However, in everyday life we rarely ask ourselves how we can better spend our time. Often, we spend it carelessly without even thinking that it will never come back to us. After spending one hour in a useless way, usually we don't notice that nor do we even pay attention to the time we've squandered. Well, what's the big difference, one hour here, one hour there, it's not that of a big deal, is it? We will have tomorrow, so we still have more time to do whatever we need to do. Tomorrow, however, we again allow ourselves to waste our time daydreaming, sleeping or just for some minor things that do not mean much in our lives in any way. Daily, one or several hours spent carelessly does not seem scary. But we do not even think about those hours adding up on a daily, weekly, monthly or yearly basis.

Here's the simple math: every day, without any exceptions, one hour adds to another hour, and with each passing day the number gets only bigger. Hour after hour, and the number is increasing into days, months and years. Let's say, during the day we spend one hour for some meaningless things. In one week, that single hour adds up almost to a full 8-hour workday. And this is if we spend only one hour carelessly. I think you will agree with me that normally, during the day we spend more than one hour for minor, meaningless things. And what if daily there are two hours spent carelessly? In one week those two hours add up to nearly two full 8-hour workdays. What do you think you could do for your goals in that amount of time? Think how much you would have achieved already, if you had used your time wisely?

Even though the saying somewhat reflects the worth of time, unlike money, time cannot be placed into a savings account. Time is given only for that day and for that day only, and each hour, minute and second or millisecond you have is a gift. With every passing day, the number of your hours is getting less, and unfortunately, they cannot be returned or somehow compensated. Can you imagine how painful it will be, if at an older age you look back into your life and see all that you wanted to achieve and experience in your lifetime, but unfortunately it all remained a wish because instead of using the given time for realizing your dreams or purpose, you wasted it for something that in fact, did not really matter?

Before it's too late, start using your given hours and days and each increment thereof for implementing that which you desire. Use your precious time not for dwelling on the problem or complaining about it.

Use your time to break through that difficulty, and continue running your race toward your solution.

As a conclusion, I want to say look at life as a journey. In your vacation journey, many unexpected circumstances might occur, right? You don't cancel your journey and don't stay in the middle of nowhere complaining about it, do you? You fix the situation, and move on. The athlete overcomes the hurdle and keeps going. It is exactly the same with problems facing you in life. Facing a difficult situation, instead of analyzing how complicated it is, remember the puzzle game that you were challenged by. The ways to improve or cope with them are always there, we just need to find them. The same situation – which is solely a fact – can be taken two ways, and your final result will depend on whether you look at it as a problem, focusing on its difficulty or you look at it as a challenge to yourself, focusing on possible solutions and taking a relentless action to resolve it.

You can change your current circumstances if you are not happy with them. Current circumstances were created by your own choices made earlier. The same way, by making different choices and taking action, you can create different circumstances. Maybe you are dealing with some events you could not control. But remember, your life is in your hands, not in the hands of your circumstances. Your choice of what you are going to do about them from now on will determine your future events, and maybe even your destiny. Do not allow them to be in charge. It's up to you to take charge of them and your life.

Please understand – you are the author of your life story. You can pick up a pen and change your next Chapter. You can change it at any time. Even today. Even this moment can be fateful for you if you make the decision to open a new page and start writing in it what you want. This is your life, your story, and nobody is going to create it for you, except you.

Your loving sister,
Inga

19

Closure. All Things Work Together for Good

Part 1 ~ Closure

1/3/2015

Hi Valdas,

It's been a long time since I wrote you a letter. I was inspired to write again, knowing what you're going through. It's very strange how this can be, but I feel you. I feel your pain. I called mom and asked her about you, and without giving me any details she said that you are going through a rough time. It confirmed the insight I had that I needed to write you and share about my new experience. The turn I recently had released me from pain I lived with for a decade and significantly strengthened my faith in what the word of God says. It surprised me greatly and confirmed once again that all things work together for the good to those who love the Lord and have faith in Him.

Your tough time has been lasting for quite a while. Feeling tired from your heartbreaking experiences and disappointments, you still try to keep on moving forward. But whatever you try to do may seem in vain. On the one hand it may seem like you're opening a door to opportunity, but as you are approaching to open and enter, it shuts right before you. Everything you do, everything you try, seems to be yet another door slammed in your face. It seems like there is no end to this repetition. Probably you are tired. And you are asking, "When is it going to come to an end?"

I know how desperate, cold and lonely it might feel. I have gone through this experience numerous times. There were countless sleepless nights from my ongoing thoughts and concerns about the unknown. There were many moments when gloomy despair looked straight at me whispering, "Your journey is over." Many times it seemed like here I see a slightly opened door to fulfill my aim, but when I approached the door to open it and enter, like you have experienced, it would shut right in front of me. There were so many times when suddenly changed circumstances pulled the ground from under my feet, pulled out of my hands everything I had and broke it into thousands of pieces. There were people in my life, who came and left, leaving me wounded and in pain. There were times when I felt I couldn't take it anymore, because it seemed it was beyond what I could handle.

Many times, I stood before my Lord in tears asking Him, "Why, Lord, why did this have to happen?" But then I would remember why I started my journey in the first place and why I needed to keep on going. And then, fully realizing that I will be the only reason for not reaching my destination if I give in to my feelings and give up, I made an arduous effort to take at least the smallest step. I kept on taking step after step. And I kept on going despite the length of my desert and the storms I had to endure. I kept on going until I reached my destination.

You know what was interesting? With time I started seeing that these events and experiences, which seemed hardly endurable, molded me, shaped my values, and strengthened me and made me who I am today. Even though it was not easy to get through them, they left a valuable imprint on my life. What's more interesting, as I have mentioned in my previous letters, the strangest thing was to realize that particularly those events that seemed destructive or seemed like endless hardships, actually brought me to my ultimate dream.

I have made a lot of mistakes, and some of them ultimately had severe consequences. But you know, the funny thing is that even those mistakes had a great value in my life. In fact, I needed to make those mistakes, because they made changes deep within me and taught me some very valuable lessons which I would not have gained otherwise. Realizing that the difficulty worked for my good surprised me each and every time.

The first time I realized this phenomenon was four years after the accident. I was sitting outside, wearing my prostheses, enjoying the gorgeous Californian weather. I was pondering my life, deeply in awe how it was changing in the most incredible way. I felt sheer joy and gratitude for what I had attained, expecting even greater, more beautiful changes in the near future. As I was thinking about certain events and how they contributed to my current circumstances, suddenly I realized something I had never seen before.

"Wait a minute," I thought to myself. "I would not have had all this if I received my answer to walk again when I wanted and how I wanted."

It was my pain combined with deep disappointment that started me looking for help. Not receiving the help I had expected from local resources, I started looking for help worldwide on the Internet. So, it comes down to the fact I would not have searched and would not have met Michael if I had not felt that unbearable pain and despair. Furthermore, I would not be in California today if I had received my answer when I wanted and the way I thought it should be. During those two years I was praying to my God asking, "Lord, I so deeply trust You. Why am I not seeing Your help? Where are You? Why don't You answer my prayers?"

It seemed to me that God did not hear my prayers and was not providing any answers. But now I see that He did hear me and He was delivering me His help. It's just that His help was coming to me in a different way and on a different timeline than I wanted. The Lord had a much more beautiful plan for my life, and He was fulfilling it. It was the plan that I could not even imagine in my wildest dreams! So, it turns out that this pain and disappointment actually worked for the better.

That was the first time I saw the beneficial value in experiencing difficult circumstances, pain and despair. It was quite unusual and not easy to admit that. However, I was thankful for it all, because I realized that the pain and despair were what motivated me to make a radical change by going on the Internet to look for help internationally. For the first time I felt sincerely grateful for those two long dark years of hard work and countless hours of strenuous training, learning to walk wearing prostheses that left me with bruises, cuts, sores and swollen thighs. I was feeling sincerely thankful that my desire to walk was not fulfilled in the way I thought it should be, because what I have now is so much better than what I could have had, if I had received my answer when I wanted.

And the best part of it – my aim to have comfortable prostheses brought me to sunny California, where I could continue my journey and fulfill my ultimate dream of restoring my independent, fulfilling life. At that time, I returned to see how I could establish my life in the United States. Even though there were a lot of unknowns, I knew I would live in California and make it my new home.

Observing it all, it looked like this pain, hard work and deep disappointment had to take place in my life, because it motivated me to take action, which brought me to fulfilling my desire to walk and it opened the doors to fulfill my ultimate dream.

That was the first time I paid attention to what was written in the Scriptures:

> *"And we know that all things work together for good to those who love God, to those who are the called according to His purpose." (Romans 8:28)*

I again experienced exactly what the Bible says. Since that time, I started observing what was behind events and circumstances and where they ultimately brought me. Time and time again, I saw events that occurred and people I met, the experiences I went through all played a pivotal role in my life, and to my surprise all of it really worked for the good.

Another example of everything working together for the good was my move out of the Flamingo Hotel into a home with my roommate, Bruce. When I got to rent my first home, I was wondering why everything was going the way it did. I stayed at one of the best hotels in the city while I was visiting, and from there I moved into a house with a nice man, but he had one habit that irritated me quite a bit. You know me well, and you know that I personally like to have my home clean with no unnecessary things around, so I throw things away or donate them if I don't use them or no longer have a need for them. He, however, was exactly the opposite – he would bring home a variety of things, whether he needed them or not. So, in addition to the fact that the house was totally cluttered, it was difficult for me to get around in a wheelchair. To say that the house was cluttered like a garage would be an understatement. So many times, in my prayers I was asking God why He arranged my living situation like this, and why this particular person ended up as my roommate. But, no matter how much I prayed about it, nothing changed, and I had no answers to my questions. So, I just decided to trust my Lord, that everything was in His hands and somehow this was supposed to work for the good. Not long after, I saw the reason why.

When my initial plan to stay in the states was abruptly terminated, Bruce was the one who was there with me day and night talking with me and consoling me, which I desperately needed. Along with Kathryn and Vanessa, Bruce carried me through my darkest time. Furthermore, during that time Bruce invited me to volunteer at the organization where he worked, so I could get my mind off my drama by helping others who were disabled, and that helped a lot. Later I saw even more why it was for my good – that organization ended up hiring me – where I still work.

Finally, it was Bruce who said the words, "You are one of them, you are unstoppable. You can't give up, Inga you must go on."

These words made that one-of-a-kind impact in my life, which held me together when I felt I couldn't go on anymore. And later, Bruce became like my big brother-friend. I was so thankful that the Lord arranged my living situation the way He did. God saw a much bigger picture, and I could see only what was in front of me at the moment.

Another example is my work place. When I was hired as a Program Assistant to help one of the staff members with organizing different documents and handling various office duties, on the one hand I was very thankful for it, because due to my physical challenges I could perform only particular kinds of tasks, and did I have an American higher education. Besides, I did not know American English well and I had to speak, write and understand everything using my third language. Looking from a bigger perspective, I was thankful for it.

But, admittedly I was so devastated that plans to work with Michael on the organization were terminated that I did not want to work for any other company. I didn't like the office environment and I did not want to be there. In addition, very quickly I started getting bored.

I knew I could do much more than organizing files. Racing thoughts of why everything worked out in such a way that I was placed to do this kind of job in this organization when I was supposed to do way bigger and more responsible and more interesting work, periodically would create a raging storm within me. The more I thought about it, the more my dissatisfaction grew. But, it seemed like there was a dead silence from the Lord despite my continuous prayers and questions; I had no other opportunities and nothing was changing. It felt like I was locked in those circumstances. I again said to myself that everything was under God's control and if this is where I was, and nothing was changing despite my prayers and my efforts, that meant for some reason I needed to be here.

When my dissatisfaction was like a roaring storm inside of me, I would calm myself with my faith saying that my life was in God's control and He knew what was better for me, where I needed to be and how I needed to start my life in this country. My trust in the Lord was the rock-solid foundation I was standing on. My hope that better yet was ahead, created the endurance within me to go through those circumstances.

I set standards for myself to do my job duties 101%, no matter the task I was asked to do. I was committed to learn everything I needed to know to do my job well and always went that extra mile. Before long, I received my first promotion, and then soon I received another promotion to the position I hold today, which I truly enjoy.

Even though this organization and a job were not what I wanted, with time it turned out to be exactly the opposite. With time, many things have changed in the company, once the new Executive Director stepped in, the organization totally changed, and today it's nothing like it was when I first came seeking help. I do enjoy working there, and I love my co-workers and the environment there.

While many people usually complain about their boss, I have to say that our Executive Director is the best anyone could ask for. The understanding administration and flexibility for my schedule is like nowhere else. I truly can say that this is a great workplace for me.

And during the economic crash in the U.S. that started in 2008, when businesses were going bankrupt, people started losing jobs, losing their homes and various assets, and many non-profit organizations were closing their operations – our company was thriving. I had a stable and secure job and we even had pay raises. It seemed like a harsh economic hurricane was sweeping everything around me, but the trouble did not even touch me.

I again saw something that still remains a mystery to me – circumstances that seemed to me to be not good turned out to be for my benefit. You know the funniest thing? I ended up having the position that is similar to the one that Michael had created for me in the organization that he had established.

These are a few situations I encountered when I did not like my circumstances, but after some time, I sincerely thanked God for them, because I realized they worked together for the good. In fact, thanks to them I have fulfilled the achievement of my dreams.

And now, I want to tell you about one of those experiences. It came into my life recently and surprised me greatly. Maybe what I am going to share with you will give you hope and endurance to keep moving on through whatever desert you are walking through right now, knowing that there comes a day when you will understand that even this long difficult time was for your good.

An Unexpected Turn of Events

Recently, I received closure to the story that nearly broke me. This time, after ten long years, I saw that the event which seemed desperately destructive and painful beyond what I could even describe, really worked for the better.

For ten years I waited for the closure of that story, and what a shocking surprise it was to see that it was actually a blessing and God's grace, not a loss. I will never forget that amazing moment when I understood it. It felt like I breathed in a new life the moment I realized the truth that was behind this devastation. It released me from the gut-wrenching regret and grief that I lived with for over a decade.

As you know, the car accident did not break me down, but such an unexpected and dramatic break-up with Michael nearly did. In addition to the betrayal, it was a total destruction of my first attempt to establish myself in the United States.

All these years I considered this event to be the second crash in my life. It altered my destiny. Even though by God's grace my life took an amazing turn and I did have many victorious and beautiful experiences in spite of it all, I continued in silent agony of the heartbreaking loss, abandonment and deep regret. I lived with the awareness that I could have continued in a totally different, graceful, exciting and fulfilling way, if not for that hurtful separation with Michael and his decision to terminate my involvement in the non-profit organization that he had established.

My deep regret was like an unseen, quiet torture for my soul. It was an enormous pain to wake up every morning, knowing that I betrayed Michael's wife, who joyfully accepted me and sincerely trusted me. It was nearly unendurable to continue my life after being betrayed by the person who convinced me of his love and unconditional faithfulness and then, in a cold-blooded way abandoned me when I became a threat to his well-being. You could call it a double betrayal, in that we betrayed Michael's wife, and he cold-heartedly betrayed me. For a long time I did not know how I was going to live further because I simply did not see my life without Michael.

Ten years have passed since then, and it seems like I should have let that go long ago and moved on, right? Yes, I moved on, but that was not because I was free from the pain or because I was able to forget, but because I could not allow myself to give up on my life because of another person's treachery toward me. My life was way too precious for me to allow anybody or anything to stop me from making it blossom again.

I moved on because I realized that it was not his choice to forsake me and it's not his choice to call off my life-changing opportunity what will prevent me from attaining my aspiration. But it is my choice to give up after his betrayal. I took responsibility for my life, and vowed that I would attain my vision anyway. Yes, the pain seemed beyond what I could take. To be forthcoming, Michael and this story were part of my awareness day and night for a long time. Often it seemed I could no longer live with it, but there was nothing I could do to hide from it. Every day seemed unendurable. The anguish of abandonment was engraved in my soul so deeply that I still feel it, even after ten years.

I simply could not see my life without him. My previous intentions did not make sense to me anymore and I did not want to do anything that I used to be excited about. Even my ultimate dream of having an independent life again no longer was desirable without him. But I knew that "my want" or "don't want" was simply the emotion, affected by these events. I could not allow my emotions to determine my decision whether I get up and continue my fight for life or align with my feelings and give up.

I was very much aware that giving up would lead me into even deeper misery. The only way for me to get out of that pit was to be resilient and become relentless again. I already have learned from my own experience that we can achieve what we resolve to reach, if we relentlessly work toward the goal and never give up. This time, the price nearly reached my limit of what I could take. But I had to be resilient if I was serious about my decision to recover my life.

Like in the beginning of my journey, I understood that by giving up and allowing some event or person to overpower me, I would sentence myself to a life of misery. Through tears and the anguish of abandonment, loneliness and disappointment, I decided to keep going. Since I was depleted of strength, I got down on the knees of my heart, asking the living God to grant me endurance to break through that dark time and give me the desire to live.

The Lord my God heard my cry and He gave me strength to make a step, then another one, and another one, and He lifted me up and then He re-lit my enthusiasm for life once again. He created new opportunities for me, I met new wonderful people who became my friends, began achieving my goals and, my new life which I had dreamed about, was finally established. While I made my steps building my life all over again for the second time, I held that secret within me.

For ten years I could not forgive myself for the mistakes I'd made. I couldn't understand how I could possibly allow myself to justify my choices the way I did and take part in such a despicable act. I could not forgive myself for betraying his wife nor could I forgive Michael for how he betrayed me. Even though I successfully implemented my vision despite what had happened, this story was like a gray shadow, constantly reminding me of my mistake and whispering that I was worthless, and that I should be ashamed of myself. However, nobody knew about it. Since Michael suddenly disappeared as if he never existed, I had to push everything deep within and live as if he'd never existed. I deleted Michael from my awareness and all memories of that time were erased as though they never happened and I forbade myself to even remember anything that related to them. I did whatever I could to delete him and this story from my conscious memory, so I would be able to move on with my life. I did not talk about him or this story when I was sharing my life with someone; it was a secret when it began and it remained a secret after it was over. He was mentioned only when people would ask me how I ended up in the United States or in my speeches at churches when the Lord began opening up the opportunities to share my testimony. I moved on, but I always carried that question I wanted to ask Michael, "How could you possibly do it?"

The pain never left as well. Time after time I was wondering if he would ever try to find me, or at least try to talk to me to explain what had happened and bring it all to closure. Michael never approached me again. But the Lord did.

There came a day when this story finally got closure. In addition to receiving the best closure I could have received, I realized this event was not just God's discipline to me, but it was actually His grace, because it pulled me out of a situation that would have made my life unbearably miserable. After all, this story played a significant role in my life, which I am very thankful for. It's hard to believe, isn't it? And I imagine you are curious how I can possibly be thankful, after all.

As you know, the Lord gave me another chance by creating a new opportunity for me, and after four months I returned to the United States. The Lord once again pulled me out of a desperate situation which seemed to be absolutely not resolvable. Having received another chance to establish myself in California, I knew this was God's grace. I treasured it and no way was I going to jeopardize it again. Now, after being strongly disciplined by the Lord for disobeying His word, I was carefully considering my decisions and did not take His commandments negligently.

After seeing how my own choices can impact my destiny, I considered the choices I made far more seriously. My mistake with Michael I took as a lesson of what to be aware of and what not to do. I started looking at it as one of the many experiences through which I learn. Changing the perspective about my experience empowered me tremendously. Feeling much stronger, I made a deliberate, arduous effort to push away my past experience and directed my focus on that which I desired to create. I set new goals for myself, directed my focus and efforts on achieving them, and in few years I met with success. Since then, my life was completely transformed.

I have neither seen Michael nor talked to him since the last time we spoke in 2004. Not even once. He never contacted me nor have we met. Sometimes I would ask myself if he ever wondered how I was doing, in which country I ended up living, and whether I was alright. Sometimes I would ask myself, "How can this be that we live in the same area, but don't meet, even by accident?" Then again, trusting that everything is in God's power, who could easily create circumstances for us to meet if that was His will, I would let it go. Memories of him could not be separated from the anguish of losing him, so I did everything I could possibly do to keep my mind away from it all.

I always hoped there would come a day when I finally got the closure to this story. I hoped that one day he would find me to at least explain what had happened and say, "Please forgive me." If truth be told, even though I made the effort to not think about Michael and this experience, I always wanted these things to happen: I always wanted to tell Michael's wife, Margaret, how deeply sorry I was for how I betrayed her. I absolutely hated what I did and wanted to ask her to forgive me for the pain that I caused her. In my opinion, what I have done is one of the most disgusting things one woman can do to another. Second, I always wanted him to look into my eyes and talk to me. I wanted to know how and why he could possibly do what he did. My long-awaited wish was granted when I least expected it to happen.

After seeing our mom off, back to Lithuania from her vacation in California visiting me, and after feeling rested and happy having had the opportunity to spend time with her, I was excited to dive back into my activities. I put all my focus back on my work and it felt great being back at work again.

One day, as I was busy taking care of a variety of tasks, I noticed the red indicator on my cell phone that I had a notification from my professional social network. I noted it and dismissed it, because I had other, more important things to do and kept putting it off to whenever I had a free moment. One day, I finally opened it to see what it was. The notification was to show me who was checking my profile.

It seemed like the whole world stopped when I saw who that person was. I stared at the picture of a person who was like a stranger and yet, who was so dear to my soul. The last time I saw those once warm eyes was the last day of July in 2004. In July of 2014, almost exactly a decade since I saw Michael the last time, in the notification I saw that he had checked my profile three times.

To my surprise, I did not feel anything except shock. I had pushed him and this story so deep within my psyche that I had to make a deliberate effort to return back to that time and remember what he meant to me.

After returning to that time, my shock started turning into pain and anger. His choice to abruptly end our relationship and everything we were in the process of creating together, left me totally broken and deeply wounded. My soul was carved with scars from his decision. Now, anger was all that was left.

By the grace of God, I was able to pick myself up and successfully continue on my life journey. Over the years I was able to push that story far away from my awareness and I did not have any particular thoughts or feelings about him or the experience. However, seeing his picture and knowing that he was checking my profile was enough for memories to come up. Along with memories, the pain re-surfaced as well. When I shared my news with a few of my closest friends, they both had the same question: "How do you feel about it?"

I told them the truth as I am telling you: I wasn't sure. The pain and anger were still so strong and inextricably entwined that I didn't even know what I would say to him if given the chance. I wasn't sure if I wanted to talk to him at all.

After analyzing this unexpected turn, I decided to leave it at that and let it go. There is no way I would initiate conversation with him, after all. If he really wanted to talk to me, he knew how to connect with me, but I was not going to make the first move. I was able to push all of this away and be okay, and I did not want to go back to that nightmare and go through those feelings again. It took me an enormous effort to recover after that and maintain myself in a good inner state, and I was not going to jeopardize all that I had accomplished. I did not see any point to think about him or that story. He made his choice, it's over, and I was not going back.

I just had this one question – what for? All these years he never appeared in my life, and now, ten years later he decided to do what he did. Why? Why did the Lord God allow him to appear in my horizon once again?

Several days later, a friend called and invited me to join her in a workshop organized by some Christian Ministries. I have been to their workshops before and they have always made a great, positive impact in my life. The opportunity to go was quite unexpected, but I told her I would think about it and let her know. I've always wanted to participate in that particular workshop and I was open to the idea of going, but there were several obstacles that were in the way. I was not sure how all of this would work out. I brought this before the Lord in my prayer, asking Him to show me whether I needed to go there. I asked Him to give me solutions to those obstacles if I needed to go, or leave things the way they were if this was not something I needed to do at the time. To my big surprise – and I would say to my astonishment – I started seeing how those obstacles, which prevented me from going to the workshop, started resolving themselves one after another. It seemed like some invisible hand moved all the obstacles out of my way.

At some point I realized that the only obstacle left was actually me – all that was needed was for me to make the final decision to go. Seeing how all the obstacles were no longer there, I took it as a sign for me to go to this workshop. I called my friend and told her that I would love to join her on this trip. Now, I had the second question lined up – Why do I need to go there? What's out there waiting for me? Little did I know what was ahead for me.

In the evening, after the workshop, a fellow named Joe, whom I'd met once before, came up to me and we started talking and sharing our experiences. Suddenly, he looked at me with this profound look and said, "The Lord just now showed me a vision of you walking up the stairs toward the light. There is darkness all around you and you are only two steps away from completing that path and reaching the top, where is a bright light. You are only few steps away, Inga. You are getting close. Also, it was revealed to me that there is someone whom you have not forgiven."

"Have not forgiven?" I looked at him, feeling caught off guard and bewildered.

"Yes, you have not forgiven someone," he continued. "It's a man."

"A man?"

"Yes, man," Joe replied. "You need to forgive him, because your lack of forgiveness prevents you from moving forward."

At the core of my being I was wondering if that man was the one about whom I told my girlfriends a few days earlier, sharing with them that I was not sure if I wanted to talk to him after all he had done.

"I don't know what this person did, but whatever he did was much more painful to you than the car accident," in a moment Joe added.

Joe's last words struck me like a lightning bolt. It seemed like I froze at the core of my being. I just couldn't believe what I heard! Now I knew. I knew exactly who that man was. Three years ago, when I was writing a chapter for my book about my first unsuccessful attempt to establish myself in the United States, Joe's last words were exactly how I described the impact that Michael's choice to abruptly cut me off had on me. Being suddenly abandoned by the love of my life and watching how at the same time my new life was shattering right in front of me was far more painful than the time when I realized that I no longer had my legs.

"Okay, okay. Yes, now I understand everything. I know who that is, thank you, Joe," I quietly responded after being totally astounded, trying to grasp what was going on in my life.

Joe looked at me with a question in his eyes. He saw my reaction, but he did not have any idea what this kind of revelation was about or what it meant to me.

But it was all very clear to me. The Lord had spoken to me through a stranger in such a way that I would immediately understand and have no questions or doubts about it. None of the people around me knew what this was all about, and especially Joe, whom I met for the second time in my life. But the spirit of the Lord knows everything about our lives, including our hearts and our minds. My Lord spoke to me using details which only I knew and this particular detail pertained to only one person in my life.

That moment I understood everything, I received my answers to the questions I'd asked the Lord. First, the reason the Lord allowed Michael to show up in my horizon was for me to see that I still had that pain and anger. I was only not aware of it, because I numbed it, did not think of him on a daily basis and thus, I could not feel anything about him. Second, the reason I had to come to this workshop was so that the Lord could speak to me directly through His vessel, because otherwise I would continue to live in denial as long as I refused to bring this subject back into my life.

It seemed like someone arranged events and circumstances so precisely that it was impossible to run away from them. No longer could I deny that I had not forgiven Michael. I was at the point in my life when I needed to forgive him, because this was a big obstacle for me to move forward. I had only few steps left until the fulfillment of whatever the Lord had planned for my life. But before I reached it, I had to forgive Michael.

All these years I lived with this numbed agony in my heart. I was so afraid to feel it again, and I protected myself by pushing away my thoughts of Michael. I thought I had let it go. Now, I faced the truth – I have not really forgiven and did not let it go. I had it all within me, numbed as a stone. I needed to forgive. I had to let him go and free myself from the silent torment, and from the numbness, so I could become a whole person once again.

That workshop had classes where I was able to work through my feelings. I cried as I had not cried in a very long time. I cried for the heartbreaking abandonment, the anguish of losing him and my new life, the guilt of my betrayal to his wife and the ultimate shock of being betrayed by him. I felt again an emptiness, cold loneliness, fear of the future, complete despair. Everything came back. I felt it all over again as though I'd been placed in a time machine and taken back ten years into the eye of that nightmare.

I brought it all to the cross, asking my Lord to take it away, because no longer could I live silently carrying all of that. Finally, I was able to let go of the anger and a big portion of the pain, which had been numbed deep within me all these years. A lot of heaviness was taken away from me. By the end of the workshop, I felt much lighter and at peace.

The last night of the workshop, something interesting happened. As I was lying in bed, preparing for the night sleep, I was thinking about Michael and my latest events related to him. Deep inside I still felt the pain. It was not completely gone. I still had the question, "How could you possibly do this?" I could not find the strength in me to let it go. It felt like the anguish was engraved in my soul, it had become a part of me.

As I was remembering the separation and the experiences I had to go through because of what I perceived as nothing less than his act of treachery, I asked the Lord to help me forgive him. Suddenly, it was unexplainable and at the same time so real – I began feeling how compassion was filling my heart.

Instead of a combination of anger and pain, I started feeling compassion for Michael. Since the day of his last phone call, I have never felt that feeling toward him and I knew this was not my feeling. It seemed like someone had performed an invisible "feeling transfusion," just like the blood transfusions in the hospitals. This was a transfusion of raw emotion. I could neither explain it, nor could I deny it – I felt that genuine compassion towards Michael was replacing my previous feelings.

It was quite unusual for me to feel this way toward Michael. I was so astonished and surprised by what had happened that all my tiredness was gone. I have not felt that kind of lightness in a long time. I felt so incredibly good and at peace that none of my questions to Michael or feelings that "it's not fair" were worth rejecting this incredible heavenly transformation of how I felt. Gratitude and sheer joy filled my heart. I knew that was the answer to my supplication to the Lord to help me forgive. Soon my earlier feelings were replaced by peace and compassion and gratitude to my Lord. It felt so good that I even tried to stay awake for as long as I could to delight in that feeling.

The next morning, I woke up feeling like a different person. It was even hard to believe that the way I felt was really true. I returned home from the workshop feeling joyful, uplifted and free from invisible shackles of pain and anger. Now I was even more ready to get to work and continue moving forward working on the book.

Little did I know, though, that I was living my new life chapter, yet to be written in the book. And this workshop was only the beginning.

Will You Overstep Your Pride to Receive Freedom?

In a few days, my friend Diana called me to hear about my trip to the workshop. After I finished sharing with her how I'd finally received freedom from anger, my friend asked me how I felt now when I thought of Michael. I did not even know how to answer her question, because I no longer felt that anger. The anger, which became a normal feeling when I thought of Michael, had completely dissipated and I didn't even know how to define what I felt now. Diana listened to what I had to say, and asked me another question, "Imagine, you are on stage in front of a large audience, and suddenly you see him coming in. How would you feel?"

Being joyful for my new experience, I was about to announce out loud, "I would continue speaking with no problem."

But something stopped me. I knew I had to really think about it before giving a rush answer. I held myself from responding and imagined myself speaking to the audience, and suddenly saw Michael coming in. I looked at him and, my room started becoming blurry.

Barely holding back tears and trying to quench pain in my throat, I had to admit that the quick answer that I was about to shoot out of my mouth like a bullet, was not how I truly felt. After a moment I said, "You know my friend, the truth is, I think I'd burst into tears. I don't think I would be able to continue speaking."

I had to admit that my journey of being released from this pain was not over yet. I realized there were many layers of pain that were still part of me, deeply etched in my soul. There was something else that yet had to be done for me to be fully free from the pain. I needed to deal with it personally so I could give a different kind of response to her question.

Diana said now she understood why she felt the urge to call me and ask how I was doing after the workshop. She shared with me what she had learned about the process of forgiving according to the Scriptures and how critical it was for us to forgive others and to ask for forgiveness. As she was speaking, a clear memory of a verse in the Bible came to me.

> *"Therefore if you bring your gift to the altar, and there remember that your brother has something against you, leave your gift there before the altar, and go your way. First be reconciled to your brother, and then come and offer your gift." (Matthew 5: 23-24)*

That moment I realized that I could not start my ministry yet. There was something else I needed to do before I published my book and started sharing my message with the world. It seemed like the whole world was diminished by a clear, consuming awareness that I needed to contact Michael and finish that story according to the Scriptures.

I could hardly even hear what Diana was saying; I could not even pay attention to my own feelings as this thought of what I needed to do completely overshadowed everything else. All I could comprehend was that

I needed to contact Michael and Margaret and reconcile with them before I did anything else.

After our conversation, I sat there for a moment feeling completely stunned by new awareness, which I never would even have thought of. But it was so strong and clear that I could not dismiss it, pretending like it didn't happen. Reconciliation was the next step I had to take.

Reaching out to Michael to reconcile was something that I could not even think of doing. There was no way I was going to make a first step to connect with him, and what's even more – to reconcile our relationship. He was the one who cut it off and deeply hurt me, so why is it me who needs to reach out and try to reconcile? I felt so bewildered that I immediately brought this before my Lord to "discuss this." In my prayer, I tried to dispute with God, by bringing my arguments and questions of why I needed to do this and what I was supposed to say to him.

As I was arguing with God, suddenly a memory came to my mind how Michael was telling me how the communication with Margaret had been getting hard and tense at his house because he was spending so much time with me. He wanted to slow down with our romance by reducing our relationship to a friendly and business-like manner, but seeing that our efforts were in vain and we continued living the lie, I began insisting that he needed to reveal the truth to his wife. I had to ask Michael to forgive me for that.

Another memory came to me how I kept saying to Michael that observing how we met, how deeply we got connected and fell in love, and where everything was going in our relationship, probably it was God's will for us to be together as a couple. What we did was adultery pure and simple, and in the Holy Scriptures the Lord God states that adultery is a sin in the eyes of the Lord and therefore cannot be His will. Here I had another awareness that I needed to tell him that I was wrong making those kinds of statements about the Lord God. And then immediately after, another feeling came to me – I needed to ask his wife to forgive me.

This awareness was crystal clear. I knew exactly what I needed to do next and even what to say. As much as I wanted to dispute this, I couldn't. Deep inside I knew this was all true and I was wrong in these matters. I was aware that now was the time for me to contact both Michael and his wife and finish that story according to the Scriptures.

This insight that I received in my conversation with my friend and in the prayer, struck me to the core of my heart. I knew that the latest events, immediately followed by this kind of insight, were not a coincidence. I was well aware what I needed to do. Yet, I did not want to write Michael. I did not want to initiate any conversation with the person who cut me out of his life. I decided to wait and think about it more.

The next several days the latest events were constantly on my mind. Mixed feelings were like roaring waves overshadowing one another. On the one hand, it was hard for me to even consider initiating contact with Michael. In my understanding, he was the one who ought to make the first step toward our reconciliation, by apologizing or at least explaining how he could possibly do what he did. My self-respect as a woman would never allow me to initiate contact with any man, who did something so despicable. On the other hand, observing what was happening behind these coincidences, I absolutely knew this was not happenstance. I knew that a divine power was arranging events and circumstances for me to put closure on the experience that had such a significant impact on my life.

Even though for many years I did not remember this story and I thought it was all behind me, now I faced the truth that it was deep within me, quietly tormenting me. I simply got used to it so much that I no longer noticed it. Now, when everything was brought back to the surface, I realized how much damage it had done over the years. This shadow of the past exhausted me. Pain and anger kept me imprisoned for so many years. I felt so tired of it and I so wished I could break free from it all. I was longing for that indescribable feeling of lightness and pure conscience.

As unthinkable and out of character as it seemed for me to contact Michael and Margaret, the more I thought about it, the more I understood why it was important for me to do exactly that. After considering all my options, I could not see myself publishing my book and standing before people sharing the message, knowing that there was someone whom I immensely hurt and who might be hurting up to this day because of my actions, and I did not even have the courage to ask for forgiveness.

Michael and I both were equally responsible for our act, but I wanted to accept responsibility for my personal mistakes and wrongdoing, and ask for forgiveness for that. The verses in the Bible were not leaving my awareness.

> *"Therefore if you bring your gift to the altar, and there remember that your brother has something against you, leave your gift there before the altar, and go your way. First be reconciled to your brother, and then come and offer your*

> *gift. Agree with your adversary quickly, while you are on the way with him, lest your adversary deliver you to the judge, the judge hand you over to the officer, and you be thrown into prison. Assuredly, I say to you, you will by no means get out of there till you have paid the last penny." (Matthew 5: 23-26)*

I had to make a choice either to do what was right or neglect these 'coincidences' and move on. It was so difficult to do what I knew was the right thing to do; in fact, I don't think I have ever faced such a challenge. Yet, I could not fight my awareness of the truth. I could do whatever I wanted, reasoning and justifying why I did not do what was right. But when at the end of our lives we stand before the living God, each of us will have to answer for every idle word and for our deeds.

> *"But I say to you that for every idle word men may speak, they will give account of it in the day of judgment. For by your words you will be justified, and by your words you will be condemned." (Matthew 12: 36-37)*

I don't think we will be able to blame anybody or circumstances or justify it. I believe deep in our hearts we all have a crystal-clear awareness of what is the right thing to do in any circumstance. It's just that we often choose what is less painful and what's easier, or what gives us more pleasure. And then we justify it so we are comfortable with it.

We can lie and justify it to ourselves or others, but we won't be able to lie to God by justifying our choices, because we will be aware that He knows we fully understand the truth. And so now, when I looked in the eyes of the truth, I knew that I needed to ask for forgiveness regardless of how difficult and painful it was for me.

In addition, I always wanted to tell Margaret how deeply sorry I was for what I did and ask her to forgive me. Many years have passed, but this burden of guilt was still carried in my awareness and my heart. I absolutely do not tolerate hypocritical people and I did not want to be one. I needed to push my pride aside and do what was right, to do what the Lord directed me to do according to the Scriptures. Watching how circumstances were pointing me that direction, I decided to do whatever it takes to go along with what Lord was doing in my life and reach the light that was ahead of me.

Breaking the Wall of Silence

One summer morning, I woke up early, fully aware that this was the day when I was going to reach out to Michael and Margaret. For some reason I knew I couldn't wait longer; I had to do it without hesitating or wasting time. In my morning prayer, I said to my Heavenly Father that I would obey Him. I was not planning to reach out to Michael, but I will do it because He says so. After doing some research online, I could not find Margaret's email, but I found Michael's. That meant that I'd need to ask him to pass on the letter to her.

I started writing to Margaret. I knew this was the moment when I could express my deep regret, which I had been carrying within for so long. I don't remember how many hours it took me to write. I cried with almost every word I wrote. The month of August 2004 was filled with continuous tears and many sleepless nights, and it was right in front of me, as if it all had happened yesterday. I knew why I allowed my connection with Michael to develop into a relationship and why my love for him became stronger than anything I valued and yet, I kept asking myself how I could possibly do something so despicable.

The pain of me betraying her was so much stronger than the pain of being betrayed by him. I did not write any explanation or justification nor did I try to blame anyone. It didn't matter what explanations or excuses I had, since none of them would have really made any difference. Besides, this was not even important. The fact was that I hurt her and I wanted to apologize for it. In my letter, I shared my feelings for what I had done to her and asked her to forgive me.

After completing my letter, I continued writing. But this letter was to Michael. In my letter to him, I shared with him the life-long lesson this experience had taught me about severe consequences of justifying wrong choices. Also, I acknowledged my mistakes and asked him to forgive me for them. Even though I still had the pain from how he treated me, my apology and acknowledgment were sincere. In the same way as in my letter to his wife, I did not blame anyone nor did I try to rationalize what was right and what was wrong. My letters to him and his wife had a very clear and definite purpose, and assessing blame or starting a heated discussion were not my intent.

I worked on those letters non-stop and I read them over and over again to make sure every word was exactly what I wanted to say. Ten years had passed since we last talked, so I naturally wondered how they would accept my re-appearance in their lives.

I had questions; plenty of them. How was Margaret going to react? Am I going to remind her of what she wants to forget and be left alone? Will he be glad to hear from me or he will dismiss it? What was he going to do when he sees my letter? How shocking and unexpected might this letter be in both their lives?

Numerous thoughts were racing through my mind as I looked through the window. It was dark outside. I realized that I did not even notice how the day had passed by. I did not eat anything in all day. I was tired. After re-living everything all over again, I felt emotionally drained and vulnerable once again. Remembering a popular saying that we used to say back in my home country, "Morning is always wiser than the night," I decided to save my letters, and in the morning, I would take another look at them with a fresh mind, and then send them.

After spending hours in poring over every word, I went to sleep feeling as though I was in the midst of some emotional storm, but at the same time in my spirit I felt peace and some relief. For the first time I had hope that this nightmare would finally come to the end.

"You Have Received an Email"

On the next day I woke up feeling refreshed and even more determined and at peace to complete my task. I made my cup of coffee, and immediately opened the final drafts of my letters. With both mind and emotions refreshed, I improved both and now they were ready to be sent. I saved my letter to Margaret into a Pdf file and attached it. I didn't want one word of my apology to Margaret to be changed. My palms were sweating. What I was about to do pushed my limits of what I thought I could possibly do. It would be so much easier to leave it alone and forget about it, than go through all of this.

With my trembling heart, in my prayer I asked the Lord that these letters would fulfill their purpose and clicked the send button. On August

11, 2015, almost exactly to the day ten years after I'd spoken with them the last time, I emailed Michael and his wife my conversation from the heart. It felt like a heavy stone rolled off my heart when I saw the notification, "Your message has been sent." My big, fearful task was accomplished. I did what I had to do. Soon I felt an easiness and even joy, which was quite strange. I felt joy that I was able to push aside my pride and showed my obedience to the Lord.

The remainder of the day I checked my inbox a bit more often to see whether I had received any response. Nothing. But I still felt joyful knowing I had done the right thing. You can only imagine my surprise the next morning to see Michael's name in my list of received emails. I received his response. I did not know whether he would respond at all. Michael's message was as kind and warm just as his letters always used to be. It sounded like my letter had made an impact on him. He said he read my message several times, and had been thinking about it since he got it. He said he wanted to take time to reply in a way that respects my letter, and as I requested he had forwarded my message to Margaret.

Brother, something incredible happened after I read his message: It felt like the invisible shackles were broken and I was let out of a prison. I have never experienced this before. It was invisible and not tangible in the physical world and yet, it felt like it literally happened – my chains were broken and I was let out into freedom.

I felt an indescribable easiness in my chest. Brother, believe it or not - it was literally easier for me to breathe! I cannot find any other way to describe what it felt like but to say, I was let out of the prison after ten years. It felt so real!

I emailed Michael, thanking him for responding to my message and forwarding my letter to his wife. Reading that he passed on the message to Margaret gave me a great relief. I always wanted her to know how much I regretted what I did, and now she finally knew. I wasn't able to look into her eyes, but at least now she knew my truth.

As years passed, time after time I would think how great it would be if we ever reunited and reconciled, but it seemed impossible after all that heartbreaking drama for everyone whose lives were impacted by our affair. And here you are; it was right around the corner now. That amazing feeling of easiness and joy was so new to me. This new sudden turn in my life was on my mind all day. I was contemplating on how much power forgiveness has. It is invisible, and yet what a huge difference did it make.

Along with enjoying this indescribable easiness, I was wondering about Margaret. Probably receiving my message to her was like a lightning bolt out of the clear sky. Maybe it brought back that horrible experience and she's in pain? Maybe she still hates me and doesn't want to speak with me? At the end of my letter, I wrote that I would understand if she decided not to write me back, but her response would make a big difference to me. I knew my actions were horribly wrong and I would not be surprised if she would decide not to speak with me ever again. Even if I heard silence from her, the most important thing for me was that she received my letter, where I finally was able to tell her how much I hated what I did.

Throughout the day I was wondering how my letter affected her and what her response (if any) would be. I prayed for Jesus to heal her pain and give her the strength to forgive me. I was trying to work on my project, but all my thoughts were about this new turn that unexpectedly took place in my life. The day was coming to its end and there was still silence from Margaret. I guess I should not have expected to hear from her. Still, I was holding on to hope that it's not the end yet. I fell asleep at peace, putting my trust in the Lord that He was going to complete what He had started and fix the impossible as only He can.

The Impossible Reconciliation Becomes Reality

"I forgive you." I felt her words as Margaret was looking into my eyes with compassion, with her eyes full of tears. And then I woke up.

Feeling totally astounded I tried to come to my senses. I saw Margaret in a dream, and it was so real, as if I had just met with her. In my dream, I was busy with my projects and talking to someone and then, somehow, I turned my head to the left and saw Margaret was quietly standing there beside me. I was caught by surprise that she was near me all this time while I was speaking to others and doing my business, and I did not see her. Then, as I was looking at her, tears started rolling down my cheeks for my deep regret for what I had done. She cried with me as I asked her to forgive me. We cried together and we both understood each other. Margaret was compassionate and understanding. The awareness I had was as if she would say that we all make mistakes, and she forgives me. As she forgave me, I woke up.

I knew this was the sign for me to know that I would receive her forgiveness. I had to get ready for my speech that I was scheduled to give a week later, and my thoughts about this situation and constant wondering about her did not allow me to focus on my preparation. I believed the Lord gave me the answer ahead, to calm me down and let me know that I will receive forgiveness from her, so I could prepare for my speech.

A few days after our initial contact, Michael wrote me a message, answering my question which was the reason of my letter. He said he was not angry with me at all, but since I asked him, he wanted to answer that yes, he has forgiven me for what I asked him to forgive me for. He said he took equal responsibility for what we did and he held nothing against me. Michael's message gave me even stronger relief, and now, I had a clear answer and did not have to assume anymore.

After ten days since my initial contact, a day before my scheduled presentation, as I was preparing for my speech, suddenly I saw Margaret's name in my inbox. I looked again to see if this was really true. It was her message. I interrupted whatever I was doing to read it. Nothing was more important than her message.

"It took a lot of strength for you to write that letter," she began. Margaret wrote a warm and kind message. Reading her message, I could sense my letter surprised her. She said my letter certainly made her think of the value and purpose of forgiveness. She said she realized that harboring negative feelings serves no purpose, and in fact, it only destroys a person inside. She added that she did not regret the kindness that she showed me, and she wished me success and happiness, just as she wished me in the past. At the end, Margaret said she forgave me and hoped that this burden that I carried for such a long time would be lifted.

"Thank you, thank you!" In my gratitude I kept repeating those two words in my mind. I have been waiting for this moment for so long. I've been waiting, and yet, my desire to be forgiven was like a dream that could not be realized, because I did not really think she could ever forgive me. But, as impossible as it seemed, it happened and what a relief this brought into my heart. Her not only forgiving me, but also wishing me success on top of that was far more than I deserved.

It's hard even to describe how different I felt after I reconciled with two very important people in my life, from whom I was separated by the invisible wall of dead silence. The easiness, feeling of freedom and joy I felt were simply indescribable.

"How could I live for so long carrying such a heavy burden?" I thought, seeing what difference forgiveness made. I kept asking myself the same question all day, day after day. It felt as if I got out of some dark place, and now I again could see the light, and could even see colors. Over the years I got so used to the imprisonment of pain and regret that I forgot what it feels like to be free from it. I remembered my dream that I had the day after I sent her my letter; her message was a confirmation of it. I took a deep breath and smiled.

This was one of the hardest things I had to do, but what a life-changing experience this was. I was so happy that I obeyed the Lord my God and reached out to them to reconcile. Margaret was right. It required a lot for me to make this step. In fact, I believe God gave me the strength to do it when I decided to obey His word by reaching out to them, because this step was beyond what I could do myself. Sure, it would have been much easier not to do it. But this time, I obeyed what God commanded in the Scriptures, regardless whether I felt like it or not. And where would I be now, if I had made my decision based on what I felt or what I personally thought about it? I would still be in the dungeon of my past mistake, in shackles and darkness.

It was interesting to notice what a different outcome I had in both choices. Choosing to obey God's word and do what He says was not easy. I had to initiate the conversation after many years of estrangement, take full responsibility for my own mistakes, and humble myself before another person. No, it was not easy to initiate contact with the person and ask him to forgive me for my personal mistakes that contributed to the fall. Given the situation I was in, without a doubt it was easier not to reach out, not to humble myself, not to acknowledge my mistake and not go back into that anguish. But then, the outcomes of both of these choices were so different.

Obeying God's word gave me such freedom and joy that I cannot even describe it! It delivered me from the guilt and heavy burden that I had to carry for so long. On the other hand, choosing to neglect the Lord's direction and stay with my pride and base my decision on my own personal understanding, would have kept me imprisoned by the heaviness of the past, consumed by my shame and guilt. Doing what is easier would have had me continue living in deep regret and silent agony.

Was it worth it for me to obey the Lord and choose what the right thing to do was, even if it required for me to have complete humility and courage? Absolutely yes. I wish I would have had the courage and insight to have done this earlier. But, I guess there is a time for everything. I was so glad that I chose to overcome my personal ego, the fear of rejection and do what is right.

Brother, as I am writing this, a thought came to me. Isn't this the same in our lives? It is easier not to get into depth of unpleasant situations trying to resolve them and let them go without resolving them. It is easier to relax and not do the work. It is easier to stay with what you know and what gives you security and not take the risk. It is easier to say "I will do this tomorrow." It is so much easier to do the job carelessly without putting extra effort in it. It is easier to stay in your comfort zone. It is easier to miss the phone call and not to take time or effort to develop relationships. It is easier to make the choice that is easier at the time, but what is the ultimate outcome of that kind of a choice? A fake relationship while pretending that everything is fine, poverty, missed opportunity, wasted time, misery, mediocrity and loneliness.

It is not easy to be open, vulnerable and make an effort to build an honest relationship that lasts. It is not easy to choose to do the work that needs to be done. It requires courage and it's not easy to take the risk. It is not easy to be disciplined and get things done on time. It is not easy to keep pushing yourself and make an extra step. It's not easy and it might be scary to get out of your comfort zone in order to reach your desired outcome. It does take time and effort to develop and strengthen your friendships. It is not easy to make these kinds of choices, but where do they bring us? Ultimately, they bring us strong, honest and loving relationships, successful results and economic well-being, opportunities that lead us to new places, wisely managed time, and memorable experiences.

What if facing choices of "easy" and "not easy," we ask ourselves, "The choice that I am going to make now, where is it going to bring me ultimately?"

Now, even more I saw what a powerful impact our choices make in our lives.

It was indescribable joy that I chose a step which ultimately brought me a great relief and freedom. I was simply astounded by such an unexpected turn. It seemed like an invisible hand once again moved events in my life, like a chess game! I was fascinated how incredibly this painful and unresolved part of my life suddenly got a perfect closure. But it was not the end.

Part 2 ~ The Choice

As we all do at times, I have built an expectation for the situation. Ideally, I had imagined that we both would acknowledge that we have done the wrong thing, apologize to each other for our mistakes, wish each other success and having reconciled, we move on, leaving the pain and guilt behind.

I did my part, and since Michael said he wanted to take time to give me a quality, well-thought response, I decided to wait for his letter. It was more important to me than he could imagine. It took me an enormous effort to move on with my life. Having no closure made it even harder. For a decade I waited to have that closure, and it looked like finally I was going to receive it.

I was very pleased to read his intention to write me a letter that "respects my care and sensitivity" (as he wrote in his response). I always wanted to know what had to happen that a person, who was constantly reassuring me of his love and unconditional devotion, overnight has a radical turnabout and in a cold-blooded way just cut everything off, throwing me out like an unnecessary, inconvenient, piece of property, without even caring what's going to happen with me. I never had experienced such betrayal, abandonment and humiliation. In the same way as I hoped for the day when I would be able to ask Margaret to forgive me, I hoped for the day when Michael would tell me what made him do what he did and ask for forgiveness. Even though I knew it would not have changed my life in any way; nor would it have changed my decision not to ever repeat my mistake, I felt I needed to hear him, what happened at that time that would allow me to become free from the agony of the past and be able to let it go.

A big portion of my anger was gone after the workshop. I was excited beyond my ability to describe the freedom I received from the anger that I unconsciously held against him all these years. However, this gut-wrenching pain was not gone. There was something else to be done until I become fully free and I felt this step was to talk with Michael about it all and make the closure which I never had. So, after reading his intention to write me a letter, I decided to wait for it.

Soon I received one email, but it was not the letter I expected. I received another, it wasn't, either. And then, another message. It was not what I was waiting for. To my surprise, I began seeing Michael's name in my inbox again. It was quite strange to see his name and speak with him after a decade of silence. This name and this person were buried for a long time; since then, my life has radically changed and it was very unusual to be brought back to that earlier time. I had to admit though, in some way I felt a relief. Michael said he also felt a relief after "breaking the wall." On the other hand, I knew me breaking that wall of silence was not for me to re-establish constant communication with him.

I wasn't sure what was going on in his mind and heart, but to my even bigger surprise, Michael was emailing as though he was interested and eager to remain in continuous communication as if a decade of our estrangement and complete silence didn't even exist. However, I could not eliminate the heartbreaking separation and a decade of total non-contact. I needed to receive his letter and get my closure to be free from it all.

Through his messages, I learned that he continued the non-profit he was establishing then. He said he was very happy, as he got to travel internationally and do what he loved. I told him I was happy for those people, whose lives were changed by the organization's mission. I was glad he continued establishing it and fulfilling the mission once we together had. On the other hand, him sharing how happy he was traveling and doing this work without even acknowledging his abrupt decision to get me out of it, was like a slap to my face. A wave of memories of his words, "I can't see you, can't talk to you and we no longer will work on the organization," was still heart wrenching. Memories of me being the reason the organization was born, and how I was there with Michael at the very beginning when together we envisioned the organization's mission and discussed ways how we were going to fulfill it, how we were going to travel together and do this good work together, hearing about it as though I was never planned to be a part of it, was very painful. I was so emotionally attached to it that even after the break-up, I kept the organization's bylaws, job descriptions and other. And I still have them.

The more I saw his messages, the more the pain grew. After his first several messages I saw he did not even address the drama that took us apart. Nor did he ever ask how I survived then and how I was doing. I did not ask him questions because I didn't want to open the door again to our past way of bonding, but I continued responding and stayed in touch with him. All this time, I was patiently waiting for the letter he promised to write, keeping in mind the purpose of why I broke the silence.

One day, while I was in the kitchen cooking, I was thinking about this unexpected turn and analyzing it, suddenly a thought came to me, "Inga, doesn't it seem familiar to you? One email, then another, and then another one. That's how it all started, remember? They were daily emails; innocent, but constant. It's the same situation where it all began, can you see?"

"Wait a minute," I even stopped what I was doing. "Isn't this interesting? Ten years ago, the morning when Michael called me to tell me it was over, I was utterly broken when I realized where my choices had led me, and there was no return. I realized everything could have been so different if I had recognized the power of choice when given the opportunity. I knew it was impossible, but I still cried on my knees before the living God almighty pleading Him to give me one more chance to appear in the same position when everything started, so I could make the right choice. And today, even though it seemed absolutely impossible, I am in the exact same situation! With the same person!"

Shivers went through my body realizing this. I sat there in the middle of the kitchen totally astounded. It looked like the Lord fulfilled my prayer. I was at the same crossroads that has two paths: to continue my constant communication with Michael behind his wife's back, and to set the appropriate boundaries at the outset. Which choice was I going to make now? Am I going to do what I want and what feels good at the moment? Or am I going to do what is right?

Am I going to continue daily emailing, which ultimately might open the doors of renewing our heart connection again? Or am I going to make a different choice this time and draw the line where it should be drawn? Which way of the crossroad – left or right? Yes, breaking that wall of silence brought some relief. And our emails seemed to be harmless, since there was nothing inappropriate in our messages. But that's exactly how it started a decade ago.

I remembered my flight back to Europe ten years ago when I was totally lost and desperate, and saw the results that my choices had incurred in my life. My choice to bend my own standards and forsake the Lord's commandments demanded the price of anguish and personal destruction. I knew that the same way as a decade ago, my choice now might direct my life again one or another direction. I felt so thankful to be given an opportunity to face the same crossroads! I knew that this time I would make a different choice. I knew my decision without the slightest doubt or hesitation. I just needed "the letter," something for which I had been waiting for over a decade.

After two weeks of exchanging messages, I still did not have the letter he had promised to write. Not even a paragraph. Every time I opened his message, I was met with disappointment at the end of each message: it was not the letter that I was waiting for. My waiting brought me a decade back to the time, when I was desperately in tears, waiting for him to walk up the driveway or at least call me, to simply talk to me, all with no avail. There was a dead silence from Michael then. And it seemed like there was now as well.

This time, I had heard from Michael, but at the same time there was a dead silence: there was no sense of remorse, no explanation and no apology. As I continued receiving Michael's messages, I started feeling again, but in an entirely different way. That part of my life had been frozen and numb for many years, and now it felt like it was being re-awakened and started pulsating all over. Our deep connection and devotion to each other, and then sudden abandonment and utter destruction of my new life kept bringing me to tears every time I thought of it. This immense agony I tried to push back and hide all these years now started coming to the surface.

I realized I could no longer carry on this nightmare. I needed to deal with it and I was ready to face it once again for the very last time. I only needed him to talk to me like we did in the past, and give me the answer to my one question that I carried for a decade. But there was no letter and no suggestion we have a conversation. It looked like his one sentence was all he felt he needed to write, "I am truly sorry for the abrupt ending, but there was no other way."

The more messages I received with no letter, the more my pain grew. Finally, one night after being in tears until 2:00 AM after reading his newly sent email, I knew I couldn't go through this anymore. I couldn't handle anymore watching, how instead of coming to me with an open conversation about the choices he had made, he was emailing as though we had no painful history together. It was as though my first letter opened the door to return to our previous constant communication.

My awareness of the crossroads I was standing at was on my mind every day. I knew the Lord had given me a second chance to make the right choice. Waiting for his letter started turning into our constant emailing back and forth just like it was ten years ago. And it was not right, especially when it came to Margaret, his wife. I received her forgiveness and felt relief from this heavy burden, but here I am, staying in touch with her husband while waiting for his letter. I was put in the same position, continuing my daily conversation with him behind her back. Truth be known, I still could sense the strong bond between us. A decade of estrangement was not able to erase it. But in the same breath, I hated going behind her back. It felt like I was betraying her all over again. The lesson about the power of choice kept coming into my consciousness.

Having concluded that he had plenty of time to write at least a paragraph in response to my initial letter, one night I wrote him a letter to end our constant emailing. My reason for connecting had served its purpose and it was not to re-establish our constant communication or relationship behind his wife's back.

It is hard for me to even describe the delight of watching that the Lord has given me that second chance to appear again in the same situation to make the right choice, and that this time, I made the choice that was right before the Lord my God and was true to Michael's wife. What an amazing relief I received from the mistaken choices I've made in the past! In addition to receiving the freedom from the invisible chains and imprisonment, that night I received even greater freedom, from shame.

By doing what I did, I got my dignity back. I am not a toy that you can pick up, throw away and take back whenever you feel like it.

Battle to Forgive

Early the next morning, as I opened my email account, I saw a message from Michael was waiting for me. Finally, it felt like the invisible wall was broken and he had spoken up. In his response, Michael said he had written numerous letters asking for forgiveness, and he re-wrote them over and over from the day I first emailed him. But he deleted it each draft, because he has never been able to forgive himself for his abrupt ending and how he has ignored me. And he felt none of his letters could possibly justify his act.

He did not see how he could be forgiven for what he had done and he felt that he had no right to ask me to forgive him. In his perspective, it was unfair to me for him to ease his conscience by asking me to forgive him. He said after writing and deleting his letters over and over, he wrote that one sentence, which was short but sincere.

After ten years, I learned his family gave him notice: they would have nothing to do with him again if he said another word to me. He said he had to become a different person, as it was not in his character to treat me the way he did and he could hardly live with himself after that. He said he did love me and that he never lied to me or to himself about it. After that day, he could hardly move on with his life and had to seek professional help. Michael said he was happy to see that I survived and moved on successfully, and that he would stop this frequent emailing, wishing me all the best.

His short explanation told me more than I ever could have imagined. Reading Michael's message, I understood that it was an immense pain for him to do what he did. Through his words, I could feel his pain and see what an enormous impact this had on him. There could be many thoughts, but at this point it did not matter anymore. I knew that the choice that Michael made was the right thing to do regardless of what we thought, felt or wanted.

We both paid a very high price for what we had created. But we deserved to pay that price, because what we did was wrong, regardless of what we felt. The person who got hurt the most who did not deserve this was Margaret. I was just glad that this nightmare was behind us. My life has totally changed since then and I hope that they also had some good experiences that overshadowed the negative aspects of this drama.

For a few days, I had an ongoing battle within. Feelings of heartache and my wish to let go were wrestling in my mind tirelessly. My question, "How could you possibly do this?" was like a roaring wave trying to overshadow my attempt to understand Michael.

In the midst of my emotional storm, a laser sharp thought came to my mind, "What would you have done if you were him?" I tried to imagine what it would feel like if I was in his position and what I would have done. Just as I imagined myself in Michael's skin, I realized that this kind of ultimatum from my family would have simply torn me to pieces, were I in his position. Only then I could see how difficult it was for him to do what he did.

I again had to face a very simple fact, which is so easy to neglect and difficult to practice when we are hurt by someone - we look at the situation from our point of view, accusing or blaming the other person for our pain, without trying to understand that person's motives. It is always easy to say a person did wrong when we look at the situation from our perspective. But we don't know what that person was going through and what made him/her do what was done. There is always a reason why people do what they do. We don't know, or most of the times don't even want to know, because what we see and feel is our pain.

Still, my own hurt spoke up, "But how could you not even try to find me at least talk to me, explain to me what had happened. You knew I was in the States, you knew how to find me! How could you live with yourself without even making an attempt to at least apologize and bring about some form of closure?"

"Did you make an attempt to connect with Margaret to do the same?" Another quiet, but sharp thought interrupted my mental dialogue with Michael.

Did I do that? No. I did not. I could not dial Margaret's number that day and I could not try to reach out to her all these years, because I thought I was the last person she wanted to hear from. I also could not forgive myself and did not see any possible way how she could forgive me and so I did not even make an attempt to ask her to forgive me.

The roaring storm within me immediately was silenced. I was exhausted. Those memories and emotions were draining the life out of me. I was so tired from the anger. When I looked at myself as an observer, I saw that holding on to the anger kept me imprisoned and it was destroying me from within. I suffered greatly when it all exploded and I continued suffering quietly for ten more years by holding on to the anger and memories of horrible consequences.

It was time to forgive Michael and receive the freedom from the pain that I carried for so long. The shock and agony was so immense that it still choked me up when I remembered those days. But what was the point for me to continue carrying on those feelings into my future? I keep that experience alive in my heart and memory, and it is going to remain vivid as long as I continue holding on to it.

There comes a point in life when you have to let go the past experience and allow a new beginning to replace that. Yes, it is part of my life, and I am not going to deny it or neglect it. In fact, it was a significant and valuable experience, which I am honestly very thankful for. The pain served its purpose and I will carry on the lesson I learned to protect myself from making the same mistake, but the anguish of this experience had to be left where it belongs – in the past. I wanted to be free from it, so I could simply live at peace and joy, and accept a blessing that is to come.

In analyzing what the Scriptures say about forgiving others, I realized that forgiving is a conscious decision to let go. It is a matter of our will, not our feelings. Also, it's the decision we ought to make not because someone deserves it or only when a person asks for forgiveness. Forgiving is the decision we make by simply us showing mercy to the person who may have wronged us. Our forgiveness doesn't mean we agree with what the person did, nor does it mean, "It's okay, never mind." It's simply showing compassion and mercy to that person and letting it go.

If you go deeper into what the Scriptures say about forgiving others, it is very clear that the forgiveness of our own trespasses depends on whether we are willing to forgive others. And so I thought, "What's going to happen to me if I refuse to forgive others?"

> *"For if you forgive men their trespasses, your heavenly Father will also forgive you. But if you do not forgive men their trespasses, neither will your Father forgive your trespasses." (Matthew 6: 14-15)*

> *"For judgment is without mercy to the one who has shown no mercy. Mercy triumphs over judgment." (James 2:13)*

I knew the Lord brought Michael back into my life to show me I unconsciously was holding my anger against him and I needed to forgive him. Not forgiving Michael and not letting go of the past were preventing me from moving forward. And it also could have been a test to see whether I would follow the path of His commandments or relapse back to where I used to be.

After an ongoing battle with my own feelings and a new understanding about forgiveness and its power, I took the initiative and wrote Michael a letter. I told him that I felt I did not deserve forgiveness from Margaret, because that was the most disgusting betrayal that one woman could do to another. But she rose above it all and forgave me, wishing me success. I said I would rise above it as well, even if he felt he didn't deserve forgiveness. We all make mistakes. We need to learn from them.

I said I was rising above it all, saying to him out loud, "I forgive you, Michael. For everything." That was the purpose of my contact after ten years. I hope that in the future we will make much better choices.

Part 3 ~ All Things Work Together for Good

That afternoon, after sending my letter to Michael, for the rest of the day I was totally consumed by the latest events of reconnecting and reconciling with both of them. It was hard for me to really grasp that all of this was true. I received easiness after connecting with them and breaking down a ten year wall of dead silence. What a priceless experience it was to receive freedom from a decade of guilt! I felt even more relief after sending my letter to Michael that I chose to forgive him for everything.

But, the pain and horrible memories were brought back to the surface, my hope to have Michael speak to me about it all was not met, and now I didn't know what to do with it all. All night I was wrestling with my feelings, flashbacks from the past and ongoing thoughts. It was another night of tossing and turning over the loss and destruction of my then-planned life, and I didn't know what to do to get rid of this pain.

In the middle of the night, as I was half-asleep, I was awakened by a voice from within, which told me that I needed to bring all this in my prayer before the Lord. I was directed to put my trust in the Lord, who would take the pain away and heal me, instead of hoping and waiting that Michael could help me work through the pain. Only Jesus can take that pain away and heal my soul. Soon I fell asleep.

I woke up with a very clear awareness what I needed to do next. I felt so vulnerable and exhausted that I did not really want to get out of my bed. I just wanted to hide from everything. Remembering the direction of the voice that I felt in the middle of the night, I decided to get up and do what I was directed to do.

Feeling fragile and emotional, I made myself a cup of coffee and went to my desk. As I started reading our recent messages, I couldn't hold it anymore. Tears uncontrollably started rolling down my cheeks. The screen of my computer faded away, like in 2004, when I was in the airplane, and I could no longer see the map of my flight from the United States back to Europe. Just like then, every part of my being was wailing from the abandonment and such heartbreaking destruction of my life which-was-to-be.

"God, why, why did it have to end like this? My life would have been so much different if this break-up would not have taken place!" I cried just like ten years ago in deep anguish from being forced to lose him, from a destroyed opportunity and broken new life.

"I contacted Michael because I obeyed You, Lord. You know I didn't want to contact him, but I did because I wanted to obey You. I asked for forgiveness and I chose to forgive because I obeyed Your word. I choose to forgive Michael even though it's so difficult, even though he did not really ask for forgiveness. But I choose to forgive him, because Your Word says so. I did all this because I obey You, God, but now because I did all this, I have all these memories and pain brought back and I don't know what to do with them. Michael left me alone to deal with them, but I cannot handle it alone God, I don't know what to do! I ask you Lord, please take it away, no longer can I live with it. I need your help Jesus… I need Your help."

After a moment, I started noticing how my inner anguish gradually started diminishing and peace gently came into my heart. It was a strange and yet astounding experience how my inner feelings started changing into peace and lightness. It seemed as my inner storm was being silenced. I stopped crying. I felt at ease. Suddenly a word came to my mind, "Perspective."

"Perspective? That's my power tool, yes. But what about perspective, how else can I look at this situation?" I snapped back to that thought with slight irony. But knowing what a tremendous impact a change of perspective can do for you and how it has helped me in the past, I decided to step out of the "Me Zone" and find a different perspective.

"Okay. Perspective. How else can I perceive this situation?" I was ready to consider different outlooks. At that moment another clear thought came to my mind, "What it would be like if nothing had happened?"

"What it would be like if no break-up had happened and I remained in that situation? Well, we would continue working on the organization that he founded. And that would be my way of getting the green card and further establishment in the United States. And, I would not have had this heartbreaking separation with Michael," I mentally responded.

"Okay. And what would it feel like?" All this time, it seemed like a sharp yet very gentle voice continued coaching me. As I thought of my response, that moment seemed like a veil was lifted from my eyes and mind – in a flash I realized something that I could not see all these years.

I would have had to continue hiding the truth. I would have had to continue pretending. I would have had to continue living a lie, which I so hated! And I would have continued living in sin, while justifying it to numb my conscience. I would have to continue watching how he lied to his wife. Even if we somehow would have been able to stop our romantic relationship – which I very much doubt that we could - I would have had to work side by side with the man with whom I shared deep, mutual feelings and with whom I had a romantic history, but be forced to pretend we are only friends and business partners.

"My Lord, this was going into such painful trap! What it would feel like? It would have been misery. It would have been simply unbearable, but I know I would not be able to break my relationship with Michael because I couldn't stand even the thought of not having him in my life. And there is no way I would be able to have another relationship with any other man, because I was so in love with Michael. Even if I wanted to leave, I would not be able to, because my immigration process would have totally depended on him and the company he was establishing. I would be living in a state of endless misery and emotional torture!"

I sat there as though I was fully paralyzed as I was coming to the new realization of what my life would have been like if we had continued on our plans to work together. It made me sick to think what my life would have been like if this break-up didn't happen. I didn't even know that my relationship and future career were turning into a trap of endless lies and emotional quicksand. And what if his family would have given him that kind of ultimatum when I was in the process of obtaining a green card and he would have dropped it all?

"Oh Lord," I thought. "You pulled me out of the triangle and you protected me from even bigger trouble! And even if we made it somehow and I did receive the green card, I would have to live knowing that my life in the United States was built on a lie. That behind the good work we were doing there was a secret love affair. If he had left his wife and chose to stay with me – I know I would not be able to live with myself, knowing that I was the reason behind a broken marriage and shattered family. There is a saying in my culture, that "You can't build your happiness on other people's sorrows."

Where would I be today in my professional life and in my personal life if everything would have remained the way it was and we would have continued fulfilling our plans? How would I be standing before the living God if I had continued walking that path? It felt like my body froze from the shock of what I was discovering. I was sitting, staring somewhere into the horizon while having this new awareness about the experience that I cried about so many days and nights.

The process of someone revealing to me the blessing in the destruction continued, though. I realized, I felt torn apart that my relationship with Michael was broken, but because this relationship came to an end, I realized that I was living in a trap of a lie and doing a horrible abomination before the Lord God, while justifying my choice. By having this break-up,

I was awakened from a deep, all-consuming sleep and saw what was really happening. I was deeply hurt and angry that Michael suddenly and completely cut off any kind of contact with me, but because of such an abrupt ending, all my ties with everything that we had created with our lie were severed, and I was able to start my new life in a new and honest way without holding on to my past.

That moment I had an awareness that our work together would have been a great blessing to many, but because we were living in a lie and living our transgression in secret, the Lord God stopped it and shut the door to it. By doing so, He pulled us out of potential trouble and misery that our transgression had in store for us. Therefore, the break up and sudden, abrupt ending of everything we had established was for the better.

I just held my breath while realizing all this. Ten years I lived thinking that the break-up with Michael and the abrupt ending was the second most destructive event in my life. For so many years I considered it to be an even bigger crash in my life than the accident. All these years I could easily speak about the loss of my legs and my despair realizing that my life would never be the same. But I couldn't speak to anyone about my relationship with Michael and its devastating ending. It was way too painful for me to even remember this heartbreaking story. And there came a time when I realized that this was actually God's grace and a blessing.

My deep connection with Michael and the anguish of losing him grew in me so tightly that it was hard for me to think this way. However, when I compared what it would have been like if our break-up had not happened, and how the separation had impacted me and directed my path toward my current life, I simply could not deny that what had happened was only for the better.

A verse in Romans came to my mind:

> *"And we know that all things work together for good to those who love God, to those who are the called according to His purpose." (Romans 8:28)*

I smiled. For the first time in ten years, I felt sincere gratitude for this story coming to an end. Suddenly the heaviness was lifted. I started breathing easier. The pain that was strangling me for so long gradually started leaving. I felt sheer lightness. I felt gratitude, instead of the deep regret for the destroyed opportunity and my endless, agonizing question, "How could you do this?"

In my mind I saw my life in one big picture watching how events, certain circumstances, experiences, people and simply all that had happened worked together for the good. Even situations that seemed bad at one time, turned out to be for my benefit. But this event? This was also for my benefit? Yes. It was. This relationship had played a significant role in my life. I am happy that I have experienced what it feels like to love and to be loved. The deep connection and love that united us is still like a gem to me. However, being in the position that we both were in, it had to be terminated. This relationship coming to an end pulled me out of a lie and life of misery. It taught me one of the most valuable lessons in my life. It shaped standards and values that will be part of my life forever.

This kind of ending made me much stronger than I ever was. It made me unstoppable. And once again my experience showed me God's immeasurable mercy and grace even if you make a horrible, unpardonable mistake. At the same time, it also showed me that the Lord God is just. He is not some 'sugar daddy' who disregards our transgressions because He loves us. He is long patient and merciful, but He will not be mocked. Sooner or later everyone reaps what he sows. With no partiality. Through it all, I also witnessed how mighty the Lord God is – even if it seems impossible to receive resolution to a situation, He can make it happen. It showed me again that people's hearts, circumstances, events and absolutely everything is in His power.

Finally, the end of this story was the beginning of the new life I had dreamed about, and the one that has no lies and is blessed by the Lord. In fact, when I looked at my life from a bigger perspective, the fact that my secret relationship was destroyed and how it all ended was one of the most valuable things that has ever happened to me.

That is how, brother, after a decade, when I least expected, I received all my answers and the best closure I could possibly want. It seemed like some invisible hand arranged circumstances like in a chess game, and my silent ongoing regret and pain turned into sheer gratitude, realizing that everything worked together for the good. And it all happened in only two short weeks. After a decade of silent suffering and dead silence, I was able to:

- Reconnect with people with whom we were estranged for a decade and with whom reconciliation seemed impossible.
- Receive forgiveness from a person whom I hurt, and whose forgiveness seemed absolutely impossible.
- I had the opportunity to acknowledge my mistakes with Michael and receive forgiveness.
- I was able to forgive and receive freedom from the anger and grief that had strangled me and kept me imprisoned for many years.
- I got to appear again in the same position just as I had asked the living God a decade ago, so I could make the right choice and this time, by recognizing the potential beginning of the fall, I stepped back and made the right choice.
- I saw that the abrupt end of my relationship with Michael and termination of our future plans was actually a blessing not a destruction of my life.

I still don't have the answer why it had to take ten years to have this closure. But you know, I trust there was a good reason for it. In fact, I don't think I was ready for this kind of closure until now. And probably it was a good thing that I did not hear from him for all these ten years.

I admit that it was good that I never saw him or heard from him, because I was not ready yet; his re-appearance in my life would have broken me again. I guess only now I was strong enough to have him come back to find closure. I had grown during this time. Many things have changed in my life. I changed. And when the time came, the Lord God cleared up the darkness of the past mistake, gave me freedom from pain and put everything back into its place. And, I finally left my experience and my feelings where it belongs – in the past. Holding on to it serves no purpose and keeps me unavailable for the blessing that is prepared for me yet to be received. It's time to move on and have my heart free.

Through this experience, the Lord showed me that He is a righteous God and yes, He can be very strict at times. Yet, He is very patient, caring and loving. He teaches as a father teaches his child – in addition to his love and care about his child, father chastises him as well, in order to correct and teach him.

> *"My son, do not despise the chastening of the Lord, nor detest His correction; for whom the Lord loves He corrects,*

> *just as a father the son in whom he delights." (Proverbs 3: 11-12)*
>
> *"No discipline seems pleasant at the time, but painful. Later on, however, it produces a harvest of righteousness and peace for those who have been trained by it." (Hebrews 12:11 NIV)*

You know, this reconciliation experience brought to me another testimony, which confirms that all things work together for the good, even if situations do not seem good at the time they occur.

I see another gem in destruction. Do you remember, I wanted to publish the book few years ago and it didn't work out? I am so thankful I did not get to publish this book when I wanted to do it! Why? Because it was not complete yet. If I had published it – this story and messages I have with this chapter would not have been included in the book. There would have been no closure.

It was May 2012 when I finished writing the manuscript and I thought it was complete. I wanted to start the editing and publishing process, and because I did not have the money to cover the expenses, I created a fundraising project to raise funds to cover the editing and publishing costs. I was confident I'd raise funds and was ready to jump into professional editing and get it out to the world. However, as soon as I published my project online, in my spirit I knew this would not work out. I did not delete the project, but I knew money would not be raised.

It was interesting to watch that I have received supportive messages and heard many excited congratulations, but funds were coming in very slowly. Considering the amount that I set as a goal, I could say, funds were not coming in at all. It seemed like some invisible hand was keeping funds from coming in, so I would not be able to proceed. It was even funny to watch having many people telling me, "I am so excited about your project; I can't wait to read your book!" But funds were still not coming in.

My reaction was confusion. I couldn't understand why it wasn't working out. It was very strange, and it confused and surprised many. I had to make the effort to pull myself out of my state of disappointment and confusion, and look at it from a different perspective. I reminded myself that all things were in the hands of the God, and if funds were not coming in, it meant the Lord was not opening that door; it was not time yet to publish it.

Seeing that nothing was coming together to publish it despite my prayers and efforts to spread the word about the fundraising project, I decided not to push it. It was obvious to me that the doors were shut, and I knew there was a reason behind it. Instead of pushing this project forward, I decided to humble myself and seek the Lord's will. One day, in my prayer I had a crystal clear insight, just like I've had at times before, that the Lord has prepared it all – and the editor and the funds, and I will not even have to do the fundraising; it will come all at once, only it will come when it's time. Meanwhile, I had to leave it all aside and focus on seeking what His will was for my future. I decided to trust, left it aside and to my friends or anyone who inquired about the book I told that I trusted that everything would come together when it's time. I simply trusted, and did not resist what was happening.

For many months, it was like a winter time. I was not producing anything and not very involved in any projects, except my duties at my primary job. I was examining myself, my values, my aspirations and my intentions behind them. It was hard for me to be still, but I knew this was the time when I needed to be still and listen.

As I was examining myself according to the Bible, very soon I learned something that totally caught me off guard and rather shocked me. Imagine, the airplane has a route to its destination. At some point, the pilot looks at the compass and sees that the plane is very slightly off course. The shift might be very slight, nearly to the point that it's not worth worrying about it because it wouldn't make any big difference. But what if the pilot would not make any changes and let the plane continue flying slightly off course? The shift might be unnoticeable at first. But after thousands of miles, that airplane would be totally off course. The arrival would be far away from the destination it was supposed to arrive. That's what I saw in my life; the arrow of my compass was slightly shifted off the course. I spent a long time re-evaluating everything, and by changing my aspirations and intentions behind them, I brought back my arrow to the course of my purpose in life. Instead of aiming to reach success in my selfish, ambitious goals, I chose to help others to go through their hardships and fulfill the promise that I made to the Lord my God to bring His glory to the nations.

It was not easy to be still and hear people's questions what's happening with the book. It is not my nature not to pursue my goal and accomplish what I set out to do. But I knew I had to stop for a while and re-evaluate where I was going in life. It wasn't easy, but this time changed the direction I was taking in life, and I am so grateful today for this time period.

Two years since then, once I've gone through some internal work and set for myself new intentions and new aspirations, I have this beautiful closure. When I was inspired to write you this letter, I had an awareness that this letter and the closure of this story had to be included in the book as well. While I was writing it, I kept thinking how thankful I was that I did not get to publish my book when I wanted to do it. I don't see this book without this particular chapter. If I had pushed seeking for funds and had published it anyway, today I would have been in deep regret that I did. Once again, circumstances that seemed bad at the time they occurred really were for the better.

You are Becoming His Precious Diamond

As I write about all these experiences, I have to pause and take a deep breath. It astonishes me to see how everything worked together for the better. As I look at my journey from the perspective of an observer, I am in awe.

As you already know, trusting the Lord that all things work together for good was not easy. In fact, I didn't really think so until much later on. The delays I experienced waiting for His answer bewildered me, annoyed me and tested my patience. What's more, it greatly tested my faith. It seemed the Lord did not hear me, but He did. God was always there with me at all times. He was caring for me and bringing me to the fulfillment of His will and the answers to my prayers. He was making it all work for me to receive what I had asked for, and only gave me what He knew what was better for me. He had a much better plan, and so His answer was different than mine. Now as I look back, I see it's like a puzzle – every situation, every person, every circumstance be it good or bad, when assembled properly they came together and made a beautiful picture.

I mentioned earlier that even problems, hardships, circumstances that seemed to be not what I had asked in my prayer – everything together served a purpose and brought me to where I am today. I only made it harder for myself by allowing my concerns and frustrations to disturb my peace. And now, after a decade, I saw that the event that I perceived as one of the most destructive one I had ever experienced, actually was a blessing and directed by my Lord in a way that I would not trade for anything lost.

Even the car crash. I am thankful for it. There are many things I cannot do, due to my physical limitations, but what an incredible life journey I've had since that dreadful event. It feels like an incredible adventure and I truly love my life. I live as if I do not have physical limitations. I learned how to do the things I must to live the life I want to live. In fact, my life is even more interesting than before the crash. I am not saying it is easy. Yes, it is tough and often challenging. At times my life seemed to be one destined to suffer pain and hopelessness for the rest of my life. However, memorable experiences, meeting wonderful people, meaningful relationships, new exciting opportunities, travelling and visiting places that I did not even dream about visiting, the sweet taste of success when attaining almost impossible goals, astonishing changes and witnessing answered prayers in the most incredible ways totally overshadowed the pain and loss.

But out of all remarkable experiences I've had, for the way I got to know my Lord and seeing Him manifest in my life in this journey, makes it all worth it. I am not sure where I would be today, if I had not gotten into that crash, but something tells me I would have wandered far away from Lord. At times, I thought to myself that if someone came up to me today and said, "You will receive your legs and your arm back and return to where you were in your life and be who you were then if you renounce Christ," I would not trade. Knowing Him and receiving that which He gives cannot compare to anything else. I do not want anything, if my Lord is not in it. Today I am sincerely thankful for everything that I've gone through, because it all worked for the better and I've gained so much.

By sharing this experience with you, I want to give you hope and encourage you. I know it's been a while since you've had to face your own personal life desert, and you probably have the same question that I had, "Why? When is this going to end?" Maybe you still blame yourself for the mistakes you've made. Maybe you feel lost and confused, but you don't have the answer.

I was inspired to write this letter to pass on to you the lesson that I had to learn the hard way – do not fear, but remain in peace fully trusting that the Lord your God has everything under control. And if you love Him, everything is going to work out for the better; you will see it when the time comes. Meanwhile, while being steadfast in your faith, do your best doing whatever you need to do to continuously improve your situation.

Since you have given your life to Jesus Christ and surrendered your life to His will, God has your life in His hands. Trust Him. He has a plan for your life, which you are not aware of. None of us are aware of His plans for us, and even though you might have a vision of what direction your life will take, it's in His hands how things should go or what role certain people will play in your life.

You probably have some expectations of how you want your life to evolve, and it's frustrating when it doesn't work out the way you thought, isn't it? I want to encourage you not to stress over it, but go into your prayer room and seek the Lord with all your heart, with all your essence. Remember, in His Word God said He will be found by those, who seek Him with their sincere hearts. Ask Him to direct your life according to His will, ask Him to help you understand things you are bewildered about. My experience taught me that our vision might be very different from His will for our lives, and His will is so much better than our understanding of what would be good for us. And at times, the Lord by His grace is not allowing our plans to be fulfilled, or they are delayed. Or, if the vision that we have aligns with the Father's will, then the path to that vision being fulfilled might be different than what our Father's plan is.

I once had a vision for my life which I believe the Lord put in my heart, but the path to that vision becoming my reality was very different than what the Lord has planned. I could not even dream about what the Lord had planned. I would not have believed this could be possible if someone had told me in advance that this is how events were going to evolve.

> *"'For My thoughts are not your thoughts, nor are your ways My ways,' says the Lord. 'For as the heavens are higher than the earth, so are My ways higher than your ways, and My thoughts than your thoughts.'" (Isaiah 55:8-9)*

Please hear me out – walk by faith. You do not know what God is doing in your life and where He is leading you. Certain events at times have a significant impact in our lives and yes, it feels scary when bad things happen. Circumstances have the power to shape our destiny, and it may cause anxiety and worry when they evolve not the way we anticipated. We feel and see only that which we experience at the moment, and usually those situations cause a lot of pain when we go through them. That's where faith must come in – walk by faith, not by sight.

"For we walk by faith, not by sight." (2 Corinthians 5:7)

Going back to the metaphor of a house, have your faith lay a strong foundation for the perspective that will empower you. The foundation that you stand on must be unshakable faith that God has your circumstances in His power and all is going to be well no matter what storms are around you.

> *"For the Lord loves justice, And does not forsake His saints; They are preserved forever, But the descendants of the wicked shall be cut off." (Psalms 37:28)*

> *"Keep your lives free from the love of money and be content with what you have, because God has said, 'Never will I leave you; Never will I forsake you.'" (Hebrews 13:5 NIV)*

Having full confidence that your Lord will help and that all things will work together for good, go through this time learning your lessons and doing your best. I want to point out one thing, when I talk about the verse, "All things work together for good." There is a condition, which many are not aware of or simply neglect. It says that all things work together for the good for two kinds of people: those who love the Lord God and those who are chosen according to His purpose. Loving the Lord is not just mere emotions of how delighted you are of how good God is. Loving the Lord is to keep is commandments. Jesus clearly stated what means to love Him:

> *"He who has My commandments and keeps them, it is he who loves Me. And he who loves Me will be loved by My Father, and I will love him and manifest Myself to him." (John 15:21)*

> *"Jesus answered and said to him, 'If anyone loves Me, he will keep My word; and My Father will love him, and We will come to him and make Our home with him. He who does not love Me does not keep My words; and the word which you hear is not Mine but the Father's who sent Me.'" (John 15:23-24)*

So, I urge you not just merely read the Bible or go to church on Sunday, but to live every day keeping Lord's commandments and trusting Him at all times. As I wrote in one of my earlier letters, merely going to the church while not knowing Christ is a religion that makes no difference in the life of a person. It is knowing Christ and keeping His commandments that will transform your life.

I do not know why there are so many painful experiences in your life. But you know, I believe that when the Lord allows certain events to happen, He provides help for us to deal with them. With God's help you and I are strong enough to take whatever happens in our lives.

I sincerely believe that later you will see that those difficulties and experiences were for the higher good. I believe that you will be grateful for all those difficult times and challenges, because you will see they made you only stronger and taught you that which you could not have bought for any amount of money. I already see in you such big changes that sometimes I find it hard to believe that it is actually my brother who I just spoke with. I know that as the time goes and you will walk your life journey with the Lord, you will be transformed.

God is shaping a diamond out of you. I think I mentioned in one of my letters to you that a diamond is nothing more than a piece of coal which was under highly intense work. No matter how strange it may sound, but both coal and diamond are one and the same. Coal and diamond look completely different, but they both are exactly the same chemical element (carbon atom), it's just they are in a different form. Changing the crystal structure with high pressure and high temperature, coal becomes a diamond. No matter how unbelievable it might look, a diamond is really a black stone, which has gone through the intense process of high pressure and high temperature before it became a beautiful jewel. I want to pass on to you something that strengthened me greatly when I was going through a rough time.

On my desk at home I keep a bracelet with Swarovski diamonds, which was a gift to me from my friend, National Mary Kay Director Gillian Ortega. Years ago, she visited us in California from Kansas City, Missouri, and we had a special event for the beauty consultants who had achieved a certain status in the company. After that night, Gillian and my director Trish Reuser drove me back home. After we parked, finishing our discussion about the benefits and challenges of the business, Gillian took off a beautiful sparkling bracelet from her hand, profoundly looked at me and said, "Inga, this is a National Director's bracelet covered with Swarovski Diamonds. Do you know what a diamond is?"

She looked into my eyes and continued, "A diamond is simply coal in another form. But before it becomes such a beautiful diamond, it needs to go through a very high pressure and high temperature, and it takes a long time for it to become so beautiful. You are going through a very tough period of time right now. You experience difficulties, obstacles and disappointments. But know that this is how God is teaching you and is working with you to develop necessary character traits within you. It is difficult for you now, but there will come a day when you will become as beautiful as these diamonds are and you will shine just as they are. Take this bracelet, and when things become difficult for you, put it on and remember that coal becomes a diamond only by going through the intense process of heat and pressure."

She gave me the sparkling diamond bracelet and hugged me wishing me to stay strong and reach success in pursuing my dream. I will never forget that moment. This time with Trish and Gillian is one of those precious moments that I always keep in my heart and will always treasure. Both of these women greatly influenced my life. I will never be the same because I had the privilege to meet and get to know them. I knew that this night and conversation with Gillian was arranged by my Lord; at that time I really needed to hear the story about the diamond. Since then, this diamond bracelet is like a symbol to me, which gives me patience and endurance.

I want to pass on this message to you and encourage you not to fear and firmly know that God is bringing you through the tough pressure and heat for a reason. He has chosen you to be one of those precious diamonds. And when you feel you have no strength to withstand the adversities you're facing, remember, that only through high temperature and high pressure a coal transforms into a beautiful diamond. And that you are strong enough to go through it.

I want you to be grateful for these difficulties that you are facing, knowing that they are here in your life to fulfill their purpose. Remember, they are opportunities for you and they are here not to break you down, but to make you stronger and wiser. I know, it's tough and it might frustrate you and bewilder you. However, trust your God in spite of it all. You don't know what work God is doing behind these scenes. Hold on. Do not give up what you are working on. Do not give up hope. Choose life. Choose to trust, not to fear.

Choose to make your best effort in any given situation, knowing that all things work together for good to those who love God and are called according to His purpose. Your morning might be right around the corner. But you will see the victory only if you stay long enough to see that beautiful sunrise in your life.

So, Be strong. Keep moving forward, fully trusting in your God.

Love you,
Inga

20

Choices and Your Destiny

Make Your Life an Extraordinary Work of Art

It was yet another gorgeous day. As the bus was bringing me to my destination, I gazed through the window, consumed by my thoughts of the latest events in my life. My decision to overstep my pride and reach out to Michael and his wife made such a significant difference. What a relief! How could I live all these years in the silent torment of being not forgiven and not forgiving myself?

My decision to cut communication with Michael hadn't been easy. Part of me wanted to know how he was doing all these years, and how his life turned out after we parted ways. But I will not know, because this time I chose to draw the line before he became part of my life once again. I wasn't going to make the same mistake twice.

I was reflecting on my decision, watching how the brightly colored trees and hills far off in the horizon played with the sunlight, changing their colors as the sun announced the end of the day. What a magnificent sunny day it had been! California's breathtaking beauty made October my favorite month. I was fascinated by the gorgeous trees clothed in their bright magenta, gold and red colors. Delighting in the Lord's creation and analyzing the latest events in my life, a memory came to me. It felt like the whole world came to stand still. Ten years ago, around this time, through the window I looked at the beautiful trees and rolling hills covered with their brightly colored vineyards and through tears and pain was asking myself if I would ever see them again. I was on my way to San Francisco International Airport with a one-way ticket out of America. My entire being suffused with regret, I watched how the consequences of my earlier choices had mercilessly swept my blessing away. If only I had known that my choices would bring me to this point of personal anguish and destruction!

This time I am again at the same crossroads: where I have exactly the same choices, and now I know which road to take. Just a memory of the consequences I had to face then made me sick. Furthermore, thinking of what possible consequences I would have to face if I made the same choice again was unbearable. This time, I am making a different choice, the right choice.

"Wait a minute," a clear realization intervened. "A decade ago I was in tears wondering if I get to see my land of sunshine ever again. And here I am today, living amidst the stunning beauty of California! I get to see this beauty every day now for many years. I have returned and I get to live my dream life in spite of all. Why? Because of the same reason - my choices.

It was my choice not to give up when I wanted to. My response to all the destructive circumstances surrounding me then was even greater determination to fulfill the vision that the Lord inspired in me. It was my choice to hold on to my faith that all things were possible with God and that I would return, if that was His will. It was my choice to be resilient no matter how heartbroken I was. It was my choice to take persistent and consistent action, even when I did not feel like it. It was my choice, my resolve to fight for my life that won the battle over what many perceived as my destroyed destiny. It was a conscious decision to break through any obstacles when they stood before me like a brick wall, preventing me from moving forward. It was my choice to get back up no matter how many times I fell. My ultimate vision and purpose was way more important than the setbacks I experienced. And, I was ready to go against the storm and break through all of my obstacles if that's what it took. It was my choice to not allow anything to stop me. I knew I had a much bigger purpose in my life than spending my days in sadness, regret and despair. I get to live my miracle simply because I chose to fight for my life and make it whatever I chose to make it.

While watching through the window as the beautiful trees passed by, I understood how my life had changed; it was because of the choices that I made. It felt like I had an epiphany. "It's my own choices that brought me to where I am today, isn't it?"

In my mind I stepped back and looked at my life through the eyes of an observer.

I always knew I shouldn't have dated Dalius. Yet that was my choice despite the unexplainable fear and cautiousness that were like shadows every time he called inviting me out. I wonder how my life would have turned out if I had listened to that inner voice.

When I returned home from the hospital to meet a different life, I was devastated. My life seemed completely broken and I did not see how I could possibly continue living. Yet I had the choice between that fine line of becoming a victim and becoming a fighter. It was my choice to fight, and not accept the belief and mindset that this was my fate. It was my choice to fight and not accept the circumstances created by the crash.

It was my choice to never give up and keep going on despite any difficulties. My decision to fight for my life directed my life in an absolutely incredible direction. Who would I be today if I had adopted the mindset of a victim? How would I have handled my life if I had chosen the far easier path of brokenness and blame?

Losing both legs and one arm left me totally helpless. I was not able to protect myself from those injuries, but now when I faced the result, I had the choice. There was a choice of accepting the mindset that I was disabled, to remain being helpless. Another choice was to say, "Yes, I can and I will." I chose the latter - to make continuous, daily relentless efforts to learn take care of myself independently.

Many wonder how I can do all the things I do with only one functioning hand. It's my choice not to take the easier route by asking someone to help me, but finding a way to do what had to be done myself that made me self-sufficient. When I was physically strong enough to do that, I chose to persevere and learned to sit up from a lying position by myself rather than doing it much easier and faster with someone's help. I chose not to have my breakfast unless I made it myself. I chose to get up earlier in the morning to have enough time to get myself ready independently rather than sleeping longer and have someone else do things for me. I wonder what my life experience would have looked like if I had chosen to be a disabled victim, instead of choosing to be self-sufficient and making a continuous effort to do things on my own?

When that professor lifted his eyes from my medical papers and stated that I would never walk again because my physical condition made it impossible, it seemed like I had no choice but to go home accepting his statement as the truth. Yet I did have a choice, and that was to pursue my dream, anyway, anyhow, anywhere that I could. How would my life be different had I not asked him to give me a chance, if I did not insist on my aspiration to walk again?

Later, my daily choices to train relentlessly to walk with prosthetic legs despite the excruciating pain it caused, over a certain period delivered an outstanding outcome. Would I have reached that outcome if I quit, justifying that it was unbearably painful and too exhausting? Would I have reached my goal to walk if instead of doing research on the internet trying to find help somewhere else, I had chosen to give up?

That morning, when I received Michael's invitation to come to Istanbul, I was at the crossroads. The choice between fear of disappointment and taking a chance directed my destiny. Where would I be today if I had chosen not to go to Istanbul and never met Michael? A different decision would have directed my destiny in an entirely different direction. What would my life look like today if I had not trusted the Lord and rejected the inspiration to return to California to establish my life, instead choosing to stay home and not be proactive in improving my life? My life's story would have been so much different, wouldn't it?

When ten years ago I was sitting in the airplane completely heart-broken, shocked and devastated, I faced a simple, but powerful truth: Our consistent choices and decisions direct our lives in one or the other direction. Sure, I could shift the blame onto Michael that I was going back to Europe with a one-way ticket, but the truth was that this was the subsequent consequence, not the root of the problem. The foundation for where I found myself was my earlier daily choices made on continuous basis.

One innocent email followed by another one and then another one compounded created its fruit. And then, when those daily insignificant choices brought us to a crossroad of choosing whatever we felt or doing what was right, we chose the path we wanted, underestimating, even disregarding its cost. At the time it didn't seem to me destructive; actually the opposite – I have not been happier than at that time. However, this deceitful, alluring, satisfying choice delivered its result much later, one that resulted in a devastating, emotional brokenness.

What a shock it was to watch how my one decision directed my life in an entirely different direction than it could have gone. I know my story would have been much different if I had made a different choice, a choice that was right before the Lord God.

My decision to be unstoppable in spite of the total destruction of my first attempt to establish myself in California again directed my life. I had absolutely no control over the choice of the person who had the power to make it or break it, and yet I had the power of choice, what I was going to do afterwards. I was brought again to another crossroads – one path was to give up and choose to continue my life in misery; another path was to get back up and continue pursuing my dream in spite of it all. It is scary to imagine where I would be if I had chosen to let my emotional brokenness overpower me. My decision to be resilient and relentlessly continue my pursuit – a one single decision - brought me to a different path, and for many years now I live my dream.

My daily choices to work hard and continuously aim to improve my performance and results for my personal growth, delivered results. The Lord's blessing and my continuous efforts to grow and do my best brought me to the realization of my dream. In all these situations my faith gave me hope, which developed my endurance, strengthened me and empowered me to take action for a change and continue on my journey.

Yet in all cases I had to make the effort to manage myself. I had the choice of how I was going to manage myself and what I was going to do in each of these situations. I intentionally managed my thought pattern, my focus and my choices. I had to make a choice between trusting and losing faith, between fighting for my life and giving up, between giving in to my bleak feelings and make the decision to be resilient in spite of it all. The truth is that if I had chosen fear, disbelief, depression or accepting the role of one who is disabled, losing sight of my goal or giving up, my story would be much different today.

"It all comes down to our choices, doesn't it?" I asked myself as though confirming my realization, as I was contemplating on all my decisions and how they had affected my destiny.

Even though it was not easy to admit, I couldn't deny the simple fact: My life today is the result of my decisions which directed my life. It is the fruit of my own daily choices and consistent actions, even if at the time it didn't seem like they were making any significant difference.

When Michael again came into my life, I was at a crossroad once again. And I knew then that what direction I took would be up my choices once again. I could have continued our constant daily innocent emailing with Michael, who remained married and I had a choice to do what was right before the Lord God, Michael's wife and everyone else. I had a choice to waste my time dwelling on past events and other meaningless things. And I have a choice to appreciate the present and focus on the future, taking consistent action to bring my new vision into fruition.

It is not easy for me to make the right choices like resisting to have renewed contact with the person, with whom I'd had a deep love connection and with whom I have been estranged for so many years. It is not easy to discipline myself daily choosing to get up at five in the morning in order to have more time to work on my goal. It is not easy to choose to work, instead of watching a movie or going out and having fun.

But knowing why I make those choices gives me strength to persevere. I also am very well aware of what it's going to cost me if I choose whatever I want or whatever is easier. The pain of regret is enormous compared to any efforts. Regret is unbearable. Therefore, I will choose the effort to do the right thing. I will choose to persevere doing what must be done rather than choosing what's easier or more comfortable. My decisions today and subsequent daily choices will direct my future. Therefore, I will make a conscious effort to make choices that will lead me in a beautiful direction and fulfill my purpose. And then, when my time comes to see the Lord, I will see Him smile and hear Him say to me, "Well done."

Make Your Life a Masterpiece

Dear Reader,

By sharing my experiences with you in this book, I want to inspire you to choose wisely. I don't understand many things. But what I do know is that our own daily choices and decisions create subsequent events and ultimately direct our destiny.

Sometimes one choice – one single decision – can literally direct our life journey in one or another direction. Also, consistent choices we make compounded over time deliver their results as well. They may seem insignificant, and even they may not even appear like choices. But they are. And, those little choices repeated on a continuous basis over time soon will deliver their results. Every time we decide to do or not to do something is a choice. We stand at those crossroads many times in life. They might not even feel like crossroads; yet, they are. Therefore, before you make those choices or make a decision which path at the crossroads you want to take, ask yourself where your choice will bring you ultimately.

I know there are many different life stories and at times it seems confusing why some destinies are filled with joy and extraordinary experiences, and some are very sad. But what I do know is that it's not what happens to us and not really what people do to us that determine the quality of our lives, but how we choose to respond to it all. We always have a choice to complain, blame others or circumstances, and wind up spending our lives in misery and regret.

But we also have a choice to get up and shake off the dust, accept the responsibility and relentlessly move on creating the life we desire. And that will make us either a victim who lives in misery blaming someone else for our unhappiness, or it will make us an unbreakable fighter, who gets to fulfill our life's purpose in spite of all because we decided to be resilient and never give up. It's what you choose to do with all that happens in your life that will make your life worth living. Or miserable.

The times when you face despair, when it seems like no longer you have the strength to endure, when your aim will seem to be impossible, when your journey will be beyond challenging and difficult to bear – instead of rushing to make choices based on how you feel, step out of your emotions and understand that those hard times are crucial because your decisions now on how you handle those times will set the course for your further journey. I will repeat myself – it's your choice whether you give up or become relentless in your battle that will be decisive factor. Your destiny might depend on it.

Set a firm standard for yourself that you will always make choices that align with your purpose. Choose to overcome any adversity and do the best you can under any circumstances. Make a non-negotiable decision that you will never give up, no matter what it takes for you to take another step.

You may face insurmountable obstacles, but from experience now I know we can achieve anything we set our minds to, if we truly desire it, and do whatever it takes to achieve it and have unshakable faith that we are going to succeed.

I know that all things are possible with God, if we believe. I don't understand how it works out that way, but I've experienced this countless times and now I know that all things work together for good to those who love God and are chosen according to His purpose, just as it's written in the Bible. Don't be stressed or terrified when things don't go your way. Trust the Lord your God that He has a plan and a purpose for your life, and that all will work together for good, even seemingly insurmountable problems.

You will make mistakes yet and yes, you will fall down, but it's not your mistakes that determine who you are. Who doesn't make mistakes? It's whether you choose to get up each and every time and learn from your mistakes that shows what's truly inside your heart.

Don't waste your precious time doing things that don't matter. This way you only create a life that doesn't really matter. Use your given time to design a purposeful and fulfilling life. Make your life count.

There are many things I don't understand about God. And I do not claim to be a Biblical scholar or theologian. But I know the Lord and He knows me. I've learned that our destiny will greatly depend on whether we choose life in obedience before the Lord God or life according to our own desires and ways. What I do know is that living in a righteous way before the Lord God and trusting Him wholeheartedly at all times is going to bring a much more secure, fulfilling and purposeful life. And after all, by trusting Jesus Christ and following Him we will have a blissful life that will last for all eternity, because our soul's existence does not end the journey here on the earth. By bringing you my experience, I want to inspire you to choose wisely. Our Father God has His will for us, and yet He has given us a freedom of choice.

> *"I call heaven and earth as witnesses today against you, that I have set before you life and death, blessing and cursing; therefore choose life, that both you and your descendants may live; that you may love the Lord your God, that you may obey His voice, and that you may cling to Him, for He is your life and the length of your days." (Deuteronomy 30: 19-20)*

We all have choices, and we are going to have what we choose. So, I invite you to take a deep breath with me. Let's you and I choose life. Let's continue on creating the lives that the Lord has called us to live. Life is not a rehearsal. You get to do it only once.

Life is like a precious painting. Your decisions and daily actions shape and create this unique piece of art.

Make your life a masterpiece.

With love,
Inga

Keep Going Forward, Trusting in Your Creator

Keep going forward fully trusting your Creator. Fight for your future no matter what happens or how difficult or painful it may get. Do not fear anything because the Lord holds you in His hands. He directs your path and leads you the way you need to go.

I am not saying your life path is going to be easy. Nor am I saying you won't meet any difficulties if you live a righteous life in the sight of God. Life is a journey, and you will experience heat and cold, sun and rain, valleys and hills, and also the dessert with no water, devoid of life. But the Lord will be there with you at all times, He will protect you and help you to go through any adversities you might encounter. At the same time remember that in a way life is a battle, and it depends entirely on you whether you win or lose.

There will be sleepless nights, when you will lie awake thinking that what you want is nearly impossible to achieve. But trust that your Creator is all powerful and with His help and your efforts, anything is possible.

There will be times when circumstances will not turn out the way you would like them to. But trust that sometimes events, which seem bad to us, really are for the better; we simply can't see it at the time. Accept what happens and always do the best you can.

There will be days when you will feel tired from continuously trying to do your best, and you will have days when you want to just let it go, or do your job carelessly. But rise above mediocrity. Win by doing the job better than you did yesterday.

There will be disappointments. But do not allow them to break down your determination. You will have thoughts that will try to discourage you when your circumstances may seem too complicated to be solved in your favor. But don't give up. Look for the solution until you find it. You will not find it if you believe there is no solution and will give up on finding it. From experience, I know your solution could be only a prayer away. Or, one action away.

There will be people who will try to convince you it is not worth doing what you are trying to accomplish. And there will be people who will try to tell you what you should or shouldn't do. But that's only their opinion. And it's based on their beliefs and their attitudes. However, only you know what the right thing for you to do is. You have your vision; you know what you believe in and where you are going. So, hold on to that and do not let anyone talk you out of your purpose.

You will meet obstacles that will try to prevent you from achieving your goal and will do everything in their power to get you off track. But overcome those obstacles and just keep going.

Remember: No one can break you down and stop you unless you allow it.

And even if you slip and fall down – ask the Lord to give you strength to get up and continue moving forward. Extract the value out of every situation and move on toward your goal.

Just do not give up. Never give up.

When you face difficult times, remember that you have a source of strength. Seek help from your Lord, for only He is an inexhaustible source of strength. He is not going to leave you alone when you're in trouble and He will not forsake you. Jesus said He will not cast out anyone who comes to Him, those who come to Him with a sincere heart. The Lord is fully aware of your situation and He will be watching what you are going to do when difficulties come – are you going to sink into sadness and fear, or you are going to decide to fight your battle and look to Him to seek His help? The choice is yours.

As you continue your journey through life, certain people or events can impact your circumstances, and even direct your life in a certain way. But they can't determine how you will live your life. Remember, it is not what happens to you or what people do to you that has the power to determine the quality of your life. They only have power if you let them.

Don't join those who choose to dwell on the problem and wallow in the mud of self-pity, blaming others for their failures and unhappiness. Rise above it. Always know that the story that will be written in your life book depends on you, not on other people or circumstances.

When you do face a challenge – accept it with courage, because it was given to you as a learning experience, not to break you down. Things that happen can impact your life one or another way, but nobody and nothing can take away from you that, which is within you. No people, troubles or difficulties can take away from you your faith and positive attitude, which is a foundation for your life. When you have unshakable faith and a mindset that empowers you, you will always have the courage to accept any situation in life and the strength to move on, no matter what happens along the way. And if you protect and guard your faith, and make it the rock on which you stand, no life's storm will be able to break you down.

So, cherish and protect that which is within you. Be like a ship that hoists its sails and moves forward despite any storms.

Be Strong. Be Determined and Relentless.

Be Unstoppable.

Your Inga

Edwards Brothers Inc.
Ann Arbor MI. USA
February 27, 2018